T0329937

Greening East Asia

Greening East Asia

THE RISE OF THE
ECO-DEVELOPMENTAL STATE

Edited by Ashley Esarey, Mary Alice Haddad,
Joanna I. Lewis, and Stevan Harrell

UNIVERSITY OF WASHINGTON PRESS
Seattle

Greening East Asia was made possible in part by a Taiwan Studies Grant awarded by the Taiwan Ministry of Education to the University of Alberta and by funding from the China Institute at the University of Alberta.

Additional support was provided by the Donald R. Ellegood International Publications Endowment.

Composed in Chaparral Pro, typeface designed by Carol Twombly

24　23　22　21　20　　5　4　3　2　1

Printed and bound in the United States of America

UNIVERSITY OF WASHINGTON PRESS
uwapress.uw.edu

LIBRARY OF CONGRESS CATALOGING-IN-PUBLICATION DATA
LC record available at https://lccn.loc.gov/2020013197
LC ebook record available at https://lccn.loc.gov/2020013198

ISBN 978-0-295-74790-3 (hardcover), ISBN 978-0-295-74791-0 (paperback), ISBN 978-0-295-74792-7 (ebook)

COVER PHOTOGRAPH: Hong Kong at sunrise, ca. 2017 (iStock/MediaProduction)

The paper used in this publication is acid free and meets the minimum requirements of American National Standard for Information Sciences—Permanence of Paper for Printed Library Materials, ANSI z39.48–1984.∞

CONTENTS

PREFACE

ASHLEY ESAREY

East Asia is one of the world's most populous and densely populated regions, one where economic output, resource extraction, and environmental degradation have grown rapidly since World War II. First Japan, then Taiwan and the Republic of Korea, and now the People's Republic of China have experienced rapid economic growth and increasing integration with the world political and economic order. This process has brought a large number of environmental challenges, from pollution of air, water, and soil, to resource extraction and degradation, to biodiversity loss, to contributions to and effects of global climate change. As the environmental challenges have grown, however, so has awareness of them and determination in some quarters to address these challenges and return local, national, regional, and world environments to a sustainable course. This has led to serious governmental concern with environmental degradation in all four countries, to robust environmental movements in Japan, South Korea, and Taiwan, and to politically inhibited but determined local activism in China.

East Asian environmentalism has dual significance for the future of the earth. First, East Asia's environmental impact is arguably the world's largest. Addressing the region's environmental problems is thus crucial to building a sustainable future for the earth as a whole. Without bringing East Asia's environmental challenges under control, there is little chance for environmental improvement at the global scale. Second, East Asia—having increased its affluence after much of Europe and North America but before South Asia, parts of Latin America, and most of

Africa—can both learn from the countries whose development came earlier and serve as an example for those likely to increase resource consumption in the coming decades. Just how multiple actors and stakeholders in the four East Asian countries have addressed, and are addressing, environmental problems is crucial to any global sustainability solution and provides invaluable lessons for a world that is considering its ecological footprint with a new sense of responsibility, trepidation, and urgency.

At the conference "Environment and Environmentalism in East Asia" held at the Banff Centre for Arts and Creativity in Alberta on June 4 and 5, 2016, an international group of scholars from East Asia and North America presented research on multiple environmental challenges and the responses to them in Japan, South Korea, Taiwan, and China. The Canadian Rockies provided a superb vantage point, as it were, from which to survey environmentalism in one of the world's most populous and dynamic regions. The Banff conference also fostered collaboration (and one snowball fight) among this book's editors, as well as among many of the twenty contributors.

As is often the case, the research presented in Banff evolved after the organizing principles for this volume took shape. A greater understanding of efforts to protect the environment and raise environmental awareness at regional, national, and local levels prompted the editors to rethink the nature of commonalities among state and societal actors that pursue sustainable growth. The articulation of the book's central concept of eco-developmentalism then emerged as an effort to capture the prioritization of environmental protection in such areas as law and policy, energy production, infrastructure, architecture, community design, school curricula, food production and consumption, and waste storage and treatment. Efforts were then made to place chapters in "conversation with each other" as well as with the volume's central theme. In this fashion, we curated a selection of research from the conference, while soliciting additional contributions from experts to fill in key gaps.

Taken as a whole, this book explicates the environmental threats facing an economically vibrant and generally resource-poor region and highlights the ways in which governments, activists, and indigenous communities have addressed these challenges. The volume's introductory chapters by Mary Alice Haddad and Stevan Harrell will appeal to readers seeking a historical and comparative overview of environmentalism in East Asia, while the case studies from Japan, Taiwan, South Korea, and China reveal the scope and complexity of efforts to ameliorate environmental deterioration from the grassroots to central government policies. Harrell's concluding chapter hails key improvements in the region to date, flags possible future stumbling blocks, and encourages us to hope that a new state-society, eco-developmentalist consensus is here to stay, even in China, where per capita income lags behind that of the region's democratic polities. Although East Asia's environmental challenges are in some ways unique, scholars and policy makers of other regions may find in these chapters inspiration for eco-developmentalist strategies applicable to the constraints and opportunities of diverse political contexts at different stages of economic development.

As the conference organizer, albeit one who drew heavily on guidance from Stevan Harrell at all stages of this project, I gratefully acknowledge support from a Republic of China (Taiwan) Ministry of Education Taiwan Studies Grant administered through the University of Alberta's Department of East Asian Studies, as well as from the China Institute at the University of Alberta, which provided funding and assistance with conference logistics. The following individuals helped to make the Banff conference a success: Mickey Adolphson, Erin Asselin, Vivien Chiew, Mi Kwi Cho, Elizabeth French, Joanne McKinnon, Michaela Pedersen-Macnab, Vivian Su, Qian Tang, Tim Tang, Jia Wang, and Noureddin Zaamout. Additionally, special thanks go to conference participants Jeffrey Broadbent, Ya-lin Chen, Chien-san Feng, Koichi Hasegawa, Gordon Houlden, Shih-Jung Hsu, Wei-chieh Lai, Florence Lowe-Lee, Myung-Jae Song, Ian Urquhart, Joohoo Whang, Rupert Wingfield-Hayes, Xiao Qiang, Emily Yeh, and Xiaobo Zhang for insights and advice.

The University of Washington Press editorial team, including executive editor Lorri Hagman, assistant editor Neecole Bostick, and production editor Julie Van Pelt, made the publication of a book with a large group of contributors an enjoyable process.

The views expressed in this book are those of the editors and the contributors; we bear sole responsibility for any errors.

Greening East Asia

PART I

OVERVIEW

INTRODUCTION

The Evolution of the East Asian Eco-developmental State

MARY ALICE HADDAD AND STEVAN HARRELL

EAST ASIA'S FOUR LARGEST COUNTRIES—THE PEOPLE'S REPUBLIC
of China, the Republic of China on Taiwan, Japan, and the Republic of
Korea[1]—contain some of the most densely populated regions in the
world and support 21% of the world's population. Their estimated GDP
constituted about 24% of the world's total in 2018 (World Bank 2019;
Plecher 2019),[2] up from just 7% in 1960 (World Bank n.d., b; CEIC 2019).
The dramatic growth of East Asia's economy in the past half century is
widely attributed to the economic success of the East Asian developmental states, which have staked their popular legitimacy on economic
development and the material benefits that such growth brings to their
citizens. At the same time, the developmental states' extreme focus on
material growth, particularly in the early decades of their existence, led
to intense pollution and environmental catastrophes. Betting on the
populace's propensity to value increases in material living standards
above all, state planners and corporate enterprises often externalized
the air, water, soil, forests, and biodiversity of their territories as something that they could take care of later, perhaps much later, after they
had achieved material prosperity.

Later has come. All of the countries in the region have reached mid-
dle- or even high-income status, and the pollution and environmental
degradation have become so intense that they threaten the health and
livelihood of residents in urban as well as rural areas. Citizens across the
region no longer automatically prioritize additional material wealth over

cleaner air, water, and soil, more buildings over more green space. Beginning in Japan in the 1960s, and spreading to Taiwan and Korea in the 1980s and China in the 1990s, citizens and civil society groups began to demand that their governments shift priorities away from growth at any cost. The governments were slow to take notice at first, but by the 1970s in Japan, the 1990s in Korea and Taiwan, and after 1998 in China, East Asia's states began to moderate their emphasis on growth and incorporated environmental restoration and preservation into their policies and practices.

This pro-environmental shift in policy orientation represents a fundamental change in the nature of these states—from purely developmental to what we call eco-developmental ones, which recognize that greater environmental sustainability is critical if they are to continue to grow economically while maintaining their political legitimacy. East Asia's eco-developmental states have thus committed themselves to some sort of balance between economic development and environmental sustainability. Under these regimes, civil society groups have continued and frequently expanded their environmental action, sometimes in active opposition to and sometimes in wary or even enthusiastic cooperation with state environmental agencies. The case studies and synthetic analyses presented here demonstrate East Asia's historical trajectory from developmental states focused exclusively on rapid economic growth, through the birth of environmental opposition, to the formation of eco-developmental states.

The Importance of East Asia

As mentioned above, East Asia has a fifth of the world's population and produces a quarter of its goods and services. In 2018 it consumed 28% of the world's total energy, including 55% of the world's coal, 23% of its petroleum products, and 12% of its natural gas (Enerdata 2019b, 2019c, 2019d, 2019e). In 2014, it produced 36% of world greenhouse gas (GHG) emissions (EPA US 2018; Boden et al. 2017),[3] making it a major contributor to climate change. China is by far the world's largest emitter of GHG, having surpassed the United States in 2013. East Asia has many of the world's most polluted rivers, and twenty-one of the fifty world cities with the worst air pollution in 2016 were in China (WHO 2018). These big numbers in themselves mean that what happens in East Asia is important for the entire natural world. Furthermore, East Asia is important not only because of its global ecological connections, but also because of its economic, political, and social ones, which ensure that what happens in East Asia influences the entire planet. Thus, it is imperative that anyone studying world environmental trends take account of East Asia.

East Asia's Environmental Connections to the World

Despite its prominence in the world economy and the relative wealth of the four countries included in our analysis, East Asia is resource poor. The region imports 9% of all the energy produced worldwide, almost all in the form of fossil fuel. Japan and Taiwan both import 93% of their energy, and Korea 81%. Although China imports a much smaller percentage of its total primary energy (around 16%), the total volume of imports—264 million tons of coal in 2018 (Enerdata 2019a) and 3.06 billion barrels of crude oil (MAREX 2018) in 2017—still makes China the world's largest total net energy importer (IEA 2019: 13, 15, 17; Enerdata 2019f). East Asia's thirst for fossil fuel thus contributes to environmental degradation and economic imbalance in oil- and gas-producing countries. All four countries also import a large percentage of the wood they use in construction and manufacturing, something that has allowed Japan, Korea, and Taiwan to restore the forest cover lost before and during the early days of the developmental state and has allowed China to increase its forest cover from 8% to 11% in 1960 to over 21% today (Robbins and Harrell 2014). The result is that all the East Asian countries are causing deforestation abroad—their construction and furniture industries have depleted the forests of Indonesia, Malaysia, the Solomon Islands, and particularly the Russian Far East, and have negatively impacted forests as far away as Gabon in west-Central Africa (ibid.). Finally, food imports, especially China's enormous appetite for soybeans from Brazil and Argentina (Rapoza 2015; Gu and Thukral 2018), have contributed to deforestation and land degradation in those areas as well. All four countries, in their enthusiasm for seafood, have put pressure on world marine fisheries resources, threatening biodiversity (Cao et al. 2017).

The East Asian region also accounted for 38% of the world's manufacturing *exports* in 2017 (WTO 2018: 138), a major reason for its polluted cities and rivers and its high GHG emissions. In 2017 through 2019, China,

Japan, Korea, and Taiwan accounted for 51%, 6%, 4%, and 1.5% of the world's steel production (World Steel Association 2018, 2019, 2020), and all four ranked among the top ten net exporters of steel, meaning that the toxic effects of coal burning on the air and of steel manufacture on the soil and water resources are concentrated locally. Similar effects result from automobile manufacture in Japan and Korea, which respectively account for 10% and 4% of automobiles produced worldwide (OICA n.d.),[4] and 12.6% and 5.2% of automobile exports ranked by monetary value, ranking second and sixth in the world (Workman 2019). Other manufactures such as leather goods, textiles, machine parts, and electronics, all of which are major East Asian exports, also contribute to the region's high rate of pollution from producing goods that will be consumed abroad.

Because of the intensity of their local environmental problems and their rapid economic growth in the postwar era, all the East Asian countries except Taiwan have become important participants in international forums dealing with the environment. China, Japan, and Korea have participated at least since the initial United Nations Conference on the Human Environment in 1972 (UNEP 1972), and although China participated only in very limited ways during the Maoist era of high socialism and self-reliance from 1949 to 1979, it began to take an active role starting in 1992 at the Rio Meeting on Environment and Development (Lewis, chapter 2) and has been an active participant ever since.

East Asian countries' international connections work in two directions. In some cases, the desire for international recognition and integration has led these countries to adopt more progressive policies on the environment. In other cases, as their economic and political influence grows, East Asian countries have been able to influence international dialogues on the environment in their desired directions.

As Joanna Lewis shows in chapter 2, on the specific issue of climate change, China's position has shifted from its initial insistence in the 1990s that economic development should take priority over environmental sustainability to its more recent proactive involvement with international efforts to decrease GHG emissions. China's commitment to reduce its own GHG emissions has also been a big force in driving down the global cost of wind and solar power generation, thus contributing to rising use of renewable energy across the globe. China has also become a leader in endangered species conservation, having cooperated with international conservation NGOs such as The Nature Conservancy (Litzinger 2004; Moseley and Mullin 2014) and the World Wide Fund for Nature (formerly World Wildlife Federation). In particular, China has gained international respect for its efforts toward the restoration of the iconic megafaunal species *Ailuropoda melanoleuca* (giant panda) which has become a national symbol as well as an object of environmental concern (Songster 2018).

In addition to the renewable energy sector, Japan and Korea (and to a lesser extent Taiwan) have focused on helping manufacturing firms adjust their products and processes to be more eco-friendly. Just as Japan was the first of the East Asia's developmental states, it was also the first to adjust its developmental policies to incorporate environmental priorities into its co-development plans with manufacturers. For example, its investments in high-efficiency and electric vehicles paid off in a big way with the explosive popularity of the Toyota Prius. That model sold just three hundred vehicles during its launch year in 1997; twenty years later, in 2017, more than 1.5 million Priuses were sold globally, and the total electric vehicle market worldwide had risen to almost 12 million vehicles, representing a reduction of 90 million tons of CO_2 (Toyota 2018). In the construction industry, Japan's policies to encourage waste reduction and recycling also offer important models that other countries follow; Japan now recycles 100% of its industrial concrete (Tam 2009).

Although they followed Japan's lead by a few years, South Korea and Taiwan have also developed extensive green growth initiatives. South Korea's 2009 National Strategy for Green Growth, along with its associated Five-Year Plan. was perhaps the most comprehensive in the region, articulating clear goals for conservation of resources and reduction in emissions, as well as significant public and private investment in green technology (UN-ESCAP n.d.). Similarly, Taiwan has found that nurturing "green" industrial products and related services promotes economic growth and helps buffer against the decline of more polluting traditional industries (Chao 2017; Hu et al. 2017).

In Japan, Korea, and Taiwan, interactions between state and civil society show important interplays with global environmental organizations and agendas. As Yves Tiberghien (chapter 13) shows, the governments of Japan and Korea were initially reluctant to sign international protocols on labeling of genetically modified organisms, but pressures from civil society groups that were linked to international environmental organizations led both countries to ratify the Cartagena Protocol on Biosafety. While sometimes at odds with those advocating for CO_2 reductions, antinuclear activists in Japan, Korea, and Taiwan have advocated for renewable policies across the region, as Chang Hsi-wen (chapter 14) and Noriko Sakamoto (chapter 6) show.

East Asia as a Region in Environment and Environmental Politics

A skeptic might question the value of covering all of East Asia in a single book, since these four countries have such different political systems and political cultures. We believe, however, that there are three strong reasons for writing about East Asia as a region. First, despite their obvious differences, East Asian countries have a number of historical, cultural, political, economic, and ecological similarities. Second, because of geographic proximity, the countries in the region are highly connected to one another and have been for centuries. Those interconnections tend to be obscured in country-specific books, underscoring the value of a volume that covers the entire region. Finally, given the similarities among them and the close connections between them, the differences among the countries allow for a valuable, controlled comparison of their environments along with their environmental cultures and politics.

First and foremost, East Asia is a climatic and ecological region that shares air, water, fauna, flora, and natural resources. The whole region is affected by the geologic fault lines that separate the Asian continent from North America, the Pacific Ocean, and the Philippines. The region shares a typhoon season, heightening its collective exposure to climate change–related risks. Dust storms originating in the Loess Plateau of North China and the Inner Mongolian Desert to the north are major contributors to lowering air quality in Korea (Lim, chapter 3) and Japan, and on certain days can even be detected in Seattle and San Francisco.

Similarly, East Asia's economies are highly interconnected—China is the top trading partner for Japan, Korea, and Taiwan; and those three countries represent China's number 2, 3, and 4 trading partners after the United States. Just as European- and American-owned manufacturing companies exported their air and water pollution to more permissive regulatory regimes in Japan, then to Korea and Taiwan, those countries are now exporting their pollution (and also many of their manufacturing jobs) to the looser regulatory regime of China. Much of Taiwanese-owned manufacturing, particularly in the electronics and apparel sectors, now takes place in China, along with substantial amounts of Japanese- and Korean-owned manufacturing. These activities of course affect China's environment in negative ways, primarily through pollution.[5] Prevailing westerly winds mean that the pollution produced by these companies then drifts back to their home countries. Thus, unlike when the US and Europe outsourced their polluting industries to Japan, outsourcing manufacturing from Japan, Korea, and Taiwan to China does not entirely outsource the related pollution. Relatedly, when Japan (and Korea and Taiwan) invest in cleaner supply chains, greener technology, and improved transportation methods for their subcontractors in China, it can contribute to the improvement in the quality of Japan's own air, water, soil, and marine resources.

Historically, the eastern half of China, along with all of the Korean Peninsula, Taiwan, and Japan south of Hokkaido, has maintained an unusually high population density for multiple centuries, based on an agrarian order in which large numbers of peasant farmers grow grains intensively and pay rents and taxes to a landlord elite and to a centralized state staffed by members of that elite. Many of the specific problems of East Asia's environment, including pollution, deforestation, and species loss—are related to the high population density recently compounded in its effects by rapid economic growth and urbanization.

East Asian countries also share both elite and popular cultural ideas about human-environment relations. Unlike the rural indigenous cultures on the peripheries of the region (Chang, chapter 12; Taiban et al., chapter 7), the elite cultures of East Asia were dominated by a tradition that we can loosely call "Confucian," which expresses diverse views that political leaders have drawn upon to promote different agendas at different times. During China's imperial era and Mao's rule (1949–76), elites promoted the perspective that nature exists to serve humanity and thus people must prevail over nature. This attitude was exemplified by the slogan "humans are destined to triumph over nature" (*ren ding sheng tian*), which can be found on a seaside monument to engineering on the east coast of Taiwan as well as in Maoist propaganda from 1960s and 1970s China (Shapiro 2001; Weller 2006).

More recently, pro-environmental leaders and activists in all four countries have touted another aspect of the Confucian tradition, one that promotes harmony or even unity between humans and nature. This idea is embodied in the slogan "unity of nature and people" (*tian ren heyi*), which has evolved in China into the modern cry to build an "ecological civilization" (*shengtai wenming*) (Schmitt 2016). At the popular level, peasant proverbs and notions of village ecology and balance, such as the Japanese "village and mountain" (*satoyama*), stress the ecological integrity of the agrarian community (Sakamoto, chapter 6).

Interestingly, the interconnection between humans and nature, and the emperor's historical responsibility for maintaining harmony in both, meant that in contrast to the Christian view of natural disasters as "acts of God" for which leaders were not responsible, natural disasters such as floods and earthquakes were seen as a sign that a leader had lost the Mandate of Heaven, and should perhaps be replaced. Thus leaders across East Asia, even those not subject to democratic political pressures, have felt a responsibility to address environmental pollution and environmental disasters that threaten people's "right to subsistence" (Tu 1989; Perry 2008).

As Mary Alice Haddad shows graphically and quantitatively in chapter 1, although they operate in a diverse set of political regimes, advocates across the region rely on a remarkably similar set of strategies to influence policy and state action in the four countries. Everywhere, more organizations use informal networking—either with or without state involvement—and public education as their primary advocacy strategies than use more direct forms of action such as public protest, lobbying, and litigation. Whom you know has always been more important than what you know in East Asian societies (and elsewhere), and this general cultural trend is reflected in the strategies utilized by environmental activists in the region.

Additionally, East Asian nations all lack a tradition of citizen participation in governance above the very local level. Thus, across the region mechanisms of citizen participation through electoral democracy or other formal means to influence national legislatures or bureaucracies are relatively new and tend to be underdeveloped, even in the democratic states. At the same time, all the countries have strong traditions of local governance (Abramson, chapter 10). Also, perhaps significantly, the region has a long and diverse tradition of millenarian rebellions and other popular movements based on religious or other local solidarities (Perry and Harrell 1983). This paradox—high levels of civic engagement at the local level and low levels of activism at the national level—may contribute to some of the specific forms of environmental action that Haddad describes in general in chapter 1, and we see in more detail in all of the case study chapters in the volume.

Finally, since World War II, the East Asian states have all shared the consensus of the developmental state, a governing body that derives its legitimacy from its ability to improve material consumption among its citizens. The developmental state's initial bargain—asking citizens to accept environmental degradation in return for an increased standard of consumption—began to fray as economic prosperity increased and environmental conditions deteriorated (Harrell, chapter 15), leading to the formation of the eco-developmental state as a new basis for policy and state legitimacy.

Variation within East Asia

Although they share many similarities, the differences among East Asian countries also make the region productive for academic inquiry. Precisely because a regional focus allows scholars to control for the many historical, ecological, economic, and cultural variables that the countries all have in common, it becomes possible to engage in a detailed investigation into the ways that biophysical, sociocultural, administrative, legal, and geopolitical differences affect political behavior.

Perhaps most obviously, there are large biophysical differences between the countries. Because of China's continental size and location, in contrast to peninsular Korea and insular Japan and Taiwan, there are large differences in resource self-sufficiency: China is much more self-sufficient and less dependent on trade than its smaller neighbors. It produces more of its own energy, forest resources, and even food than the other nations, and this difference affects each country's ability to determine its environmental policies, especially with respect to energy (Lewis, chapter 2; Lim, chapter 3). This is particularly apparent in nuclear power politics. Historically, Japan has relied heavily on nuclear power, getting as much as 30% of its electricity from that source before the 2011

Fukushima triple disaster (WNA [World Nuclear Association] 2019), and since then has emphasized conservation. Korea generated 29% of its electricity from nuclear plants in 2017, but the Moon administration has announced plans to gradually eliminate nuclear generation as a power source (*World Nuclear News* 2018). Taiwan built three nuclear plants during its period of authoritarian rule before 1987, but popular protests have rendered a fourth plant infeasible since democratization, and the regime is now committed to a fast transition to heavy reliance on renewables, though the means for achieving that goal are only vaguely defined (Chang, chapter 12).

Socioculturally, the differences among the countries are quite complex. Many of them stem from their recent histories of governance models: Japan as a bureaucratic state with democratic elections for the whole postwar era, Korea and Taiwan with traditions of authoritarian governance and transition to democracy in the late twentieth century, and China as an authoritarian state that nevertheless changed its economic model from state socialism to bureaucratic capitalism after 1980. These differences influence the nature of regulatory regimes, ministerial turf wars, and most importantly environmentalist opposition to, and cooperation with, state agencies in the four countries. Democratic politics—its institutions (e.g., elected legislature, free press, independent judiciary, and autonomous advocacy organizations) as well as its practices (e.g., electoral politics, public protests, community organizing, etc.)—are commonly thought to be fundamentally important when determining the environmental politics of a country. East Asia allows us to examine that assumption critically: although all four countries have very different experiences with democracy and hence with popular action, they all initially followed a developmental state model and have made the transition to eco-developmental states.

Central-local government relations also differ. All four countries have strong central governments and a common practice of local policy experimentation prior to national policy making. However, the center-local political game is played very differently in the four countries, and the capacity for local innovation varies as well. In China, localities can practice what we might call "guided autonomy," or a limited ability to experiment with policy implementation, so that policies such as the emissions trading markets described by Iza Ding (chapter 4) or the renewable energy subsides described by Lewis (chapter 2) are often tried out locally before being implemented on a wider scale. In Japan local municipalities frequently experiment with waste, emissions, and building ordinances in an effort to increase the quality of their local environment. When those local models are effective, they can be adopted by multiple localities and eventually become national policy (Sakamoto, chapter 6; Avenell, chapter 5; Tiberghien, chapter 14). Similarly, in Taiwan, local governments are able to experiment with environmental policies, and their models of what to do as well as what not to do can be adopted nationally (Chiu, chapter 11). In Japan and Taiwan, pioneering local governments often "guide" the national governments in the area of environmental policy. Although Korea has also seen a rise in the autonomy of its local governments in recent years, they remain highly constrained and have the least capacity to act as environmental policy innovators of the four countries in this study (Choi and Wright 2004).

The role of law and lawyers also varies. In none of these countries has litigation traditionally played as great a role in society as in the Euro-American world, and its importance differs considerably from one country to another. Although environmental lawsuits have been permitted in China and Taiwan since the early aughts (Economy 2004a; Lee Chienliang 2010), they play a minor role in comparison to popular protest. In contrast, in both Japan and Korea, lawyers and lawsuits have played vital roles in the environmental movement and in environmental policymaking. Victory in the early 1970s by pollution victims in what came to be known as Japan's "Big Lawsuits" (Upham 2009) served as a critical turning point for the reorientation of the developmental state away from growth-first towards a model that promoted more sustainable development. As Simon Avenell describes in chapter 5, legal battles have reshaped the discourses on the environment, which facilitated this shift in policy goals. In Korea, lawyers' associations were crucial players in the successful democratization movement (Lee et al. 1999; Ku 2002), and they continue to influence the evolution of Korea's eco-developmental state (Cho 1999). These differences have implications as all four countries increase their participation in rights-based international forums and join various treaties and protocols.

Diachronic differences are also important to any comparative project, and especially here as we compare and contrast the transformation of developmental to eco-developmental states across the region. Countries that experienced this transition later have done so in a different world context, particularly with regard to climate change and its effects. Since Japan was the first East Asian country to develop economically and the first to face the environmental legacy of the developmental state, it was a pioneer in developing environmental policies, based primarily on regulation (Harrell, chapter 15). But it was not until the end of the twentieth century that the bureaucratic processes of regulation became transparent enough, and global environmental NGOs became powerful enough, to allow popular participation to influence policy significantly (Tiberghien, chapter 13). Korea and Taiwan not only developed later, they democratized later. It is partly because of this timing that they have been much more closely connected to worldwide environmental movements (Lim, chapter 3; Tiberghien, chapter 13). China has not democratized, but its government is eager to be seen as a player in international environmental politics. It has developed a system of top-down environmental regulation that also allows a small amount of popular environmental protest (Lora-Wainwright 2017), but activism has generally been restricted to the local level (Dai and Spires, chapter 14).

All of these differences mean that the basic structure of the environmental politics in the four countries varies widely. While there are remarkable similarities in the specific strategies utilized by citizens to advocate for pro-environmental policy change (Haddad, chapter 1), the configuration of environmental politics in the four places is very different. In Japan, which experienced its environmental crisis first and has been ruled by the Liberal Democratic Party for nearly all of the post-war period, environmental organizations have found it most effective to find allies among the ruling LDP members and inside the bureaucracy. While advocacy organizations have connections to opposition parties, electoral politics has not been a defining element of the environmental movement (Lim, chapter 3; Avenell, chapter 5; Sakamoto, chapter 6; Tiberghien, chapter 14). In contrast, in South Korea and Taiwan, the environmental movement became fully incorporated into those countries' pro-democracy movements, creating much closer connections between environmental groups and progressive political parties (Lim, chapter 3; Chiu, chapter 11; Taiban et al., chapter 7; Chang, chapter 12; Tiberghien, chapter 13).[6] In further contrast, after a brief period of opening up in the 2000s, the

Chinese Communist Party (CCP) has spent much of the last decade tightening state control over environmental organizations and increasing party involvement in their activities. As a result, environmental groups in China tend to be small and local, and if they grow larger they must find ways to work productively with the government or face shutdown (Ding, chapter 4; Efird, chapter 8; Abramson, chapter 10; Dai and Spires, chapter 14).

In sum, East Asia is an excellent region in which to study the complex dynamics of environmental politics and particularly the way that developmental states can evolve into eco-developmental states. The four countries in the region share many ecological, social, cultural, and political characteristics, but they vary in size, resource wealth, history, and especially political systems. This enables us to study in detail how these various factors can influence environmental politics and how national policy can become reshaped by environmental advocacy.

The Recent Trajectory of East Asia's Environment

Because of their geographic proximity and cultural commonalities, and in spite of the differences in size and regime type, the East Asian countries have all experienced a similar trajectory in environmental politics and policies—and in the state of the environment itself—since World War II but at different times and at different speeds, roughly corresponding to the timing of industrial growth. As a result, East Asian countries have followed a similar pattern where growth-first developmental states have evolved into eco-developmental states, modifying high-growth policies to include pro-environmental goals and promote more sustainable economic growth.

First in Japan, then in Korean and Taiwan, and most recently in China, all of the East Asian states supported rapid industrialization and high-speed economic growth that emphasized export-oriented manufacturing industries. As they grew economically, they suffered from increasingly intense pollution that endangered the lives and livelihoods of their citizens, threatening the stability of their political regimes. All of the ruling political regimes struggled to incorporate these new environmental concerns into their governance strategies. Japan's Liberal Democratic Party managed to hold onto power by passing sweeping environmental regulations in 1970 during what came to be known as the "Pollution Diet." The military/Nationalist regimes in South Korea and Taiwan failed to get ahead of popular dissatisfaction—the environmental movements merged with pro-democracy movements that resulted in political democratization in the late 1980s in both places. So far the Chinese Communist Party has managed to keep ahead of the mounting political pressure with increasingly ambitious pro-environmental policies designed to reduce the pollution that can lead to political unrest. This process of transformation from a developmental state to an eco-developmental state is described briefly below and is elaborated on in more specific detail in the subsequent case study chapters.

The Developmental State in East Asia

Central to our understanding of environmental degradation and mitigation in East Asia is the idea of the developmental state—a state that derives its legitimacy primarily from its ability to improve the material consumption standards of its citizens and hence promotes heavily state-led programs to accelerate material growth. In a certain sense, all states in the postwar period have had development as a goal, but when we think of the developmental state, we usually think of states ruling countries that are materially poor and seek, through "development," to make them richer. As Kristin Looney (2012, 11) has pointed out, the term "development," which is almost synonymous with "modernization" or "industrialization," usually boils down to the transition from an agrarian to an industrial economy, although developmental states also pursue social welfare goals such as public health and the spread of education, as an adjunct or sometimes as a means to the main goal of material enrichment. In pursuit of industrialization, states everywhere often neglect other goals such as rural livelihoods and, most important for us here, environmental sustainability.

Beginning with the seminal work of political scientist Chalmers Johnson on Japan (1982), which he (Johnson 1986) and others later extended to Taiwan (Gold 1986) and Korea (Haggard and Moon 1997; Suh and Kwon 2014), the idea of the developmental state has been central to analysis of East Asian economic growth. East Asian developmental states other than China have been characterized by private ownership of most of the means of production; policies set and enforced by a meritocratically selected bureaucracy; and active intervention, through both regulation (including import substitution followed by export promotion) and economic incentives, to guide economic growth in the directions they deem desirable. In service of their development goals, these states have promoted universal education, including both technical and nationalistic content, ensured relative income equality, and limited citizen political participation (Johnson 1986; Beeson 2004).

Developmentalist programs in East Asia began in Japan in the Meiji period (1868–1912), which saw rapid industrialization and urbanization, with little if any attention paid to the environment (Avenell 2013). Modernizers in China in the early twentieth century sought to emulate Japan's progress but had little success outside a few coastal enclaves, and Korea's and Taiwan's early development, undertaken by the Japanese colonial regimes there, was heavily skewed by its primary purpose of supplying the Japanese Empire with agricultural (and to a lesser extent mineral) raw materials from Taiwan (Ho 1975) and timber and minerals from Korea (Fedman 2018; King 1975).

After the Second World War, as the idea of development took hold in poor countries worldwide (Escobar 1999; Bebbington 2000; Blaikie 2000), Japan made a remarkably quick recovery from the devastation of a lost war and continued to pursue rapid industrialization, very much at the expense of air, water, and soil quality. Newly independent regimes in Taiwan and Korea experienced initial periods of war in Korea and the violent consolidation of power over a hostile populace in Taiwan, but by the mid-1950s, they too were headlong committed to development, with similar disastrous environmental results. By the 1980s, the problem had intensified significantly as Japanese and other multinational corporations shifted manufacturing operations from Japan, where labor was becoming more expensive and environmental standards had risen, to Korea and Taiwan. Since Korea had already been largely deforested by the Korean War, and Taiwan's forest cover had also diminished due to logging and agriculture, the growth of intensive petrochemical and other manufacturing to source global multinationals threatened an already-degraded, fragile environment. Air and water quality declined rapidly in both places, and there were few controls on polluting industrial and transport activities (Harrell, chapter 15).

In China, developmentalism of a different kind pushed environmental concerns almost entirely into the background. Marxist theory emphasized that capitalist greed was the primary cause of environmental degradation (Whitney 1973), and as Judith Shapiro showed so devastatingly in *Mao's War against Nature* (2001), a combination of utopian urgency, dogmatic uniformity, and political repression led to a lack of governmental concern for the environmental costs of industrialization. When global multinationals reacted to the rising costs and stricter environmental regulations implemented in Korea and Taiwan by the 1990s and shifted their industrial production to China, the combination of political devaluation of the environment with intense, highly polluting industrial manufacturing led to what, beginning with Václav Smil (1993), has become known worldwide as "China's environmental crisis." China's water, air, and soil all became severely polluted, groundwater was mined to dangerously low levels, minimal forest cover was reduced even further, heavy pesticide use became the norm for farmers, and environmental diseases greatly increased in prevalence. In addition to toxic pollution, all four countries experienced an exponential increase in their greenhouse gas emissions as rapid industrial development combined with significantly higher consumption levels.

The Rise of Environmental Consciousness

Environmental consciousness worldwide typically arises in reaction to local pollution and resultant environmental disease, as local communities organize spontaneously to demand that governments and corporations take responsibility for the suffering they cause (Dalton et al. 2003; Hager and Haddad 2015). This was certainly the case in Japan in the 1960s, as Avenell (2013) has graphically described: "Throughout most of Japan's modern history the state has pursued an overtly developmentalist agenda which privileged unbridled industrial and, for a time, military expansion at the expense of human wellbeing and the environment. Ordinary citizens bore the full brunt of such policies and it was in their visceral reaction to the resulting suffering and destruction that the Japanese environmental movement was born" (398).

Japan's postwar environmental movement was triggered both by general deterioration of urban air quality and by a series of industrial pollution incidents (Avenell 2012, 27), two of which have become iconic in the world history of environmentalism. In one incident, the Mitsui Company's mines polluted the waters of the Jinzu River in Toyama Prefecture with cadmium, causing the outbreak of a local epidemic of *itai-itai* (ow, ow!) disease, which led first to local citizen protests and eventually to litigation in which Mitsui was found culpable and forced both to clean up the river and to pay a large amount of compensation (Yoshida et al. 1999). In the other incident, the Chisso Corporation, a plastics manufacturer in Kyushu, released large amounts of methyl mercury into Minamata Bay, and local people ingesting fish became afflicted with what came to be known as Minamata disease, a potentially fatal degenerative disease of the nervous system. This led to local protests and eventually to the formation of a national environmental movement with important political allies (Almeida and Stearns 1998), one that began to include citizens' groups agitating for nature preservation and food safety in addition to opposing industrial pollution and its negative health effects (Avenell 2012, 429).

In Korea, the rise of an environmentalist movement followed its own rapid industrialization, about two decades after Japan's. There were local protests as early as the 1960s and 70s, in response to pollution around industrial sites and local demands for contamination. Just as pollution in Minamata galvanized the Japanese, Korean farmers demanding compensation for pollution caused by the Ulsan Industrial Complex mobilized others to demand redress, including residents of Seoul and Inch'on affected by poor air quality. Citizens began to establish organizations to pressure the government and demand change (Ku 2002; Lee 2000). But in the atmosphere of a repressive military dictatorship that lasted until 1987, only local action was possible, and the regime purposely interfered with any attempts at coordination between local residents of polluted areas and any national or international environmental organizations, seeing them (correctly) as connected with the pro-democracy movement and hostile to the dictatorship (Ku 2004, 191). Once the Chun Doo-hwan dictatorship fell in 1987, the space for political organizing around the environment expanded, and during the 1990s Korea's environmental movement grew rapidly, as part of the growth of civil society organizations generally in the newly democratic country. Now, the Korean Federation for Environmental Movement (KFEM), which was formed in

1993 by the merger of eight national environmental groups, is the largest environmental organization in East Asia by far, boasting more than eighty thousand members (KFEM n.d.).

Taiwan's environmental movement developed around the same time as Korea's but in different ways. Like its counterparts in Korea, the Nationalist-ruled state ignored environmental concerns in its headlong (and successful) push for development, setting the stage for environmental opposition. This opposition began, as did environmental movements in Japan and Korea, around local issues, primarily those of water pollution. In Taiwan, the pollution cases that served to spark the national movement formed against Sunko Ink in Taichung County (1982–84) and DuPont in Lukang (1986–87). Both cases saw local villagers organize and successfully force companies to scrap plans to locate factories in their towns (Ho 2010). Throughout the 1980s victims as well as opposition intellectuals began to raise issues of local water and air pollution along with nuclear power and nuclear waste, the latter prompted by the 1980 proposal to build Taiwan's fourth nuclear power plant. This nascent environmental movement was a primary issue in the programs of the "Outside the Party" (Dangwai) political movement that developed into the Democratic Progressive Party, which was tolerated when it formed in defiance of a ban on the founding of opposition parties in 1986 and was allowed to organize and run candidates when martial law was lifted in 1987. After full democratization in the late 1990s, the environmental movement, among many other social movements, began to resort to mass demonstrations on the one hand, and to formal organizations on the other, becoming, as Ming-Sho Ho (2011, 120) puts it, "a vital component of political life."

Unlike Korea (but like Hokkaido and Okinawa in Japan), Taiwan has a significant indigenous population, which was deprived of much of its rights to land and resources by the Japanese colonial government and then by the Nationalist dictatorship after 1945. As civil society organizations of all kinds blossomed beginning in the late 1980s, the Aboriginal Rights Movement grew along with them. Because of both resource extraction and storage of nuclear waste on aboriginal lands after 1979, indigenous rights and environmental rights became closely connected political issues and have remained so to the present day (Chang, chapter 12).

China's environmental movement, like its economic development, has taken place most recently. Propelled by the Marxist assurance that only capitalism could despoil the environment, along with the ideological valorization of sacrifice for the revolution, the Communist-ruled state paid little attention to environmental concerns even after the transition to bureaucratic capitalism in the 1980s. Informed by what happened in the other countries as pollution intensified—especially how the environmental movement provided significant support to what became successful pro-democracy movements in South Korea and Taiwan—the Chinese government began to establish a series of environmental protection agencies and laws. The first officially permitted environmental NGO, Friends of Nature (Ziran zhi You), was established in 1994, although it worked primarily on the politically safer issues of biodiversity conservation and nature education rather than antipollution advocacy (Weller 2006: 128–29).

The CCP state is notoriously fearful of *any* kind of national-scale organization or movement, environmental or otherwise. The primary focus of environmental organization and protest (as with other forms of protest), therefore, has always been local. Grassroots organizations formed to address issues of industrial pollution and its effects on agriculture, food safety, water quality, and population health (Lora-Wainwright 2017). Although China, like Taiwan, has large indigenous minority populations, indigenous peoples have not been allowed to organize for environmental causes, lest their organizations develop into movements for local autonomy. When national-scale environmentalism emerged after 1998, it was thus inevitably incorporated into the state's developmentalist system, and belongs to the next section of our overall history—the evolution of the eco-developmental state.

The Evolution of the Eco-developmental State

Nowhere in East Asia did the state respond quickly to the environmental concerns brought up by direct action, journalistic exposés, and increasing public awareness. Instead, all of the states, attempting to continue their policies of promoting economic development through collaboration with industrial corporations and enterprises, initially reacted by trying to ignore and minimize the problems. The states claimed that pollution was a temporary sacrifice populations would have to endure if people wanted to continue to raise their standards of consumption, and continued to study environmental problems without doing anything concrete about them (Avenell 2012, 434–35).

Eventually, however, spurred on by a combination of mounting public pressure from growing environmental movements and realization that things were getting bad enough to harm further development, governments began to act to address environmental problems, reaching "[environmental] tipping points" (Tiberghien, chapter 13). Japan, having been first to pollute, was also first to begin cleaning up, but it did not really begin until the late 1960s and early 1970s, initially at the local level and then only later at the national level. At that time, the Japanese developmental state began to become eco-developmental—passing antipollution laws, creating an environmental protection agency, and ruling in favor of pollution victims who had brought lawsuits in the courts (Avenell 2012, 435; Wakamatsu et al. 2013; Avenell, chapter 5). Within only a few decades, Japan went from being a "toxic archipelago" (Walker 2011) to one that enjoyed some of the cleanest air, water, and soil among advanced capitalist countries (Schreurs 2002).

In spite of this dramatic improvement, Japan has not fully replaced its developmental goals and policies with environmental ones. The Japanese state still prioritizes economic growth, although it now takes environmental concerns into account in the ways that it supports that growth. As a result, international and national NGOs, local citizen groups, environmental lawyers, and other activists continue to put pressure on the state and large corporations to live up to their environmental promises (Edahiro 2009). Stories of some of these state-private relationships are told in this volume by Avenell (chapter 5), Tiberghien (chapter 13), and Sakamoto (chapter 6), while Stevan Harrell evaluates the results in chapter 15.

In Korea, the Chun Doo-hwan regime (1980–88) actively worked against the environmental movement. For example, in the face of the "Onsan disease" caused by heavy metal pollution in Gyeongsamnan-do, the government's environmental agency officially and erroneously announced that the disease was not caused by industrial pollution (Ku 2004, 196). After democratization, however, the state reaction to environmental concerns began to evolve. President Roh Tae-woo condemned the Doosan Electrical Materials company for spilling phenols into the Nakdong River in 1991. That same year local residents and national NGOs organized to block a proposed dam on the Donggang River, and won their fight on Environment Day when President Kim Dae-Jung announced that plans to build the dam had been scrapped. That same day he laid out "The New Millennium Vision for the Environment" in 2000 (ibid., 199–201).

Since that time Korea's state regulation has been successful in combating air pollution and partially successful in combating water pollution (Harrell, chapter 15). Programs to restore Korea's forests to something resembling their condition at the beginning of the colonial era have succeeded remarkably, partly due the transformational New Village Movement (Saemaul Undong) implemented by Park Chung-hee's dictatorial regime in the early 1970s, which reduced local usage of forest products while increasing dependency on imported energy (Kim, chapter 9).

As in Korea, Taiwan's environmental movement played a key role in democratization itself (Weller 1999). Its political system rather quickly evolved into a "two-camp" structure with splinter parties forming coalitions with the two major parties—the reformed Nationalists leading the so-called "blue" camp and the Democratic Progressive Party leading the "green," both named for the colors of the respective parties' flags and not for any affiliation with environmental movements. While Korea's environmentalists formed a powerful organization in the Korean Federation of Environmental Movements (KFEM) that usually supported the Democratic Party, in Taiwan environmentalists formed an independent Green Party. Taiwan's Green Party has never gained representation in the national legislature, but they have elected representatives to city and county councils and work with the Democratic Progressive Party to run and support candidates for national office. Through their partnership with the Democratic Progressive Party, they have promoted such programs as "trash doesn't fall to the ground" (*lese bu luo di*) under then-Taipei mayor Chen Shui-bian (which was partly responsible for his successful bid for the presidency in the 2000 elections, ending fifty-plus years of Nationalist Party rule). Significant air and water quality regulations were adopted during his mayoral and presidential tenures.

The most prominent recent focus of environmental movements in Taiwan, however, has been the antinuclear power movement (Chang, chapter 12). The Nationalist dictatorship heavily promoted nuclear power as a solution to Taiwan's lack of fossil fuel resources and built three nuclear power plants in the 1970s. When the fourth plant was proposed in 1990, however, the country had democratized, and all sorts of popular protests were possible; some of them successfully forced the postponement of the fourth nuclear plant (Fell 2017). Since then, nuclear power politics has varied with party politics; Nationalist governments, both national and local, have tried to push ahead with more nuclear power construction, while the Democratic Progressive Party has positioned itself as antinuclear, leading to current President Tsai Ing-wen's pledge to denuclearize Taiwan's entire energy sector by the mid-2020s. Not surprisingly, the 2011 Fukushima disaster in Japan considerably strengthened the antinuclear movements across the islands. As in national politics, local governments take diverse and shifting positions, alternating between support for continued development of nuclear power and promoting renewable and sustainable energy.

China has followed a similar trajectory to the others but for very different reasons and with a starkly contrasting outcomes. All through the transition from state socialism to bureaucratic capitalism in the 1980s and early 1990s, China's environmental degradation accelerated. Throughout this period, it continued to be impossible for any but the most local and spontaneous groups to engage in protest, let alone organize effectively in opposition. Thus, unlike the other three countries, China has not seen any coordinated environmental or antinuclear movements emerge to play a serious role in politics. However, a transformation in state policy orientation did happen, beginning in the mid-1990s and galvanized by disastrous floods in the middle-Yangzi provinces in 1998 that killed more than three thousand people, left fifteeen million homeless, and negatively affected more than two hundred million people (UNCHA 1998). After researching the cause of the floods, state scientists (perhaps wrongly) attributed (see Henck et al. 2011) much of the damage to upstream deforestation caused by the logging booms of the 1970s and 1980s. The state at this point did an about-face and began to take environmental regulation seriously. The State Environmental Protection Administration (later elevated to ministry status) began aggressive campaigns to stop deforestation, followed after a few years by policies emphasizing decarbonization of the nation's energy mix, as well as attempts to address excessive water use for irrigation (which had caused the Yellow

River, for example, to run dry before it reached the ocean), and measures to clean up some of the world's worst urban air pollution. But much of China's recent push to green its coal-based energy sector though efficiency and renewables has been driven by green industrial policy, in line with overarching economic development and reform goals (Lewis 2013b).

Unlike the eco-developmental states in Japan, Korea, and Taiwan, however, there has been little coordination between any central-level state agencies and national environmentalist groups because there are no powerful national environmentalist groups. Formally organized local groups do exist from time to time, and local protests continue to be very common (Mertha 2008; Lora-Wainwright 2017). Local state agencies are often eager to compromise and to pay compensation to victims of pollution or occasionally to shut down the most egregious polluters, in fear of retribution from higher-level state agencies.

At the national level, a small number of the largest and most professional global NGOs such as The Nature Conservancy (n.d.) and the Natural Resources Defense Council (NRDC 2016) have been able to work with the Chinese government to promote better environmental policies. But unlike the other countries, China has not swayed uneasily between opposition and collaboration of state branches and environmental organizations, except in the area of species conservation. Instead, environmental mitigation in China has been largely state-led, using methods ranging from legislation to broad policy initiatives, including the state's proclamation that China is an "ecological civilization" (*shengtai wenming*) (Schmitt 2016).

In general, environmental groups and the general public and have only been able to exercise influence when they work through the channels already provided by the state, which tends to reinforce the legitimacy and authority of the central government while directing the criticism to local authorities (Haddad 2015b; Teets 2018). Widespread unrest has largely taken a virtual form—including Chai Jing's 2015 film "Under the Dome" (Chai n.d.), WeChat and Weibo discussions, and crowdsourced reporting (Tyson and Logan 2016) of environmental pollution. Citizens unhappy with the government have not been allowed to form organizations to express that unhappiness—Chinese citizens can express their unhappiness as individuals, but if they want to organize, they must form groups that work with, not against, the government.

Since China's transformation into an eco-developmental state is only about a decade old, we have not yet seen the kind of dramatic improvements in air, water, and soil quality that Japan, Korea, and Taiwan have enjoyed. In general, the environmental situation in China remains in "crisis" mode. That said, we have seen considerable improvements in some areas (e.g., reduction in SO_2 emissions, increase in forest cover) even as the overall situation remains dire (Harrell, chapter 15).

While the overall story of the environmental cleanup made possible by the transition from a developmental to an eco-developmental state may be impressive, we must emphasize that in no case has the state become a fully environmental state committed to sustainability as its highest goal. The eco-developmental state views green technology as an important industry for continued economic growth and is concerned about the costs and risks related to climate change and pollution cleanup. In other words, the developmental state's shift in perspective did not proceed from pro-economic growth to pro-environment. Rather, the eco-developmental state now recognizes that many pro-environmental policies are also beneficial for the economy and that sustainable economic growth requires more sustainable environmental policies and practices. Because the eco-developmental state is still very strongly progrowth, all of these states continue to face both environmental challenges and significant, growing pressure from their citizens to respond to those challenges.

We can see East Asian states' emphasis on growth over environment in their active promotion of "smokestack-less" industries such as tourism. The tourist industries in all four countries have skyrocketed in direct proportion to China's affluence, which has enabled middle-class Chinese to travel for leisure much more often and created Chinese tourist destinations for Japanese, Koreans, and Taiwanese. According to World Bank data, international arrivals to China were 84 million in 1997, 177 million in 2007, and more than 320 million in 2018 (World Bank n.d., c). Not surprisingly, the rise in air travel—one of the most carbon-emitting forms of transportation—rose correspondingly: 53 million passengers were carried in China in 1998, 191 million in 2008, and 611 million in 2018 (World Bank n.d., a). This means that the equivalent of slightly less than half of China's population flew sometime during 2018.

All four countries have been actively promoting their domestic tourism industries as an alternative to manufacturing and other polluting "smokestack" industries. While tourism does not create the kind of intense local pollution of air, water, and soil that manufacturing might, it does contribute negatively to the environment through increased emissions, depletion of natural resources, and degradation of delicate ecosystems (Thomas 2013). Air travel, which has become increasingly accessible, is particularly damaging. Not surprisingly, since the potential economic gains are so great and the human health impacts are relatively small (even though the ecological and climate impacts are large) the eco-developmental states in the region have done very little to discourage aviation travel and instead are actively promoting it.[7]

Overall, the observed pattern of evolution from developmental to eco-developmental state is based on three main factors: industry support, state capacity, and party incentive.

1. Industry support. In many cases, pro-environmental policy has the potential to generate economic growth (e.g., renewable energy industries or increased energy efficiency), and in fact, the success of these industries and initiatives has very much been driven by "green" industrial policy. In other cases, there are real tradeoffs to be made between environmental protection and direct economic gain (e.g., land conservation or pollution-control equipment), and in these areas state support has remained lukewarm.

2. State capacity. In industries and issues where the industry is fairly consolidated and/or the state has a lot of influence, it has been a lot easier to shift policies (e.g., energy, forestry). In industries and issues where the sources of pollution are more diffuse (e.g., car emissions) or the industry is more fragmented (e.g., farming), it has been a lot harder for the state to convince industry to change behavior.

3. Party incentive (resulting from threats to political stability). If the issues are negatively affecting an important political constituency, then the ruling party will deal with the issue in order to maintain political

legitimacy/support. If the issues are not very visible or affect politically marginalized communities, then the ruling party will be much less likely to deal with the issues.

When these three factors combine, we can observe a wholesale shift away from a growth-at-any-cost policy towards one that regularly includes environmental concerns. Indeed, in some policy areas where these three factors coalesce, we see East Asian countries become global leaders, such as low emission and hybrid vehicles in Japan and solar energy in China. In contrast, in areas where we only see a few of these factors coming together (e.g., biodiversity), we see much less inclusion of environmental concerns into state policy.

Thus, the governments of East Asia have remained developmental states. They continue to base their legitimacy on their ability to bring material prosperity to their people. They continue to work closely with industry to coordinate efforts to bring about economic development. In areas where the state can work with industry to promote green growth policies, where efficiency and conservation can cut production costs, where short-term environmental investments can reap long-term economic gains, we see tremendous progress towards a model of sustainable development. In other areas, where it is more difficult for industry and/or government to collaborate for a policy that is good for the bottom line as well as good for the planet, when people, plants, and animals can only win when industry loses, we continue to see activists across the region seeking to pressure corporations and governments to make more ecologically positive choices. They frequently lose those fights, but they keep fighting.

Notes

1   We take no position on the status of Taiwan in international law. We treat it as a separate country because one, it has its own government, political and judicial system, enforced borders, armed forces, and currency; and two, its trajectory of development and environment has been unique— different from China, Japan, and South Korea. We wish we could include the Democratic People's Republic of (North) Korea in our analyses, but data are very slim where they exist at all. In this introduction and elsewhere, we often use "Korea" as a shorthand for the Republic of Korea.

2 GDP is calculated by the Purchasing Power Parity (PPP) method. By the nominal method, East Asia's share of global GDP is slightly less, around 24%.

3 These figures do not include emissions from land use change, which are difficult to quantify, but may comprise about 25% of total emissions.

4 China produces more motor vehicles than Japan and Korea put together, but almost all of these are used domestically.

5 Hatch and Yamamura 1996; Reardon-Anderson 1997; Terao and Otsuka 2007; Wilkening 2004; Lora-Wainwright 2017.

6 See also Ku 1996; Lee 2000; Lyons 2009; Grano 2015; Haddad 2015a.

7 Ch-Aviation 2019; Falcus and Wong 2019; Lee Hsin-yin 2018; *Telegraph* 2019.

1

East Asian Environmental Advocacy

MARY ALICE HADDAD

EAST ASIA HAS GAINED GLOBAL NOTORIETY FOR BEING ONE OF THE most polluted regions on the planet—from Japan's Minamata disease in the 1960s to China's current records in terms of carbon emissions and pollution from $PM_{2.5}$ (fine suspended particles). And yet, in the last decade East Asian countries have become the world's largest producers of green energy, have established hundreds of government-protected nature reserves, and are at the forefront of municipal waste management and sustainable urban design. Operating in a context of pro-business governments, their cutting-edge environmental policy is particularly remarkable and has been made possible by their evolution into eco-developmental states.

This chapter examines the landscape of environmental organizations in East Asia—the causes they pursue and the advocacy strategies they utilize to realize their aims—and compares their strategies to those used elsewhere in the world. The comparative context highlights the remarkable similarity of advocacy topics and strategies across the region, foregrounding environmental organizations' extensive collaboration with governmental actors and utilization of organizational networks and cultural tools. While subsequent chapters offer details on particular cases of environmental advocacy and policy innovations, this one offers a broader frame of reference, demonstrating that the forms of environmental advocacy found in the case studies can be found in every region of the world. Thus, while East Asia's political constraints are unusual, the solutions that activists have found to overcome those constraints and enact positive change can be emulated elsewhere in the world.

Environmental Advocacy Strategies in East Asia

Seen in comparative context, East Asia's environmentalism conforms with patterns of environmental activism found in other regions in the world. Interviews with more than one hundred advocates, journalists, government officials, businesspeople, grassroots volunteers, and academics, as well as two original datasets, inform this analysis. The first dataset gathered information from about one hundred environmental organizations in China, Japan, South Korea, and Taiwan. The goal was to (a) capture the most influential organizations and (b) provide a fairly representative sample of the rest. For Japan and South Korea, I began with a small number of environmental organizations (five and seven, respectively) that I knew to be highly influential and then added organizations randomly selected from official databases of environmental organizations for a total of 103 Japanese groups and 100 Korean groups.[1] For China and Taiwan, which do not have official lists of environmental groups from which I could randomly select organizations, I worked with native research assistants to generate a list of environmental organizations that included the most influential groups as well as a fairly representative sample of the rest. The final lists were then circulated to several prominent academics in both places to ensure that the list included all of the most influential groups and was fairly representative of other groups. In the end, the list had 108 groups from China and 32 groups from Taiwan. In all four countries, there is a bias towards groups with better resources (i.e., sufficient to have a website and/or to be registered with the government) and against local, all-volunteer groups.[2]

Which issues are the focus of environmental organizational activity in East Asia, and how does that compare with the rest of the world? Drawing on the data gathered from the environmental organizations in the region, figure 1.1 illustrates the percentage of environmental organizations in each country that are engaged with each issue area. Percentages can add up to more than one hundred because most organizations are involved with more than one issue.

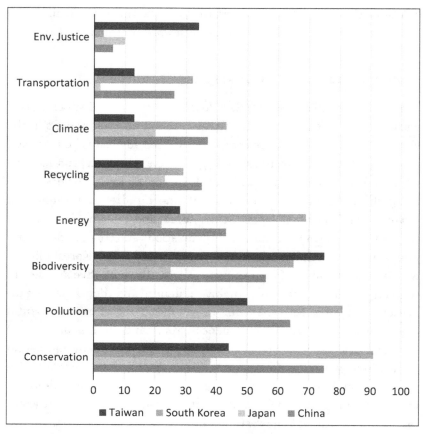

FIGURE 1.1   Issue foci of East Asian environmental organizations (%)

Figure 1.1 illustrates both the diversity and congruence of activity of environmental organizations in the region. On the one hand, there is diversity across the countries concerning their engagement on particular issues, for example, while 77% of South Korean environmental organizations are working on pollution issues, only 38% of Japanese organizations are. As the concluding chapter discusses in more detail, this variation makes some sense developmentally. Of the countries in East Asia, Japan developed first, so its pollution got worst first and has improved the most. South Korea's and Taiwan's period of rapid development followed Japan's, so their economic and political resources have focused on pollution issues more recently—it still receives significant emphasis in their environmental activism. China is the most recent of the four places to experience rapid industrialization, so its pollution levels are now (hopefully) reaching their peak, and their capacity and political will to combat that pollution have grown only in the last decade or so. As a result, pollution is likely to remain a significant focus of their environmental activism for many years to come.

In contrast, while 34% of organizations in Taiwan are active on environmental justice issues, only 10% of groups in Japan, 6% in China, and 3% in South Korea are dealing those issues. Because Taiwan has a much larger indigenous population compared with the other three places—as chapters 7 and 12 show in their discussion of social justice issues in Taiwan—environmental justice has long been an important concern.

With respect to other issues, it is somewhat difficult to determine the underlying reason for the patterns revealed in the data. China and South Korea were the two most active countries with respect to five of the seven issue areas—conservation, pollution, energy, climate, and transportation. Recycling, one of the politically easiest areas of advocacy, and also one of the most commercially viable, was not particularly well represented as an advocacy issue in any of the countries.

Turning from the types of issues to the modes of advocacy, as shown in figure 1.2, we see similar patterns; while there is some diversity across countries within East Asia, that diversity is less than might be expected and cannot be easily explained by regime type. We do not see advocates in democracies using substantially different advocacy strategies from non-democracies in systematic ways. Similarly, we do not see poorer countries like China using consistently different advocacy strategies from richer countries like Japan.

Some of the reasons for these similarities are revealed in the case studies in the rest of the volume. All of the chapters dealing with national-level policy (chapters 2, 3, 9, and 13) reveal the complex interactions that environmental advocates face in cultivating policymakers and persuading them to adopt a pro-environmental stance. A common theme in research on policymaking in East Asia is the key role that formal and informal networks among policymakers, advocates, and industry play in developing and transmitting policy ideas and shaping general goals into concrete policies. They talk about how international organizations can create policy papers that often serve as models for local-level advocates

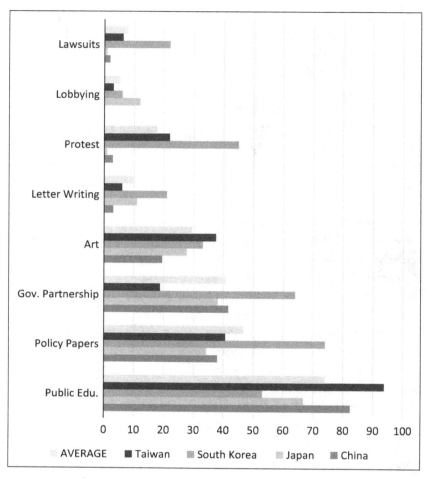

FIGURE 1.2 Advocacy strategies in East Asia by country (%)

and policymakers and the critical role that public-private partnerships can serve in facilitating both the development and the implementation of environmental policies.[3] As the findings here and the case study chapters demonstrate, these partnerships and collaborations are important irrespective of whether the advocates and policymakers are operating in a democratic or nondemocratic context.

Similarly, nearly all of the chapters in this volume emphasize the importance of personal and organizational networks in developing and implementing environmental policy. They also highlight the critical role that successful pilot projects at the local level play in developing and disseminating environmental policy both nationally and internationally. The grassroots-focused chapters also reveal the prevalence of media and letter-writing campaigns, as well as art and culture. While public protest and political lobbying can sometimes be a critical component of an overall advocacy strategy (e.g., chapter 11),[4] for the most part political lobbying, public protest, and lawsuits play a much smaller role than the other forms of advocacy (chapters 5 and 11).[5] The data presented here about different advocacy strategies found among environmental organizations in East Asia offer an overview of the prevalence and relative distribution of these different strategies across the region.

Although there is remarkable similarity in the different countries, we do see some notable outliers. South Korea's and Taiwan's environmental organizations engage in significantly more contentious behavior such as public protests and lawsuits than those in China and Japan. It is likely that their willingness to engage in political contestation is a result of the evolution of the environmental movements in those countries, which was closely linked to the democratization process and the development of strong two-party systems (Haddad 2015). Although Japan is a democracy and has free and fair elections, its political system has been dominated by a single party, the Liberal Democratic Party, for most of the last sixty years, while the Chinese Communist Party has held political control of China for seventy years. It is likely that the necessity of working closely with ruling parties is one of the reasons why in South Korea and Taiwan, we see much more engagement with collaborative forms of advocacy such as policy papers, working with government, and organizational networking.

Environmental Advocacy Strategies around the World

Moving from intra-East Asia comparisons to comparisons between East Asia and other regions of the world, this section examines data from a different dataset. Rather than looking at information gathered from specific environmental organizations, this second dataset used the Factiva database to collect two hundred cases of environmental advocacy from around the world. The search for cases was conducted in the following manner: Factiva's major English-language news and business publications[6] were searched, and the search was limited to (a) articles with word counts of greater than 1,500 to ensure there was sufficient information to identify a case; (b) articles that mentioned the environment (or variants thereof) five or more times; and (c) articles published between January 1, 2005, and December 31, 2009. These five years were chosen because they are recent enough to be able to capture advocacy strategies used in contemporary environmental politics, the focus of this study, and they are old enough such that there would be a good chance that the outcome of the advocacy could be determined. The search generated 3,567 relevant articles with 177 duplicates for a final pool of 3,390 articles. Articles were then randomly selected until the dataset contained two hundred cases of environmental advocacy, which is a large enough sample to ensure sufficient variation on key variables while small enough to code. The cases were then coded for a variety of descriptive information including the location, scope, issue, and the strategies employed by advocates. The "issue" variable was refined to be more precise (e.g., waste/ trash was added as an issue when it became clear that many of the "pollution" and "conservation" cases were fundamentally about handling waste/ trash rather than the effects of pollution or the desire for preserving greenspace).

Examining a slightly different set of issues, figure 1.3 shows that global patterns of environmental advocacy are similar to those found in East Asia. Thus, just as there was broad similarity in environmental activism across East Asian countries, despite their different political regimes, there is also broad similarity across the world—conservation, pollution, energy, and climate issues tended to be the focus of environmental activism in most regions, while waste and environmental justice issues generally garnered less attention. Although there is some diversity across regions within single issue areas (e.g., focus on conservation issues ranges from 83% of cases in the Middle East and Africa to 41% in East Asia), the patterns do not correspond with the assumption that the liberal capitalist democracies of Western Europe and the Americas have fundamentally different patterns of activism than the pro-business developmental states in East Asia and the developing countries of Africa and South and Southeast Asia.

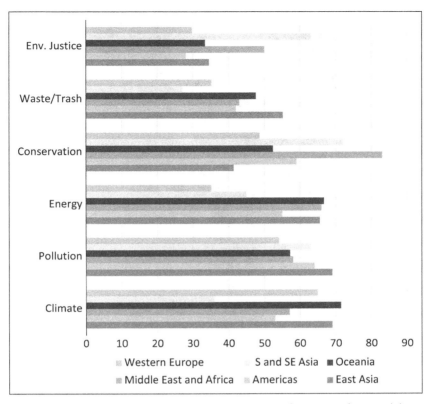

FIGURE 1.3   Types of environmental events 2000–2009 by issue and region (%)

Finally, when we examine the global patterns of environmental advocacy strategies (figure 1.4), we once again find that the patterns found in East Asia are also common around the world: local pilot projects, cultivating government allies, networking with other organizations, writing policy papers, collaborating with business, and public education are common advocacy strategies everywhere—more than 40% of advocacy events involved one or more of these strategies in nearly every region. In contrast, the advocacy strategies that have traditionally generated the greatest academic interest, such as political lobbying, public protest, and lawsuits, are much less common across the world—fewer than 40% of advocacy events involve any of these strategies in most regions of the world.

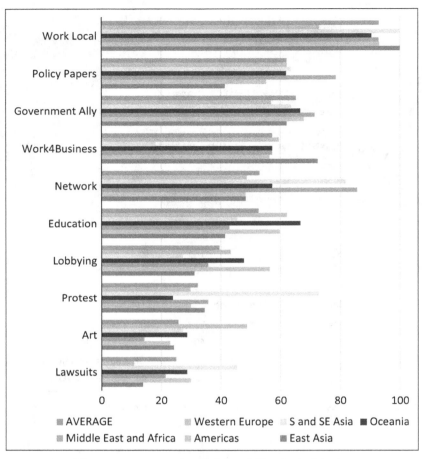

FIGURE 1.4 Advocacy strategies around the world by region (%)

Discussion

The commonalities that we see both across East Asia and across the world require that we question some of our basic assumptions about environmental advocacy. While much of the literature on environmental politics commonly suggests that social mobilization, especially in the form of public protests, lawsuits, and lobbying political parties, plays a critical role in a country's environmental policy development,[7] these comparative data and the case studies themselves suggest that these factors are frequently not the most important areas of environmental activism.

Additionally, scholars have generally assumed that the process of influencing environmental policy in democratic systems—where legislators are held accountable by citizens during regular electoral cycles—should be fundamentally different from the process in countries where most policy is made by unelected bureaucrats or legislators who are not facing regular competitive elections. However, once again, the large-n comparative data as well as the case studies in this chapter suggest that many of the most effective advocacy strategies, such as cultivating elite political insiders, piloting successful local projects, creating personal and organizational networks, and developing policy papers, are effective advocacy strategies in democratic and nondemocratic countries alike.

Therefore, while the case studies in this volume were gathered to offer a diverse, detailed, and nuanced view of environmentalism in East Asia, their insights should resonate with scholars of East Asia who are interested in issues other than the environment as well as scholars of environmental politics and policy who may not study East Asia. Finally, these findings suggest three interrelated themes that are explored in more depth in the case study chapters.

First, personal and professional networks are the channel through which policy is made, changed, and implemented no matter where you are. The boundaries between governmental policymakers, civil society actors, and even business are porous and malleable. Individuals can shift their sector (business, government, nonprofit) location over time and can sometimes exist in several sectors simultaneously (e.g., an academic who is on the board of a nonprofit organization, sits on a governmental policy-advisory committee, and engages in private-sector consulting). Organizational networks among grassroots organizations can magnify their influence far beyond what one would expect from a tiny, all-volunteer group.

Second, environmentalism is simultaneously global and local. On the one hand, environmental issues are universal not just in terms of their planetary impacts but also in the way that they connect with fundamental human existence—the air we breathe, the water we drink, the food we eat, the spaces we inhabit. Global environmental organizations are large, well-resourced, and can be accessed by elite governmental policymakers and local housewives alike. On the other hand, environmentalism is fundamentally local—we each experience the environment in the specific location where we are at any given moment. Thus, the meaning of "the environment" will be quite different for a young office worker peering through Shanghai's smog, a Rukai elder seeking to teach a young generation where the traditional hunting grounds are, or a town planner in rural Japan who is attempting to use a renewable energy project to stem the depopulation of his town.

Finally, energy is at the heart of many environmental problems and solutions. Whether it is nuclear waste dumped on an offshore island where indigenous people live or urban smog produced by coal-fired power plants, many of the worst pollution issues currently faced around the world have energy at their source. Tackling these problems requires a combination of simple, individual solutions (e.g., walking and biking to work instead of driving), complex national policies that engage multiple stakeholders (e.g., feed-in tariffs and cap-and-trade policies), and everything in between.

Not every chapter in this volume touches on each of these themes, but the diversity of cases of environmentalism presented here offer a tapestry of perspectives on how a wide variety of different actors in East Asia are seeking, and often succeeding, to improve the environment for their local communities, their countries, and the world. They are working on a range of different issues from food safety and renewable energy to cultural preservation and wildlife protection. The heroes in the stories are equally diverse: they are central government officials, politicians, city planners, environmental activists, suburban housewives, indigenous leaders, and schoolchildren. Together, advocates at the elite and grassroots levels are working in collaboration and in opposition with one another to chart the evolution of East Asia's eco-developmental states.

The environmental challenges facing the planet are enormous and can be overwhelming. The chapters in this volume underscore the complexity of the problems we are facing and the difficulty of finding solutions. And yet, they also demonstrate that no matter what a person's social location or political context, there are ways to engage productively. We can all learn from their examples.

Notes

1 More precisely, NPO Hiroba (www.npo-hiroba.or.jp/) generated 3,597 organizations that included "environmental protection" as a focal area; every thirty-sixth organization was sampled to ensure geographic

diversity (a random sample could result in an over-sampling of Tokyo-based groups) for one hundred groups; since two of these were already in the original five, a total of 103 groups were used for Japan. For Korea, the Ministry of the Environment maintains a list of environmental organizations that contained 373 environmental organizations when I accessed it in September 2014 (www.me.go.kr/home/web/policy_data/read.do?pager Offset=0&maxPageItems=10&maxIndexPages=10&searchKey=&search Value=&menuId=10260&orgCd=&condition.code=A1&seq=6330).

2 For more detailed information about the dataset, see Haddad (2017).

3 Busch, Jörgens, and Tews 2005; Carter and Mol 2008; Eisner 2006; Ho 2007; Schreurs 2002.

4 Alagappa 2004; Broadbent and Brockman 2010; Lee and So 1999; McKean 1981.

5 Harris and Lang 2015; Hildebrandt and Turner 2009; Ho 2007; Kim 2009; Schreurs 2002; Terao and Otsuka 2007.

6 Factiva's "Major News and Business Publications" (https://professional .dowjones.com/factiva) subset of news sources was selected because it offered the greatest geographic diversity of sources and stories. If the full set of available articles or other publication subsets had been used, results would have been highly skewed toward North American news sources and stories.

7 Agrawal and Lemos 2007; Bosso 2005; Keck and Sikkink 1998; Kingdon 1984; Lemos and Agrawal 2006; Miller 2002; O'Neill 1997; Rodrigues 2003; Schreurs 2002.

PART II

POLICY AND LAW

2

China's Low-Carbon Energy Strategy

JOANNA I. LEWIS

CHINA HAS HISTORICALLY BEEN A RELUCTANT PLAYER IN GLOBAL environmental forums and particularly in international climate change negotiations. Even as international pressure and attention shift to China as the largest global carbon emitter and a potential leader on climate change, the country's actions internationally are still predominantly shaped by domestic, rather than international, factors. China's energy system, still highly reliant on fossil fuels, is the main constraint on the government's adoption of an aggressive climate policy position. However, changes in the domestic energy policy agenda in the last decade have led to a transformation in China's approach to global environmental diplomacy.

China's contribution to climate change, namely greenhouse gas emissions from fossil fuel combustion and industrial activity, is inherently linked to the country's economic development strategy. Beijing's approach to climate change therefore must be understood in the context of its energy development strategy, which is driven by its overall economic development goals. Recent national economic plans increasingly place low-carbon development at the forefront. China's 13th Five-Year Plan (FYP) sets peak targets for carbon emissions, energy usage, and water consumption, as well as goals for eliminating outdated industrial production, increasing energy production from renewables, and developing green infrastructure. It also tasks the government with developing the rules and regulations to manage China's new carbon emissions trading system (ETS)—soon to be the largest such program in the world.

Despite these aggressive goals, China still faces real challenges in curbing carbon emissions and reducing its reliance on fossil fuels, to the detriment of the local environment, the health of its people, and the global climate. China's clean energy ambitions and its commitment to climate protection must be seen against the backdrop of the country's broader ambitions for economic growth and industrial reform.

The Emergence of China's Low-Carbon Energy Strategy

The concept of a low-carbon economy began taking hold in the last two decades. Some have traced the political origins of China's low-carbon strategy to the emergence of what was called the "scientific viewpoint of development" (*kexue fazhan guan*) promoted by former president Hu Jintao around 2003 (Fewsmith 2004), though in practice low-carbon development was already emerging by then out of market opportunities in the clean energy space supported by strategic industrial policy. China's economic growth model since the 1980s was based on the high-volume consumption of energy and raw materials, causing heavy pollution, low output, and low efficiency (*People's Daily Online* 2004a). In contrast, the vision of a low-carbon development model is based on conservation, science, and technology (*People's Daily Online* 2004b).

Energy is directly tied to economic development, and the relationship between energy use and economic growth is very important in the Chinese context. Although China quadrupled its GDP between 1980 and 2000, it did so while merely doubling the amount of energy it consumed during that period. This allowed China's energy intensity (ratio of energy consumption to GDP) and consequently the emissions intensity (ratio of carbon dioxide–equivalent emissions to GDP) of its economy to decline sharply, marking a dramatic achievement in energy intensity gains not paralleled in any other country at a similar stage of industrialization (figure 2.1a and b). This achievement has important implications not just for China's economic growth trajectory, but also for the quantity of China's energy-related emissions. Without this reduction in the energy intensity of the economy, China would have used more than three times the energy that it actually expended during this period (Lewis 2007).

The twenty-first century has brought new challenges to the relationships between energy consumption, emissions, and economic growth in

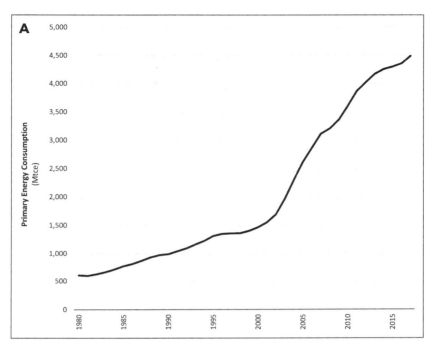

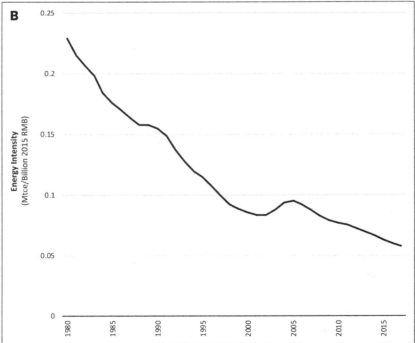

FIGURE 2.1   Trends in China's (a) primary energy consumption in million tons coal equivalent (Mtce) and (b) energy intensity in million tons coal equivalent per billion of 2015 RMB (Mtce/billion 2015 RMB)

China. China's current environmental challenges are fueled not only by domestic demand but also by the global demand for its products, and a concerted effort to shift the country away from energy-intensive manufacturing and towards high-value sectors was enshrined in China's 11th FYP (2006–10) (Pan et al. 2017). A cornerstone of this plan was the identification of low-carbon technology sectors as "strategic emerging industries" (Government of the People's Republic of China 2010).

With the 11th FYP and the simultaneous Renewable Energy Law (State Council of the People's Republic of China 2005) came the rise of China's renewable energy industries. Renewable energy, and wind and solar power technologies in particular, were identified as strategic technology sectors for China. Since then, they have become only more critical as initiatives to reduce the country's reliance on coal due to concerns about climate change and air pollution have been introduced. China's green innovation strategy has propelled its clean energy sector to be among the largest in the world. A latecomer to the clean energy innovation field, cooperation with many of the foreign companies that pioneered wind and solar technology has been a very important way for Chinese firms to enter this sector (Lewis 2017, 2013a). Technology transfers to China from overseas firms have led in many cases to fruitful cooperation and occasionally to tense relationships over intellectual property. China's entry into the manufacturing of wind and solar technologies has led to significant cost reductions and increased "learning by doing" globally. This rise has also launched international trade battles with its biggest green technology competitors (Lewis 2014).

In 2017, China accounted for a record 45% of global investment in clean energy by investing US$162.4 billion that year—its highest amount ever and almost half the global total (REN21 2019).[1] In 2018, this number declined due to a slowing of solar project investment, but China still led the world with US$110.1 billion of clean energy investments (BNEF 2019). Of the "non-hydro" renewables, wind and solar have been particularly successful in China in the last decade. By the end of 2018, China had constructed 206 gigawatts (GW) of wind power, more than all the EU countries combined, and almost twice as many as the second largest installer of wind power capacity, the United States (GWEC 2019). China is also becoming the largest market for offshore wind power development, with US$11.4 billion in investment and thirteen new projects being constructed in 2018 (BNEF 2019). China is now by far the leading country in installed solar capacity, installing 53 GW of solar in 2017 and 43 GW in 2018, bringing the total national capacity to about 170 GW or about 35% of total global solar capacity (Bellini 2019; McCrone et al. 2018; Reuters 2019).

China is experimenting with the large-scale deployment of renewable energy as no other country has before it. As a result, it is a de facto global laboratory, experimenting with the challenges of large-scale renewables deployment that will benefit the rest of the world should they follow China's path. For example, one of the biggest challenges facing China's wind and solar sectors today is integration, that is, making sure the green electricity being produced by China's wind and solar farms is absorbed by the grid and consumed. Curtailment leads to major economic losses, and from an environmental perspective, it leads to wasted pollution-free electricity (Lewis 2016). The location of China's wind resources leads to difficulties in transmitting China's wind power to population centers, and many completed wind farms sit idle while they wait for the construction of long-distance transmission capacity. In spite of these difficulties, curtailment rates for 2018 were around 7.7% for wind and 2.9% for solar, which is a notable improvement on recent years where a fifth of total wind power produced was wasted (Bloomberg News Editors 2018). In contrast, solar can work very well as a distributed source of power. As a result, recent Chinese government policies have targeted increasing the use of distributed solar and building-integrated (solar) photovoltaics (BIPV) so that the electricity is consumed at the point of generation and not transmitted over long distances.

Most recently, there is pressure to decrease the wind and solar industry's reliance on subsidization. The feed-in tariffs for wind and solar have recently been reduced, and the National Energy Administration has released a development plan for "subsidy-free" wind and BIPV projects, with the first batch of projects (20.76 GW total) spanning sixteen provinces (NEA 2019).

China's Evolving Role in International Environmental Diplomacy

The modern era of international environmental diplomacy began with the 1992 United Nations Conference on Environment and Development (UNCED) in Rio de Janeiro. At the conference Chinese premier

Li Peng emphasized that economic development should not be neglected in the pursuit of environmental protection and that international cooperation should not interfere with national sovereignty, thus setting the stage for China's subsequent international environmental diplomacy (Cai and Voigts 1993). The United Nations Framework Convention on Climate Change (UNFCCC), with the ultimate objective of stabilizing greenhouse gas concentrations in the atmosphere at a level that would prevent dangerous anthropogenic interference with the climate system, was also opened for signature at the Rio Conference (UNFCCC 1992).

For many years, including during much of the 11th FYP period, China's positioning in the international climate negotiations lagged behind its domestic energy and climate action. It was not until the lead-up to the 15th Conference of the Parties to the United Nations Framework Convention on Climate Change in Copenhagen in the fall of 2009 that China's domestic climate and energy undertakings began to make their way into the international climate negotiation process. Taking many observers by surprise, the Chinese government came forward that year with its first ever carbon target, pledging a 40% to 45% reduction in national carbon intensity from 2005 levels by 2020.

Scholars have long speculated about the extent to which Chinese domestic policies are shaped by international regimes, trying to reconcile international policy stances with China's domestic policy making processes.[2] China's increased involvement in international environmental negotiations around issues such as ozone depletion, biodiversity, and climate change has likely broadened the range of policy alternatives that China considers in response to these environmental problems and has provided it with access to new technologies and funds that will be crucial to any response that it might undertake (Economy 1997). At the same time, it is important to understand "both how the state is influenced by the emergence of new kinds of environmental problems . . . and how states are using the internationalization of environmental politics to forward their own policy priorities" (Economy and Schreurs 1997). In the case of China, at times its own policies directly respond to the actions of other countries, but the influence of the international community still remains sharply constrained when compared with the role of domestic interests (Economy 1997). For example, China has long aligned itself with the developing world in negotiating blocs such as the Group of 77 (G77) and the "BASIC" countries (Brazil, South Africa, India, and China) and since 2012 joined in coalition with the "Like-Minded Developing Countries," though it has deviated from such coalitions when necessary to protect its own interests (Lewis 2007; Olsson et al. 2010).

Since the beginning of the climate talks, China historically was unwilling to adopt legally binding commitments as part of a future climate change agreement. The G77 has consistently emphasized the historical responsibility that the industrialized world bears and the disparity between per capita emissions that persists between the developed and developing world, resisting any commitments to reduce the group's own greenhouse gas emissions. The Kyoto Protocol institutionalized this firewall in 1997, and this entrenchment remains a key obstacle to engaging developing countries in international climate negotiations. However, at the 2011 UNFCCC meeting in Durban, South Africa, China signaled a potential shift in its negotiating position. This same year, China also revealed a new openness toward discussing absolute greenhouse gas emissions targets, rather than just intensity targets. This shift toward more proactive engagement, both with other country delegations and with the global civil society community, pointed to an increased willingness on the part of China to explain its domestic climate and energy challenges and to articulate its accomplishments. These changes were very likely a result of the programs that were implemented domestically in the wake of China's carbon intensity target and since the Copenhagen negotiations in 2009 to both measure and monitor domestic emissions and to implement domestic carbon trading programs, resulting in a new confidence on the global stage. The importance of this newfound confidence became evident in the lead up to the 2015 Paris Agreement, the first new international climate treaty under the UNFCCC since the 1997 Kyoto Protocol, where China increasingly played a leadership role alongside the United States.

Multilateral participation most certainly shapes Chinese policymaking via the transmission of new ideas, and new norms introduced by the multilateral economic institutions often are used to provide leverage for domestic political actors (Pearson 1999). These observations also hold for

China in the climate change sphere. Many have pointed to China's use of environmental policy to help promote domestic policy priorities that are generally considered more important than environmental issues, including protecting Chinese sovereignty, acquiring foreign aid and technical assistance, and promoting economic development (Economy 1998). Others have argued that domestic reforms have led to more proactive engagement in international negotiations. For example, domestic institutional reforms that moved climate policy responsibility into the National Development and Reform Commission (NDRC) (the ministry responsible for energy policy) may have "eased China's integration into climate negotiations" (Tamura and Zusman 2011); though as discussed later in the chapter, new reforms announced in early 2018 once again put the role of climate change in the broader policy agenda in question. While domestic reforms have certainly facilitated China's engagement in the climate negotiations, the added technical capacity that energy experts brought to the climate change challenge perhaps explains this more than institutional reforms (Lewis 2013b).

A New Era of Domestic Action and International Engagement

At the beginning of the 12th FYP period in early 2011, China was in a very different position than it had been in just a few years before. The results of the 11th FYP were by then evident, and the leadership was increasingly confident that the national energy intensity target had been achieved. China was emerging as the de facto global leader in renewable energy technology. Also underway was a shift in the national statistical system used to measure energy consumption and energy efficiency, including the development of a more robust system to measure and estimate greenhouse gas emissions. As a result, we saw two significant changes in China's climate policy at home and abroad. At home, provisions for the regulation of carbon explicitly appeared in China's core national economic plan for the first time. Abroad, for the first time, China signaled in the international climate negotiations that it would be willing to take on a binding international commitment. Not only were China's international proclamations now being more directly linked to domestic policies, but the previous decade's achievements in energy efficiency and renewable energy, and the scientific basis for both action and assessment, had put China in a far more confident position in the international climate negotiations.

China's 12th FYP (2011–15) established the goal of gradually establishing a national carbon trading market, and seven provinces and municipalities launched pilot carbon-trading schemes (NDRC 2011). The implementation of a carbon-trading scheme in China, even on a small-scale or pilot basis, will not be without significant challenges. For example, there is still limited capacity to measure and monitor carbon emissions in China, although it is rapidly improving. (See Ding, chapter 4, for a discussion of the limitations associated with emissions trading programs to control other air and water pollutants in China.) The 12th FYP established an improved system for monitoring greenhouse gas emissions to help assess compliance with the carbon intensity target and to serve as the basis for a national reporting system under the forthcoming ETS. This puts China is a better position to adhere to new transparency guidelines stipulated by the Paris Agreement. Under the Paris Agreement and the associated "Paris Rulebook," national greenhouse gas inventories must now be reported more frequently to the UNFCCC, and Nationally Determined Contributions (NDCs) must include detailed information on how targets were calculated (Yang 2018; UNFCCC 2019).

The 13th FYP (2016–20) builds upon the programs enacted under the 12th FYP, including new energy intensity, carbon intensity, renewable energy and non-fossil energy targets as outlined in table 2.1 (National People's Congress 2016). These targets are in line with the longer-term pledge made in the lead up to the Paris meeting, where China committed to reduce total carbon emissions per unit of GDP by 60% to 65% from 2005 levels by 2030 and peak its overall carbon emissions by 2030 (NDRC 2015).

On December 19, 2017, China launched its long-awaited national ETS following several years of experimenting with regional pilots. The program has big ambitions but modest beginnings in terms of sectoral coverage and stringency. As a result, the cap-and-trade program alone will likely be insufficient to deliver sizable emissions reductions in the near term. It is, however, being implemented alongside multiple other policies aimed at increasing coal efficiency and reducing demand, including those discussed above.

*Table 2.1 Key climate and energy targets in the 12th and
13th Five-Year Plans*

TARGET TYPE	12TH FYP TARGET (2010–2015)	ACTUAL LEVEL ACHIEVED BY 2015	13TH FYP TARGET (2015–2020)
Hydro power	260 GW	319 GW	350 GW
Wind power	100 GW	129 GW	200 GW
Solar power	35 GW	43 GW	100 GW (150 GW)*
Nuclear	40 GW	26 GW	58 GW
Carbon intensity	17% down from 2010	20% down from 2010	18% down from 2015
Energy intensity	16% down from 2010	18.2% down from 2010	15% down from 2015
Non-fossil share of primary energy	11.4%	12%	15%

Sources: National People's Congress 2016; US-China Economic and Security Review
Commission 2017; Seligsohn and Hsu 2016.
GW = gigawatt.
*The solar target was increased during the 13th FYP period.

The fundamental key to decarbonization in China will be a shift away
from coal. After many years of exponentially increasing coal demand, the
past five years have seen a marked change in consumption patterns. Just
a few years ago the US Department of Energy was projecting China's emissions in 2030 to be 25% higher than they are projecting now (EIA 2011,
2019). In contrast, their most recent analysis now projects a 3% *decline* in
carbon emissions between 2015 and 2050 (figure 2.2a). This outlook would
have been unheard of just a few years ago.[3]

This is in no small part due to the sizable and unexpected decline in
coal consumption in both the power and industrial sectors in China—the
two largest drivers of coal demand in China's economy—between 2013
and 2017 (figure 2.2b). As a result of these trends, many researchers

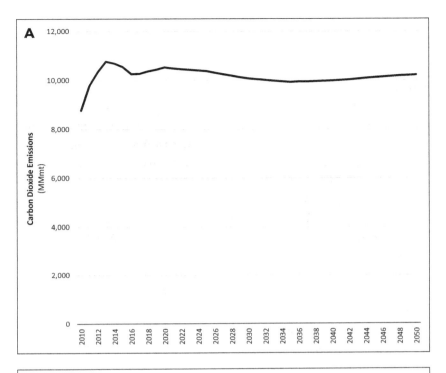

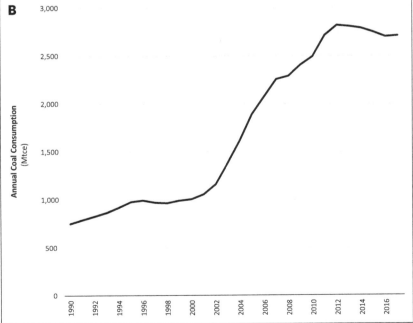

FIGURE 2.2   China's (a) carbon dioxide emission projections in million metric tons of carbon dioxide (MMmt) and (b) annual coal consumption trends in million tons coal equivalent (Mtce)

have claimed that coal use in China likely "peaked" in 2013 (Green and Stern 2016; Wang and Li 2017; Qi et al. 2016), though such claims remain controversial in the literature, particularly since it appears coal consumption is increasing again.

Indeed, there are many pressures on China's largest coal consuming sectors to reduce coal consumption. Coal power plants are being targeted by a number of government policies aimed at increasing efficiency and reducing pollution and will likely soon be the target of carbon dioxide standards under the new national emissions trading scheme. In addition, many energy-intensive industrial sectors including iron, steel, and cement plants are being ordered to shut down as part of a broader goal to transition the economy away from heavy, energy-intensive industry.

What is less clear is whether these trends are sustainable. Reduced plant operation and closures around the country are putting huge pressures on local governments to deal with slowing economic growth and unemployment. Overcapacity in these sectors, and particularly an over-build of coal plants, means there is pressure to increase coal electricity production, which is often done through the curtailment of renewables (Lewis 2016; Davidson, Kahrl, and Karplus 2016; Qi et al. 2018). The COVID-19 outbreak in early 2020 initially resulted in a reduction in emissions as factories were shut down, but as the government attempts to stimulate the economy, emissions are likely to rebound. As a result, China's long-term CO_2 emissions trends are unclear at best. It would be premature to assume China's emissions trajectory is on a path of long-term stagnation or decline, yet there is growing momentum and numerous reasons for the country to get serious about making a permanent transition away from coal.

A Reluctant Climate Leader

The Chinese government is taking a long-term approach to economic restructuring, which should eventually deliver emissions reductions. The question is whether China and other countries can accelerate reductions so that the world has a chance of moving towards an emissions pathway that avoids the most dangerous impacts of climate change.

China has deepened its commitment to decrease carbon emissions through domestic policies and reaffirmed bilateral and multilateral cooperation with other nations. In early 2017, President Xi Jinping gave a compelling speech at the World Economic Forum in Davos where he referred to the Paris Agreement as a "hard won achievement" and heralded his country's efforts to "pursue green development" (Xi 2017). His comments were a stark contrast to the "America First" policies promoted by US president Donald Trump that led to the US withdrawal from the Paris Agreement a few months later.

China's increasingly constructive engagement in international climate policy extends well outside of the UNFCCC. In 2016, China played a significant role in drafting an agreement to curb civil aviation emissions under the International Civil Aviation Organization (ICAO) and to reach the historic Kigali Amendment to the Montreal Protocol to phase down HFCs (ICAO 2016; Davenport 2016). In a high-level UN climate event in New York in late March 2017, China's UN ambassador reaffirmed the country's position to remain "steadfast in its determination to advance global climate governance" and to continue to "engage in pragmatic cooperation in such areas as energy efficiency, renewable energy, low-carbon cities and carbon markets" (Lewis and Li 2017). In 2017 China also hosted two key international clean energy meetings, the 8th Clean Energy Ministerial and the 2nd Mission Innovation Ministerial, both of which were originally conceived by the United States (Mission Innovation 2017). Meanwhile, China is strengthening ties with US allies such as the EU and Canada (Lungu 2017; Government of Canada and Government of China 2017). As American policies under the Trump administration have deprioritized climate change, China moved into the spotlight, poised to become a leader for climate action.

China's increasing involvement in international settings and the great strides in domestic climate policy under the 13th Thirteenth FYP raised expectations across the world for China to step into a leading role in climate negotiations. Despite this, China is still hesitant to play a leadership role on the international stage, which may once again be rooted in part in recent domestic reforms. In March 2018 at the first session of the 13th National People's Congress (NPC), a plan to reshuffle the entire government institutional structure was revealed (J. Zhang 2018). The plans included some of the most drastic reforms to China's environmental governance this decade (Ewing 2018), including the establishment of a new environment "super ministry," the Ministry of Ecology and Environment (MEE). While the ministry may see a staff increase over the former Ministry of Environmental Protection (MEP), it is also expected to take on new functions previously held by other ministries. This notably includes responsibility for climate change and emission reduction policies previously under the jurisdiction of the NDRC.

While some have lauded the change, which certainly could increase the efficiency with which pollutants are controlled in China since CO_2 will now be under the jurisdiction of the same ministry in charge of regulating other air pollutants (see chapter 4), the concern is that climate change is not just an environmental problem but also a development problem, and it is intrinsically tied to China's coal-based energy structure. The NDRC is one of China's most powerful ministries, overseeing national development strategy including for energy infrastructure and energy policy. Previously, when the NDRC was in charge of climate change policy, it had the ability to ensure energy policy and climate policy were at least somewhat aligned. In addition, NDRC's stature gave climate change a higher profile nationally, and helped it leverage cooperation from local governments and from powerful State-Owned Enterprises in the power sector. Now that the responsibility for climate policy has shifted to MEE, there is concern from local environmental activists and climate policy experts alike that "the hard-fought momentum of climate action could become the unintended casualty of this reshuffle" (Li 2018). The future of China's new cap-and-trade program may also hang in the balance, as NDRC was the longtime champion of this otherwise politically unpopular program.

In conclusion, China's energy challenges are shaping the way its leadership is approaching climate change mitigation at the domestic level, which in turn is shaping its positioning in international climate negotiations. For many years, China's climate change negotiating position favored inaction over action. However, changes in China's domestic energy situation over the past decade, including its successes in low-carbon technologies and its improved capacity to measure and predict energy and emissions trends, have permitted China to legislate with more confidence domestically and to be more engaged internationally. Despite the real challenges that the country faces in limiting emissions growth, all signs point to an intensified, multifaceted domestic effort to promote a low-carbon economy in the coming years.

Notes

1   This does not include hydropower projects larger than 50 megawatts (MW).
2   This is a common theme both within the broader international relations literature as well as in global environmental politics literature; this chapter focuses on the latter.
3   The 2019 International Energy Outlook projects that emissions will decline until 2035 and then gradually increase through 2050; most other scenarios show a peak and then gradual decline in emissions.

3

Energy and Climate Change Policies of Japan and South Korea

EUNJUNG LIM

JAPAN AND SOUTH KOREA, TWO OF THE MAJOR ECONOMIC POWER-houses in Northeast Asia, face similar energy and environmental concerns. Both are heavily dependent on fossil fuels and yet have also pledged to make significant reductions in their greenhouse gas (GHG) emissions internationally.

Such comparison of energy and climate change policy approaches of Japan and South Korea is valuable for several reasons. First, the two countries are significant players in the global economy. In 2018, Japan's gross domestic product (GDP) was approximately US$4.97 trillion and South Korea's GDP was US$1.61 trillion, ranking them as the third and eleventh largest economies in the world (World Bank 2019). Considering the economic scale of the two countries, their energy policies have large global economic consequences. Second, both Japan and South Korea are highly industrialized economies that are notably resource-poor, making them heavily dependent on energy imports. Understanding how these countries have tried to overcome their inherent disadvantages provides insights into a specific resource-poor economic development model.

Overview of Energy and Emissions Trends

The Japanese and South Korean economies are structurally very similar. Japan ranked as the world's fourth largest merchandise exporter and its fifth largest importer in 2016; it exported merchandise worth US$644.9

billion and imported merchandise worth US$606.9 billion, resulting in a surplus of US$38 billion. In 2015, 87.2% of Japan's total exports were manufactures, the most valuable of which were motor vehicles, motor vehicle parts, and electronic integrated circuits. Also in 2016, South Korea ranked as the world's eighth largest exporter and tenth largest importer—exporting US$495.4 billion and importing US$406.2 billion, recording a surplus of US$89 billion. In 2015, 89.4% of South Korea's exports were manufactures, including electronic integrated circuits, motor vehicles, and refined petroleum. Table 3.1 details the top five export manufactures of Japan and South Korea and shows similarities and differences between the two countries.

Manufacturing these products requires extensive energy resources. In 2016, Japan used 445.3 million tonnes of oil equivalent (Mtoe) of primary energy, whereas South Korea consumed 286.2 Mtoe in the same year (BP Global 2017). Moreover, a comparison between the two countries' primary energy consumption portfolios reveals a notable similarity in their energy mixes (table 3.2). Since the Fukushima Daiichi nuclear accident (hereafter the Fukushima accident), the most severe nuclear accident in the world since the 1986 Chernobyl disaster, Japan's dependence on nuclear energy has been replaced by expansion of natural gas consumption, which creates differences between Japan and South Korea, but table 3.2 shows that their dependence on petroleum and coal are comparable.

Since neither country has sufficient domestic energy resources, they are both leading energy importers. Among these resources, the largest share is petroleum, making both countries reliant on imports of crude oil, major reserves of which are concentrated in the Middle East. Japan ranked as one of the top four importers of crude oil, the largest importer of liquified natural gas (LNG), and the third largest importer of coal after China and India in 2015 (EIA 2017) while South Korea was the fifth largest importer of crude oil and condensate, the second largest importer of LNG after Japan, and the fourth largest importer of coal following China, India, and Japan in the same year (EIA 2018).

At the 2015 United Nations Climate Change Conference in Paris, the two countries pledged to substantially reduce their GHG emissions by 2030; Japan pledged a 26% reduction in GHG emissions from 2013 levels by 2030, and South Korea pledged a 37%[1] reduction from the business-as-usual (BAU) level—850.6 metric tons of carbon dioxide

Table 3.1 Top five export manufactures of Japan and South Korea (in million USD)

JAPAN				SOUTH KOREA			
TOP EXPORT MANUFACTURES		TOP IMPORT MANUFACTURES		TOP EXPORT MANUFACTURES		TOP IMPORT MANUFACTURES	
Motor cars for transport of persons	91,900	Petroleum oils, crude	50,768	Electronic integrated circuits	52,307	Petroleum oils, crude	44,295
Parts for motor vehicles 8701–8075	31,667	Petroleum gases	34,323	Motor cars for transport of persons	37,496	Electronic integrated circuits	30,027
Electronic integrated circuits	24,151	Electronic integrated circuits	17,112	Petroleum oils, other than crude	25,528	Petroleum gases	14,884
Laser machines	13,132	Medicaments in measured doses	17,047	Vessels for transport	25,140	Petroleum oils, other than crude	11,744
Machines with individual functions	12,305	Radio-telephony transmission tools	16,820	Parts for motor vehicles 8701–8075	21,838	Motor cars for transport of persons	9,342

Source: WTO 2017.

Table 3.2   Total primary energy consumption of Japan and South Korea by fuel type

	JAPAN (2015)	SOUTH KOREA (2017)
Petroleum and other liquids	42%	44%
Natural gas	23%	14%
Coal	27%	29%
Nuclear	< 1%	11%
Renewable sources	8%	2%

Sources: EIA 2017, 2018.

($MtCO_2eq$)—by 2030 across all economic sectors.[2] Accordingly, the South Korean National Assembly ratified the Paris Agreement on November 3, 2016, and the Japanese Diet ratified the Paris Agreement five days later on November 8, 2016. Considering the two countries' current dependence on fossil fuels, 92% out of total primary energy consumption for Japan and 87% for South Korea (table 3.2), this could be a double-edged sword because it could mean reducing production of their major export items, which would in turn damage their economies. Therefore, given the growing challenge of climate change, it has become increasingly imperative for Japan and South Korea to diversify their sources of secondary energy, especially sources of electricity.

Explaining Earlier Policy Differences between Japan and South Korea

In spite of similar energy challenges—high reliance on fossil fuels and international commitment to reduce emissions—Japan and South Korea have adopted different policy priorities. Japan has focused largely on curbing consumption, while South Korea has focused more on increasing generation efficiency. Their policy difference can be explained by several factors. First, South Korea's later economic development partially explains the difference in the two's energy policy priorities. Currently, both countries are experiencing low GDP growth rates, 0.52% and 2.95% for Japan and South Korea respectively in 2016 (World Bank n.d., d and e), indicating that both countries are in a mature stage of industrialization. Due to its long-lasting low GDP growth rate, Japan has tried to make its energy and electricity consumption more efficient. On the other hand, South Korea's economic growth rate dropped to the 2% range only in 2012, and it has been enjoying relatively higher growth rates for the last decade (World Bank n.d., e), encouraging energy policy makers to expand capacity based on growth-oriented calculations.[3]

Second, demographic changes contribute to different energy and electricity demand prospects for the two countries, in turn resulting in different policy priorities. Japan's population growth rate has been continuously lower than the South Korea's since 1975, turning to negative growth in 2011. Meanwhile, the two countries' fertility rates are similarly low, 1.5% and 1.2% respectively for Japan and South Korea in 2015. This statistic suggests that South Korea's population is likely to be shrinking even faster than Japan's once it hits its peak; however, South Korea's population is still growing and was expected to grow by an average of 0.69% per year between 2013 and 2020 (World Bank n.d., e). Furthermore, South Korea expects that the number of single-person households will increase rapidly, contributing to growth of electricity demand.

Third, after the Fukushima accident, all nuclear reactors in Japan stopped operating, which became another major motivation for energy conservation or electricity saving (*setsuden*) (Sakamoto, chapter 6). Since nuclear power had supplied about a third of Japan's electricity from the 1980s to 2011, when all its nuclear power plants shut down, Japan needed to adjust its electricity usage.

Fourth, energy conservation can be more viable for Japan than for South Korea because the Japanese economy is relatively less dependent on exports. Between 2014 and 2016, 17.7% of Japanese GDP consisted of goods and services for export, whereas South Korea exported 43.3% of its goods and services during the same period (WTO 2017). Given that their exports require extensive raw materials and energy, South Korea may face greater negative externalities from attempting to curtail total energy consumption.

Last but not least, structural differences in their respective electricity markets contribute to the divergence between the two countries' energy and electricity policies. Japan's electric utility industry began to liberalize in 1995 through the revision of the Electricity Business Act of Japan, and privatization of the electricity market has continued since. After the Fukushima accident, liberalization of the electricity market has accelerated: specifically, the Japanese Diet passed legislation in 2015 requiring the nine major power companies[4] holding monopolies over their own regional grids to spin off transmission operations and proceed to full privatization. By contrast, South Korea's electricity market is vertically integrated and its transmission and distribution sectors are monopolized by the state-owned Korea Electric Power Corporation (KEPCO), which comprises six power companies and four other subsidiaries in related fields.[5] This structural feature of the South Korean electricity market is an important reason why South Korea has highlighted stabilization of the electricity supply rather than encouraging changes to consumer behavior because there is almost nothing consumers can do in terms of price setting. In addition, the structure of the South Korean electricity market has encouraged policy makers and industry to expand nuclear power generation instead of converting to renewable energy because nuclear power has been regarded as a baseload source of electricity, since it is more lucrative and stable than other sources.

However, as the South Korean economy enters a more mature stage, and after the progressive Moon Jae-in administration came into power on May 10, 2017, after the political turmoil that ended up with the impeachment of Park Geun-hye, South Korea's energy policies have changed substantially, increasing similarities between the two countries' energy portfolios.

Similarities in Approaches to Energy and Climate Change Policy

Japan

Japan's strategy for energy and electricity can be seen in the energy white paper, published annually by the Agency for Natural Resources and Energy under the Ministry of Economy, Trade, and Industry (METI), as well as in the basic plan for energy published triennially by the same agency.[6] According to the latest iteration, *The Fifth Basic Plan for Energy* (METI

2018), Japan first aims to adhere to its "3E plus S" principles: energy security, environment, and economic efficiency "plus" safety, which was added after the Fukushima accident. Second, Japan aims to control total energy consumption by fully applying advanced energy conservation (*shō enerugi*, or *shō ene*, in a shortened form) technologies in every field, particularly in end-use electricity consumption. Third, Japan aims to expand electricity generation from low-carbon sources, mainly renewable energy and nuclear power. The plan emphasizes that renewables should become major sources for electricity generation through reducing costs and improving the transmission system. Though the plan clarifies that Japan needs to reduce its dependence on nuclear power and strengthen its safety regulations, nuclear power still remains one of the most important options to reduce carbon dioxide (CO_2) emissions.

The Fukushima accident was a critical event that almost irreversibly hurt the reputation and credibility of the Japanese nuclear industry and brought harsh public criticism against Japanese regulators. Before the Fukushima accident, the Japanese nuclear industry operated fifty-four nuclear reactors, and nuclear power supplied almost one third of the total electricity generation in Japan. The Democratic Party of Japan was the ruling party immediately following the Fukushima accident, and its position on nuclear energy was passive and inconsistent. However, since the Liberal Democratic Party (LDP) regained its position as the ruling party and Shinzō Abe returned to the prime minister's office in December 2012, Japan's nuclear policies have gradually returned to their original track. Abe's "nuclear U-turn" probably resulted from two factors. First, nuclear host communities are conservative—they vote LDP—and the majority of them continue to support reopening nuclear power plants. Second, Japan's plutonium stockpile has been rising continuously, and Japan wants to reduce the stockpile by recycling plutonium in mixed oxide (MOX) fuels and restarting halted nuclear power plants (Lim 2018).

South Korea

South Korea's policies for energy and electricity are found in its published basic plans for energy[7] and basic plans on electricity demand and supply,[8] by the Ministry of Trade, Industry, and Energy (MOTIE), as well as its *New and Renewable Energy White Paper*. A critical event that influenced the formation of South Korea's current energy and electricity policies occurred in 2011 as well, when it experienced a power outage across the country for several hours on September 15, 2011. Even before the blackout, stabilizing the electricity supply had been a high priority, but after the crisis, this priority became an imperative. The government realized that it needed to calculate and forecast domestic electricity demand more accurately and manage its electricity consumption more efficiently by applying various types of information and communications technology and creating a market for demand management.

Like Japan, South Korea has announced its intention to expand the use of electricity resources that emit less GHG, mainly renewable energy. Since the Moon Jae-in administration came into power, "nuclear phase-out" has become a political slogan. Though the South Korean government currently uses "energy transition" instead of "nuclear phase-out" because of contentious interpretations and domestic opposition (Lim 2019), the Moon administration aims to reduce South Korea's dependence on nuclear energy, but only gradually. Also, it is eager to expand the use of renewable energy. According to *The Third Basic Plan for Energy* released in June 2019 (MOTIE 2019), South Korea has declared the following five major policy goals from now to 2040: (1) reforming energy demand; (2) transitioning toward a cleaner and safer energy mix; (3) developing the energy supply system through enhancing channels for distribution and participation; (4) strengthening energy industries' competitiveness in the global market; and (5) improving material and immaterial platforms of the energy market. Following these goals, South Korea set 30% to 35% as the target for power generation share by renewable energy by 2040, but it did not set up any numeric target for nuclear (MOTIE 2019).

In summary, there has been a noticeable convergence between the energy policies of Japan and South Korea in the era of climate change. Renewable energy has received comparable attention from both countries as a major alternative source, while nuclear is likely to remain for a while as one of the major sources for power generation in spite of the massive scale of the Fukushima accident and consequent public concerns.

Emerging Policy Changes in Japan and South Korea

Both Japan and South Korea have faced difficulties in meeting the targets they pledged at the Climate Change Conference in Paris. For Japan, one of the major concerns is growing dependence on imported natural gas. Japan's natural gas consumption has been rapidly rising mainly for the power sector after the Fukushima accident and reached 4.4 trillion cubic feet per year (Tcf/y) of natural gas in 2015 (EIA 2017). Electricity generation from natural gas emits less GHG than coal but nonetheless, emits more than nuclear energy.

In reality, however, restarting nuclear reactors after the period of suspension is challenging to Japan on sociopolitical, institutional, and legal fronts. Any halted nuclear power plants need to get the approval of Japan's Nuclear Regulation Authority (NRA) and the agreement of host communities before restarting. Composed of five commissioners, the NRA finalized its safety requirements for reoperation on June 19, 2013, but it takes substantial time to inspect each power plant. Moreover, there is often local opposition. As mentioned above, nuclear host communities in Japan tend to be politically conservative and support restarting nuclear power plants, mainly because of their economic interests.

In one case, however, reoperation was vetoed by opponents. In early 2016, reactors 3 and 4 at Kanden's Takahama power plant in Fukui Prefecture resumed operation after the NRA's safety investigation. However, these two reactors were stopped again by a local court injunction in March 2016, citing safety-related issues. They were brought back online on in mid-2017 after legal disputes. As of March 2019, nine reactors including Takahama 3 and 4 and Sendai 2 are in operation, with seventeen reactors in the process of restart approval and thirty-seven reactors operable (WNA 2019). Meanwhile, Japan made a significant change in its system for renewable energy; Japan abandoned the renewable portfolio standard (RPS) and adopted feed-in tariff (FIT) instead in 2012. The Japanese government considers this change to be a success: average annual increase of installed capacity of renewable energy had been between 5% and 9% during the period of RPS (from 2003 to 2012), but the rate grew remarkably after FIT began in 2013, to 29% (METI 2017b). The most outstanding growth has been in solar power.

In contrast, the South Korea's original plan of expanding its nuclear power capacity has been modified by the new leadership. The Moon Jae-in administration has committed to significantly reducing coal and nuclear power plants as responses to increasing concerns of air pollution and nuclear safety among South Korean public. South Korea's fine dust, 70% of which comes from China (Kim 2017a), has caused serious health problems, and people's concerns have been increasing. Meanwhile, the record-breaking earthquake (5.8 on the Richter scale) that occurred in Gyeongju City[9] on September 12, 2016, exacerbated public concerns about nuclear safety that had grown following the Fukushima accident. The new government decided to shut down aged coal power plants (older than thirty years) immediately after its inauguration (Kim 2017b) and subsequently to shut down the country's oldest nuclear reactor, Kori 1 (Kim 2017c). Almost one year later, in June 2018, the country's oldest heavy water reactor, Wolsong 1, was also closed. Additionally, the Moon administration aims not to construct new reactors.[10]

Instead, the new administration is trying to expand gas thermal power and renewable energies. *The Eighth Basic Plan on Electricity Demand and Supply* was completed in December 2017, and according to this plan, South Korea will review the total electricity demand with more conservative calculations, will gradually reduce its dependence on nuclear and coal for electricity generation, and will expand use of natural gas and renewable energy (MOTIE 2017). Also, Moon appointed Paik Un-gyu, an engineering professor and an expert on renewable energy, as the administration's first minister of Trade, Industry and Energy, which indicates that the new administration will prioritize renewable energy.

Unlike Japan, South Korea adopted the RPS system in place of FIT on January 1, 2012, requiring larger power producers with installed capacity more than 500 megawatts (MW) to generate a minimum portion of their electricity from renewable energy sources. The results of RPS system are still mixed in South Korea. While the capacity of renewable power plants has grown substantially after South Korea adopted the RPS system, only biomass has been utilized at scale, primarily due to cost concerns; relatively less cost-efficient sources such as solar and wind power do not show significant growths compared to biomass.

Looking Ahead

As stated above, Japan and South Korea face common challenges of tackling energy security and reducing GHG emissions, and their policies have both similarities and differences. First, the two countries are likely to continue or even expand consuming natural gas while trying to expand renewable energy uses. Second, South Korea has previously assumed that its energy and electricity demand will grow, but recently, it has also tried to control demand as Japan does. Third, both Japan and South Korea, as inherent resource-poor but energy-consuming economies, are eager to reduce their dependence on imported natural resources, which has attracted them to nuclear power. However, South Korea's Moon government set a new policy goal, reducing nuclear dependence, whereas the Abe administration is working on restarting halted nuclear reactors. The two countries' attitudes toward nuclear power differed along with their political leadership. Fourth, coal is likely to remain a cornerstone of the two countries' energy portfolio mainly because of energy security concerns, though it is not helpful for their commitment to mitigate climate change.

Following the Fukushima accident, Japan's energy and environmental security situation faces some dilemmas. Specifically, while most of its operable nuclear reactors still remain dormant, Japan needs to import a substantial amount of natural gas in order to fully utilize gas-fueled power plants that are more efficient than coal-burning plants. In addition, since April 2016, the electricity market in Japan has been fully liberalized, causing large-scale electricity producers to lean more toward natural gas instead of rigorously expanding renewable energy. However, the expansion of power generation from gas-fueled plants can undermine both energy and environmental security because Japan relies on imports to meet the demand of natural gas, which emits much more GHG than nuclear or renewable energy. Nevertheless, the legal and institutional process of restarting nuclear reactors is complex in Japan and local opposition remains another barrier to overcome. These dilemmas have pushed Japanese people to practice exhaustive energy conservation and power savings on a daily basis. However, it is unclear whether Japan can accomplish its pledged goal from the 2015 Paris Climate Change Conference solely with these policies.

Ultimately, Japan seems to need to work on reoperation of its nuclear reactors while aggressively expanding renewable energy. Restarting nuclear reactors, however, can bring another burden—increasing the amount of spent fuels. Besides spent fuels that will strain storage capacity, the Japanese plutonium stockpile has been accumulating significantly as well; it was 47.8 metric tons in total as of July 2015, which marked Japan's stockpile as the fifth largest in the world and the largest among countries with no nuclear weapons (Lim 2016). Japan therefore needs to substantially reduce the total amount of plutonium; otherwise, concerned voices from other countries and domestic civil society will become louder. Moreover, Japan may need to show its strong commitment to reducing its plutonium stockpile and avoiding further buildup during its bilateral negotiations with the US (Acton 2015; Kobayashi 2017). Therefore, prioritizing MOX fuel-burning reactors, which can consume part of the existing plutonium stockpile, can be a recommended policy option for Japan (Lim 2016).

Meanwhile, the South Korean economy is now entering a long-term slow-down phase, and its population is likely to peak very soon, so electricity demand is also likely to stabilize. Scattering power capacity and spreading grids can help South Korea better deal with its current energy and climate change challenges by simultaneously increasing the efficiency of its electricity distribution system and promoting low carbon power sources. Since South Korea's inflexible energy pricing system and strict entry regulations interrupt entry and expansion of new businesses that are related to the consumption side of the electricity market (Lee 2015), demand-side reforms can bring higher and faster returns (Pittman 2014). However, how fast South Korea should accelerate liberalization of its electricity market remains a question without clear answers. As the Japanese case has shown, liberalization of an electricity market can bring about increases in fossil fuel use rather than promoting renewable energy sources, mainly because of cost efficiency. As long as the current government wants to reduce nuclear power uses, there is very limited room for South Korea to reduce its GHG, since it will continue to use large amounts of natural gas and coal for its electricity supply. South Korea needs to work on reforms of its electricity market and pricing, but hasty liberalization might not be the right answer.

Japan and South Korea, with limited access to natural resources, have strenuously worked on their economic development through manufacturing and international trade. Their economic development path, however, made them more vulnerable to external challenges such as energy supply crisis and fluctuating prices of natural resources. As they have turned to eco-developmentalism, this problem has not gone away. Instead their energy dependency has shaped the way they have implemented the turn: by technological innovation and increasing efficiency. Japan and South Korea should keep initiating technological innovation that can contribute to overcoming these external risks and continuing their economic growth. The two countries' experience can provide meaningful guidance to newly developing countries with limited natural resources.

Notes

1   Out of 37% reduction of GHG emission South Korea pledged at COP21, 11.3% (approximately one third of the target) will be accomplished through international carbon trade mechanisms. This decision made by the South Korean government has been criticized domestically as a compromised solution (Choi and Lee 2015).

2   Some critics view neither country's target as very aggressive. For example, the Climate Action Tracker, an independent analysis consortium composed of Climate Analytics, Ecofys, and New Climate Institute, evaluates Intended Nationally Determined Contributions (INDCs) of both Japan and South Korea as "highly insufficient" (Climate Action Tracker 2017).

3   When the South Korean government was preparing for COP21, it was assuming that South Korea's GDP would increase by an average of 3.08% per year for the period between 2013 and 2020 (Government of the Republic of Korea 2015).

4   In Japan, the electricity market was previously divided up into ten power companies that are regionally monopolies: Chugoku Electric Power Company (CEPCO), Chubu Electric Power (Chuden), Hokuriku Electric Power Company (Hokuden), Hokkaido Electric Power Company (HEPCO), Kyushu Electric Power (Kyuden), Kansai Electric Power Company (Kanden), Tokyo Electric Power Company (TEPCO), Tohoku Electric Power (Tohokuden), Shikoku Electric Power (Yonden), and Okinawa Electric Power Company (Okiden). The "major nine" excludes Okiden, which has no nuclear plants.

5   Following the government-led restructuring initiatives for the electricity market and the Electricity Business Act of South Korea, liberalization in the generation sector began. By Act on the Promotion of Restructuring

the Electric Power Industry that was proclaimed on December 23, 2000, KEPCO's power generation business was spun off into six power generation companies: Korea Hydro and Nuclear Power (KHNP), Korea South-East Power (KOSEP), Korea Midland Power (KOMIPO), Korea Western Power (WP), Korea Southern Power (KOSPO), and Korea East-West Power (EWP). Additionally, the Korea Power Exchange (KPX) was established on April 2, 2001, as a hub for the management of a relatively privatized electricity market. However, the South Korean electricity market remains still very centralized and vertically integrated.

6   Japan legislated the Basic Act on Energy Policy in June 2002, which requires the Japanese government to set up its basic plans for energy at least once every three years. Since then, METI has published plans five times: in October 2003, March 2007, June 2010, April 2014, and most recently, in July 2018 (METI 2014, 2018).

7   South Korea legislated the Basic Act on Low Carbon Green Growth in January 2010. Based on this law and its Energy Act, the South Korean government decided to establish its basic plans for energy for the coming twenty years quinquennially. The first one was published in 2008, the second in January 2014, and the latest in June 2019.

8   The South Korea's MOTIE is supposed to establish the country's basic plans for electric power supply biennially according to the Electricity Enterprises Act. The latest one, the *Eighth Basic Plan on Electricity Demand and Supply*, for 2017–31, was published in December 2017.

9   Gyeongju City is located in Northern Gyeongsang, very close to existing nuclear power plants in eastern coast areas and it also hosts a low and intermediate radioactive waste disposal facility.

10 Moon pledged to stop the plan to build new nuclear reactors, Shin Kori 5 and 6, during his presidential campaign (Shim 2017). After Moon's inauguration, his administration established the Shin Kori 5 and 6 Public Task Force, composed of 471 citizens, to publicly discuss whether or not to continue the construction of the two reactors. The task force finally concluded in October 2017 that the construction of the reactors should continue to run, but nuclear power generation should be reduced in the longer term (Lee and Lee 2017). The government followed the recommendations, and construction resumed.

4

The Politics of Pollution Emissions Trading in China

IZA DING

DURING A SEPTEMBER 2015 VISIT TO THE WHITE HOUSE, CHINESE president Xi Jinping announced to the world that China would develop a nationwide carbon cap-and-trade system for carbon dioxide by 2017. Experts celebrated Xi's pledge as a promising step towards a greener planet by the world's biggest greenhouse gas emitter (Davis and Davenport 2015). In December 2017, Xi's promise was realized when the National Development and Reform Commission (NDRC) held a news conference to announce the initiation of China's national carbon trading system.

China has had almost two decades' experience in local emissions trading pilots for pollutants other than carbon dioxide. Yet the government's fervid push for a cap-and-trade model of environmental regulation generates interesting questions about environmental politics in China. First, why did the Chinese government, operating in a quasi-market economy, embrace the market-based system of cap-and-trade? The success of a carbon market requires a well-developed legal and regulatory system, as well as local bureaucracies capable of enforcing the discharge cap of pollutants to create value in emission credits—both of which China currently lacks. In the realm of pollution control, command-and-control measures and top-down crackdowns have been the norm (Mol and Carter 2006), and in many cases have proven to be far more effective (van der Kamp 2017), leading to real improvements in air and water quality in recent years. Second, how do localities respond to central government advocacy of cap-and-trade, and what kinds of lessons can we generate about policy making and implementation in China?

The directed experimentation with local cap-and-trade programs in China—one type of policy strategy among the vast array of environmental and energy policy instruments employed in China—seems to be awkwardly placed within a quasi-market economy. Poorly aligned local political economic incentives, combined with the local government's need to fulfill policy targets, have created a situation in which emissions trading often serves as a type of "policy theater," whereby political authorities recruit stakeholders to act out the key processes of a policy in order to convince key audiences of the effectiveness of policy implementation. Localities then send inaccurate feedback to the central authorities, who in turn call for the policy's further expansion—partly based on its perceived positive results, partly based on the symbolic value of "market mechanisms" on a second, international stage. However, the lack of success in cap-and-trade pilots has meant that *local* initiatives to expand the policy have been few and far between.

Cap-and-Trade in China

In recent years, China has taken bold strides towards reducing pollution, curtailing carbon emissions, and shifting towards cleaner energy sources (discussed in detail in chapter 2). Debates about policy effectiveness aside, China's pledge to pursue a greener future is not mere symbolic rhetoric; sometimes it even seems to be willing to reduce emissions at the expense of social stability (Buckley and Hernandez 2016). In various public and intra-party speeches, President Xi has affirmed his commitment to environmental protection, which sends a positive signal to China's environmental regulators. On his first day in office, Xi declared in a speech about the "China Dream" that "our people love life and expect . . . a beautiful environment."[1] Since 2013, there has been a consistent decline in coal consumption, and China's policy to eliminate outdated industrial capacity (*taotai luohou channeng*) led to the reduction of 290 million metric tons of coal production capacity and 65 million metric tons of steel production capacity in 2016 alone (*Xinhua Net* 2017). During 2016–17, "central inspection groups" (*zhongyang ducha zu*) from the Ministry of Environmental

Protection (MEP) visited all provinces, leading to the temporary shut-down of 40% of all factories in China and a noticeable improvement in air quality during the months of the inspection (Nace 2017).

Meanwhile, the government is rolling out a plan to marshal market forces for emissions control through various cap-and-trade programs. In most versions around the world cap-and-trade works as follows: each year, the regulators set a ceiling on certain types of emissions. Each emitting firm is allotted a certain amount of emission permits; firms can then trade emission permits with each other on an exchange market, and over time, the government lowers the cap.

China's cap-and-trade programs have some distinct features. For example, regional caps are centrally determined such that they add up to the national targets of "total emissions control" (*zongliang kongzhi*) of each type of emission (set every year). The targets themselves are a defin-ing feature of the command-and-control system of emissions reduction used in China. Subsequently, the local Environmental Protection Bureaus (EPBs) may assign firm-level caps in the form of emission permits. Some-times the government sets more stringent caps on specific industries that it wants to phase out.

China has implemented two distinct types of policies using cap-and-trade: pollution cap-and-trade (*paiwuquan jiaoyi*) and carbon cap-and-trade (*tan paifang jiaoyi*).[2] Pollution cap-and-trade, or pollution trading, is a policy program that facilitates the regional trading of emissions permits of key air and water pollutants, including sulfur dioxide (SO_2) and nitro-gen oxides (NO_x) in industrial waste air, and ammonia nitrogen and chemical oxygen demand (COD)[3] in industrial wastewater. Carbon cap-and-trade facilitates the trading of carbon dioxide emissions permits in the form of "energy use rights" (*yong neng quan*) within specific indus-tries or regions. Until 2018, pollution cap-and-trade fell under the juris-diction of the MEP and local Environmental Protection Bureaus, whereas carbon cap-and-trade fell under the jurisdiction of the NDRC and local Development and Reform Councils (DRC). In 2018, a new environmental superministry—the Ministry of Ecology and Environment (Shengtai Huanjing Bu)—was established in part so that all emissions trading pro-grams would now fall under the purview of the same ministry.

Although the two different types of policies share similar goals and mechanisms, they have evolved somewhat independently (figure 4.1).

FIGURE 4.1   Evolution of pollution trading and carbon trading pilots

As early as the 1980s, China began research on emissions trading with the help of international organizations and experts (Zhang et al. 2016). In 2002, the central government formally rolled out the "4 + 3 + 1" program of pollution trading: SO_2 trading pilot programs in four provinces, three cities, and one state-owned company. One of the earliest firm-to-firm trades took place between two power plants in the eastern province of Jiangsu: a power plant in Taicang City purchased three years' worth of SO_2 emissions permits from a power plant in Nanjing City at ¥1,000 (US$143) per ton—a price arbitrarily set by the provincial EPB.[4] In 2004, two textile dyeing mills in Jiangsu participated in the first water pollution cap-and-trade: they signed a three-year contract that allowed one plant to sell its excess COD discharge permits to the other plant for ¥1,000 per ton (Jiangsu Price Association 2016). The Jiangsu EPB has since adjusted the price of permits every year, varying by industry: chemical plants pay six times as much as paper mills for COD permits. In 2007, eleven provinces launched pollution trading pilots to facilitate the trading of SO_2 and COD permits; the 12th Five-Year Plan (FYP 2011–15) further piloted the trading of ammonia nitrogen and nitrogen oxides. To date, fifty-three cities across thirteen provinces have piloted pollution trading, and eight other cities have officially announced plans.

These ten years of experience with SO_2 trading should have provided substantial lessons learned for the country to initiate carbon trading. However, since SO_2 and greenhouse gas emissions operated in separate policy domains—being governed by separate bureaucracies, in particular—until recently the sharing of knowledge, expertise, and institutional resources was minimal. This stands in contrast to the US experience: the US Environmental Protection Agency initiated SO_2 trading in the 1990s, and began preparations for carbon trading decades later, using very similar principles and drawing on shared expertise.[5]

Although it was not until a decade after the first pollution trading pilot that China initiated carbon cap-and-trade, the program expanded much more rapidly than pollution trading. Carbon trading was first featured in the 12th Five-Year Plan (FYP). In 2011, the NDRC approved seven pilot programs in five municipalities and two provinces, covering 2,052 firms; by 2014, all programs had become operational. In September 2015, Chinese officials met with US environmental officials in California to learn lessons from that state's cap-and-trade program (Davis and Davenport 2015).[6] In 2016, five more provinces established provincial cap-and-trade centers; eventually, all provincial pilots will be merged into a nationwide carbon market. In December 2017, the NDRC announced the start of the national carbon market covering the power sector. However, the actual document still reads like a draft plan, with key policy elements—such as the allowance allocation protocol—missing (Pizer and Zhang 2017).

Carbon trading has expanded much more rapidly in China than pollution trading, in part due to the relative strength of the NDRC vis-à-vis the MEP: powerful bureaucracies like the NDRC have stronger administrative capacity, better local and international connections, and hence stronger support for their policies. In Shenzhen, for example, the local DRC enjoyed support for the NDRC's carbon cap-and-trade program from industries and firms that had strong ties to municipal and provincial governments, as well as from its linkages with academic institutions and international organizations.[7]

Champions of cap-and-trade believe that this type of policy allows for the maximum amount of market efficiency yet incentivizes firms to save energy and invest in pollution abatement (Stavins 2008). Theoretically, for emissions trading schemes (ETS) to be considered a success, we should observe a few features of a mature market, including large numbers of voluntary participants, regular transactions in each trading period, and price fluctuations based on the supply and demand of emission credits. As the government gradually lowers the caps on emissions, we should expect firms to adjust their pollution levels and/or invest in pollution abatement in anticipation of the rising prices per unit of emissions. If local ETS prove to be more effective than command-and-control methods, we will likely observe the diffusion of such policies through bottom-up initiatives.

It may be too soon to evaluate the efficacy of the national ETS, but research on local cap-and-trade pilots in China (especially in pollution trading) shows that the results are lackluster. Local markets are generally thin, with small participant pools and few transactions per period. Local governments usually play the matchmaker, with transactions brokered by local EPBs, and prices set (or negotiated) before the trades take place. Trading in most localities has been irregular, and both firms and regulators are uncertain of the future of the trading programs. Inconsistent implementation and regulatory uncertainties result in low trust in the program and prevent firms from engaging in long-term planning. Not surprisingly, there is little evidence that "market mechanisms" in themselves have led to a reduction in emissions. China's reduction in SO_2 emissions was achieved mainly through government subsidies for desulfurizing equipment purchases by power plants rather than through emissions trading programs (Zhang et al. 2016). Similar issues emerged during carbon trading pilots, notwithstanding strong support and higher overall volumes traded (Lo 2016; Munnings et al. 2016). Poor data quality, state control of electricity prices, and the lack of private finance participation further exacerbated the issues (Guan et al. 2012).

Policy Theater

The lack of clear success in pollution trading in China after a prolonged period of experimentation raises the question of why the Chinese government continues to push for such a policy. The framework of "policy theater" can be used to make two related arguments about the development of pollution trading through its adoption, piloting, feedback, and expansion. First, "market mechanisms" (*shichang jizhi*), through which cap-and-trade operates, give the Chinese government reputational gains in the audience of the international community. Second, the policy theater of local ETS pilots—whereby local governments recruit stakeholders to act out pollution trading in order to convince upper-level authorities of the policy's efficacy—sends inaccurate feedback to the center, perpetuating a policy that has not shown effectiveness despite nearly two decades of experimentation.

A wealth of social science research interprets politics as "symbol-laden performances whose efficacy lies largely in their power to move specific audiences" (Esherick and Wasserstrom 1990, 839). Political theater can be found in political campaigns (Alexander 2010), social revolutions (Esherick and Wasserstrom 1990; Thompson 1978; Tilly 2008), and street-level governance (Ding, forthcoming). Some argue that symbolic performances in politics have the powerful effect of helping perpetuate existing political systems (Geertz 1980; Wedeen 2015).

Cap-and-trade in China plays out on two stages: the international stage, where the key audience is the international community, and the domestic stage, where the key audience is the upper-level authorities who evaluate the performance of their subordinates. In the case of domestic politics, although the success or failure of a market, by definition, should not impinge on non-market actors, local authorities were not given the option to truly fail. Therefore, in order to fulfill policy decrees set by the center, they invest resources and recruit key stakeholders to act "as if" the policy has been effectively implemented. At the same time, the actual efficacy of the policy pilots may be overlooked by the actors and audience alike. This is analogous to the concept of "security theater"—for example, increasing security measures at airports following the 2001 terrorist attacks, which projects an image of security but does not actually increase security according to some (Blalock et al. 2007; Schneier 2006).

Evidence of the lack of substantive effectiveness of local cap-and-trade pilots abounds. Close studies of local ETS pilots show an overall lack of enthusiasm among key stakeholders. The absence of local initiatives in policy expansion puts ETS pilots in sharp contrast to other policies that expanded through bottom-up initiatives during the Reform era—most notably, the return to household farming (Kelliher 1992; Yang 1998; Zhou 1996).[8] In the realm of environmental governance, China's "River Chief System" (Hezhangzhi) is an example of a local policy innovation that has organically diffused to other localities.[9]

Adoption

As latecomers in the development of an environmental regulatory system, Chinese regulators often looked to the advanced market economies (especially those in Western Europe and the United States) for solutions.

Since the beginning of the Reform era, Chinese regulators and academic institutions have been working with experts in the US and EU to design China's environmental policies.

Foreign organizations and experts have long advocated the adoption of market-based policies. The Environmental Defense Fund (EDF), for instance, played an instrumental role in introducing cap-and-trade to China in the 1990s. The head of EDF's China office, Dan Dudek, writes: "To understand China's environmental solutions, you have to think big," referring specifically to cap-and-trade (Dudek 2013). Through high-level exchanges, the experiences of SO_2 trading in the US and the EU emissions trading scheme were introduced to Chinese regulators. Local regulators also participate in training programs in Beijing or abroad coordinated by experts from foreign organizations like the EDF and US EPA.[10]

For those familiar with Chinese political economy, the image of the Chinese government racing full speed towards a full-fledged emissions market seems rather strange. Absent a well-functioning legal and regulatory system, command and control is significantly cheaper and much more effective. However, China's environmental policy—climate change policy, in particular—cannot be understood in isolation from international relations. Central authorities' enthusiasm about emissions trading can only be explained by its reliance on foreign expertise and by reputational demands arising from the international system. Adopting cap-and-trade signals China's desire for international cooperation and its asserted commitment to addressing climate change.[11] In the domestic arena, policy instruments relying on "market mechanisms" also help legitimate deeper economic reforms. However, recent developments in China suggest that economic conservatives (who favor state control of the economy) have gained the upper hand.

Piloting

In both pollution and carbon cap-and-trade schemes, central authorities selected provinces, and provinces selected municipalities to pilot the policies. This type of guided policy experimentation—first in selected localities, and then nationally from "point to surface" (*you dian dao mian*)—is familiar in the Reform era (Heilmann 2011). In the late 1970s and early 1980s, approximately half of China's regulations were in experimental status (Heilmann 2008, 6). Policy experimentation allows the Chinese Communist Party to take risks with controversial policies without jeopardizing its legitimacy since failures may be contained at the local level (ibid.). Yet the degree and ways in which policies expand from isolated local experiments to national coverage often vary from one policy to another, depending on the existence of central, local, and sometimes international stakeholders, their level of support, and their power.

In pollution trading, localities had full autonomy over the design of the policy instrument. Three components are central to the design of cap-and-trade: initial allocation, price setting, and firm participation. In the first stage, local EPBs allocate pollution permits to each firm within the pilot while maintaining the ability to adjust this allocation for future years based on overall pollution control targets (such as those outlined in the FYPs). In the second stage, a price is determined for each unit of pollution (the price often varies based on the type of pollutant); in some pilots local EPBs set the price, while others use auctioning. In the third stage, firms can buy or sell pollution permits on some sort of local exchange: some localities established "pollution rights exchange centers" (*paiwu quan jiaoyi zhongxin*) specifically for emissions trading, while others use existing local "equity exchange centers" (*chanquan jiaoyi zhongxin*), where pollution permits are traded alongside apartments, patents, and land.[12] Some pilots only allow trading between firms and EPBs, while others allow firms to trade with each other, with EPBs acting as facilitators. Theoretically, should market mechanisms activate, the second and third stages should be merged, and the prices of pollution permits should be determined by the number of free-floating permits, the number of participating firms, and firms' projection of future emission and future price changes. A healthy market would benefit from a large number of participants and a large volume of frequent transactions.

However, a few complications impede the creation of market mechanisms at each stage. First, because most pilots only allow new firms and existing firms that have expanded to purchase additional allowances, most of the local polluting enterprises are not in the market to buy. Furthermore, in order to pass their environmental impact assessment (*huanping*), firms have to invest heavily in pollution abatement facilities, leaving them few economic incentives to invest in pollution permits as well. Second, from the firms' perspective, there is significant uncertainty with regard to future price changes and cap adjustments. In recent years, command and control measures have become more stringent each year; environmental crises and ad hoc government decisions may lead to the abrupt shutdown of specific industries and firms.[13] Policy experiments can also be abolished altogether, especially when they lack powerful and supportive stakeholders. Therefore, firms have few incentives to buy pollution credits when there is uncertainty over whether they may hold value in the future. Finally, local EPBs lack the enforcement capacity to prevent illegal pollution: if wastewater can be discharged through secret pipes into local rivers without a high likelihood of severe punishment, firms may prefer the risk of fines than to purchase extra permits.[14]

As a result, voluntary firm participation in pollution trading is extremely low in most pilots. Even pilots that use auctions for price setting have not seen substantial frequency or volume of trades. For example, the Hubei pilot for pollution trading in COD that uses auctioning has only had six transactions between 2008 and 2016 (Zhang et al. 2016). Meanwhile, Jiaxing County, one of the COD pilots that has produced the largest amount of transactions, uses fixed prices set by the government. A few years into the pilot, although thousands of firms in Jiaxing are officially enrolled in the emissions trading program, few participate in auctions. Local EPBs broker trades between firms that can be easily mobilized, either because they are well-connected with the firms (asking for participation is equivalent to asking for a favor), or because the firms are weaker (asking for participation as a form of payment for environmental violations).

Nominally, pollution trading uses market mechanisms, but its actual implementation often does not differ from a policy of pollution taxes or fees based on command-and-control methods of permit allocation. In fact, a firm-level survey in Zhejiang found that 36% of firms view pollution trading as another instrument through which the local government raises revenue (Han and Hu 2011). Nevertheless, localities use market language in their articulation of the policy, invest substantial amounts of money to establish trading platforms, and use connections and influence to broker trading between firms that would otherwise not participate.

Although other policy goals—such as meeting pollution reduction targets and preventing public environmental crises—are far more important to local EPBs' performance evaluation, pollution trading is one item to be checked off the bureaucracy's to-do list (which usually contains at least a few dozen goals). Local EPBs often set targets on the number of transactions to be achieved in a year or month, as it would with the Total Emissions Control (Zongliang Kongzhi) policy, which means that at the end of the time period any unmet targets will have to be brokered by the EPB.

Feedback

Indeed, case studies of pollution trading report that local governments have to play matchmaker for there to be any transactions (Tao and Mah 2009), which raises the question of why localities invest significant resources into policy theater. For starters, unlike local initiatives, top-down experiments leave little room for localities to fail: failure is never explicitly stated as an option. An extreme version of such information asymmetry may be seen during the Great Leap Forward (1958–61), when localities exaggerated grain production to hide policy failure, which led to the over-procurement of grain by the center, contributing to one of the greatest man-made famines in human history (Becker 1998; Bernstein 1984; Kung and Chen 2011).[15] In the much less extreme case of pollution trading, the power imbalance between the MEP and local EPBs combined with the lack of actual local government interest in pollution trading causes the localities to over-report the substantive implementation of the pilots and to exaggerate their positive impacts.

Of course, the center is never completely blind to local politics—in fact, it has abundant mechanisms to keep local officials in check, such as the petitioning system and inspection teams. Further, the information environment is much freer in the Reform era, and local officials can speak much more freely to the center. Yet, local EPBs—given their lack of authority in the bureaucratic system—seldom resist central directives, discard the policy, or report it a failure; instead, they focus on positive reporting. Such information asymmetry in policymaking complicates the "experimentation under hierarchy" model, which assumes that the center has good information on local policy implementation. Even in cap-and-trade, it would be far-fetched to argue that the center is blind to the lack of clear local success. Yet, without significant negative costs, the policy will likely continue for its symbolic value.

Expansion

The lack of accurate and timely feedback—as well as path dependency—helps to explain why the center continued to push for the expansion of pollution trading. Yet in reality, the expansion has been painfully slow, without meaningful diffusion across localities or initiatives shaped by local priorities. In other words, despite decades of experimentation and central government encouragement, pollution cap-and-trade has not scaled up, with the exception of Zhejiang Province, which established a provincial-level trading platform for COD, SO_2, nitrogen oxides, and ammonium nitrogen. Currently, only a sixth of all Chinese cities have plans for pollution trading. In 2016, of the seventeen provinces that had pollution trading pilots, only six reported any transactions; only slightly over half of the cities that had ever piloted emissions trading reported any transactions (figure 4.2).

The slow expansion (if not retrenchment) of pollution trading is partly due to the nature of China's pollution control policy, which is still defined by geographic command and control: at the beginning of each year, central authorities set nationwide pollution reduction targets based on goals outlined in the FYP. These targets are then divided among provinces, and provinces divide them among cities and counties. Therefore, a local government's primary environmental goal is to meet the target reduction for each pollutant; over-implementing emissions trading or facilitating interjurisdictional cooperation generate few benefits for local officials' career prospects.[16] As Shin (2013, 928) summarizes, local EPBs lack the "infrastructure, resources, transparency, and sometimes willingness" to enforce emissions trading. This inertia is felt at the local level by firms and neighboring governments: given the policy's lack of success, they tacitly resist participation. A provincial EPB official candidly described emissions trading as "bogus prosperity" (*xujia fanrong*) and "a numbers game" (*shuzi youxi*), a reference to its theatrical implementation and the lack of substantive effects on firm behavior (MEP Official 2016).

Many localities that claim to have implemented pollution trading policies also seem to conflate the policy of paid pollution permits (*paiwu quan youchang shiyong*) with market-based emissions trading (*paiwu quan jiaoyi*). China is clearly moving toward a system in which polluters have to pay for each unit of pollution. However, allowing market forces to set

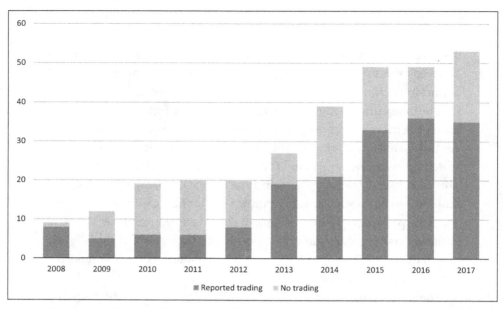

FIGURE 4.2   Number of municipal pollution trading pilots, 2008–17

prices in the inter-firm exchange of pollution permits is a separate matter. The overuse of the word "market," however, legitimates the push for an otherwise ineffective policy experiment.

China's experience with pollution cap-and-trade illuminates the convoluted and often opaque process of policy making and implementation during the Reform era. Despite almost two decades of local experiments across a variety of conventional air and water pollutants, cap-and-trade has yet to demonstrate its effectiveness.[17] However, central authorities have continued to push for the expansion of emissions trading in both carbon and pollutants, including an ambitious plan to establish a nationwide carbon market. One explanation for this push is that adopting cap-and-trade helps establish China as a credible player in the international system and an endorser of the free market. Another is that local policy theater in the process of policy experimentation sends inaccurate feedback to the center, which pushes for the policy's expansion—partly based on its perceived positive outcomes, partly based on its symbolic benefits—while overlooking its lack of substantive effectiveness.

Policy experimentation should be viewed as a dynamic process of central-local communication through which information may be skewed due to each side's particular position and associated incentives in the bureaucratic hierarchy. In the case of pollution trading pilots, local authorities treat the policy as a performance target to be fulfilled rather than an experiment to be tested, which leads to policy theater. However, the environmental bureaucracy's lack of administrative capacity means that emission caps cannot be strictly enforced, and environmental violations often go unpunished, leaving firms few incentives to voluntarily exchange emission credits.

To make emissions trading work, central authorities will have to empower local environmental bureaucracies with greater administrative capacity, foster greater vertical accountability and transparency, streamline bureaucratic responsibilities, and increase policy consistency across localities over time. Such changes seem to be well under way. The 2018 "Super Ministries Reform" (Dabuzhi Gaige) led to the new Ministry of Ecology and Environment, whose bureaucratic purview will encompass a plethora of policy issues previously not under its jurisdiction, such as carbon emissions control (previously under the NDRC), the protection of groundwater (previously under the Ministry of Land and Resources), and the protection of oceans (previously under the State Oceanic Administration), etcetera (*Xinhua Net* 2018). Recent reforms of "vertical accountability" (*chuizhi guanli*) have also increased the power of the central environmental bureaucracy over its local subsidiaries through measures such as shifting the power of appointment of local EPB officials from local governments to the EPB one level above. While it is too early to assess the influence of the ministerial restructuring on the efficacy of China's cap-and-trade programs, it is very likely that this new bureaucracy will be in a better position to enforce China's environmental regulations, including its cap-and-trade programs.

Notes

1   A full transcript of President Xi's speech is available at BBC News (www
.bbc.com/news/world-asia-china-20338586).
2   I use "pollution cap-and-trade" or "pollution trading" to refer to the
MEP-administered policy that facilitates the local trading of industrial
emissions. I use "carbon cap-and-trade" or "carbon trading" to refer to the
NDRC-administered carbon emissions trading policy. The Chinese government uses these two terms to refer to two distinct policy programs.

3   Chemical oxygen demand (COD) is used to quantify the amount of oxidizable pollutants in surface water or wastewater as a way of measuring water pollution.

4   Records of these earlier cap-and-trade pilots make very little mention of the setting of caps. In fact, regional cap setting is meaningless if not all firms in the region participate in the market.

5   However, carbon trading in the US has yet to happen at the federal level due to the pushback from entrenched political economic interests. Several states have their own programs or participate in regional programs.

6   Dudek (2013) wrote that the Environmental Defense Fund (EDF) helped develop Shenzhen's carbon cap-and-trade program and broker an agreement between California and Shenzhen to collaborate on the design and implementation of carbon cap-and-trade.

7   Interview with academic expert in Shenzhen, 2016.

8   Dali Yang (1998) finds that the return to household farming in the Chinese countryside began as spontaneous local initiatives in areas that were most devastated by the Great Leap Forward famine. In the Reform era, a hallmark of the policy making process is "experimentation under hierarchy," in which the local experimentation of controversial policies precedes their nationwide expansion (Heilmann 2008).

9   The RCS divides a waterway into specific segments and assigns the protection of each segment to the care of a local official. The policy was the brainchild of Qiu He, who served as deputy governor of Jiangsu Province and deputy party secretary of Yunnan Province before he was ousted at the end of 2016 on corruption charges. After its initial implementation in Jiangsu in 2007–08, various neighboring provinces adopted this policy before central authorities called for its expansion at the end of 2016 (*China Daily* 2017).

10 For example, the EDF coordinates training programs for local regulators in the carbon pilots launched in 2007.

11 Donald Trump's decision to withdraw the United States from the Paris Agreement seems not to have derailed China's Paris commitment; however, China's plans for a nationwide carbon market by the end of 2017 fell behind schedule.

12 See, for instance, the website of Hangzhou's equity exchange (www .hzaee.com/) and its subpage for the exchange of pollution permits (www.hzaee.com/311/).

13 During 2016–17, the MEP temporarily shut down about 40% of all factories in China in an environmental campaign.

14 Although the "online monitoring" system (*zaixian jiankong*) sends emissions data to local EPBs, tinkering with the program is not hard. Firms can also create secret source points that are not monitored by the program.

15 Ideological reasons and elite politics also played a role.

16 The lack of interjurisdictional expansion of the policy, however, is not the biggest problem, as Chinese localities are large in size, often housing thousands of polluting enterprises in an individual city.

17 It would be far-fetched to characterize most current local ETS pilots as failures. Prior research demonstrates wide variation in the design and implementation of local cap-and-trade pilots. Chongqing, for instance, is one of the few pilots with regular, frequent auctions and what seems to be a healthy longitudinal fluctuation in the pricing of SO_2 and COD permits (Zhang et al. 2016). However, the scholarly consensus is that, overall, emissions trading has not demonstrated itself to be an effective policy instrument.

5

Legal Experts and Environmental Rights in Japan

SIMON AVENELL

AMONG THE DIVERSITY OF ACTORS IN THE JAPANESE ENVIRON-
mental movement, lawyers and legal scholars have received surprisingly
scant attention. While earlier research has thoroughly analyzed antipollution and antidevelopment lawsuits in the country, we still know very
little about the significant role of legal experts as agenda setters and
influential actors in Japanese environmental activism more generally.
This is an unfortunate lacuna because legal experts have contributed in
myriad ways both inside and outside the courtroom. Beyond their popular reputation as "guns for hire" in environmental litigation, legal experts
have been at the forefront in proposing provocative new principles and
discourses that have pushed environmental knowledge in Japan in new
directions. They have stimulated and supported environmental protest
and activism, oftentimes as active participants, and they have served as
conduits between the domestic and international arenas in an era of burgeoning global environmentalism. In terms of Japan's eco-developmental
state, legal experts have influenced policy makers through their involvement in litigation and public advocacy. In the late 1960s and early 1970s
they forced policy makers to address the industrial pollution wreaking
havoc on the environment and human health. Thereafter they continued to shape policy makers' (and others') attitudes towards the environment through ideas about environmental rights, which moved beyond
the narrow issue of industrial pollution to include such notions as the

right to sunlight and scenery and even the inherent rights of nature. Policy makers did not adopt all of these proposals, of course, but environmental rights did find their way into Japan's eco-developmental state, for instance in the Environmental Impact Assessment Law of 1997, which requires not only consideration of environmental conservation and human health but also factors such as the maintenance of the landscape and spaces for people to interact with nature.

Legal experts—their activism and their conceptual innovations—have contributed to and have shaped environmental knowledge and activism in contemporary Japan over the past half century. Like medical doctors, chemical engineers, economists, and other specialists, legal experts must be understood both within and beyond their specific professional and disciplinary fields as critical producers of environmental knowledge and as influential environmental activists in their own right. Their role in fostering a language and consciousness of rights is particularly important within the Japanese environmental movement where there had primarily been a sense of victimization or even acquiescence. This rights discourse served several objectives: it connected the struggles of pollution victims to the burgeoning human rights movement worldwide and gave them the courage to litigate; it facilitated provocative reconceptualization of the human-environment relationship within policy making communities and society at large; and it offered local activists a powerful language that connected to the highest democratic principles of the postwar constitution.

Legal Experts, Rights, and the Environment

In their important study on cause lawyering and social movements, Austin Sarat and Stuart A. Scheingold (2006, 11) point to the role of lawyers in helping social movement actors to collectively connect their grievances to legality. Lawyers and legal experts become the principal architects of what Scheingold (2004, xix) calls a "myth of rights" that activists can deploy in the political realm when legal channels have been shut down. The animal rights movement is a case in point. In *Unleashing Rights*, Helena Silverstein (1996, 18) shows how activists in this once-marginalized movement applied the legal language of rights to animals, thus expanding this discourse to a completely new realm. Legal experts' advocacy of environmental rights in Japan has mirrored this process of movement empowerment through rights articulation. Important too, although legal experts often propagate rights discourse with specific litigation objectives in mind, the discourse has influence well beyond judicial institutions (Silverstein 1996, 19). In a sense, once set free, rights take on a life of their own in society and especially within movements—oftentimes to the surprise of their legal creators. In connection to Japan, rights discourse has provided activists with a "vocabulary of social protest" along with strategies for mobilization and public advocacy (Feldman 2000, 10, 39) Even though many of the asserted rights—like environmental rights—may have lacked judicial or constitutional affirmation, they have stimulated political action and given practical clarity to vague feelings and frustrations (Feldman 2000, 5).

Japanese legal experts played an especially critical role in stimulating a kind of rights revolution in their country in the 1960s and 1970s. Japanese people had long been asserting their rights, but in this period the rights asserted were new. Along with environmental rights, legal experts and activists began to advocate entitlement to privacy, sunlight, ventilation, views, serenity, waterfronts, and beachfronts as well as nonsmokers' rights, access rights, and rights of rebuttal (Senba 1989, 42). The rights were new because they were not stipulated in the constitution or associated with existing legal theories or decisions (Feldman 2000, 39). These new rights met with mixed success in the courts, but for many advocates legal legitimization played only second fiddle to the more important objectives of swaying public attitudes and shaping policy (Foote 2014, 171).

The evolution of environmental rights discourse is best understood in this way. Even though some legal proponents of the idea have been skeptical about its utility as a legal principle in litigation, as committed activists they have recognized how the idea of environmental rights has the potential to precipitate change through policy innovation and the fostering of attitudinal change in society. Given the evolution, diffusion, and growing sophistication of environmental rights discourse in Japan coupled with Japan's transition to an eco-developmental state, their expectations have not been misplaced.

The Challenge of "Environmental Rights"

Legal experts' advocacy of environmental rights grew out of Japan's ago-
nizing encounter with industrial pollution in the 1960s and early 1970s.
This history has been told in great depth elsewhere (Avenell 2012; Iijima
2000; Tsuru 1999; Ui 1992), but for our purposes it is important to note
the extraordinary role played by pollution victim case lawyers and their
professional associations nationwide during this period. In the courts,
lawyers—usually working pro bono (Foote 2014, 173; Nakajima 2010,
11)—facilitated momentous victories in the so-called Big Four pollution
cases instigated in the late 1960s. Most infamous among these was the
tragic methylmercury poisoning of communities scattered around the
picturesque Minamata Bay in Kyushu. Yet it was not an environmental
agenda per se that drew cause lawyers to these cases but instead, a commitment to addressing the flagrant violation of pollution victims' fundamental human rights. Prior to the 1960s, the environment was
essentially absent from the legal imagination in Japan other than in private property law and a few local ordinances regulating factory emissions (quite ineffectively). Thus, lawyers' involvement in environmental
issues grew out of their extant initiatives and associations for the defense
of human rights. In fact, the first statement from lawyers demanding a
legislative response to industrial pollution came at the 7th Annual Congress on the Protection of Human Rights of the Japan Federation of Bar
Associations (JFBA) in 1964. Along with a demand that authorities immediately institute systems of industrial oversight and legislation, the
JFBA Human Rights Protection Committee (HRPC) designated industrial
pollution a "serious violation of human rights" demanding immediate
action by federation members (Nichibenren 2010, 3). In 1967 the JFBA
established a Special Subcommittee on Pollution within the HRPC and
only in 1969 did this become an independent Pollution Countermeasures
Committee (PCC). Evidencing the magnitude of the industrial pollution
problem, by 1971 the PCC boasted a membership exceeding one hundred
lawyers nationwide (Nichibenren 2010, 4). Although human rights concerns continued to dominate legal experts' involvement in antipollution and environmental litigation thereafter, over time their agenda
expanded to include concern for environmental protection and nature

conservation. The introduction of environmental rights discourse greatly encouraged this transformation.

Despite their victories in industrial pollution lawsuits, by the early 1970s many lawyers and activists had become frustrated with the compensation-based approach to pollution which only provided remedies after human injury and environmental degradation. A common refrain among antipollution lawyers at the time neatly encapsulates their exasperation: regardless of courtroom successes, they said, "pollution begins with suffering and ends with suffering" (Nakajima 2010, 21). Particularly vexing was the principle of "tolerable limits" utilized by the courts in pollution cases to weigh up damages against the utility or value of the polluting industry or infrastructure. In a growing economy, activists too struggled to articulate a language powerful enough to challenge prevailing notions of the "public interest" and the "harmonization of economy and environment" used by industry and political leaders to justify new industrial developments and infrastructure projects. Some local activists even resorted to the appropriation of conservative criticisms (Miyazaki 1975). Opponents of a freight line development in Yokohama, for example, celebrated their "local egoism" (i.e., not in my backyard, or NIMBY, logic) as the only pathway to a genuine "public interest" reflective of citizen preferences. This was a clever appropriation of conservative discourse, but the negative—for some, even unpatriotic—connotation of "local egoism" undoubtedly undermined the broader appeal of their cause.

Against this backdrop, legal experts' proposal of environmental rights as human rights in 1970 was a groundbreaking intervention. In terms of providing a new legal principle for litigation, environmental rights promised to transcend earlier notions of tolerable limits, since the primary question now became environmental degradation regardless of the objective value of a project. The inherent threat to the establishment, of course, was that local communities might be able to invoke their environmental rights to halt all forms of public works or industrial development, hitting at the heart of Japan's seemingly invincible postwar "construction state" (Woodall 1996). As one influential activist put it, the environmental rights concept threatened nothing less than a "massive social transformation" (Matsushita 2008, 267). Discursively, environmental rights offered a potent new language to activists. Rather than appealing to a negative "local egoism" and the language of victimization, they could now couch their struggles in the lofty human rights principles of the postwar constitution and, later, international instruments such as the Declaration of the United Nations Conference on the Human Environment (1972).

In the first instance, then, legal experts' adoption and advocacy of environmental rights emerged from frustration with the domestic environmental crisis and the existing pollution litigation framework. But it was also a product of their attentiveness to developments in environmentalism worldwide. Activist lawyers became aware of the idea through the International Symposium on Environmental Disruption, sponsored by the International Social Science Council and held in Tokyo in March 1970 (Tsuru 1971). This symposium brought together world experts on environmental matters and served as an important launchpad for the United Nations Conference on the Human Environment (UNCHE) convened in Stockholm two years later. Among the participants in Tokyo was Joseph L. Sax, a young legal scholar from the University of Michigan at Ann Arbor, whose work focused on the development of an environmental rights agenda (Sax 1971a, 1990). Sax (1971b, 223) told participants about a novel form of litigation in the US instigated by citizens not based on "conventional private interest" but "as members of the general public asserting rights simply *as* members of the public." He described these lawsuits as "citizens' revolts against the official protectors of the public interest," similar in many respects to Japanese protests in the name of "local egoism" but different in their appeal to rights (Sax 1971b, 224). The Tokyo Resolution of the symposium likewise urged "the adoption in law of the principle that every person is entitled by right to the environment free of elements which infringe human health and well-being and . . . nature's endowment, including its beauty, which shall be the heritage of the present to the future generations" (Tsuru 1971, 319–20).

Attentive to the utility of this idea, legal scholars and activist lawyers began conceptualizing "environmental rights" (*kankyōken* in Japanese) in earnest only months later. Two antipollution lawyers from Osaka, Nitō Hajime and Ikeo Takayoshi, first proposed the idea at the JFBA's 13th Annual Congress on the Protection of Human Rights held in Niigata in September 1970 (Nitō and Ikeo 1973, 41–60). Soon thereafter Nitō, Ikeo, and colleagues in the Osaka Federation of Lawyers established an

Environmental Rights Study Group which subsequently published the influential volume *Environmental Rights* (Kankyōken) in 1973 (Osaka Bengoshikai 1973). Along with advocating environmental rights as a tool for obtaining injunctions in antidevelopment lawsuits, the volume evidences a nascent ecological perspective among legal experts at this time. As one of the authors noted "to date we have believed that the resources of nature were infinite. But, in reality, these are limited things within the finite space of the globe." Reconceptualizing pollution problems under the wider issue of "environmental destruction" and struggling for "environmental rights," he said, represented a new consciousness of the "ecological crisis" among Japanese lawyers (Osaka Bengoshikai 1973, 63). The JFBA released its own Proposal for an "Environmental Right" in 1972, which its delegation presented to the NGO Environmental Forum at UNCHE in 1972 (Gresser et al. 1981, 146–47). In 1973 the lawyer Yamamura Tsunetoshi and his colleagues went a step farther, proposing three new pieces of draft legislation based on environmental rights principles: the Basic Law for Environmental Protection, the Planning Law for Environmental Protection, and the Law to Ensure Participation of Residents and Others in Determinations for Local Development (Nichibenren 2010, 14). Although the Japanese Diet would not pass the Basic Environment Law (Kankyō kihonhō) until 1993 (which does not contain the term "environmental rights"), proposals such as this opened up a broader discussion on environmental protection where there had primarily been debate over pollution abatement before. It should be noted too, that involvement in the environmental rights issue had a transformative effect on legal experts. Yamamura Tsunetoshi, for example, thereafter became a leading advocate of nature conservation and global environmental issues in Japan and internationally, notably as director of the influential Japanese NGO, the Citizens Alliance for Saving the Atmosphere and the Earth (CASA) (Yamamura 1998).

How then did these legal experts define environmental rights? The JFBA's 1972 Proposal for an "Environmental Right" stated that "the natural environment such as air, water, sunshine and natural scenery is an indispensable and valuable resource for human beings. It must be completely separated from the ownership of the real estate. The right to utilize the environment must be a common property to be distributed equally to everyone regardless of whether or not he is an owner of real estate. . . . The Environmental Right, therefore, must be established as a community's collective right, giving the people a position substantially equal to that of industry" (translated in Gresser et al. 1981, 147). Proponents argued that environmental rights had a basis in both constitutional and private law. Constitutionally, they pointed to Article 25, the right to maintain the minimum standards of wholesome and cultured living, and Article 13, the right to life, liberty, and the pursuit of happiness. In terms of private law, they also asserted that local residents could seek injunctions on public works or corporate developments that threatened to damage to their local environments (Nichibenren 1978, 231).

The environmental rights idea met with a degree of resistance among legal experts, including lawyers involved in antipollution litigation, not to mention in the courts. Many noted the absence of any reference to environmental rights in the constitution and, even if these rights were implicit in Articles 13 and 25, skeptics said they were merely "programmatic rights" that the government was required to strive towards but could not become the basis of specific rights assertions in litigation (Nichibenren 1978, 232–233). There were also questions about the extent of the "environment" claimed under environmental rights suits, the demarcation of rights holders, and the degree of damage subject to injunction (Awaji 1995, 9). Moreover, because environmental rights pertained to public and/or communal benefits as opposed to specific individual benefits, skeptics also doubted whether environmental rights could form the basis of civil lawsuits for injunctions against specific environmental disruptions (Yoshimura 2010, 60). Japanese courts echoed these misgivings and have yet to recognize environmental rights.

In a famous case to prevent evening flights out of Osaka International Airport begun in 1969, the Supreme Court in its 1981 decision rejected the plaintiff's request for injunctive relief and stated categorically that it was not making any determination on the violation of so-called "environmental rights" (Senba 1989, 52). Although courts have clearly been sensitive to environmental rights claims by local communities, to date their preference has been to utilize existing rights relating to "personal integrity" (i.e., the right to health) and/or individual property rights rather than to take the radical step of creating a new right (Ōsugi 2012, 31; Koiwai 2012, 57). Japan is no exception here. The United Nations is yet to approve a "general normative instrument on environmental rights"

(Shelton 2009, 4). Moreover, although the constitutions of South Korea, India, Spain, Brazil, and Turkey indeed call on their governments to strive for a healthy or pleasant environment, none of them appear to create "justiciable environmental rights" (Boyle 2007, 478–81).

Environmental Rights Beyond the Courts

Despite such hesitancy and even resistance within legal circles in Japan (and elsewhere), the idea of environmental rights has been a powerful tool for legal experts and activists to galvanize support for specific local struggles and pressure officials and corporate executives to genuinely address environmental problems in the country. Furthermore, the numerous lawsuits invoking environmental rights, although unsuccessful, have served as lightning rods for raising public awareness about the environment (Fujikawa 2013, 39). Indeed, as with litigation in other spheres, defeat in court may actually work "to the advantage" of litigants "by stoking a sense of outrage among movement members, their allies, the general public, and even erstwhile opponents" (Maclachlan 2014, 140).

Beyond the courts, the idea of environmental rights has attracted significant attention in the Japanese media, in political and bureaucratic circles, and especially in environmental movements. *Asahi shinbun* ran front page stories on the idea immediately after the initial JFBA-HRPC congress in 1970 (*Asahi shinbun* 1970a, 1; 1970b, 1). Thanks to this reportage, activists around Japan became aware of the idea. Environmental rights lawsuits such as the Osaka Airport case and the Date and Buzen cases discussed below, although unsuccessful, had the effect of exerting great public and media pressure on officials to institute environmental assessment ordinances and to adopt other pollution abatement countermeasures (Shimizu et al. 1981, 60). National land development and infrastructure projects began to incorporate environmental considerations (environmental impact assessments) within their planning processes (Nichibenren 1978, 231). Some prefectures and municipalities even included the concept of *kankyōken* in their environmental ordinances, as in Tokyo and Saitama Prefectures, and the cities of Kawasaki, Yokohama, and Osaka (Awaji 1995, 9). And, although arguably lip service, some government officials expressed a recognition of the concept. When questioned about the government's position on environmental rights at an Upper House budgetary committee meeting in 1974, Miki Takeo, then deputy prime minister and Environment Agency director, stated that although "environmental rights are recognized as a political principle," there were still "ambiguities" from a legal perspective that needed to ironed out (Nasu 2007, 5).

Local movements opposed to infrastructure and industrial developments have wholeheartedly embraced the idea of environmental rights. As one observer in the mid-1970s noted, the concept offered local residents' movements both "legitimacy" and a "realistic symbol" of their objectives in protest and in the courts (quoted in Senba 1989, 54). Two movements that unfolded over the 1970s are emblematic of this enthusiastic adoption. In 1972, local fishermen, farmers, and residents opposed to the construction of a thermal power plant in Date, Hokkaido, filed a lawsuit in the Sapporo District Court demanding that the construction permit issued by the Date City Council be cancelled. As grounds for the injunction, the plaintiffs and their lawyers cited the potential impact on fisheries and farming. But they also alluded to their "right to enjoy an environment adequate for maintaining a healthy and comfortable life," their so-called "environmental rights" (Koshida 2005, 18).

Although environmental rights had been part of the earlier Osaka International Airport case, this lawsuit really brought the concept to national attention for the first time. It brought into question the "solution" of the pollution prevention agreement signed between the power plant operators and the Date Council. Activists ridiculed this as a "pollution prevention smokescreen" because it directed attention away from the fundamental fact that Date's natural environment would be profoundly and irreversibly impacted, even in the total absence of pollution. The power plant was eventually constructed and the residents' lawsuit unsuccessful, but the use of environmental rights discourse by Date residents and their legal team helped push forward environmental discussion in Japan in important ways. Broadly speaking, the case contributed to a shift in Japan from discussion about "industrial pollution" to a more holistic consideration of the "environment." The environmental rights claim formulated by legal experts in the case was arguably a critical catalyst here.

Even more influential was another local protest and lawsuit against a planned power plant in Buzen, Kyushu, instigated in 1973. Different from

Date, this was the first purely environmental rights-based lawsuit, since the plaintiffs made no other claims to fishing rights or the like. Like Date, however, the lawsuit was unsuccessful, and the plant was completed for operation in 1977. The movement's leader, bestselling author Matsushita Ryūichi, used his high national profile and the publicity surrounding the case to propagate an innovative ecological vision based on the environmental rights of present and future generations. His prolific writings in popular magazines, scholarly legal journals, mainstream newspapers, and book-length works, helped cement the idea of environmental rights in the activist community and advance public discourse on the environment in Japan during the 1970s and 1980s (Matsushita et al. 1975; Matsushita 1999, 2008). Interestingly, Matsushita's decision to file a lawsuit with fellow residents solely based on environmental rights proved too radical even for environmental lawyers, who argued that the courts were not ready for this standalone rights claim and that defeat would be a great setback (Matsushita 1999, 134). But by 1973 environmental rights discourse had taken on a life of its own and, accordingly, Matsushita and his six coplaintiffs represented themselves (Matsushita 2008, 289). Although the group certainly wanted to stop the construction in Buzen, they also clearly had a larger environmental agenda they wished to propagate by litigating on the basis of environmental rights. They hoped that their lawsuit would precipitate a flood of similar cases—which it did, with some forty environmental rights lawsuits underway by the mid-1970s— in turn forcing officials and industrialists to modify their development strategies (Matsushita 2008, 289).

As Matsushita noted, environmental rights offered a "systematic written definition" of an ethic contained within the daily lives of local residents; it gave a vocabulary to their innate attachment to the local environment (Matsushita 2008, 281). Environmental rights, Matsushita argued, were about more than utilitarian rights to use and consume nature (such as fishing rights), connecting instead to the fundamental right of all people to "enjoy" (*tanoshimu*) the environment. Indeed, evidencing his embryonic ecological vision, Matsushita said that the value of nature was not only in its "enjoyment" but in the very existence of nature "in itself" (Matsushita 2008, 137). Matsushita likened his movement to the "national consensus" that the Japanese Crested Ibis should be "protected." Similarly, for residents of Buzen, the shoreline was something "precious" (*aisubekimono*) that they wanted to preserve for later generations (Matsushita 2008, 135). "If we eliminate the Buzen coastline," he argued, "we will have taken away this 'precious thing'" from future generations "for eternity," and "obliterated their environmental rights." "Who is allowed to deprive the children of the future their right to play on the beach?" (Matsushita 2008, 136–37). Matsushita admitted that without the idea of environmental rights Buzen residents would not have gone to court. I would also suggest that, in the absence of this concept, nor would his ecological philosophy have developed with such alacrity and sophistication.

The Evolution of Environmental Rights

Legal experts in academia and the JFBA continued to advance and expand their environmental rights agenda in the subsequent decades. Internationally, as I noted earlier, the JFBA delegation to UNCHE energetically publicized its Proposal for an "Environmental Right" at the NGO forums run parallel to the conference. They repeated this process again at the United Nations Conference on Environment and Development (UNCED) in Brazil in 1992, enhancing environmental rights advocacy with a Proposal for Global Environmental Protection (Nichibenren 2010, 30). Prior to UNCED, in 1988 the JFBA convened an international human rights conference in Kobe devoted solely to the new global environmental problems such as stratospheric ozone depletion and climate change. One of the three principles adopted at this conference was that global environmental protection be understood as a "human right" (Nichibenren 1988). Regionally, in the 1990s lawyers in the JFBA became involved in environmental rights issues in Southeast Asia, conducting field surveys on rainforest destruction in Borneo and Japanese ODA infrastructure projects in Thailand (coastal development), Indonesia (dam construction) and the Philippines (electrical power infrastructure) (Nichibenren Kōgai-Kankyō 1991). As discussed earlier, environmental rights lawyers such as Yamamura Tsunetoshi now also took up the cause of nature conservation and climate change. Together with another lawyer, Asaoka Emi, in 1996 Yamamura and others established the Kiko Forum group involved in lobbying and public advocacy in the lead up to the intergovernmental deliberations on the Kyoto Protocol adopted in 1997 (Yamamura 1994; Saitō 2001, 24).

Inspired by attention to the global environment, legal experts also continued to push conceptual boundaries in environmental rights. In the mid-1990s, the legal scholar and activist Awaji Takehisa began to address the link between environmental rights and nature conservation through the provocative notion of the "rights of nature." Awaji's ideas built on efforts among environmental lawyers in Japan throughout the 1980s to define a human right to "enjoy nature" (*shizen kyōyūken*) At the JFBA-HRPC congress in 1986, participants agreed that "in order for citizens to sustain their existence and to live humane lives they have a right to enjoy the benefits of nature" (Yoshimura 2010, 61). The background to this proposal was rooted in emerging global attention to the importance of nature conservation over and above the impacts (or lack thereof) on human health and daily life. Another important element was growing awareness of the desirability of preserving biodiversity for future generations. Such discussion provided a conduit for legal experts to move from concepts of environmental *rights* to environmental *responsibilities*— in other words, the responsibility of humans toward nature and the inherent rights of nature and natural things, distinct from considerations of human enjoyment (Fujikawa 2013, 38). In the mid-1990s Awaji (1995, 8) suggested three bases for such "rights of nature" (*shizen no kenri* in Japanese): (1) that "nature as a whole and natural things are endowed with legal rights"; (2) that "in principle, humans have a one-sided legal duty to protect the whole of nature"; and (3) that humans possess an "inherent right" to "defend nature as a whole and natural things from harm."

Some Japanese lawyers have even begun to theorize on how the rights of nature might be established in the legal system. Mami Ōsugi (2012, 31) suggests four litigation scenarios: (1) where an individual or group is a proxy plaintiff for nature; (2) where an individual or group is a plaintiff in their capacity as trustee over nature; (3) where a natural entity and an individual or group are co-plaintiffs; and (4) where a conservation group responsible for the management of nature is plaintiff. Needless to say, Japanese courts have rejected lawsuits for the rights of nature outright on grounds that natural entities cannot have legal rights (for example, as in the case of the Bean Goose in the Mito District Court in 1996 where the plaintiffs sued Ibaragi Prefecture for failing to create a wildlife sanctuary for the geese to utilize during their winter hibernation resulting in a steep decline in flock size (Ōsugi 2012, 32). Yet, as with environmental rights, judges have at least shown a sensitivity to the larger environmental questions involved. A case in point is the lawsuit initiated by lawyers and environmental advocates on behalf of the Amami black rabbit and four other species seeking an injunction against forest development which threatened their habitats. The court dismissed the case but in its verdict, noted that the concept of the "rights of nature" raised important questions about the adequacy of existing law based only on providing remedies for infringements to the benefits of individuals and/or legal persons (Yoshimura 2010, 61). Just as environmental rights raised questions about the adequacy of compensation-based pollution law, the rights of nature principle challenges the anthropocentric basis of environmental rights in law and society more generally. Japanese legal experts have pursued this conservation agenda outside the courts too, conducting research on blue coral reef destruction from airport construction near Ishigakijima (Okinawa) and rainforest depletion in Shiretoko (Hokkaido) and the Shirakami (Aomori) Mountain Range from the late 1980s onward. Reflecting this broadening agenda, in 1985 the JFBA Pollution Countermeasures Committee changed its name to the Pollution Countermeasures and Environmental Protection Committee (Hiwatashi 2010, 4).

Litigation has and will remain the central concern of Japanese lawyers and legal scholars, but as the development of environmental rights discourse reveals, the impact of these cases has spread beyond the courtroom, influencing the evolution of Japan's eco-environmental state, grassroots activism and protest, and public attitudes on pollution and conservation. Legal experts' introduction and advocacy of environmental rights reveals the important function of this group in recognizing, digesting, and giving sharp articulation to developments on the environment unfolding both domestically and internationally over the past half century. The environmental rights concept offered a potent critique of post-pollution legal remedies that implicitly accepted a degree of environmental damage and human injury. It provided activists with a strategic language of rights that transcended earlier appeals to "local egoism," and it opened the way for new forays into nature conservation and the human responsibility to protect nature and natural things. Lawyers have also been leading activists for the environment in Japan in their own right. They have taken ideas such as environmental rights to the international community and, conversely, have injected global environmental initiatives such as flora and fauna conservation and responses to climate change back into Japan. They have not only served as a check on Japan's developmental state but also as key actors in the country's transition to an eco-developmental state by expanding concepts of environmental rights and responsibilities. For these reasons their substantial contribution to the Japanese environmental movement deserves recognition.

PART III

LOCAL ACTION

6

Local Energy Initiatives in Japan

NORIKO SAKAMOTO

ON MARCH 11, 2011, A MAGNITUDE 9.0 EARTHQUAKE AND MASSIVE
tsunami waves up to 38 meters (125 ft) high hit the northeastern part of
Japan, causing widespread devastation and loss of life. According to the
data as of March 10, 2016, the losses from the disaster were officially
reported as follows: 18,455 people dead or still missing (not including
deaths related to injuries after the earthquake) and 400,326 houses or
buildings either completely destroyed or half destroyed. By prefecture in
the most seriously affected areas in the Tohoku region, the death tolls are
4,673 in Iwate, 9,541 in Miyagi, and 1,613 in Fukushima (Edahiro 2014).

At the same time, the disaster led to an unprecedented nuclear accident at the Fukushima No. 1 nuclear power plant, owned by Tokyo Electric Power Corporation. Due to the radiation risk, residents near the
power plant had to evacuate immediately. The estimated number of evacuees was approximately 470,000 at the peak, and 144,471 people were
still living as refugees as of February 12, 2016.

The earthquake, tsunami, and nuclear accident combined significantly
damaged the electricity supply in eastern Japan. Power supply from many
thermal and nuclear power plants located along the Pacific coast was cut
due to heavy damage to their facilities. In Tokyo Electric's power system,
rolling blackouts became necessary to balance between electricity supply and demand for the day. Various problems occurred during the blackouts, including interrupted home medical care and water failure in
condominiums. It greatly impacted the daily life of the population and
caused serious economic impacts.

The accident led to a national review of nuclear policies and a strong promotion of energy conservation, a process that fed into Japan's already evolving eco-developmental state policies. Eventually Japan shut down all of its nuclear plants, and they all remained shut for more than two years. The Fukushima disaster raised public awareness about the dangers of nuclear power and the importance of energy conservation, and in fiscal year 2013, Japan saw reduction of 78.9 Terawatt-hours (TWh), the same amount of electricity that thirteen nuclear reactors would generate in an entire year, enough to supply twenty-two million Japanese households (Greenpeace 2014, 1).

As part of its new energy plan, Japan accelerated the implementation of a feed-in tariff system that had previously been under discussion and went into effect in July 2012. The new system promoted small-scale renewable energy development. In fiscal year 2013, a total of 18.1 TWh, sufficient to supply five million Japanese households for an entire year, was generated from renewable sources (excluding large hydroelectric), the equivalent to what would have been generated by three nuclear reactors in one year (ibid., 3).

Additionally, in the twenty-three months from the beginning of the feed-in tariff system until May 2014, 680,000 new renewable power stations started to operate across the country. Most of that new capacity of 10.4 gigawatts (GW) came from decentralized power stations, particularly small-scale solar photovoltaic systems. According to the Ministry of Economy, Trade, and Industry (METI) the majority (530,000 out of the 680,000 cases) were solar panels rated at less than 10 kW, made for households (METI n.d.).

Emerging Local Power Initiatives

Before the disaster in 2011, most Japanese people were largely indifferent about how their energy was supplied. After the disaster, however, many began to think about the origin of the electricity they were purchasing from power companies and other aspects of energy issues that they had previously ignored (Yoneda 2012).

At the time of the disaster, the public could not choose electric power providers for their electricity needs; their provider was automatically determined by where they lived. Seeing the need for more decentralized electricity generation and seeking to promote renewable energy the government liberalized Japan's electricity market, which became fully liberalized in April 2016 (Edahiro and Kojima 2011).

As a result, some communities began small-scale energy projects. These were developed to help Japan transition from a system of centralized energy supplied only by major power companies to a more self-sufficient system in which communities would take advantage of their location and natural resources to generate and distribute energy to local residents (JFS 2009).

Eventually, some of these initiatives across Japan grew into a movement to promote shifting energy systems from centralized and large-scale to a decentralized, network-based energy society that had the potential to achieve denuclearization and independence of local communities. Some of the key promoters of established power generation systems started to work together on a local level.

For example, a Japanese nonprofit group, the Institute for Sustainable Energy Policies, began organizing community power study meetings as a domestic and international cooperation and networking events in 2012. The group advocates for the expansion of community power across Japan. "Community power" refers to an approach for promoting renewable energy through cooperation among a wide range of people, use of local resources, and working from the bottom up. The World Wind Energy Association advocates these three principles, emphasizing the need for a mechanism to return profits to local people (Matsubara 2013).

In March 2013, an informal group of business leaders and entrepreneurs working together to build a sustainable business and energy future organized a networking event to promote community-driven, local energy production and to share experiences from such initiatives in the effort to establish community energy initiatives nationwide. They were primarily focused on renewables, such as community-funded or citizen-based investment schemes to install solar panels on the rooftops of multiunit residences and public facilities (JFS 2013). In May 2014 the following year, the National Local Energy Association launched an effort to create sustainable local communities by promoting renewable energy development and energy-saving initiatives by local citizens.

The association has over forty member groups, including Hokkaido Green Fund, a nonprofit organization (NPO) that has built citizen-funded wind power plants, and Aizu Electric Power Company, which is engaged in electric power generation using photovoltaic power systems and heat energy supply. The association aims to facilitate exchanges among business operators, relative councils, and individuals involved in the projects and to accelerate the diffusion of community-led renewable energy developments by sharing information and solving common issues (JFS 2014). The first World Community Power Conference was held in Fukushima in November 2016, and the momentum of community power continues to grow.

Regional Revitalization to Address Aging and Declining Population

The community power movement is not just about transforming Japan's energy sector and improving environmental sustainability. The movement also has the potential to address two pressing problems that have been growing in Japan in recent years: rural depopulation and the aging society.

Depopulation, especially of rural communities, has been a hotly debated issue in Japan for decades. Japan hit its peak population of 128 million in 2008, which has been declining ever since. By October 2015, the population dropped back to 127 million, a decrease of about one million people. If the population were to continue decreasing at this pace, it would drop to 95 million by 2050, and to 50 million by 2100 (Kono 2011).

In addition to this population decrease prediction, a shocking and detailed report titled "Municipalities at Risk of Vanishing" released by the Japan Policy Council, a group of business and union leaders and scholars to advance proposals to create a new Japan and stimulate a national debate based on the citizens' perspective, created a fuss nationwide. The report showed that nearly one thousand municipalities were at risk of vanishing, accounting for 49.8% of the total number of municipalities in the country. Thus, almost half of all of Japan's cities and towns were likely to disappear by 2040 (JPC n.d.; Somusho 2017a, b).

According to data released by the Ministry of Internal Affairs and Communication in April 2016, while the population of underpopulated districts accounts for only 8.9% of the nation's total, the land area of these districts accounts for nearly 60% of Japan's national territory.

Underpopulated areas suffer additionally from aging problems. Data from 2010 by the same ministry show that senior citizens aged sixty-five years or older accounted for 22.8% in Japan overall but 32.8% in under-populated areas, 10% higher than the rest of the nation. In such areas, various kinds of problems occur: closed hospitals, discontinued train and bus services, and closed shops, which makes residents' daily lives more difficult (Niitsu 2015).

In response to their alarming analysis, the government is addressing this national challenge not only at the local level but also at the national level, by establishing the Headquarters for Overcoming Population Decline and Vitalizing Local Economy under the Cabinet Office since the September 2014 (Niitsu 2015). This policy direction and shared concern over risk of vanishing municipalities across Japan triggered local munici-palities and people's efforts for revitalization. Some of such communities reviewed their local assets such as rich natural resources like water, rich sunshine, fresh agricultural products, etc. Some of them took a serious look at the possibility that local power generation could generate income for their communities by selling surplus electricity while also contribut-ing to mitigating environmental and energy problems.

Community power initiatives are among the businesses using these revitalization incentives to establish themselves across the country. In contrast to many businesses whose primary beneficiaries are outside the local area, community power initiatives offer the possibility to contrib-ute to true community revitalization as local businesses tend to reinvest profits in the local economy.

The two cases of community power generation projects examined here focus on challenges that are common in rural areas in Japan. The first is a micro-hydropower community energy project in a small village, Itoshiro, with about only 250 residents. This is one of the forerunners in commu-nity energy, driven by a sense of crisis that residents might lose their hometown due to the village's aging and declining population. The sec-ond is a community solar power generation project, which developed a unique scheme in financing construction costs in exchange for local spe-cialty products trying to energize local agricultural industry.

Itoshiro is a village located in Gujo City, in the mountains of Gifu Pre-fecture, about 100 kilometers (60 mi) from Nagoya. People have been living in this district since the Jomon period (14,000 to 300 BCE). Until around 1964, its population was about 1,200, but over the following fifty years it dropped to less than one quarter and now has only about only 250 people living in one hundred households.

The village of Itoshiro is located at an altitude of around 700 meters (2,300 ft); thus, it is cool and comfortable in summer, but the weather is harsh in winter with several meters of snowfall. The harsh, isolated environment has resulted in a culture in which villagers have long cooperated with each other to support their lives and the village. Itoshiro is also where Mount Hakusan, a sacred mountain, is worshipped. From the Heian period to the Kamakura period (from around 794 to 1333 CE) when the worship of Mount Hakusan was particularly active, many people from all around Japan, including ascetic Buddhist monks, are said to have come to the village and ultimately settled there. Therefore, Itoshiro has traditionally been open to newcomers, despite being a remote village. To this day, the village's atmosphere remains one in which residents welcome strangers and do not interfere with each other's lives.

In the past, no river flowed through the village, so local people grew common millet and foxtail millet in their barnyards. Then, in the Meiji period (1868–1912), they hand-dug a 3 kilometer (1.8 mi) canal to divert water from a river, and this enabled them to grow rice in paddies. Since then, villagers have cooperated in cleaning out the agricultural canals before flooding rice fields in spring and after harvesting rice in autumn. In this way, they have operated and maintained the canals by themselves. From the Taisho period (1912–26) to 1955, there was an electric power utilization union in the village, and waterwheels powered by water diverted from a valley through these canals were used to run a timber mill in the daytime and for residential electricity in the evening. When light bulbs would grow dim at night, someone in the village would go to a water wheel to clean it out, and the lights would grow brighter again. In this way, villagers have created, operated, and maintained the canals by themselves, providing themselves with water for agriculture and electricity.

In 2007, an NPO established by young people in their twenties from Gifu Prefecture to revitalize regional development, went from village to village in the area upstream of Gujo City to encourage villagers to launch micro-hydropower generation projects, and people in Itoshiro responded positively. The NPO promoted micro-hydropower generation based on the idea that, in the past, money circulated within each community, whereas at present money flows out because people purchase things coming from outside. One of the most commonly purchased items is energy. Generating electric power within communities may help restore value to farms, mountains, and villages, and at the same time help solve global environmental and energy problems. The villagers of Itoshiro decided to launch micro-hydropower generation not because they were interested in the energy itself but because they knew that they needed to do something to attract and retain young people or their community would disappear.

In the summer of 2007, the NPO helped the local community install three waterwheels for micro-hydropower generation. Unfortunately, the waterwheels did not work very well. Therefore, NPO members searched for advice and undertook an independent study to find a more practical design. As a result, in June 2009, a spiral water turbine for run-of-river power generation was installed in a canal running beside rice paddies to generate power for a single household.

After some trial and error, the spiral design worked much better. The power supplies a private house that is also used as the office for a local nonprofit organization called Peaceful Village Itoshiro (Yasuragi-no-Sato Itoshiro), which is located across the road from the waterwheel. Even though its head is only 50 centimeters (20 in), it provides all the electricity generation needed for the NPO/household.

In June 2011, another waterwheel was installed beside a food processing factory, which had been closed because of high electricity costs. This installation generated 2.2 kilowatts (kW) of power, taking advantage of an elevation drop of 3 meters (10 ft). As a result of their new waterwheel, the factory restarted operations, creating a place to work for four people for six months a year producing processed food items using sweet corn, a village specialty.

These locally produced food items are served at a café operated by local women. This café opens usually only on weekends but started to take reservations for lunch on weekdays. Recently, the number of people visiting the village to observe their micro-hydropower systems is increasing, but there is no place for them to have lunch. In the spring, when the café receives lunch reservations, local women operating the café go to a nearby mountain together to gather edible wild plants. "If our activities only deal with energy, it will be difficult to win sympathy from the community. But if power generation can be connected to an interest of local people or something else they want to do, we can receive much more understanding and cooperation from them," Akihide Hirano told me in a 2015 interview. Hirano has been a driving force of community activities in the village. He first became involved in Itoshiro's community activities in 2007 and settled in the village in 2011.

A piece of good news is that the number of people relocating from other areas is now increasing. Ten households with twenty-five members are newcomers who have relocated from other areas to this village with its population of 250. In this year, four babies are to be born in the village. "We are having a baby boom here," smiled Hirano.

The two micro-hydropower generators presently installed in Itoshiro are not connected to a grid because the power is not for sale but for in-house consumption. Both generators were constructed by local builders/technicians, and local people well-versed in electric control systems manually developed the control panels. The slogan in Itoshiro is "Let local people do what they can do." This allows local people to fix the generators on their own in case they break down. These two power generators are owned by the Regional Renaissance Agency (RRA), an NPO to which Hirano belongs, and they are managed by the Yasuragi-no-Sato Itoshiro on commission from the RRA.

Gifu Prefecture touts itself as a "Land of Clean Waters," and the prefecture is certainly blessed with rich water resources. It was in fact officials from the prefectural government who approached the community in Itoshiro about generating power with a micro-hydropower system utilizing an irrigation canal in the village. At the beginning, local people were not very enthusiastic about the project and indeed found out later that all the profit from selling power generated by these systems would go to the government (national, prefectural, and municipal) in exchange for funding 100% of the cost for the systems. Some local people claimed that the plan should be abolished if the systems utilizing the local canal, which local residents have maintained since the late eighteenth century, would not benefit the community. In the end, however, the community decided to accept the project on the condition that it would also take part in the funding so that profits would be returned to the community, although this was a risk for the community.

The result was a decision to divert the irrigation canal to make two channels and begin micro-hydropower generation at two places. One station was constructed by the prefecture and provides provide power for eighty households.

The other station was constructed with the funds raised by the people in the Itoshiro community. The total construction cost of the power station was ¥240 million (about US$2 million) and Itoshiro needed to bear ¥60 million (about US$500,000), the amount after subsidies, etc. were deducted. Gengo Uemura, the chairperson of the neighborhood community association at the time and sixteen other people became promoters, holding discussions for a half year as to how they should raise funds for this investment and decided to ask residents of the district for contributions. They explained the proposal to each of the one hundred households, saying, "Our community's ancestors built the irrigation canal for the sake of their descendants. For the sake of our descendants we will build a power station." As a result, almost all households decided to make a contribution and the necessary amount of money was collected. To manage the collected funds, the Irrigation Canal Agricultural Cooperative was established in April 2014.

Operation of the power stations started in June 2016. Although it is expected that the station will make an annual profit of approximately ¥20 million (about US$167,000) by selling electricity to the Hokuriku Electric Power Company, this profit will be used not for dividends to the investors but rather to promote community-based agriculture, including training sessions on farming, support to food-processing factories, and development of new products.

Hirano said,

> Micro-hydropower generation facilities using spiral water turbines, etc. are reliable as independent facilities where power is generated and used on the spot and suitable for environmental education since we can directly watch them work. However, from the viewpoint of bringing money back into local circulation, it will be necessary to generate and sell power on a larger scale in order to return profits to the region. For this reason, we decided to build a power station to generate income to support projects in the community by selling power. Having this station means we can pay management costs to clean and otherwise maintain the water canal. Cleaning the water channels stabilizes the flow, and this profits local agriculture as well as the independent

micro-hydropower generation facilities. Since the Itoshiro community is rich in water and has uneven land, I believe that many independent micro-hydropower generation facilities will be built in various places.

This system, in which hydropower generation station supports local projects, could develop into an instructive example informing local residents elsewhere who wish to club together to start micro-hydropower generation using water canals that have been maintained over the years to generate profits for agricultural promotion in their region. It could also help promote independent micro-hydropower generation facilities designed to generate power for local residents' homes and workplaces.

Community Happy Solar!

Another example of community power generation is the Tokushima Regional Energy General Incorporated Association (TREGIA), which is a business enterprise that was set up in Tokushima Prefecture in 2012 to encourage independent local energy development to enable local people to enjoy the benefits. Rather than a business model in which investors provide funding in expectation of a return on their investment once the project is completed, TREGIA "solicits donations to partly cover construction costs in exchange for local specialty products"(*JFS Newsletter* 2015) This system draws many people into the solar power generation business and helps make it more acceptable to the community.

TREGIA raises donations in units of ¥10,000 (US$84.03) from people interested in supporting villages dependent on primary industries. These donations contribute to the working capital needed to manage a solar power plant, and the names of contributors are posted at the power plant to express appreciation. The power generation capacity and profits from selling the electricity are publicly disclosed, and profits are used to support local agriculture, forestry and fisheries in ways determined by a management council that includes representatives of local public bodies and agricultural organizations. When the power generation is going well, TREGIA sends contributors local specialty products (agricultural or fishery products) that are safe and secure. Procuring these products locally provides further support to local industries.

The first project that called for donations under this system was Sanagochi Mitsubachi Solar. Sanagochi Village, with a population of about 2,600 people, is about one hour by car from Tokushima Station. It is the only village left in Tokushima that has not been consolidated into a larger local government entity. This village is blessed with a rich natural environment and an agricultural industry that produces fruit, mushrooms and green onions.

When TREGIA initially offered three hundred units, they received 322 contributions in only two months, exceeding the number offered. Operation of a solar array started in March 2014. Among the 322 contributors, 7 are residents of the village, 254 live elsewhere in Tokushima Prefecture, and 61 live in other prefectures. This shows that many people even outside the village support the initiative.

In return for their contribution, supporters receive specialties of the village such as kiwi fruits, strawberries, and *sudachi*, a citrus fruit similar to a lime. For contributors living outside the prefecture with few opportunities to visit the solar facilities, the village uploaded an airborne video to their website. TREGIA plans to implement Community Happy Solar! projects at five locations in the prefecture. Three of them, including Sanagochi Village, are now underway.

Mugi Town, one of the three operational locations, is a coastal town located about ninety minutes by Japan Rail train from Tokushima Station. With a population of just over 4,500 people, the town is mainly dependent on its fishing industry. The town's mayor, Masahiko Fukui, describes the current severe situation on the town's website: "Just as in other depopulating places, many young people have been leaving town since Japan's rapid economic growth period started in the mid-1950s. Currently the population is less than half of what it used to be, and with the declining birthrate and aging population, the town is suffering from a depopulation spiral and having a hard time pulling out of it" (*JFS Newsletter* 2015).

According to Kazumi Toyooka, TREGIA's administrative officer, after the mayor of the town consulted her about the matter, the town started to collect donations to operate solar arrays at places such as the rooftop of an abandoned elementary school and vacant lots owned by the town. The target amount is ¥3 million (about US$25,210). The town government and local association of fishing cooperatives are collaborating on implementation. They plan to send gifts to contributors in return for their donations, including fresh marine products, dried fish, and processed seafood (*JFS Newsletter* 2015).

Another case is Community Happy Solar! Naruto, located in Naruto, a city on the northeast edge of the prefecture and famous for the whirlpools in the Naruto Straits. It is promoting the installation of photovoltaic facilities at four elementary and junior high schools in the city. The annual power generation is expected to total up to 162,500 kilowatt hours (kWh). It collected donations, with a minimum unit of ¥10,000 (US$84.03), until the end of March 2016, and hopes to collect ¥4 million (US$33,613.45). Currently, TREGIA and Naruto are discussing what local specialty gifts will be sent to contributors.

Toyooka said she has a sense of crisis, thinking, "Local communities will never be free from exploitation by the central government, for example by accepting profligate public work projects or radioactive wastes, unless we create systems that circulate money through the local economy on our own."

The major reason why Toyooka and her colleagues started this initiative was because they were inspired by a case in the town of Yusuhara Town in Kochi Prefecture. Although it faces depopulation and an aging population, Yusuhara has managed to avoid falling into debt and succumbing to a municipal merger. Yusuhara has promoted electric power sales by installing wind power generator systems funded by the town together with subsidies from the national government. It also has implemented various environmental policies, such as installing photovoltaic facilities and granting subsidies for forest plantation thinning. Hoping to recreate Yusuhara's success, Toyooka said, they launched Community Happy Solar!: "It is said that renewable energy businesses do not create jobs, but I think they do depending on what kinds of systems we adopt. We hope to make the best use of systems like Community Happy Solar!, so that each community can earn enough money to be financially independent. This would help vitalize local communities, leading to a decentralized society."

The Community Happy Solar! initiative is particularly well done because the profits from electric power sales are returned to the community, and also the locally produced gifts sent to contributors support local businesses and build community pride. Now, Itoshiro and TREGIA receive numerous requests of site visits from neighboring prefectures, towns and villages that are interested in developing their own community energy projects. Over 500 people visit Itoshiro every year. Members of TREGIA serves as committee members for councils for the environment and energy for other municipalities and expands their energy projects into biomass (Isoyama 2016; Sugimoto 2016).

If the promoters of the projects only focused on electricity generation, it would have been difficult for them to involve local people to gain support for the projects. Instead, they tried to integrate the local people's interests—sustaining and revitalizing their communities. As their community power projects made progress, their efforts gradually attracted attention by others, visitors, supporters and new residents.

These two community power projects are examples of how local communities can integrate small-scale renewable energy facilities with community revitalization efforts, such that generating clean, renewable energy can benefit not only the global environment but also promote local agriculture, small businesses, and community pride to sustain their communities. Their efforts are being scaled by local advocates who participate in site visits, bringing tales of success back to their own communities.

Efforts to scale these local-level initiatives are also being supported by national business organizations, such as the Japan Smart Community Alliance, as well as the government. The Ministry of Economy, Trade, and Industry is actively seeking to promote the local development using renewable energy as a core organizing principle (frequently called "smart communities") (METI 2017a). The stories of Itoshiro and Community Happy Solar! exemplify the way that eco-developmental polices can contribute to economic revitalization, community health, as well as environmental sustainability.

7

Indigenous Conservation and Post-disaster Reconstruction in Taiwan

SASALA TAIBAN, HUI-NIEN LIN, KURTIS JIA-CHYI PEI,
DAU-JYE LU, AND HWA-SHENG GAU

TAIWANESE INDIGENOUS PEOPLE CONSTITUTE ABOUT 2% OF THE ISLAND'S population, more than 550,000 people. Their ancestors have been living on Taiwan for almost eight thousand years, long before the major Han immigration from China, which began with the arrival of Dutch merchants in 1624. Since then traditional lands of indigenous people have been taken and colonized by the Dutch, Spanish, Ming, Qing, Japanese, and finally, the Chinese Nationalist rulers. Each of these successive "civilized" cultures participated in both violent conflict and peaceful economic interaction with both the Plains and Mountain indigenous ethnic groups. To varying degrees, different groups of outsiders hugely influenced or transformed the culture and language of the indigenous peoples of Taiwan, including their relationship to the natural environment and its resources. In recent years, as part of Taiwan's democratization, indigenous peoples have made great efforts to restore their sovereignty and preserve their relationship to the land. As part of this effort, some members of younger generations have carried out projects of community mapping and community-based conservation to better recognize their ancestral knowledge of traditional territories and the natural environment, which can help indigenous communities regain control of their land and resources.

The Rukai people, one of Taiwan's sixteen officially recognized indigenous groups, live along both sides of the southern mountains of Taiwan's Central Mountain Range. On the west side of the mountains, the Western Rukai reside in the Ailiao River drainage area, while the Xia-San-She group lives in the drainage area of the Zhuokou River, a tributary of the Laonong River. The Danan (Dongxing), or Eastern Rukai, reside on the Lujia River on the eastern side of the Central Mountain Range (map 7.1).

In 2009, Typhoon Morakot brought significant damage to southern indigenous communities in Taiwan, especially the Rukai. The government moved several Rukai villages from the mountains to the lowlands after the typhoon, a move that threatened Rukai culture. In response, indigenous leaders from the Western and Xiasanshe Rukai groups undertook projects of community-based conservation to alleviate the threat of lost traditional knowledge and help local communities regain sovereignty over their traditional lands.

Conventional bureaucratic approaches to conservation tend to emphasize scientific management practices, guided by government officials who rely on knowledge acquired from scientific study and applied technology to solve environmental problems. As East Asian states and societies move toward eco-developmental consciousness and practice, however, they have come to realize that professional decision-making processes often ignore the rights and benefits of local communities and indigenous people, at times even relocating them under the pretext of conservation, which always leads younger generations to lose their connection with traditional territories. Although this conventional, exclusive approach has been the norm for government officials, in the past few decades an inclusive management approach has emerged, yielding some proactive and positive contributions to conservation with local interests in mind (Borrini-Feyerabend 1996).

Inclusive management of natural resources has two primary aims: participation by local people and balancing resource conservation and development against the needs of local and neighboring communities (IUCN 1993; Murphree 1994; Western and Wright 1994; Holdgate and Phillips 1999). There are many reasons for local populations to participate in resource management work:

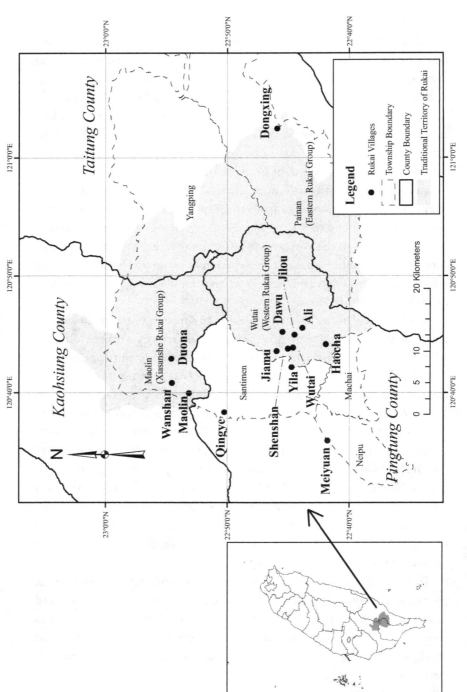

MAP 7.1   Distribution of Rukai villages in Taiwan

1. People have lost their connection with nature and have become unaware of the impact their actions have on the landscape. In order to interact more responsibly with the natural world, they must re-create a link between humans and nature. Therefore, we must understand humanity's role in ecological systems and find a mode of coexistence in order to conserve habitats and biodiversity.

2. It is difficult for central authorities to provide assistance and support in the remote areas in need of labor power, material, and financial help. Therefore, local communities can participate efficiently and effectively.

3. Conservation experts need to view local communities (especially small communities and indigenous peoples) as primary stakeholders and important partners, not as destructive actors. By emphasizing the importance of community and cultural factors, as well as the limitations of government power, scientists and managers can forge new partnerships with local people.

In Taiwan, developmentalism, under various names, such as water conservation, land security, conservation, et cetera, has long dominated the policy of land and natural resources, forcing the nationalization of resources in indigenous traditional territories, depriving indigenous communities of the legitimacy of local resources use and rationalizing its own monopoly measures. The forced invasion of colonialism and state hegemony has seriously distorted and changed the traditional institutions and cultural mechanisms of resource use in forest-dependent communities. Colonial forces and modern management science applied to traditional Rukai territories changed not only the local forest landscape but also the forest culture and land ethics on which the inhabitants have long depended (Taiban 2008). In other words, developmentalism not only leads to rapid changes in the economy, culture, and society of local communities but also causes irreparable harm to forest resources.

One promising approach to reconnecting with nature lies in traditional ecological knowledge (TEK), returning to traditional practices such as taboos and myths that indigenous societies relied on for centuries to define their position in the natural order and guide their behavior. Often, outcomes of this approach are more effective than those using conventional modern practices.[1]

Two Cases of Post-disaster Environmental Management and Cultural Reconstruction

In August 2009, several Rukai communities in Wutai Township and Maolin District were destroyed by Typhoon Morakot, which brought significant social, cultural and economic impacts to individuals and society at large. Subsequently, two Rukai community organizations, the Mountain Forest Patrol (Shanlin Xunshou Dui) and the Hunter School (Lieren Xuexiao), focused their efforts on restoring traditional knowledge connected with natural resource conservation and subsistence living. These examples can provide a starting point for Taiwan to develop a community-based conservation model.

With support from the Ministry of Science and Technology, the authors attended community meetings, official and private negotiations, academic symposiums, and NGO conferences. We also conducted in-depth interviews with local residents, including: (1) community leaders (chiefs, members of the nobility, community heads, local council representatives, and heads of community-based organizations); (2) local bureaucrats (township office staff and community officials); (3) members of the Wutai Township Mountain Forest Patrol; and (4) members of the Maolin Hunter School. We interviewed these experts mainly in Chinese; with elders who knew little Chinese, the interviews were conducted in the Rukai tongue.

Case 1: Wutai Township Mountain Forest Patrol

Wutai is an indigenous township located in Pingtung County, southern Taiwan. It currently has a population about 3,400 and an area of 278.80 square kilometers (108 mi²). The majority of residents are Rukai, and some of them currently rely on farming, tourism or work for the Township government. However, most people have moved to the cities over the past decades to seek better job opportunities. Wutai Township was devastated by Typhoon Morakot in 2009. The Rukai communities of Wutai, Ali, Jilou, Dawu, Jiamu, Shenshan and Yila near the northern drainage basin of the Ailiao River were ravaged by the typhoon, which destroyed many homes, farmlands, public facilities, and ceremonial and ritual spaces. The entire village of Haocha at the south end of the Ailiao River was buried in a landslide. After the disaster, although no resident died from the typhoon, the central government moved the people of Haocha to Rinari, and the residents of Ali, Jilou, Jiamu, and Yila from north of the Ailiao River to the Lily Tribal Community in Changzhi Township (map 7.2). About one thousand residents, nearly one-third of the total Wutai township population, were relocated to the new settlements.

Based on the perceived need for community reconstruction and cultural survival, in 2010 some local intellectuals and university scholars proposed the Mountain Forest Protection Project in Wutai Township, which would create a community-based nature conservation management model connecting with traditional hunting culture and environmental knowledge, in the hopes that the Rukai people could maintain their relationship with nature and traditional territory.

The planners believed that local people with deep traditional knowledge rather than academic training could help create a sustainable approach to resource management. In January 2010, they applied to the national Council of Indigenous Peoples for funding through Wutai Township to recruit, train, and employ eighteen Rukai (two or three men from each of the eight communities, with an average age of forty, all with hunting experience) to patrol, monitor, and collect data on forests and natural resources. The patrol headquarters and information storage were located at Wutai village. Members of the patrol team elected a chief officer who would coordinate and implement each phase of the project. Members autonomously established a conservation agreement, made uniforms, and allocated equipment for outdoor work.

In addition to relying on traditional hunting and scouting skills, patrol team members received modern training, including basic and advanced environmental monitoring skill courses, workshops, and field training for work in the dangerous mountain forest. This combination of technology and tradition helped foster an efficient but also spiritual approach to both stewardship of the land and response to immediate needs during times of natural disasters. Course content included the relationship between traditional and community forestry, the rights and obligations of the mountain forest patrol team and the law enforcement agencies, regulations and methods for forest patrols, GPS and tracking devices and data management, traditional borders for each community and patrol trails, survey methods for rare wildlife species, processing and storage

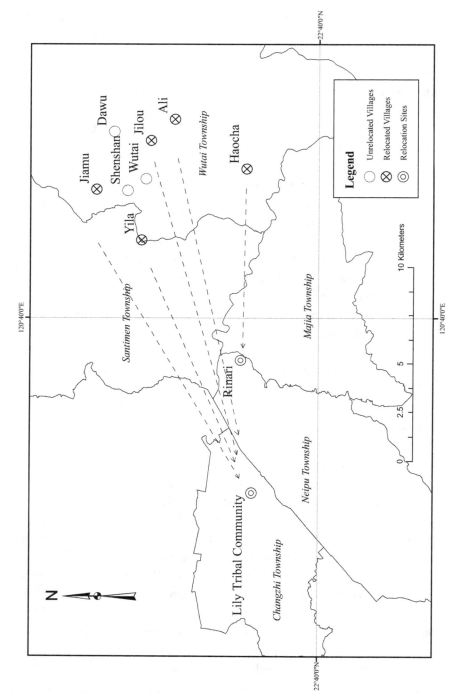

MAP 7.2   Relocation of Rukai villages in Wutai Township after Typhoon Morakot

methods for precious and ethnobotanical plants, collecting methods for community chiefs' and experienced hunters' knowledge, and locating and recording important natural resources—all within the devastated areas. The group used GPS devices to track all their patrol tasks. After each patrol, they downloaded and mapped their data. They also used digital cameras with verifying timestamps to record useful information, such as the locations of landslides, cultural ruins, or important plants and animals.

Daily tasks of the Rukai Mountain Forest Patrol included: (1) reporting illegal or prohibited actions, which aided local law enforcement agencies; (2) surveying, recording, collecting, and digitizing the damage inflicted upon Wutai Township and its traditional areas (including the homes and farmlands of community members, important landmarks and scenic areas, bridges, etc.) by Typhoon Morakot; (3) using field surveys to demarcate and digitize traditional lands, ancient sites, water sources, and historical landmarks of the Western Rukai; (4) scientifically demarcating, recording, and digitizing medium and large mammals and their tracks and rare or endangered trees and ethnobotanical plants found during patrols.

Delineating and drawing a Wutai Township Typhoon Morakot "disaster map" identified the damage and changes to the terrain, in addition to analyzing the nature and extent of devastation in each area of Wutai, the damage done to roads and waterways, and other information vital to safety. When completed, this map identified potential disaster areas and integrated local ecological knowledge into a planning framework to locate emergency shelters, evacuation routes, and preventative measures. The data can enable long-term use through geographic information systems (GIS) to analyze conditions within traditional areas and assess regional, seasonal, and annual trends. Through comparisons with past data, the scientific foundation for each phase in land restorations can be adjusted (Taiban et al. 2015, 219).

The Rukai Mountain Forest Patrol organized four short patrol routes in the area near the six villages. On each trail, four task-oriented groups of patrol team members familiar with the local community and terrain covered key locations and roads in and near Wutai Township. After the road conditions were devastated again during the 2010 rainy season, the shorter Shenshan and Yila routes were maintained within the patrol range. By mid-October 2010, the Rukai Mountain Forest Patrol had performed 187 patrols—182 in the daytime and 5 at night. When a team discovered an illegal logging operation near the Ailiao River in April 2010, they immediately informed the police station and blocked the logging trucks at the Santimen checkpoint, helping to finally bring the illegal organization to justice. Illegal logging has existed for many years in Wutai territory, but there are still no effective policing practices to prevent it, owing to the government short-handed and limited budget. The Mountain Patrol's efforts at protecting natural resources, by contrast, proved to be effective. There were no new incidents after that one, showing that daily patrols and reporting of illegal activities prevented some types of unlawful behavior (Taiban et al. 2015, 220).

Indigenous workers were able to penetrate wild lands through traditional hunting and tracking methods rather than relying on modern roads when infrastructure had failed. Extending their scope of influence, the mountain forest teams conducted four separate long-distance patrols, ranging from 40–100 kilometers (25 to 62 mi) and very different daily patrols. They found more severe landslides than expected, and at times it was impossible to locate any trails and waterways. Environmental disturbances recorded using digital cameras during the patrols were very useful since these images were the first ones taken after the disaster. The data collected include location information for at least forty-five landslides, forty-five cultural ruins, and rare sightings of wildlife and ethnobotanical plants. Area information collected through multiple patrols proved to be invaluable. In 2011, the Rukai Mountain Forest Patrol continued its second-year project. In addition to strengthening the protection of their homeland and collecting environmental and natural resource data, the patrol added professional training in emergency rescue, disaster prevention, and large tree location.

Thus, in many ways the modern training enhanced the ability of the Rukai Mountain Forest Patrol to reach and aid distressed people and contribute to community development. After several years of successful work, in 2017, the Council of Indigenous Peoples changed its name from Mountain Forest Patrol to Indigenous Traditional Sites and Ecological Resources Maintenance Project and increased its work projects to include not only ecological monitoring but also protection of traditional cultural sites and maintenance of ecological resources. The new project based on the Mountain Forest Patrol has become one of the most successful models of post disaster reconstruction projects in Taiwan. Through this project, indigenous people in the future will be able to improve responses to illegal incidents and curb illegal entry to ensure the safety and integrity of traditional territories. At the same time, the capacity of digital processing can be strengthened in order to systematically and scientifically calibrate, record and preserve information about old settlements, water sources, archaeological sites, animals, plants and precious tree species. Most importantly, indigenous people can build their own disaster prevention maps. When a disaster strikes, the maps can provide information about landslides and tell people where it is safe to take refuge. In the past, whenever the communities encountered disaster, the government always forced them to give up their homelands and evacuate to lowland areas. If local communities can master accurate disaster prevention maps and related knowledge, they can be more resilient to disasters.

Case 2: Maolin Hunter School

The advent of hunter schools marks a new direction in promoting ecological knowledge of indigenous people in Taiwan. No longer does mainstream discourse consider indigenous hunting practices "barbaric"; it now views them as complementary to modern conservation approaches. This transition highlights Taiwan's turn from developmentalism to ecodevelopmentalism, specifically taking indigenous knowledge and culture into consideration. In early Chinese society, the word "hunter" carried a negative connotation among "civilized" and imperialist Chinese, based on their subjective values and norms. In indigenous culture, by contrast, the hunter is recognized for his courageous spirit and holds a position of authority in the community. Therefore, the controversy over hunting is not about the act of hunting but over its interpretation (Lin 2005; Taiban 2006).

The emergence of an indigenous movement in Taiwan during the 1980s was followed by a new discourse on hunters and hunting at the Indigenous Are the Protectors of the Forests Symposium in 1996. This movement came at a time when the state and wider society in Taiwan were beginning to question all-out developmentalism. The negative image of hunters as destroyers changed to one of protectors of the mountains and forests. Ecological intelligence, taboos, rituals, and legends that related to hunting culture were emphasized, reflecting the coexistence between hunters and nature. These ideas resonate with the positive valuation of TEK expressed in the 1992 Rio Declaration on Environment and Development Agenda 21 and in the UN Convention on Biological Diversity.

In recent years, hunter schools, which offer traditional ecological knowledge and indigenous cultural activities, have become a marketing strategy for indigenous ecotourism in Taiwan. Maolin District, a community belonging to the Xiasanshe Rukai group, is home to the Maolin (Teldreka), Wanshan (Oponoho), and Duona (Kungadavane) villages. The village of Maolin opened a hunter school in 2010; paradoxically, its success was mainly due to the widespread devastation caused by Typhoon Morakot in August 2009. Aside from damage to roads, many tourist-dependent areas such as Lovers' Valley and Duona Springs were destroyed. As a result, economic development was needed. The driving force behind the Maolin Hunter School was a local Rukai retired schoolteacher, Chen Cheng. Chen became devoted to reconstructing and passing on traditional culture. In the late 1990s, the Purple Butterfly Research Society, a conservation organization, inspired Chen to recognize the community's ecological potential, and together with several conservation groups, he established and provided leadership for the Maolin Township Purple Butterfly Valley Conservation Association. Co-organizing events with conservation groups caused Chen to think of various ways to maintain traditional culture while stimulating the local economy.

In 2010, Chen began a hunter school and a three-day, two-night "little hunter" camp at his own De-en Gorge guesthouse with the help of Tree Valley Foundation and the Society of Wilderness (SOW), the biggest non-profit environmental organization in Taiwan. One goal was to give children an opportunity to experience Rukai ecological intelligence. Chen invited SOW volunteers and experienced community hunters to design a feasibility study which included trail routes and cultural content. The Maolin Hunter School has held five "little hunter" camps since 2010; participants are mainly Han, and each camp has served about twenty fifth- or sixth-grade children. With the help of the Tree Valley Foundation, ten children from Maolin, Wanshan, and Duona were able to attend one of these camps free of charge. In 2011, Chen added a "big hunter" camp with assistance from SOW. Eighteen people attended, many of whom were SOW volunteers, members, or their families.

The "little hunter" camp is led mainly by three indigenous hunters and two SOW volunteers who plan the program and receive room and board. The three indigenous hunters are elders in charge of camp events; the participants call them *mumu*. The two volunteers are assistants who act as intermediaries, asking *mumu* questions about traditional hunting culture and ensuring that the camp runs smoothly. The camp is focused on indigenous hunting culture, introducing children to indigenous principles and life skills through immersion. Activities include identifying plants and animal footprints, constructing hunting shelters, making *cinabuane* (hunters' breakfast), practicing rituals, and setting traps.

Community residents created the Maolin Hunter School without assistance from the public sector to promote indigenous knowledge and hunting practices using community elders and outside conservation groups. The Maolin Hunter School has much potential to impart cultural knowledge and sustainable management of natural resources in relation to society and the economy.

Social Impact

Hunter schools provide a reinterpretation of, and new platform for, indigenous culture in Taiwan (Chen and Chen 2014). To prepare for the Maolin Hunter School, Chen conducts much literary and historical research, hoping to create opportunities for conversations between indigenous elders and school participants about traditional Maolin hunting culture through camp activities with the help of various conservation groups. This message is consistent with the UN's 2002 International Council for Science report, which stressed that TEK is a complex and dynamic system. In recent years, studies on TEK in Taiwan have removed the misconception that this topic is just meant for static museum exhibits. Instead, they investigate the local social, economic, and cultural backgrounds to emphasize how this dynamic knowledge system continues to be socially constructed in a community (Chi 2005; Lee 2014; Lin 2011).

Economic Impact

Most of the revenue generated from the Maolin Hunter School activities is returned to the community in various ways; for example, indigenous elders who participate receive pay as lecturers, the food for campers' meals are mostly fruits, vegetables, and chickens purchased from the community, and the schools provide young members with temporary job opportunities such as cooking and cleaning. Economic benefits to the local community are consistent with a basic premise of ecotourism.

Environmental Impact

The Maolin Township Purple Butterfly Valley Conservation Association is passionate about ecological conservation. The association does not use any pesticides in lychee orchards, in order to give the purple butterfly a clean and natural environment. Ecological conservation is also one of the goals for establishing the Maolin Hunter School; indigenous elder hunters in the community abide by and advocate traditional hunter culture. For example, they inspect mountain areas where the hunter school activities are conducted. They promptly remove traps that disregard indigenous culture (i.e., traps not set in traditional hunting areas or set in other hunters' areas). They practice divination rituals or prayer songs before heading into the mountains; underlying these actions is the understanding that everything in the world has a spirit. Spirituality also prevents hunters from overusing the natural resources, especially when animal populations are abundant. The TEK that indigenous elder hunters advocate in the Maolin Hunter School enhances the dialogue among community residents about traditional hunting practices. For example, how hunters become aware of danger comes up frequently in the residents' dialogue because of the collective memory of disaster. Through this process, the school recollects, revitalizes and reshapes TEK based on collective efforts. All these efforts help the residents to better respond to natural changes and cope with disasters in the future.

The Rukai Mountain Forest Patrol in Wutai has made significant achievements in social and cultural revitalization in relation to natural resource conservation. According to an official from the Wutai Township Office, more than NT$20 million (US $667,000) came from the national

Council of Indigenous Peoples over the past seven years to provide job opportunities for local communities. However, the patrol faces numerous obstacles. Most of the Rukai Mountain Forest Patrol budget comes from government support, and their finances are reliant on funds provided by the government. If the provision of government resources were to decrease or stop, the foundation for the Rukai Mountain Forest Patrol would cease to exist. The temporary workforce recruited for this project is small, with only two or three members, and lacks authority. Without legislation or government support, local residents who often hunt and gather in the mountains often challenge forest patrols. Recruits are often older and unemployed, with little knowledge of modern technology such as computers, cameras, digital media, and monitoring tools. Lacking the skills necessary to record information and collect data, they have some difficulty combining traditional knowledge with modern technology. Because forest patrol members are not police officers, they only have the power of persuasion. Urging offenders to cease unlawful activity in outdoor settings is not without problems. It is difficult to recruit and retain young people who want a higher salary and stable work conditions; therefore, the turnover rate is high, and few suitable workers are available.

Although the Maolin Hunter School promotes TEK and is good example of local management of natural resources, the extent of its influence is limited. For example, Chen's De-en Gorge guesthouse has yet to offer career opportunities to community members. The scope of operation, restricted to only one business, may cause some members to feel that the Maolin Hunter School does not provide benefits for the entire community. As stated previously, few older people participate in the Maolin Hunter School; therefore, the community-level involvement may not be high enough to be an ideal model for the younger generation.

Despite these challenges, many achievements have resulted from creation of the Rukai Mountain Forest Patrol and the Maolin Hunter School. These indigenous-led efforts have contributed to habitat conservation, cultural reconstruction, and knowledge preservation. Considering that community-based conservation is becoming an important conservation strategy, both the Rukai Mountain Forest Patrol and the Maolin Hunter School represent a crucial starting point for community-based conservation in Taiwan.

Notes

We would like to thank the Ministry of Science and Technology of the Republic of China (Taiwan) for financially supporting this work under contract nos. MOST 103-2621-M-214-001 and NSC 99-2511-S-214-001-MY2.

1   For examples, see Gómez-Pompa and Kaus 1992; McNeely 1994; Ghimire and Pimbert 1997; Berkes 1999; Berkes and Folke 2002; Smith 2001; Brodt 2001; Armitage 2003; Becker and Ghimire 2003; Gómez-Baggethun, Corbera, and Reyes-García 2013; Hanna, Folke, and Maler 1996; Hellier, Newton, and Gaona 1999; and Ostrom 1990.

8

Nature for Nurture in Urban Chinese Childrearing

ROB EFIRD

"YOU ARE THE BOW. YOUR CHILD IS THE ARROW. THE NATURE educators are the archers." On a sweltering July day in 2017, Zhang Hehe stands on the dirt road leading to Gaia Nature School's Wosi Garden, nestled in the gently rolling hills of Pinggu to the east of Beijing. She is facing a group of about thirty parents who have paid RMB 350 (approximately US$50) per family to spend a full Sunday engaged in outdoor activities, with the parents mostly separated from their four-to-six-year-old children. Over the shrill of cicadas, Zhang explains that the members of her nature school have discovered a recent trend toward parental "overprotectiveness" (*guodu baohu*). Her bow-and-arrow metaphor—drawn from Kahlil Gibran's poem "On Children"—encourages parents to instead accept their children's independence and separation.

The twenty children have in fact already separated from their parents: they are assembled up the road at Wosi Garden's main building with three of Gaia's skilled "nature experience" teachers (*ziran tiyanshi*). In the morning they clamber up (and occasionally fall down on) a dirt path to a nearby summit, then descend to the sun-dappled walnut grove of the school's Forest Classroom (Senlin Jiaoshi) where—unbeknownst to their parents—they are taught, and then encouraged, to climb the walnut trees. After a brief lunchtime reunion, they separate again for the afternoon and the children engage in a hands-on investigation of insects followed by rabbit and goat feeding. Meanwhile, their parents are learning all day as well, studying the farm's operation, waste disposal, and local ecology through both lecture and self-guided investigation and experiencing farm work firsthand by cutting grass in the blazing sun.

Toward the end of the day, just before the children leave the walnut grove's cool green classroom, the nature experience teacher solemnly reminds them: "Everything that you picked up in the forest classroom needs to be returned. Whether it is a walnut that you're holding, or a stick that you've picked up . . ." "And! And!" a child suddenly breaks in, "Also: if you've picked up a blue treasure bug or a beetle you need to put them back . . ." "Because!" interrupts an older child as others begin to chime in loudly, "Because the insects here are the hosts, and we're the guests! If we treat them badly, how can we come again?"

Not long afterward, it is time for the guests to go. Following a final commemorative photo, they wearily pile into the two chartered minibuses and begin the drive back to the smog and skyscrapers of Beijing's Dongzhimen. The green hills recede in the distance, and the minibus gradually falls silent as parents nod off, sleeping children in their arms.

A rapidly growing body of multidisciplinary research (cf. Children and Nature Network 2017; Frumkin et al. 2017; Kuo, Barnes, and Jordan 2019) has persuaded many parents in Europe, North America, and parts of East Asia such as Japan and Taiwan that there is a strong connection between nature exposure and human health and well-being. Now, a growing number of mainland Chinese urban parents appear to be similarly persuaded that their children (and perhaps they themselves) will benefit from "nature experiences" (*ziran tiyan*) and "nature education" (*ziran jiaoyu*). These experiences are increasingly offered—for a fee—by organizations and companies outside of the formal school system, including so-called "nature schools" (*ziran xuexiao*) that have begun to mushroom across the country, from Yunnan Province in China's southwest to large eastern seaboard cities like Shenzhen, Shanghai, and Beijing.

Though nature schools are a new development in mainland China, similar organizations and institutions have long functioned as critical non-formal supplements to school-based environmental education in places such as Japan, Taiwan, and the United States (Zhou 2011, 2013). Mainland Chinese nature schools also have the potential to make significant contributions to formal, classroom-based environmental education by fostering pro-environmental attitudes and behaviors and offering the type of hands-on experiential learning that schools cannot. This is particularly important because concerns of parents and school administrators over student safety and test preparation have largely stymied the teaching of environmental education in China's public schools—despite the fact that it has been officially required by the Ministry of Education for over a decade.

Ironically, the failure of formal, school-based environmental education and the growth of nature education appear to share one similar source: parental concerns for the current and future welfare of their children. While some parents may be unenthusiastic or even opposed to environmental education in schools because they fear it will jeopardize their child's safety or exam scores, other parents now worry that their child's lack of nature contact may result in "nature-deficit disorder." In both cases, parents appear to be focused on their children's well-being rather than the welfare of "the environment" per se. This perspective suggests that nature educators can appeal to the public—and parents in particular—by emphasizing the ways in which nature contact nurtures happiness and healthy development.

This chapter explores the reasons for nature education's growth in China, its distinction from school-based environmental education, and the ways in which nature experience is viewed as a source of personal growth. Nature educators in China often draw upon non-Chinese sources for inspiration and ideas, including the concept of "nature-deficit disorder" (*ziran queshizheng*), which was originally developed by US journalist Richard Louv (2005). But these educators also stress that China's circumstances are unique, at least partly due to the planned birth policy and its cultural consequences. These consequences—including a perceived parental "overprotectiveness"—have prompted some nature educators to emphasize forms of "parent-child" (*qinzi*) nature education that nurture personal growth and independence in both parents and their children. What is particularly striking about the rapid rise of nature education in China, however, is the way in which it appears to resolve a core conflict in the lives of Chinese parents (and, arguably, parents throughout the industrialized world): the desire to ensure both children's happiness and their academic success. It is widely assumed that one must come at the expense of the other, but a growing number of urban Chinese parents believe nature education enhances both, at least in early childhood. And they are willing to pay for it.

Parent-Child (*Qinzi*) Nature Education

Following our day at the Gaia Nature School's Wosi Garden, I meet with Principal Zhang in the organization's main office at the foot of a non-descript apartment tower in the north of Beijing. Before our interview I'm treated to a tour of their office's ground floor patio area, a former concrete parking space that has been transformed into a "Gaia Ecological Garden" incorporating recycled materials and permaculture principles. A rainwater collection barrel catches water dripping from the air conditioners on upper floors, and there is a riot of plants with medicinal and culinary uses, a small pond with turtles, and a woodpile providing abundant habitat for bees and other life.

Zhang's first exposure to both formal environmental education and experiential nature education came in 1998, the year after she began her undergraduate studies in biology at Beijing's Capital Normal University. That was also the year that she began volunteering for Friends of Nature (Ziran zhi You), the trailblazing Chinese environmental NGO. In 2003 her volunteer work turned into a full-time staff position working on Friends of Nature's various nationwide environmental education initiatives. As a direct outgrowth of this work, in 2014 Zhang launched the Gaia Nature School, one of the first nature schools in China. Today it is arguably the most influential of these schools, as measured both by the numbers of participants in Gaia's wide variety of environmental learning programs, as well as by the several hundred "nature experience teachers" trained and certified through Gaia's introductory and intermediate training courses. Many of these teachers have dispersed to found organizations and teach in other areas of China, where they are spreading Gaia's philosophy and method of experiential nature learning.

Although children are clearly the focus of Gaia's diverse menu of nature education classes and events, Zhang stresses that "we've never given up educating parents. We call it 'parent-child education' [*qinzi jiaoyu*]." The reason, she says, is because "our critical assessment is that the basic education that today's parents experienced [in their youth] was also nature-deprived." As a result, "we've discovered that whenever we do an activity . . . if we just focus on kids, there will be a big problem. We give the children 100% of our effort, and then they go home and parents may reverse it all. So all of our curricula take parents into account. You and your child grow together; only then is it sustainable."

Zhang bases her assessment on nearly a decade and a half spent immersed in the field of environmental learning. "I've experienced a lot of the changes during the early years of environmental education," she says, "including both classroom education and education outside of schools. There was this classic expression: start with the classroom, and then the child will go home and 'the little hand will lead the big hand' [*xiao shou la da shou*]." In other words, children will influence their parents. "But we've discovered that in today's China, this is too cruel. Because the kids discover that what they're getting is contradictory: they discover that what they're learning at school conflicts with what they're getting at home. And—apparently—no one cares. It's like telling a kid not to play with an iPad, when you can't tear yourself away from your [smart]phone."

Given the importance of parents, Gaia's programming pays particular attention to their participation and ensures that they are provided with learning opportunities. According to Zhang, parent-child activities give parents "an opportunity to discover themselves—*without* their children." But they also give parents and children something they can share with one another "instead of just 'Are you hungry?' 'Are you thirsty?' 'Shouldn't you dress warmer?'" Referring to her goals for the previous day's forest preschool program, Zhang says it's enough if parents learn to see themselves as part of an ecological system and realize that they have "different choices for their relationship with their child." By making them aware of the living things around them—upon which they depend—Zhang is countering what she sees as a problem shared by both the singleton children and their (typically singleton) parents, namely that they are extremely focused on themselves (*ziwo yishi tebie qiang*): "So it's very easy for them to overlook what kind of impact they're having on things outside of themselves."

But Zhang has a larger goal. Despite the differences between classroom-based environmental education and nature education, when training nature educators Zhang is careful to maintain that what they are doing is still "environmental education" (*huanjing jiaoyu*). According to her, that's because environmental education has a specific historical background in the environmental challenges created by economic development and their resolution. "We have to meet those challenges, and we have to be able to shoulder the responsibility of resolving or mitigating them. That's something we [Gaia] really care about." This causal connection between childhood nature exposure and adult environmental stewardship that Zhang and many other Chinese nature educators have personally experienced is also borne out by a growing body of social science research (Chawla and Derr 2012).

Of course, action on behalf of the environment is also the ultimate goal of school-based environmental education. But nature education differs in critical ways. In formal, school-based environmental education, the goal of changing behavior to meet environmental challenges is explicit, and it is clear that these behavior changes often involve inconvenient or unpleasant sacrifices—sacrifices which are often justified by the threat of even greater future sacrifices if action isn't taken now. By contrast, consumers of nature education typically view it as a form of immediate enrichment, a pleasurable nurturing of growth, health, and well-being that they actively seek (and pay for) instead of passively enduring it. This fundamental difference between experiential nature education and in-school environmental education has easily imaginable consequences for participants' engagement, learning, and motivations for future stewardship, consequences that are borne out by the growing scholarly literature on nature-based learning—and acknowledged in China's official environmental education guidelines.

Nature Education and School-Based Environmental Education

In 2003 when China's Ministry of Education called for the infusion of environmental education content throughout the nation's public school curricula from the first year of primary school through the second year of high school, their guidelines emphasized firsthand experience (*qinshen tiyan*) and recommended that a full quarter of the total environmental education content should consist of "practice activities" (*shijian huodong*) as opposed to classroom work (Ministry of Education 2003a, b). Nearly a decade and a half after the Ministry's call, teachers in China rarely adopt this approach to environmental education. Even in those schools where teachers and principals are aware of the Ministry's environmental education requirement and are trying to meet it (a mere four hours per year are suggested), the method is almost exclusively classroom-based. This is largely due to parental (and hence administrative) concerns over child safety and test preparation (Efird 2011, 2012, 2014, 2015), particularly fears that taking children out of the classroom might not only endanger them but also jeopardize their all-important exam performance by squandering precious class time. These concerns largely prevent—or at least discourage—schoolteachers and principals from providing the kind of local, experiential environmental education specifically suggested in the Ministry of Education's guidelines. The result is a strong tendency towards an indoors, passive, audio-visual approach to education.

Zhang recalled touring public schools in the early 2000s as part of her work with Friends of Nature and discovering a serious problem with the way environmental education was being practiced there. As she succinctly puts it, "environmental education didn't have an environment" (*huanjing jiaoyu meiyou huanjing*). The schools she visited didn't even have any plants—they could only use images to teach about the environment. As Zhang puts it, "There's no way to use a projector or a computer to reveal nature's allure [*meili*] and foster a deep connection [*lianjie*]. You can't eat it, you can't smell it, you can't touch it." She blames conservative education authorities and their preoccupation with student safety as the primary obstacle to environmental education in schools. Under these circumstances, her organization has chosen to work outside of the school system.

Increasingly, parents too are looking outside the school system for opportunities to expose their children to nature. Ironically, while parental fears for children's safety have certainly contributed to the largely indoor nature of Chinese schooling, concerns over children's healthy development now prompt some parents to view nature experiences as desirable or even necessary for their child's welfare. According to several Chinese nature experience providers (including those interviewed for this chapter), the demand for nature education among well-educated urban parents has grown strongly over the past several years, feeding the rapid growth in hands-on outdoor learning opportunities like Zhang's nature school.

When asked about the reasons behind this recent surge of interest, several educators cite Louv's landmark book, *Last Child in the Woods: Saving Our Children from Nature-Deficit Disorder* (Louv 2005). Based on extensive research and interviews, Louv's book documented the negative mental and physical health consequences of the precipitous decline in North American children's contact with nature, catalyzing an international movement to address this "deficit" through grassroots organizing, family nature clubs, and policy initiatives. Friends of Nature oversaw the first Chinese-language translation of *Last Child in the Woods* in 2010 and facilitated the gradual nationwide spread of Louv's ideas, including the signature concept of "nature-deficit disorder." A translation of an updated and expanded second edition of *Last Child in the Woods* was published in China in 2014, and the book is now familiar not only to environmental educators throughout China but also to a growing number of urban, middle-class Chinese parents as well. Louv offers Chinese parents a compelling collection of research and anecdotes to support their sense that nature deprivation is in fact harmful to their (typically only) child. According to Zhang, this is particularly true of the primary school parents who participate in their nature school programs. Oftentimes both parents work full-time and therefore pay extra attention to their child's "growth, health, all aspects of their life, and particularly 'nature-deficit disorder': they don't want their child to be negatively affected by that."

Wang Yu, director of the Yunnan Local Nature Education Center (Yunnan Zaidi Ziran Jiaoyu Zhongxin) and the Shicheng Nature School near Kunming, agrees that nature education really began to take off in China after the first translation of *Last Child in the Woods* appeared in 2010: "At that point, traditional environmental education was facing a lot of difficulties, and it wasn't very successful." In contrast to nature education, she says, "environmental education is more formal [*zhengshi*] . . . and it's pushed by the government. Nature education is more 'popular' [*minjian*], more grassroots [*caogen*]." Wang's organization illustrates this contrast. As an undergraduate, Wang attended Yunnan University in Kunming, where she was active in the student environmental club. She later received a master's degree in Environmental Education from University of Wisconsin-Stevens Point, and after returning to China and working for the international environmental NGO Rare, in 2012 she started her own organization which offers nature education programming both in Kunming and at their nature school just outside the city.

Like Gaia Nature School's Zhang, Wang agrees that it is critical to reach parents as well as children. "Previously," she notes, "nature education focused on kids. But there is a need to consciously address adults and get them involved." She stresses that it isn't just children who are suffering from a lack of contact with the natural world: "Many people in society are increasingly distant from nature. People who were born in the 1970s and 80s grew up in a much more urban environment, and now they are parents." Like Zhang's, Wang's organization has focused on developing a core of parent-child activities as a way of meeting the needs of both generations, each of which is largely composed of city-raised singletons. Wang and Zhang are hardly unusual in this focus: in a 2016 nationwide survey of 177 organizations that provide nature education, three quarters reported that the "primary target" of their nature education programs was "families comprised of parents and children" (Wang and Liu 2017, 10).

The focus on parent-child education among Chinese nature educators exemplifies the importance of cultural context to environmental education research and practice. As with so many imported ideas and practices, notions of nature and techniques of environmental learning undergo a process of translation and accommodation to local circumstances. As Zhang puts it, the focus on parent education is "a typical (*dianxing*) example of 'localization'" that reflects the unique circumstances of China's planned birth policy. Yet as with earlier instances of Chinese borrowing, Euro-American ideas and practices of environmental learning often reach mainland China via East Asian intermediaries.

East Asian Influences on China's Nature Education

Non-Chinese NGOs have long been influential in the evolution of mainland Chinese environmental education. Perhaps the most dramatic example of this involvement was the ten-year Environmental Educators' Initiative led by the China office of the World Wildlife Fund (WWF-China) between 1997 and 2007, which trained thousands of teachers, established environmental education training centers at teachers' universities, and directly resulted in the drafting of the Ministry of Education's guidelines for environmental education in public schools (Lee 2010). WWF-China remains active in promoting environmental education and nature schools in China, but they have recently been joined by nongovernmental organizations from other areas of East Asia. One noteworthy example is an ongoing partnership between the Hong Kong–based NGO Partners for Community Development (PCD; Shequ Huoban) and the Ministry of Forestry's Administrative Office of Yunnan's Gaoligongshan National Nature Reserve to establish a nature school and spread the teaching of nature education throughout Yunnan's Baoshan municipality. Their concerns with Chinese parenting and their belief in the potential for nature to nurture children's healthy growth are evident in their original project application:

> These days, parents raise children as if they were raising pets. . . . We protect them in every possible way, carefully tend to them, leash them for fear that they will fall . . . keep them at home for fear that we'll lose them. This generation of children is both fortunate and unfortunate. Their misfortune is that, under their parents' "pet raising" educational approach, the children's future is in peril. Building the Gaoligongshan Nature School will allow children to immerse themselves in the outdoors, make nature their classroom, have class in the forest, take nature as the teacher, learn from nature, learn in nature, and learn to care for nature. (PCD 2012)

The philosophy and practice of nature education in Hong Kong and Taiwan have resonated in mainland China for reasons that include both a common language and shared cultural circumstances. Gaia's Zhang says that they tend to privilege the Chinese-speaking region (*huayuqu*) as a reference and a partner in exchange because of the many shared problems and similar "basic understandings, like how people see children and education." With the support of NGOs like PCD and Friends of Nature, environmental education scholars and practitioners have been invited to the mainland from Taiwan and Hong Kong to offer their expertise and lead trainings in a variety of areas related to nature education, from permaculture to Leave No Trace camping. But Japan's nature schools have also provided an important model, due to an influential three-year training program implemented by a Japan-based NGO and funded by the Japan International Cooperation Agency.

Between 2012 and 2015, the Japan-based nonprofit organization Japan-China Civil Society Network (CSNet) (csnet.asia) carried out an international project to familiarize Chinese environmental education professionals with Japanese nature education and promote the establishment of a nature school network in China. Despite the cultural differences, Japanese nature education offered Chinese practitioners a readily understandable model: beginning in the 1990s, widespread concern over the negative consequences of Japan's high-pressure, test-focused academic system led to the increased provision of outdoor learning opportunities for schoolchildren and the rapid growth of "nature schools" (*shizen gakkō*), which now number nearly four thousand and are linked by a nationwide network (Nishimura 2006; Tsuji 2008). Under the auspices of the CSNet project, Chinese nature educators learned about Japanese nature schools through both firsthand visits and lectures in China by Japanese experts and a wealth of materials on Japanese nature schools translated into Chinese. However, perhaps the most lasting consequence of the initiative was the networking of Chinese nature educators through a series of nature education fora held at different locations throughout China. The largest of these continues as the yearly National Nature Education Forum (Quanguo Ziran Jiaoyu Pingtai), founded in 2014, which has attracted a rapidly growing number of Chinese participants interested in presentations from both Chinese and foreign nature education experts, including such internationally prominent writers and practitioners as Richard Louv and Joseph Cornell.

The Nature Education Forum and its attendees offer a revealing window on the state of nature education in China today and its recent explosive growth. Referencing a 2015 survey of 286 participating nature education organizations (63% of which were established since 2012), one of the forum's organizers succinctly summarized the origins and growing appeal of nature education in China, as well as its contrast with traditional school-based environmental education:

Undoubtedly, Richard Louv and his work related to nature-deficit disorder has [*sic*] played a major role in inspiring people in China. Some folks who have worked for environmental education (EE) and/or education for sustainable development (ESD) now see nature education— connecting children and families directly to nature—as a means of encouraging wider participation, as well as a way of generating income to support their institutions. The ultimate aim of EE and ESD is to protect the environment and nature, which are what we call "common pool resources." Everyone is affected by them, but many individuals may find these concepts abstract, and do not necessarily see them as personal or family priorities. In contrast, parents see that nature education—which happens outdoors in the natural environment—nourishes their children's minds and bodies. As a result, nature education is becoming a voluntary choice by parents and children. Especially in the context of urbanization and industrialization, connecting to nature is now seen by many as essential to children's mental and physical health. (Yan 2015)

Conclusion: Rediscovering Nature as Nurture

Robert Weller points out that indigenous Chinese perspectives on the nonhuman world and globalizing, non-Chinese notions of nature and the environment contributed to a complex, synthetic process of "discovering nature" in Taiwan and mainland China in the late twentieth century (Weller 2006). In this process, new notions of nature drove new practices, from aesthetic consumption (e.g., "nature tourism") to "environmental protection" (*huanjing baohu*). In the twenty-first century, a second major transformation is occurring as nature is now being rediscovered as a source of nurture, and the practice of "connecting with nature" (*yu ziran lianjie*) is being valorized as essential to people's—and particularly children's—health and well-being.

This rediscovery of nature in mainland China is a watershed in the relationship between Chinese people and the nonhuman world, one with significant consequences for mainland China's environment and the people who depend upon it. Heretofore, environmental education has largely been a state-driven agenda to promote environmental protection, and environmental education initiatives in schools and society have typically taken the form of top-down, mass efforts at behavior change in which students and citizens are situated as the passive objects of indoctrination. As noted above, this approach has been largely unsuccessful. By contrast, the growth of nature education is riding a wave of enthusiasm and anxiety, both of which appear to be motivating parents to seek outdoor learning opportunities for their children and for themselves. Given the empirically demonstrated connections between nature exposure and environmental care, the growing embrace of nature education may well succeed in fostering stewardship where government-promoted, top-down, school-based environmental education has failed.

In fact, the Chinese government itself is beginning to promote nature education. Since its inception in China, nature education's rapid growth has been driven by nongovernmental and for-profit organizations. Now the newly reorganized Ministry of Natural Resources (MNR) is assuming an influential role in shaping nature education by encouraging its practice in China's national parks, protected areas, and nature parks, all of which now fall within the ministry's administrative purview. As one reflection of this new emphasis, in October 2019 the MNR held its inaugural international forum on nature protection with nature education as one of the conference subthemes.

This governmental embrace of nature education illustrates the complexity of China's emerging eco-developmental state, in which the singular goal of economic growth is now balanced—but not necessarily superseded—by other concerns, such as environmental protection. Similarly, nature education exemplifies the way in which parental preoccupation with academic performance is increasingly balanced with other concerns, such as a child's health and well-being. Nature education's appeal derives at least in part from the perception that it enhances both personal satisfaction and academic success.

As Confucius reminds us when he says that "the wise delight in water; the humane delight in mountains," this is not an entirely new perspective: nature has long been a source of delight and self-cultivation in China (Liu 2012). What is new, however, is the urban, indoor lifestyle led by most contemporary Chinese, one largely devoid of nature contact. Thus, the key question for China's nature education is not one of efficacy, but of access: will the clear benefits of nature-based learning remain the preserve of a small, privileged elite? Or will a broader share of China's public enjoy the birthright of every child: the right to form meaningful, satisfying, and mutually sustaining relationships with the more-than-human world?

9

Sustainability of Korea's First "New Village"

CHUNG HO KIM

WHAT IF YOUR HOUSE AND VILLAGE WERE DEMOLISHED AND rebuilt by the government? How would you respond to the completely new built environment? This kind of sudden, large-scale transformation happened in rural Korea during the 1970s, initiated not by residents or by natural disasters, such as typhoons and earthquakes, but by the government in the name of village-scale modernization and urbanization. The "First Saemaul Village" in Cheonan County, a showcase village intended to demonstrate the benefits of rural modernization to other villages across South Korea, provides a useful case study for examining the environmental and political dynamics of state-directed modernization programs in rural communities. Village demolition and reconstruction were driven by models and ideas of high modernist developmentalism (Scott 1998) imported from the West and illustrate both the unfaltering actions and the unintended consequences of wholesale modernization projects on rural landscapes and communities. The experience of the First Saemaul Village offers important empirical insights for sustainable rural development around the world.

The First Saemaul Village was newly built in 1974 in a compact form, demolishing existing traditional rural houses and agglomerating scattered villages. As a showcase project of the Korean Saemaul New Village Movement, the village demonstrates how traditional Korean villages were modernized and how the villagers have adapted to the completely new human settlements over the past forty years. The question remains whether this kind of rural redesign, undertaken by an authoritarian developmentalist regime, can still contribute to village sustainability in the new era of eco-developmentalism.

Village Continuity: Before the Saemaul Movement

It is estimated that people started to settle in the Korean Peninsula between 10,000 and 8,000 BCE (Jeon 2016). Grain agriculture based on rice and barley was important in sustaining people and forming human settlements, due to the temperate climate in the middle latitudes. The Korean villages discussed here evolved as farming villages during the Joseon dynasty (1392–1897), when rice farming was the main rural occupation. The villages, typically located near rice paddies in the plains, had between 50 and 150 families. The physical sizes of the villages would be controlled by the distance between each village and its residents' fields, which reached 4–5 kilometers (2.5–3.7 mi) at most (Jeon 2016). Prior to the Saemaul Movement, rural Korean villages were shaped by two main settlement logics: fengshui affected site selection, and lineage structure influenced planning of the village and its buildings.

Fengshui is a system of East Asian traditional ecological knowledge expressing the relation between cultural values and natural environments. Fengshui has played an important role in settlement patterns and site selection in Korea (Yoon 2006). Korean fengshui has focused on the theory of landforms (*hyŏngseron*). According to fengshui theory and principles, there are two auspicious patterns that are commonly observed in the location of Korean traditional villages (Hong, Song, and Wu 2007): One is *changp'ung tŭksu*, a settlement pattern surrounded by mountains and watercourses with more open spaces facing the south. The other is *paesan imsu*, in which a village is located with its back to the mountain and its front to the water, irrespective of the cardinal direction of the village.

The lineage village was the dominant type of Korean traditional settlement during the Joseon dynasty,[1] reflecting the neo-Confucian social structure adopted by the dynasty as part of its state ideology (Jeon 1992). Neo-Confucianism is an ethical and philosophical system that emphasizes desirable social relationships between people and self-discipline of humanistic persons. In this context, gentry lineage villages (*yangban* ssijok ch'on) in the Joseon dynasty, were geographical units that adopted neo-Confucianism as strong social norms. Since villagers were related by blood, the patrilineal order (chongbŏpchŏk chilsŏ) in the family hierarchy, affected all types of economic, social, and cultural relationships among villagers, regardless of the tangible or intangible features.

As a result, neo-Confucianism and patrilineal order in the Joseon dynasty substantially influenced architectural characteristics and spatial composition of traditional villages and houses (Jeon 1992). House sites, orientations, and ornaments in lineage villages were not socially interchangeable and equal, but hierarchical and exclusive. For example, gentry lineages (chaeji sajok) lived in large houses in the upper hills with panoramic views and tile roofs, while peasants (nongmin) lived in small houses in the lower hills with narrow views and thatched roofs. In addition, a leading family (chongga) had better sight lines to major landmarks or mountains than branch families (pun'ga) (Jeon 1992).

Likewise, traditional gentry houses (hanok) reflected this neo-Confucian social hierarchy.[2] For example, men's spaces in hanok—sarangchae for upper-class men and haengnangchae for their servants—were located in the front of houses, while women's spaces and kitchens were at the back. Away from these living spaces, ancestral shrines (sadang) were often located in hanok.

Village Transformation: During the Saemaul Movement

The Saemaul Movement, which took place in the 1970s, is a prime example of the application of high modernist developmentalism to human settlements. High modernism involves strong confidence in scientific and technological progress, seeks to master nature in order to satisfy human needs, and ignores existing historical, social, and cultural context in development (Scott 1998). High modernism thus grants excessive power and authority to people who have expertise in science, technology, planning, and administration. The Saemaul Movement took a radical approach to transforming existing traditional houses and villages into new human settlements aimed at modernized landscapes, urbanized structures, and industrialized materials and resources.

President Park Chung-hee, as the primary proponent of the Saemaul Movement in the 1970s, believed in a deterministic and progressive development ideology based on social evolution. For example, Park followed

Walt Rostow's ideas and theories on economic development (O 2009). Rostow was an American economist and political theorist who served as special assistant for National Security Affairs to US president Lyndon B. Johnson in 1966–69 and who proposed the use of his five-stage model of economic development, ranging from traditional society to high mass consumption society (Rostow 1960). Rostow's ideas played a significant role in the development of the Saemaul Movement, which led to the intentional eradication of traditional villages in Korea (Nemeth 2008). Park and his planners viewed traditional villages as backward and detrimental to the development of the rich, urban society that they envisioned for the Republic of Korea. Their unfaltering confidence in modern society and fundamental social transformation was connected to their belief in high modernist developmentalism.

In this historical context, the First Saemaul Village is an extreme case, selected to illustrate how high modernist developmentalism worked in Korea. Park was personally involved in the beginning of the Saemaul Movement, and this village was a pioneering case of Park's built environments experiment.[3] This was the first village-scale showcase project of the Saemaul Movement,[4] constructed according to the Saemaul Countryside Construction Plan that was published in 1972 (Ministry of Home Affairs 1972).

The First Saemaul Village is located in Samgok-ri, Cheonan-si, approximately 80 kilometers (50 mi) south of Seoul and 320 kilometers (200 mi) northwest of Busan. The village is adjacent to the Gyeongbu (Seoul-Busan) Expressway, which was opened in 1970 as South Korea's first expressway and was promoted by President Park's regime as a symbol of rapid economic development and modernization. According to a *Kyunghang Shinmun* newspaper article in 1972, the central government announced that it would construct nine model villages near main expressways across the country, and this village in Cheonan was on the list. The goal of the model villages was to agglomerate and collectivize scattered rural farmhouses. For this, each province had its own model village, which was classified according to its topographical location as either a mountain or plain type of village.

Architecturally, the new village design displays a compact urban form and a clear functional zoning. The conspicuous central area where eight main roads pass diagonally contains community facilities including a village hall, a farming tool and equipment center, and parking lots. According to the interview with the village head Kyung-uk Lim, who was a middle school student at the time of the construction and has lived there ever since, the village was completely reconstructed in 1974, including land and road realignment and house construction.

In 1974, residents were evicted from their homes and forced to live in temporary structures such as tents near the construction site until construction was finished. A house was distributed to each household according to the value of its previous house. Mr. Lim remembered that villagers were very happy when they were relocated to new houses. Although each house had a smaller yard than before, villagers were satisfied with the new built environments (houses and roads), modern in-home conveniences (tube well water, sewage, and electricity), and community facilities (a village hall, a small exercise area, and a farming tool and equipment center) in the middle of the village, which were completely new environments, services, and infrastructures to villagers. Meanwhile, this village came to have three or four times as many houses and residents than neighboring traditional villages had. Since the reconstruction in the 1970s, the village has not experienced further radical transformation of built environments, although it has had minor changes or improvements. As of December 31, 2011, the village had 89 households and 203 people (101 men and 102 women). The population largely consists of older residents who are engaged in small-scale commercial agriculture such as rice farming and grape cultivation.

The village's extreme transformation can be attributed to the authoritarian regime's strong top-down leadership. In fact, central government leadership was new to rural villages at that time. Although South Korea gained independence in 1945, it was not until President Park's military coup in 1961 that the central government gained authoritarian power over villages and their residents, replacing the rule by local gentry that had continued from the Joseon dynasty. Even though the traditional feudal system was abolished by the Gabo Reform in 1894, local power in rural communities was generally still handed down to descendants of former leaders.

President Park's authoritarian regime disrupted these long-standing social and political patterns. The Saemaul Movement itself reveals the strong centralization of political power over rural villages in the 1970s, which was made possible by the weakening of landlord rights and class power during the Japanese colonial period (1910–45) (Shin 1996; Shin 1998). The 1970s village leaders were not proponents of the old local gentry's vested interests, but loyal and passionate workers of the central government, educated through the training camp system at the Samaul Undong Central Training Institute (Asian Development Bank 2012). In this political context, President Park's high modernist developmentalism acted as a new ideology and coherent policy to rapidly modernize and urbanize rural villages. Thus, the Saemaul Movement aimed to create a complete break with traditional Korean settlements by transforming rural villages physically, providing them with new industrial materials and resources such as cement, glass, and fossil fuels. This intentional physical change was explicitly symbolic of development and modernization and served to mobilize rural people and legitimize the authoritarian regime. However, while President Park's authoritarian regime was a necessary condition for this unprecedented rural development, it was not sufficient to ensure actual and successful rural development because the regime did not heed the voices of farmers and villagers, nor did it take into consideration the ways that these rural settlements had been refined and had evolved over the centuries. In short, Park pursued an unequivocal high modernist agenda.

The Transformation of the First Saemaul Village

The way that the Saemaul Movement transformed the physical infrastructure of traditional villages in Korea is illustrated in the contrast of the First Saemaul Village with Yangdong Village, a similarly situated community which was not involved in the Saemaul Movement. Map 9.2 shows the two villages: Yangdong Village, a traditional village, in the top panel and the First Saemaul Village in the bottom panel.

Following fengshui logic, the traditional houses of Yangdong Village are scattered—sparsely distributed along the contours of the hills. Most of the houses are located in the valleys in order to gain access to water. Village roads conform closely to the terrain, curving around hills and other geographic features. Houses mostly face south and vary

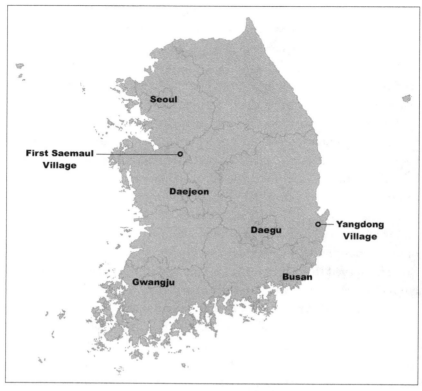

MAP 9.1   Locations of Yandgong Village and First Saemaul Village in Korea

in orientation according to the patrilineal order of houses and sight lines to major landmarks. Generally, the higher residents are in the patrilineal order, the larger their lots and the better their views. In contrast, all of the houses of the First Saemaul Village are located in the plain area near the expressway and highly concentrated near the single center of the village. Village roads are not related to the terrain, instead forming a planned hexagonal geometric pattern. All houses are generally oriented east, facing the expressway.

Despite the stark differences in settlement logic and patterns, residents of the two villages have mostly relied on agriculture for their living in recent decades, even though there has been a growing influx of urban commuters into the First Saemaul Village. Traditional villages have the advantages of convenient access to agricultural lands and conformity

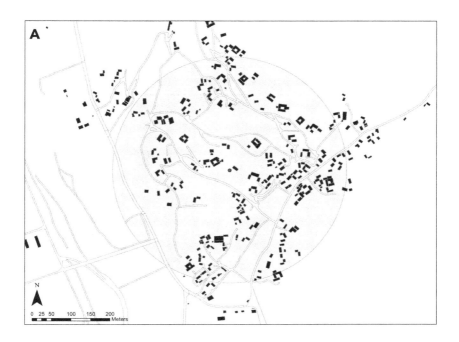

MAP 9.2 (a) Yangdong Village and (b) First Saemaul Village, showing buildings alleys, and contours. The shaded circles each have a radius of 300 meters (1,000 ft).

Table 9.1   Comparison between traditional villages and First Saemaul Village

CATEGORY	TRADITIONAL VILLAGES	FIRST SAEMAUL VILLAGE
Ideology	Neo-Confucian	High-modern, pseudo-Western
Implementation	Family-level	Top-down government
Rationale	Proximity to farming	Proximity to modern resources
Formation process	Long and incremental	Short and rapid
Village pattern	Organic and contextual	Regular and centered
Building layout	Loose and irregular	Compact and standardized
Construction materials	Natural materials	Industrial products

to local contexts, including water, terrain, and climate. By contrast, the First Saemaul Village has the advantage of easier access to modern or urban resources such as healthcare, education, and grocery stores and lower infrastructure costs relating to continuous updates in resource management. The rapid transformation of the built environment at the First Saemaul Village was aimed at creating regularity, centrality, zoning, and standardization conducive to modern, urban lifestyles and employment patterns. Although the First Saemaul Village has been more amenable to integration with nearby urban centers, its residents were also forced to confront the issue of high dependency on modern or urban resources, unlike the self-sufficiency of traditional villages (table 9.1).

Village Adaptation: After the Saemaul Movement

Residents initially welcomed the radical transformation of the First Saemaul Village because they enjoyed the modern amenities of electricity, efficient road systems, and easy access to urban areas. Over the course of forty years, villagers carried out additional adaptations, which may reveal lessons for sustainable rural development. In order to understand the transformation better, I conducted open-ended interviews in 2014 with residents who have lived in the village continuously since it was built in 1974. My interviews clearly revealed two dimensions of the transformation: village-scale and house-scale adaptation.

First, the village-scale adaptation concerned layout, road patterns, and community facilities. Speaking about challenges in contemporary village life, Mr. Lim, the village head, pointed to the issue of transportation: "Transportation is the most challenging issue. The village plaza was changed into parking lots. However, they are not enough. Some roads are just three meters wide. Two cars cannot pass through at the same time." President Park and his planners in the 1970s did not imagine significant transportation needs, which reveals that the high modernist confidence of mastering human society as well as the natural world was sometimes illusory or at least woefully incomplete. Surprisingly, the number of registered vehicles in the country had climbed from 180,000 in 1974 to 17,940,000 by 2010, which has created intense demand for parking in all parts of the country, urban as well as rural. Unlike the 1970s, today farmers own a variety of vehicles including cars, pickup trucks, cultivators, and tractors. As a result, this transportation issue could not be solved easily because it is associated with the village's physical structure and land ownership.

Next, Mr. Lim described in positive terms the continuous improvement of community facilities at the center of the village, including a village hall, a farming tool and equipment center, parking lots, and a small exercise area. In addition, he emphasized the village's advantage in updating public utility management, such as water, sewage, electricity, and fuel, because the village is agglomerated right next to the Gyeongbu Expressway. The village is currently using common resource facilities such as a common well and a common methane fuel tank. The community facilities have been easier to update and modify with the changing times because of high household density, locational advantage, and use flexibility of central spaces.

In summary, Mr. Lim emphasized that the continuous influx of people and factories acted as a main driver of transforming the village—building new houses and renovating existing ones. He thought the growth of population and industry could be largely attributed to the accessibility to the expressway. For example, it takes about only thirty minutes to commute by car from the First Saemaul Village to downtown Cheonan, the nearest urban center to the village, with a population of about six hundred thousand people in 2015. The continuous influx of people into the First Saemaul Village is in stark contrast to most rural villages in Korea, which have been experiencing population decrease. Nevertheless, Mr. Lim pointed out the difficulty of assimilating new residents and workers with long-term residents and villagers because the newcomers were not farmers living full-time in the village but rather commuters who spent their days in urban areas.[5]

In terms of the house-scale adaptation, significant changes were made to the room arrangement, building expansion, and resource management. The newly constructed village had only three building types that residents still call "Type A," "Type B," and "Type C." As shown in figure 9.1, each house type typically has two or three bedrooms, one kitchen, one bathroom, and one living room. Regardless of the specific types, the house-scale adaptation was similar. The small and compact floorplans led to horizontal building expansion over the past forty years. I observed that almost all houses in the First Saemaul Village had portions expanded by residents even though they still kept the first story of the building in its original form, marked as shaded areas in figure 9.1.

The residents in the First Saemaul Village mentioned that the original kitchens and bathrooms were too small and old-fashioned to accommodate changing lifestyles. By 2010, most houses had undergone major renovations. One major design flaw that was present in all the houses was a lack of a septic system. Planners did not include a septic system at that time, but, viewing a bathroom as an important feature of a modern house, they located traditional toilets inside the houses. Not surprisingly, within only a few years, the residents had to build outhouses. About twenty years later after that, flush toilets were added inside the houses with septic tanks that were then regularly emptied by municipal septic trucks. Meanwhile, the residents described not only continuous improvement of building materials and systems including insulation, windows and doors, and kitchens and bathrooms but also, over time, changing heating and cooking fuels from wood to coal, oil, and finally gas.

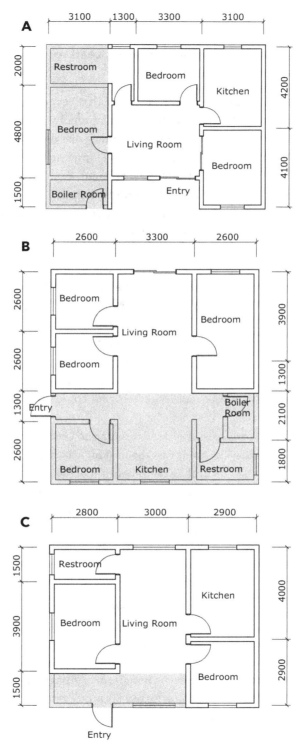

FIGURE 9.1   Floor plans of Type A, B, and C buildings in the First Saemaul Village (dimensions in millimeters). Shading indicates portions expanded by residents.

Can High Modernist Developmentalism Lead to Sustainable Rural Development?

The First Saemaul Village is an extreme case that reveals both the efficacy and limitations of high modernist developmentalism and leads to several important observations about high modernist developmentalism and the possibility of sustainable rural development: (1) strictly controlled, top-down processes can be highly efficient, dramatically improving the quality of life for rural residents and villagers, especially if they live in very poor, traditional environments without consistent access to water, sewage, electricity, and fuel; (2) modernizing rural villages with good access to transportation could be a method to slow down urban migration and encourage reverse migration, where urban residents move from expensive, overcrowded cities into the countryside; (3) specific policies should fully embrace the voices of farmers and villagers, as well as drawing on useful features of rural settlements refined and evolved over a long period, in order to make the physical transformations more appropriate to the lives of the people that live there; (4) rural residents and villagers are able to adapt to the radical reforms of rural villages to an extent, but not entirely because the reforms could deprive them of self-sufficiency.

One of the main sources of difficulties for the First Saemaul Village was that the Saemaul Movement was focused on urban or pseudo-urban development rather than rural development. In other words, the movement had no clear prescription for rural development, and in particular, no plan to incorporate agricultural life into the redesign of the village. Instead, they tried to integrate the countryside into urban economic, social, and environmental systems, compounding the urbanization problem that the programs were designed to solve. In addition, they were highly disruptive to the social systems of rural villages, creating physical and psychological difficulty for rural people who were used to engaging in small-scale agriculture, and thus contributed to further marginalization of rural residents and villagers. Further, they furnished rural villages with completely different energy and resources, such as industrial materials and fossil fuels, even though rural villages did not ask for these changes. In the end, rural residents became even more dependent on urban resources, services, and infrastructure than before, leading them to become less and less self-sufficient and more and more affected by national- or global-scale changes in resource management. Therefore, while high modernist development can succeed in integrating rural communities into urban systems, those new communities are no longer rural villages but rather partially connected suburbs. Thus, what is fundamentally required for sustainable rural development is to increase the self-sufficiency of rural residents and villagers with diversified resources, services, and infrastructures.

This Korean historical experience may provide important insights into how other authoritarian countries can use their top-down national planning structure to influence rural development. In particular, China has historically successfully maintained an authoritarian regime as a socialist country, and the Chinese New Socialist Countryside Construction (CNSCC) begun in 2006 benchmarked the Saemaul Movement in the 1970s (Perry 2011; Looney 2012). As China and other countries rethink their developmentalist ideologies, they can learn from the experiences of the Republic of Korea.

Notes

1   There were 14,672 lineage villages in 1930 (Zensho 1933).
2   Although *hanok* is a common designation of Korean traditional houses, here I use the term more narrowly to refer to the houses for local gentry that reflected Korean natural environments and neo-Confucian social structure in architectural layouts and styles.
3   Byoung-hwa Lee, interview by author, Yongin, September 22, 2014. Mr. Lee was agricultural secretary for President Park in the 1970s and has managed and operated the First Saemaul House in Yongin, which President Park designed as a secret farmhouse in 1972.
4   I call this village the First Saemaul Village on the basis of an interview with Mr. Lee in 2014 and comparative review of the Saemaul Countryside Construction Plan published in 1972. However, I could not find any government documents that officially named it the First Saemaul Village.
5   I conducted interviews with three residents who live in "Type A," Type B," and "Type C" houses in Cheonan on September 30 and October 15, 2014. The residents have continuously lived in the village since it was built in 1974. Along with the open-ended interviews, I measured the residential units and documented them in architectural drawings.

10

Eco-developmentalism in China's Chengdu Plain

DANIEL BENJAMIN ABRAMSON

ENVIRONMENTALISM IN LONG-SETTLED, DENSELY POPULATED, AND deeply coupled human and natural systems—even those subject to political revolution and rapid urbanization—is a product of historical values embedded in the local landscape as well as new values reflecting cultural and technological inputs from various internal and external sources. Such systems' resilience depends on local adaptations that contribute to feedback loops in decision-making at multiple spatial and temporal scales, including construction projects, developmental policies, and environmental management. In East Asia and other rice-growing monsoon regions, anthropogenic landscapes have supported very dense populations over long periods without the soil degradation and biodiversity loss observed in ancient civilizations around the Mediterranean, the Middle East, and parts of the world more recently colonized by Western Europeans (Montgomery 2007).

Over the past century, however, East Asia has also produced some of the world's most strident and effective developmental state regimes (Leftwich 1994). Putting their faith in the Environmental Kuznets Curve (see chapter 15), these regimes are willing to sacrifice some of the world's most robust achievements of time-tested sustainability, with the expectation that new technologies and economic growth will launch their societies into a more productive and ultimately sustainable new state of equilibrium. In China, "economic strength" and the authoritarian government's "ability to implement massive programs that can infiltrate every aspect of society rapidly" have even given particular hope to some advocates of sustainability (Liu 2010). East Asian state developmentalism emerged in a geopolitical context of European colonization, hot wars and the Cold War, and other global crises; however, it was also a response to internal crises produced by the "technological lock-in" that long-term sustainability itself produced.

Borrowing W. B. Arthur's economic concept of path dependence, in which "technological conventions . . . tend to become locked-in by positive feedback" (Elvin 2004, 123; Arthur 1990), historian Mark Elvin describes how China's highly efficient and sustainable ancient systems of agriculture, along with land and water management, simultaneously nurtured a large population and depended on that population's intensive labor input for their maintenance—an input that in turn depended on an inflexible bureaucracy and highly connected collective communal life. The low adaptive capacity of these systems, he argues, was responsible for much of the turmoil, displacement, and loss of life China experienced in the late nineteenth and early twentieth centuries. Environmental degradation did not begin with the developmental state in China (Li 2007; Pietz 2015).

The Chengdu Plain in the western Sichuan Basin, however, fared much better through these crises, and exhibits many features of resilient adaptive capacity (Abramson 2019; Whiting et al. 2019). Supported by the Dujiangyan Irrigation System, China's largest, which was built in the third century BCE and has been almost continuously maintained and expanded since then, the plain has sustained several major cities with an agrarian civilization based on irrigated rice cultivation for over two thousand years. Chengdu, the plain's metropolitan center, has remained remarkably stable in its rank among Chinese cities over this long history (Modelski 2003, 214–15). Given the environmental degradation and threats to food production that have accompanied urban growth elsewhere in China over the past century at least, Chengdu's resilience may be globally significant.

The Dujiangyan system channeled water from the Min River throughout the plain, creating a remarkably productive, densely populated, biodiverse, and forested agroecosystem with nutrient-rich soil, levee-free irrigation canals, and a spatially dispersed forested lot (*linpan*) settlement pattern (figure 10.1). This physical system has combined with

FIGURE 10.1   Aerial view of *linpan* farmstead clusters in the Chengdu Plain, Pi County, Chengdu.[1] The cluster in the center is larger than most, due to its unusual inclusion of a temple (with a large square roof), but it shows the typically tight spatial integration of dwellings with trees of different species, ages, and sizes, surrounded by a diverse patchwork of fields, rice paddies, nurseries, and irrigation channels. (Photograph by Yi Xiang, 2017)

crosscutting structures of local governance to feed and support a historically increasing population, even at times when nearby areas experienced famine. In recent decades, however, aggressive developmentalist programs of farm consolidation, residential concentration, agricultural commercialization, and urbanization have disturbed this ecosystem. In response, environmentalist movements and organizations have arisen, dedicated to maintaining, restoring, or adapting the plain's historic sustainable agroecology on the time-tested principles of past centuries. How have they fared?

The Chengdu Plain's Agroecology at a Crossroads

Just as "technological lock-in" was a threat to environmental resilience in China's imperial past (Elvin 2004), more recent developmental programs have locked the society into a new form of "dependence upon monumental engineering schemes" and bureaucratized management (Courtney 2016, 98–99). Two massive, continental-scale development schemes—the Great Western Development Program and the New Socialist Village Campaign, have imported modernist developmental thinking into the management of land, water, and agriculture in the Chengdu Plain, which was seen to be "lagging behind" the more industrialized coastal regions. These programs have fueled a particularly radical transformation of the Dujiangyan system's broader landscape through urban expansion. The late 1990s and early 2000s saw a speculative boom in housing construction in the municipality of Chengdu, including the counties and districts in the Dujiangyan system, expanding the city's built area by nearly 40% between 1995 and 2002, occupying much prime agricultural land (Schneider, Seto, and Webster 2005, 340). In the mid-2000s, the municipality also extended urban infrastructure and services to rural communities, intending to reshape rural livelihoods and living conditions on a "comprehensively planned" basis (Ye and LeGates 2013).

These programs reorganized land use according to the "three concentrations" principle: (1) concentrating rural housing and amalgamating villages; (2) concentrating rural factories into industrial zones; and (3) assembling small farm plots into larger agricultural enterprises (Bray 2013; Huang et al. 2013; Zhang and Wu 2017). Concentration of rural housing was seen as providing a number of co-benefits: it allowed for a more planned approach to urban expansion, including building roads, electrical and telecommunication lines, piped gas, and sewage treatment; it reduced the footprint of paved and built land; and, most importantly from the municipality's perspective, it allowed the scattered *linpan* dwelling sites to be converted to new fields (and often consolidated for scaled-up agribusiness enterprises), freeing up rural land elsewhere for urban construction without decreasing net arable land across the municipality.

Financing for new village construction would come from a government-mediated transfer of land development rights. Developers would be permitted to build on farmland in one location by paying to "create" new farmland elsewhere in the municipality—usually by converting rural *linpan* house lots into fields (Xiao 2014). A mid-2000s survey counted 141,100 individual *linpan* across the municipality, housing 4,490,300 residents, or 77.09% of the municipality's total rural population (Chengdu Urban and Rural Construction Commission 2007; Chen 2011, 29). In Pi

County, the closest rural jurisdiction to the urban center of Chengdu, new development reduced *linpan* from 11,000 to 8,700 just between 2004 and 2006 (Yuan and Yuan 2013, 4). The new Urban-Rural Coordinated Development (URCD) and Socialist New Countryside Construction (SNCC) plans only called for more demolition of *linpan*, and the relocation of nearly two hundred thousand *linpan* dwellers—some 74% of the county's rural population—into new concentrated settlements (Pi County People's Government, 2011). By winter 2012–13, forty-five new villages were already built or under construction in Pi County to rehouse nearly sixty thousand people (Ye and LeGates 2013, 267).

Paradoxically, these plans coincided with a new Chengdu Municipal West Sichuan Linpan Preservation Plan, which identified *linpan* as important "ecological and humanistic resources" and features of "local rural and ethnic character" to be preserved according to Chinese Communist Party (CCP) general secretary Hu Jintao's guiding principle of "scientific development" (Chengdu Municipal People's Government 2008). Except for rare cases, however, the preservation plans treated *linpan* as isolated points in an otherwise malleable landscape and community structure rather than as elements of a larger agroecological system integrating *linpan* with surrounding irrigation channels and fields to support smallholder agricultural production and habitation.

According to the municipal plan, 2,100 "gathered settlement" *linpan* would be preserved to house a total of 290,000 rural residents—that is, these "preserved" *linpan* would accommodate an average of 138 residents each, which is over four times larger than typical existing *linpan*. The plan also designated 2,885 "ecological" *linpan* where landscape elements would be preserved but residents would be relocated and their dwellings demolished. The vast majority of *linpan* throughout the municipality would be preserved only in the sense that their trees would remain "in principle" after the houses were demolished and the lots converted to cultivation (*fu geng*).

The Chengdu Municipal Planning Bureau's Rural Planning Section, struggling to reconcile the contradictions between development and preservation policies, adopted a vague principle of "concentrate where it is beneficial to concentrate; disperse where it is beneficial to disperse" (*yi ju ze ju, yi san ze san*). Planning officials, professionals and academics have discussed extensively how *linpan* might be adapted to new forms of rural livelihood, especially agritourism, and to modern transportation and infrastructure, but the great majority of visions hew to the "three concentrations" principle, including converting smaller *linpan* into cultivated land and resettling residents closer to highways (Cai 2007; Liu et al. 2017; Yang 2014).

Studies and projects that acknowledge the ecological function of *linpan* within the larger landscape mosaic, and even measure the morphology of ecological patches and corridors as factors in siting new settlements, still tend not to address the role of traditional smallholder food-producing farm households in the plain's broader ecological function (Jiang et al. 2016; Yang et al. 2011; Yang et al. 2012). Often, "cultivation" consists only of noneconomic aesthetic landscaping, which satisfies the letter, but certainly not the spirit, of the national policy to preserve agricultural land for food security.

Pushing Back against Technological Lock-in: *Linpan's* Adaptive Capacity

Whether or not farms are enlarged, or uncultivated land becomes arable, the Chengdu Plain's vaunted ability to grow a large variety of crops sustainably is threatened (Shi Ju Zhi Ku et al. 2014). Despite a subsidy for growing grain, and increases in the monetary value of agriculture and peasant incomes, total land under cultivation has decreased and agricultural labor inputs have also decreased as peasants migrate to non-farm work and cultivate less labor-intensive crops—typically non-food crops such as ornamental trees and shrubs, whose demand surged with growth in urban real estate development. After a brief period of increase *before* the subsidy program, grain production in Chengdu resumed decreasing in 2009; in 2012 it was less than half its peak level of the 1980s, and in Pi County, the plain's historically most productive area, it dropped even more precipitously, from around three hundred thousand tons in 1998 to less than one hundred thousand tons in 2012 (Liang 2015, 27, figure 3.1; Chengdu Municipal Bureau of Statistics 2014.)

During this period other types of food production have generally increased in the larger region but have moved to peripheral counties of the plain at the edge of the irrigation district or outside it entirely. The largest share of this increase is in pigs, which do not require high quality irrigated soil. Over a longer period, rapeseed, a classic crop of the irrigation system, decreased in Pi County from a sixty-year peak yield in 1987 of over twenty thousand tons (about 10% of Chengdu's total production) down to about eleven thousand tons (4.16%) in 2012, while approximately doubling in outlying Pujiang and Jintang Counties over the same period (Chengdu Municipal Bureau of Statistics 2014). The overall increase in yields, as well as the shift in production from grain to other food and from higher- to lower-quality arable land, is consistent with national trends and raises concerns for both the security and environmental sustainability of the food supply (Jiang et al. 2012; Xu et al. 2017; Zhan and Huang 2017).

A small but significant resistance to these trends has taken the form of organic community-supported agriculture (CSA) initiatives allied with environmental NGOs and activists (Schroeder 2014; Zhao 2013). The CSAs are extremely intimate: urban subscribers enjoy regular collective meals on the farm, farm-to-door delivery of produce, and the chance to rent plots to grow their own produce. Peasants and city-dwellers who participate in the CSAs also see the landscape as a place where they can forge new social relationships and bonds of trust in the wake of disruptive and alienating urbanization and global capitalism, and as a place where they can pursue a healthier balance of economic and environmental values according to New Rural Reconstructionist (NRR) alternative development principles (Hale 2013; Hu and Abramson 2015; Hu 2015).[2] Trust-building is particularly important for urbanites concerned about food safety and suspicious of official regulatory integrity (Kim 2014; Si 2017; Yasuda 2013), while the peasants who sell the produce value personal connection not only because it helps them to gain consumers' trust but also because it prevents pirating of their brand once they are successful and keeps their market niche secure from competitors.

All of these concerns are somewhat remote from the initial interests of the environmental NGOs that partnered with the local communities. The most prominent of these NGOs, the Chengdu Urban Rivers Association (CURA), began its work in the early 2000s with efforts to clean up pollution in the waterways of central Chengdu (Birnbaum and Yu 2006, 191–92; Schroeder 2014). The organization shifted its focus to *linpan* communities only after it realized that most of the urban water pollution came from nonpoint agrochemical sources upstream. Employing university-based and public participatory science and education as well as policy-oriented advocacy, CSA marketing, and construction of ecologically low-impact trails and waste-treatment infrastructure, CURA sought to convince farming communities that industrial agrochemicals were not essential to development and to raise public awareness of the value of the biodiversity and near-closed cycles of inputs that characterized traditional farming in the *linpan* environment.

CURA partnered primarily with a small group of fifty-five farmsteads mostly in Quanjia Heba, a part of Anlong Administrative Village on the Zouma River, one of the four main channels that flow out of Dujiangyan through Pi County. Its location along a small tributary facilitated CURA's measurement of the impact of organic farming on water quality in the local stream as compared to the larger river. With the support of the township party secretary, in 2007 Anlong Village became a pilot site for an official Pi County "West Sichuan Farmhouse Character Preservation and Construction District" (Pi County People's Government 2007). The official project in Anlong abutted, but did not include, Quanjia Heba. The government's intention was to take advantage of CURA's and Quanjia Heba CSA's reputation as a kind of identity branding.

By the early 2010s, however, the government's idea of a model "preservation" district showed itself to be quite different from CURA's or Quanjia Heba CSA's. From the perspective of Chengdu's experiments with "concentrate where it is beneficial to concentrate; disperse where it is beneficial to disperse," Anlong's official plan for a model new village adopted a "relatively" concentrated or semi-concentrated approach, midway between keeping all the scattered farmsteads in place and moving all residents to a single dense housing estate. The designers strove to fit the new housing in among existing large trees to maintain vegetated riparian corridors along waterways and to minimize building on farm plots and thus the need to reorganize land rights.

This design concept claimed to "preserve and display" local agrarian folk customs and landscape features of the West Sichuan Plain. Still, except for Quanjia Heba, all *linpan* dwellings in Anlong would be demolished and converted to arable land and each household relocated to an attached townhouse-style dwelling in one of eight entirely new housing clusters accommodating between 52 and 287 relocated households each. Individual new housing units averaged 55 square meters (610 ft^2) per person, approximately one-third the area of a typical *linpan* dwelling with its private courtyard and space for storing farm implements and supplies and keeping livestock—all of which were absent in the new designs. The project did include a house museum, showcasing a reconstructed traditional courtyard as well as an exhibit of information and artifacts on the developmental history and future planning of the village and Ande Town.

The redeveloped area included a smaller proportion of fields for growing food than in Quanjia Heba, with fewer and larger fields and less diversity in field sizes (Tippins 2013). Residents who moved into the new housing within the first two years of construction also took on considerable debt (Xiao 2015). Families who had already diversified their income sources to include local non-farm work and held some equity in a business were in a good position to handle the transition. Lower-income, primarily farming families, however, were pushed toward livelihoods that offered more cash in the short term, such as migrating to wage jobs elsewhere or monocropping of landscape ornamentals, which for a brief period commanded relatively high prices but were more vulnerable to market fluctuations.

While these different livelihood trajectories among households had existed before, village reconstruction tended to exacerbate local socioeconomic disparities, creating a financial trap for many peasants. When Chengdu's real estate market softened in 2014–15, demand for ornamental plants dropped, hurting those who depended on that income to repay debts. Village and town government investments also became difficult to recover when the value of the transfer of land development rights, expected to cover the cost of the construction, also suddenly dropped. Quanjia Heba residents who did not participate in the *linpan* home buyout and relocation program were seen by some of their fellow villagers as making the problem worse. The Quanjia Heba CSA nevertheless persisted, and while CURA is frustrated that it has not been able to scale up the activity, the participating peasants have found their low-growth model to be quite sustainable as long as they can fend off both efforts to consolidate and redevelop their land and competitors who cut corners and market less-ecologically grown produce under the increasingly popular label of "organic."

The new administration of Xi Jinping and Li Keqiang has wound down the SNCC campaign and discouraged local governments from conflating physical construction and economic value. In 2012, the 18th Party Congress elevated "Ecological Civilization" to one of the five goals of national development (Schmitt 2016). The new mantra for rural development planners became "Ecology, Productivity, Livability" (Shengtai, Shengchan, Shenghuo). New national programs for rural development have emerged under the names "Beautiful Villages" (Meili Xiangcun) and "Characteristic Small Towns" (CST, Tese Xiaozhen). Tellingly, when Chengdu issued CST grants to towns across the municipality, Ande Town's application did not succeed, at least in part because the reconstruction of Anlong was seen as too insensitive to the original *linpan* environment.

As their names imply, the new programs still emphasize visual aesthetics and touristic consumption of rural environments by urbanites, rather than actual ecological or even productive function. These programs also intersect with new bureaucratized approaches to environmental protection and infrastructure provision. Sandaoyan, another town in Pi County, is a case in point. Due to its location on key branches of the Min River between Dujiangyan and Chengdu, Sandaoyan is the site of the largest water treatment plant in southwest China—one of six that provide more than 90% of Chengdu's drinking water. The town has thus become a special focus for environmental protection, including proscribing all polluting industries, plans to relocate all residents from a 200-meter (660 ft) water source protection buffer along the rivers, and restrictions on construction within 500 meters (1,650 ft) of the rivers. The local government has parlayed the town's large-scale significance into a new rural touristic identity based on a clean, healthy environment that is increasingly devoid of agriculture and especially food production. Sandaoyan had previously redeveloped one of its villages, Qinggangshu, according to a "relative concentration" principle similar to Anlong's but was more radical in collectivizing agricultural production and attracted more tourists, thus justifying more of the costs of the new settlement and winning for itself a CST grant. The grant, however, was not intended to fund more such projects. The transfer of land development rights model had fueled government finance-driven overbuilding throughout Chengdu, and Sandaoyan had many vacant new apartments.

The CST was intended, instead, to leverage direct investment in rural redevelopment by nongovernmental market actors more attuned to "real" economic value. Just across the Xuyan River from San-daoyan, in Hongguang Town, the Shanghai-based Duoli Organic Farm conglomerate—one of China's highest-profile private corporate purvey-ors of luxury-brand healthy and safe food—saw an opportunity in the mandate to preserve *linpan* landscape and also satisfy the strict pro-scription on habitation and construction in the water-source protection buffers along the Xuyan River. The result was an extreme case of rural gentrification.

The town relocated 603 households of 1,800 *linpan* dwellers from within the buffer zone and elsewhere in Baiyun Village into new concen-trated housing nearby, at a cost heavily subsidized by the county, allow-ing Duoli to reorganize its fields for organic farming on a large scale. The company maintained *linpan* trees and rice paddies as attractive landscape features and rebuilt the farmstead clusters outside the buffer zone as new luxury housing sites, sold primarily to urban individual and corporate buyers for retreats and second homes. This "city-dwellers' farming village" (*shimin nongzhuang*) includes private vegetable gardens of up to five *mu* (one-third hectare; ⅚ acre) with each unit, though most buyers cannot grow or eat that much produce and have no need to sell it, so some gar-dens have been converted to lawns. Even the rice was grown only as part of the visual backdrop to the houses, not to produce food. Relocated peas-ants were given the opportunity to work as wage earners growing Duo-li's produce and maintaining the landscape of its "West Sichuan *Linpan* Cultural Preservation Model Land," but they lost all power to decide what to grow and how to market it. Sandaoyan now faces a choice of whether or not to pursue a similar approach in its own villages, but it is not at all clear how much market demand for Duoli's model exists, and farmers are increasingly reluctant to accept the accompanying tradeoffs. Other than large government subsidies and luxury market investments, there is no financial model currently able to support the relocation of so many rural residents out of water-quality protection buffer zones.

By contrast, CURA's contention, and the experience of the Quanjia Heba CSA, is that organic farming on a small scale but over a larger ter-ritory could achieve at least the same benefits to water quality that the buffers would, at a far lower economic, social, and cultural cost and with less impact on biodiversity. Local village leaders have indicated that they would welcome this option, but the obstacles are considerable. The law for environmental protection of urban water sources would need to change, to allow continued habitation of *linpan* while regulating the ecological performance of buildings and infrastructure as well as agricultural practices. The budget for buffer zone clearance and management would have to shift, to support scientific monitoring of ecological performance, and also perhaps to support programs to recover and teach local traditional agroecological knowledge to younger generations of farmers, and to help them market their products. Perhaps the greatest challenge is to incentivize town and county/district leaders to implement programs whose results may not be evident within the typical political leaders' term of three or five years. Whatever the cost, however, such programs would likely have many co-benefits beyond mere protection of urban water quality. Preservation of the basic *linpan* landscape system as a productive and inhabited environment would secure an important "buffer" in a broader sense: preserving adaptive capacity at many scales—from livelihood choice for individual farming households to food security and biodiversity for the region, nation, and world—in the face of market volatility, technological disruption, and perhaps even climate change.

Long-Term Multiscale Adaptive Capacity: A Challenge for Eco-developmentalism

The development approaches that have dominated the Chengdu Plain since the mid-twentieth century increasingly concentrate power at higher levels of government and investment centers, just as they concentrate *linpan* dwellers in larger settlements. With each form of concentration, adaptive capacity is lost, and both environment and society risk falling into new forms of "lock-in." This story is not unique to China. China's SNCC was inspired by Korea's New Village Movement (KNVM; Saemaul Undung) of the 1970s (Looney 2012; Kim, chapter 9). KNVM sacrificed important aspects of local resilience in the pursuit of a developmental "takeoff," promoted by Walt Whitman Rostow to build up US-allied national regimes in rivalry with Communist regimes across Asia (Rostow 1960; Kim, chapter 9). Despite its strange ideological pedigree, SNCC was a key element of current Chinese urbanization-driven macroeconomic policy, which continues to have strong "Rostovian" overtones. By contrast, *linpan*-style New Rural Reconstructionism as pursued by the Quanjia Heba CSA presents a kind of self-aware modern parallel to the traditional "enlightened underdevelopment" David Nemeth (2008) sees in the villages KNVM destroyed.

The efforts of CURA, the Quanjia Heba CSA, and other coalitions of activists, scientists, and farmers seeking to preserve the *linpan* landscape as functional heritage also have a parallel in the Satoyama movement of Japan, a grassroots alternative to KNVM/SNCC-type development that advocates the revival of communally managed village woodlands and small rice-producing watersheds (Takeuchi et al. 2003). These coalitions sometimes cooperate, but more often conflict, with government programs and regulations as well as economic forces (which are often indirect expressions of policy). The Chengdu Plain, despite its extent and flatness, has inspired some civil society actors and academics to a vision of micro-scale stewardship similar to that of the Satoyama but at a much larger scale (Yuan 2018). The particularly large scope of governmental power in China might suggest the feasibility of scaling up such stewardship, given the proper coordination of policies and programs.

However, governmental appreciation of the Plain's resilience has only very recently looked beyond the ancient engineering project of Dujiangyan itself, and even Dujiangyan's importance is framed primarily in terms of cultural heritage rather than ecological function (Mertha 2008). In early 2017, Chengdu's municipal development policy explicitly acknowledged the need to limit urban development in the Plain, suggesting a new awareness of the Plain's environmental sensitivity (Zhang 2017). Secretary Xi Jinping's visit in 2018, when he praised a vision of Chengdu as a "park city" surrounded and interlaced by "ecological zones," inspired a new wave of park developments and *linpan* preservation plans, but designs for these spaces largely exclude productive inhabitants and involve even more displacement (Kuo 2019). As we have seen in the policy to relocate farmers out of the "environmental protection buffers" along the waterways that they resiliently stewarded for centuries—and to replace that stewardship with an untested bureaucratic and technocratic management—the eco-developmental state continues to turn a blind eye to history, despite all its rhetoric, much as "non-eco-" developmental regimes did before.

Notes

The author gratefully acknowledges the theoretical mentorship and editorial advice of Stevan Harrell, as well as the research collaboration and assistance of Wei Li, Hong Chen, Susan Whiting, Shang Yuan, Wenjing Jiang, Shuang Wu, Yue Wang, Yang Wei, and Yuehan Wang. Many other students and faculty at Sichuan University, University of Washington, National Cheng Kung University, National Taiwan University, and Harbin Institute of Technology also participated in joint field research exercises that informed this chapter. Field research and travel support were provided by the University of Washington China Studies Faculty Research Grants, the University of Washington East Asia Center, and a Sichuan University College of Architecture and Environment guest lectureship.

1 Pi County became Pidu District in November 2016 as part of an administrative redesignation that included the county among Chengdu's central urban districts. Since this chapter discusses situations that largely predate the redesignation, the text refers to the territory as Pi County.

2 Followers of NRR and supporters of CSAs in China use the term *nongmin* in Chinese with explicit pride and respect, in defiance of modern urban-centered and global-marketist developmental discourses that denigrate or "spectralize" agricultural work and environments (Abramson 2016; Yan 2008). Consequently, scholarship in English on these movements tends to translate that term as "peasant," which has a similar pejorative and shocking connotation from a developmentalist perspective, rather than "farmer," which can be understood as expressing a modern individualistic market-oriented ideological view of agricultural identity. However, as Hale (2013) describes, even among its adherents, there is significant debate about how NRR should relate to individualism and the market. Within China studies more broadly, there is also debate about whether translating *nongmin* as "peasant" may cause confusion, as there are great historical differences between Chinese premodern and European feudal society in the way agricultural workers relate to each other, the land, and the state (Cohen 1993).

PART IV

ENVIRONMENTAL NGOS AND COALITIONS

11

Environmental Activism in Kaohsiung, Taiwan

HUA-MEI CHIU

ANTIPOLLUTION PROTESTS AT THE COMMUNITY LEVEL HAVE BEEN a crucial component of Taiwan's environmental movement in Kaohsiung, Taiwan's largest industrial city, with a present-day population of 2.77 million. Although the movement emerged in the 1980s, urban middle-class activists and professional environmental organizations have become active since the aughts. Environmental activism in Kaohsiung has included evolving participation of citizens, politicians, and environmental groups.

Kaohsiung is notorious for poor water quality and air pollution. As the result of decades of industrialization, Kaohsiung has the most contaminated industrial sites and the highest CO_2 emissions per capita in Taiwan. This inconvenient truth has significantly elevated risk awareness and perceptions of injustice among Kaohsiung residents for whom life expectancy is 4.3 years shorter than in Taiwan's capital, Taipei (Tsuang 2014).

In recent decades, environmental disputes have occurred in Houjin, Renwu, and Dashe in northern Kaohsiung and in Dalinpu and Linyuan in the south, the same locations where community-based "anti-pollution self-help protests" (*fan wuran zili jiuji*)[1] erupted in the 1980s (map 11.1). Devastating industrial accidents and pollution and, simultaneously, plans to expand industrial development since the late aughts, have not only provoked resistance from the neighborhoods around industrial parks but also raised concern throughout the city, in particular among the urban middle class.

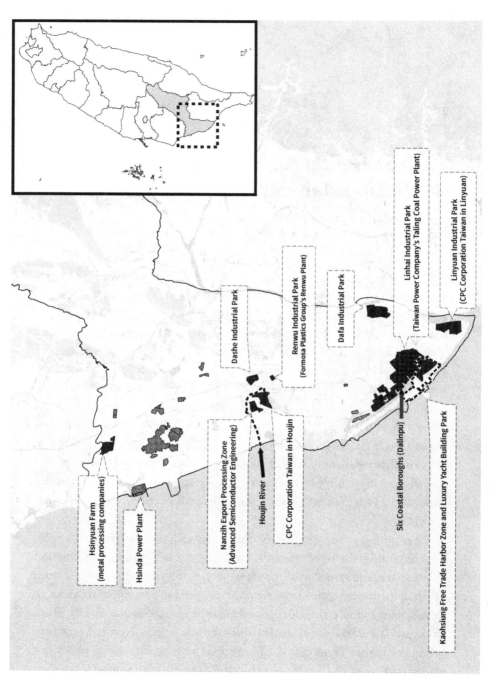

Hsinyuan Farm
(metal processing companies)

Hsinda Power Plant

Nanzih Export Processing Zone
(Advanced Semiconductor Engineering)

Houjin River

CPC Corporation Taiwan in Houjin

Dashe Industrial Park

Renwu Industrial Park
(Formosa Plastics Group's Renwu Plant)

Dafa Industrial Park

Linhai Industrial Park
(Taiwan Power Company's Taling Coal Power Plant)

Linyuan Industrial Park
(CPC Corporation Taiwan in Linyuan)

Six Coastal Boroughs (Dalinpu)

Kaohsiung Free Trade Harbor Zone and Luxury Yacht Building Park

MAP 11.1   The main industrial zones in Kaohsiung

One significant change is that urban conservation activists, who advocated for urban parks and wilderness conservation in the 1990s, founded new environmental organizations focusing on both conservation and pollution-reduction in the late 2000s. As a result, community-based anti-pollution activism and urban conservationism have merged into one urban environmental movement opposing industrial development and pollution. These circumstances have brought together two types of activists, community activists and professional activists, to promote the investigation of environmental hazards, conduct environmental monitoring, fight for information transparency and environmental democracy, and amend environmental regulations. Environmental activism in Kaohsiung has thus transitioned from isolated community-based protests to activism that pursues the broader objective of environmental justice. The new activism also advocates a transition toward low-carbon economy at the municipal level.

Trajectory of Environmental Activism in Kaohsiung

Industrialization in Kaohsiung commenced in the 1930s during the Japanese colonial period. After the Nationalist Party fled to Taiwan in 1949, its authoritarian government transformed Kaohsiung into a center for heavy industry. Since the 1960s, export-oriented industrial processing zones, oil refinery plants and petrochemical industrial parks, cement, steel and shipbuilding industries and power plants have appeared, along with Kaohsiung Port. As map 11.1 shows, the city has several industrial zones in the north and the south.

Antipollution activism in Kaohsiung before 2000 can be divided into two periods: (1) the eruption of community-based self-help protests in the 1980s; and (2) the decline of community antipollution protests and the rise of urban conservationism in the 1990s. Little interaction between members of the conservation movement and local antipollution activists took place at that time. However, after 1999 concerns over the Kaohsiung area's aging infrastructure, industrial accidents, and the expanding industrial footprint worried middle-class environmentalists and stimulated activism and collaboration among a broader range of groups. We can thus identify two additional periods of activism: (3) growing collaboration between urban environmentalists and community activists from 1999 to 2007; and (4) the convergence of urban environmentalism and community-based activism from 2007 to the present.

As the local economy took off in the 1960s, serious pollution prompted self-help protests in nearby communities from the 1970s to the early 1990s (Hsiao 1988). This time period coincided with the emergence of Taiwan's pro-democracy Dangwai (non–Nationalist Party) Movement which led to the founding of the Democratic Progressive Party (DPP) in 1986. Kaohsiung was a center for the democratization movement. The DPP won the mayoral election in Kaohsiung for the first time in 1998 and held power until 2018.

Throughout the 1990s, antipollution protests were relatively weak because of the state's dual strategies: paying compensation to victims and suppressing the community activists (Ho 2010). Meanwhile, urban conservationism was on the rise; activists called for river restoration, forest and wetland conservation, and the establishment of urban parks. The leaders of the conservation movement hailed mainly from the urban middle class, including teachers, doctors, and journalists. They paid greater attention to biodiversity and species' habitat than to the concerns of urban residents.

In the late 1990s, illegal leakage of toxic industrial waste in Kaohsiung and Pingtung Counties attracted the attention of middle-class conservation groups, including the newly founded Ecological Educational Centre of the Kaohsiung Teachers' Association. These activists formed the "Environmental Monitoring Alliance" and argued that "the beautiful island (Formosa) has become a toxic island." In subsequent years, teachers' association activists visited Houjin and Linyuan neighborhoods, with the aim of "picking up the big missing component of environmental movements in industrial Kaohsiung," according to leading activist Lee Keng-Cheng (Lee 2015, preface).

Meanwhile antipollution activists mobilized again at the grassroots level. The most notable change appeared in Houjin, which won renown for its late 1980s opposition to CPC Corporation, Taiwan's 5th Naphtha Cracker Plant, a complex for petroleum refining. Although the community's militant resistance failed to halt the operation of the 5th Naphtha Cracker Plant, the government acknowledged that Houjin had been severely polluted by the CPC's 1st and 2nd Naphtha Cracker Plants, which were built in 1968 and 1975, respectively, and thus it promised in 1990 that the 5th Naphtha Cracker Plant would be closed after twenty-five years (Ho 2005; Lu 2009, 2016).

In 1998, Huang Shih-lung was elected to the Kaohsiung city council to represent Houjin; he worked with the Houjin Social-Welfare Foundation to collect evidence of CPC pollution. By using CPC compensation funding to contract scholars at the National Kaohsiung Marine University[2] to conduct environmental research, the once powerless Houjin victims of industrial pollution were able to support scientific studies to verify their environmental claims concerning the CPC facility's soil and groundwater contamination. Long-hidden pollution has been gradually unveiled since then. In particular, a gas spill in 2004 that required the medical treatment of 8,710 residents further boosted Houjin's determination to monitor CPC operations and to see the 5th Naphtha Cracker Plant shut down.

The threat posed by hazardous waste and industrial incidents not only revitalized activist solidarity at community level but also prompted middle-class environmentalists, who had previously dealt mostly with conservation issues, to found new environmental organizations to deal with the challenge of industrial pollution. Teachers' association leaders founded a new environmental organization, Citizen of the Earth Taiwan, to focus on both ecological conservation and industrial pollution. Around the same time, a series of industrial expansion plans and industrial safety accidents compounded Kaohsiung-area pollution and provided the impetus for newly created environmental organizations to work with grassroots community activists, scholars, lawyers, and urban middle-class volunteers. New patterns of environmental activism have emerged since in response to environmental disputes in both northern and southern Kaohsiung.

In northern Kaohsiung, three severe explosions at the Houjin CPC facility in 2007 and 2008 enraged the community. Although there were no casualties, the blasts created opportunities for Citizen of the Earth to build stronger connections within the affected community. After the third explosion, Houjin residents blocked the northern gate of the CPC in a standoff that lasted for 221 days. The protest finally ended after the secretary of the Ministry of Economic Affairs visited Houjin to confirm that the CPC's 5th Naphtha Cracker Plant would be dismantled by 2015.

In subsequent years, serious incidents such as the illegal discharge of wastewater into the Houjin River during the rainy season (fifty-five times in 2013) as well as fires and explosions in 2012 and 2013, have strengthened the determination of Houjin to pressure the CPC to close its refinery complex. By working closely with Citizen of the Earth, Houjin residents have not only appealed for the dismantling of the Houjin Naphtha Cracker Plant but also advocated the transformation of brownfields into an ecological park and called for the restoration of environmental justice (Citizen of the Earth Taiwan and Houjin Social-Welfare Foundation 2015). The Houjin CPC complex finally ceased operations on November 30, 2015. However, up to 177 out of 253 hectares (625 acres) of the plant area have to undergo remediation. Benzene, phenol, petroleum hydrocarbons, and other toxins have contaminated the soil and groundwater (Lifayuan 2016). Remediation is expected to cost the CPC NT$11.2 billion (more than US$381 million) over seventeen years (Lifayuan 2017). Whether the brownfields will be transformed into an ecological park—as Houjin residents wish—remains unclear.

In northern Kaohsiung, environmental organizations have also worked with scholars, community residents, and farmers to collect and reveal new evidence of contamination. Four major industrial parks, the Houjin CPC, Renwu and Tashe Petrochemical Industrial Parks, and Nanzih Export Processing Zone, have severely polluted the Houjin River. In 2006, teachers' association activists conducted a study to identify the social impact of Houjin River pollution discovered by Professor Lin Chit-san. The investigation revealed that polluted river water had been converted into irrigation water for 1,390 hectares (3,435 acres) of farmland along the Houjin River, endangering food safety and the livelihood of farmers. It has created a disgraceful truism: "industry is consuming clean water, while farmland is irrigated with toxic water" (Lee 2007).

After the establishment of Citizen of the Earth in 2007, a series of follow-up actions have pressured regulators to examine the Formosa Plastics Group's Renwu Plant. In late 2009, the Environmental Protection Administration confirmed that the Renwu Plant has contaminated soil and groundwater heavily through the use of various chlorinated organic compounds. The worst pollutant was 1,2-Dichloroethane, which was 302,000 times higher than normal. The Kaohsiung Environmental Protection Bureau entered the Renwu Plant on its official list of contaminated sites. This devastating case led activists to appeal for a more comprehensive investigation and for greater information transparency during follow-up remediation.

Citizen of the Earth has also investigated pollution along the Agongdian River in northern Kaohsiung. Since 2012, farmers and nearby residents have worked with Citizen of the Earth activists to fight a plan to transfer the Hsinyuan and Johong farmlands to the electroplating industry. They worry that such a plan could pollute 2,000 hectares (5,000 acres) of farmland and 1,200 hectares (3,000 acres) of aquacultural land along the Agongdian River.

Citizen of the Earth's growing expertise concerning irrigation in northern Kaohsiung aided the organization's ability to respond to subsequent crises. In 2013, the world's largest provider of semiconductor testing and packing, Advanced Semiconductor Engineering was fined by the Kaohsiung city government for illegal discharge of wastewater into the Houjin River. Thanks to Citizen of the Earth's research on the irrigation system in previous years, activists speedily conducted a follow-up investigation to challenge Advanced Semiconductor Engineering by visiting affected farmers, fishermen, and the Irrigation Association and Fishermen's Association.

In southern Kaohsiung, the Linyuan, Dafa, and Linhai Industrial Parks have notorious records of pollution and industrial accidents that have provoked community-based protests from surrounding neighborhoods since the 1980s. Some health studies show that the residents in Linyuan and Hsiaogang Districts have cancer rates above the national average (Hsu 2014). In 2007, two big polluters in southern Kaohsiung, Taiwan Power Company's Taling Coal Power Plant and the CPC's 3rd Naphtha Cracker Plant in Linyuan filed Environmental Impact Assessments for scaling up capacity. These expansion plans, initiated by the DPP's central government during the Chen Shui-bian administration and later taken up by Nationalist central government in 2008, have provoked still more environmental activism. This time Citizen of the Earth worked with residents to persuade the DPP-led Kaohsiung municipal government to resist the expansion. Although environmentalist groups encountered difficulties collaborating with the divided Linyuan community and failed to stop the expansion plans, they persuaded environmental impact assessors to downsize the original plan, to reduce the permitted amounts of pollutants, and to order the CPC to conduct health risk assessments on the carcinogenic risk of residents' exposure to hazardous chemicals. Resistance to the ramping up of Taling Coal Power Plant and the CPC's 3rd Naphtha Cracker Plant in Linyuan laid the foundation for professional environmental organizations to launch their advocacy related to air pollution, climate change, and energy transition in subsequent years.

In December 2008, Chaoliao residents, who often smell foul odors from nearby factories, suffered from industrial safety lapses in which toxic gas leaked from the Dafa Industrial Zone six times within four days, requiring the hospitalization of some one hundred schoolchildren and teachers. The suspected sources of the leaks were a wastewater treatment facility, chemical manufacturers, and a pesticide container cleaning factory upwind of the Chaoliao primary and secondary schools. Environmentalists visited the affected area, interviewed residents, and for the first time used the expression "industrial refugee" (*gongye nanmin*) to highlight the plight of residents after failed government monitoring and factories' irresponsible misconduct (Lee 2009).

Although public concern over the negative impact of heavy industry in southern Kaohsiung has increased, central and local governments envision further industrial development. Since 2012, Dalinpu residents living in six coastal boroughs (see map 11.1) objected to establishment of the Kaohsiung Free Trade Harbor Zone and Southern Star Luxury Yacht Building Park, which intends to utilize coastal land reclaimed from construction and industrial waste sites. Dalinpu communities are already surrounded by over 880 chimneys from nearly five hundred plants, including power plants, steel mills, oil refineries, incinerators, and various factories to the north, south, and east. As the residents sadly complain, the establishment of the yacht production area on reclaimed land will deprive them of their last source of fresh air from the southwest and leave them with "nowhere to go, and no air to breathe."[3]

Residents created an organization called the "Golden Chimney Association"—a sarcastic name contrasting with what residents experience in daily life. The Golden Chimney Association has hosted events and staged protests to attract attention from mass media and the public. Joined by activists from Citizen of the Earth and Water Resource Conservation Union (a Tainan-based group), residents have participated in the environmental impact assessment process to express their grievances.

The controversy surrounding the proposed development plan eventually altered the deliberations of the environmental impact assessment committee, which decided to conduct an additional review of the second phase of Kaohsiung Free Trade Harbor Zone and the first phase of the Southern Star Luxury Yacht Building Park. The initiation of a more comprehensive review involving further community and public participation prompted the developers to suspend the original plan.

On July 31, 2014, the Kaohsiung gas pipeline exploded, killing thirty-two people and injuring over three hundred. This catastrophic disaster revealed to many Kaohsiung residents that the city is not only surrounded by several petrochemical industrial zones but also by a complicated underground network of gas pipelines that connect industrial zones, gas storage sites, and the Kaohsiung harbor. A public health scholar Chan Chang-Chuan has argued that the pipeline network has turned the city into a high-risk mega petrochemical industrial zone (Chan 2014). Shortly after the disaster, environmental activists, residents, and community-based groups held a press conference to vent their outrage, conducted several protests, and organized fora to express their concerns. Activists adopted the concepts "environmental colony" and "environmental injustice" to hold the Nationalist Party's central government accountable for longstanding pro-petrochemical policies. Further, environmental activists emphasized the importance of "the community's right to know," "environmental justice," and "city industrial transition" (Lee 2014; Chiu 2014a).

Ironically, the deadly explosion may not bring environmental justice to residents of Kaohsiung. After the incident, the Nationalist central government announced a plan to reclaim land in six coastal boroughs to construct a "Petrochemical Industry Zone," with the justification of removing unsafe pipelines from the city center. Given that the six coastal boroughs are already heavily polluted, Kaohsiung mayor Chen Chu expressed her opposition to the plan with the slogan "No relocation, no petrochemical industry zone" (Lee 2016). Since the Democratic Progressive Party (DPP) won the 2016 presidential election, President Tsai Ing-wen has promoted the notion of a "circular economy" to maximize the value and use of product lifecycles through recycling, reuse, energy savings, and reduction of greenhouse gas emissions. The Kaohsiung city government has considered a Circular Economy New Materials Park as a possible alternative to the petrochemical industry zone. In

November 2016, Premier Lin Chuan and Kaohsiung mayor Chen visited Dalinpu to apologize to the twenty thousand residents of six coastal boroughs for their long suffering from industrial pollution. Whether residents will be relocated to make way for municipal development, however, remains unclear. The DPP government has *not* indicated that it plans to downsize the petrochemical industry in Kaohsiung; in 2017, the CPC announced plans to scale up capacity at the 4th Naphtha Cracker Plant in Linyuan.

Characteristics of Environmental Activism in Kaohsiung

Environmental activism in Kaohsiung over the last decade has gained influence through changes in the composition of activists, the use of more flexible and diverse advocacy strategies, and greater capacity to frame public discourse.

The composition of activist groups is more diverse compared to the community-organized groups of the 1980s. The establishment of a professional environmental organization based in Kaohsiung, Citizen of the Earth, has facilitated the construction and mobilization of networks including community residents, farmers, fishermen, scholars, lawyers, and urban middle-class volunteers during environmental disputes. In 2007, Lee Keng-Cheng, the Kaohsiung Teachers' Association general secretary, and his colleagues decided to found a new environmental organization that would be more professional, politically autonomous, and financially independent. Teachers, academics, and lawyers joined him in establishing Citizen of the Earth, an NGO funded solely through donations from the public. The number of full-time employees working in three Citizen of the Earth offices in Kaohsiung, Taipei, and Hualien grew from just three in 2007 to seventeen in 2017. The Kaohsiung office, with seven employees, not only monitors and exposes local industrial pollution, but also promotes national policy on environmental, industrial, and energy-related issues. Citizen of the Earth is one of the largest environmental organizations in Kaohsiung and also participates in a cooperative network that includes other environmental organizations.

The efforts of full-time employees at a professional environmental organization have strengthened Citizen of the Earth's advocacy, credibility, and organizational capacity, and have helped to play a pivotal role in connecting societal groups to the broader movement. To integrate farmers and fishermen into the environmental movement, Citizen of the Earth employees have built cooperative relationships with community leaders, conducted research on pollution of agricultural land and fish farms, held meetings in local communities, and emphasized the impact of pollution on agriculture and fisheries in campaigns and lawsuits. Vulnerable farmers and fishermen have become prominent in protests and in pollution studies and lawsuits, creating a new linkage between environment protection and social justice. The movement has adopted more flexible strategies over time, ranging from protests and direct actions to participation in environmental impact assessments and monitoring of governmental meetings and public hearings. The movement has launched aggressive and comprehensive media campaigns, utilizing such tactics as press conferences, public statements, newspaper commentary, and social media outreach.

Campaigns have also extended the battlefield from media to the scientific arena to better demonstrate the legitimacy of environmental claims. Due to the fact that environmental problems often entail scientific uncertainty, the environmental movement—frequently accused of lacking science-based evidence—struggled in the past to identify the causes of pollution and the extent to which it posed a health risk. The ability to conduct independent testing and to research the social costs of pollution along the Houjin River has enabled the movement to contend with critics, to define pollution, and to press the government and the corporations to identify the existence of pollution. Environmentalists have also deliberately incorporated the subjective pollution experiences of residents—especially farmers and fishermen—into their environmental claims.

Activists have cultivated broader societal involvement in the movement by highlighting personal experiences with air pollution and the growing realization among Kaohsiung residents of the health risks posed by $PM_{2.5}$ (fine suspended particles). Citizen of the Earth, in particular, has carried out various creative activities, such as displaying "100 days air pollution photos," working with primary schools to raise a flag, alerting families to severe air pollution and collecting public signatures for tighter environmental regulation on air pollution. These efforts persuaded the central government to include $PM_{2.5}$ in the indicators of air pollutants in 2012 and to implement the Air Pollution Total Quantity Control policy in Kaohsiung City and Pingtung County in June 2015.

At the grassroots level, teachers and pupils at the Wen-Fu Primary School have developed a systematic method to monitor the cement factory adjacent to the school. They record the odors they smell and take photos of abnormal emissions from the factory chimney for comparison with the real-time information provided by the Environmental Protection Agency. Through the application of a simple scientific method, they were able to identify a cement factory as the source of odors. Such school-based actions as raising an air pollution status flag, integrating air pollution issues into curricula, and collecting signatures for petitions have made grassroots concerns more visible. Activism that includes a two thousand-strong, community-based demonstration and close collaboration with Citizen of the Earth compelled the city government to suspend operations for one of the area's main polluters, the Dong-Nan Cement Corporation, and to pass regulations tightening emission standards for the cement industry (Chiu 2018).

Meanwhile other campaigns have shifted contestation to the legal arena. It is notable that litigation is a new trend in the Taiwanese environmental movement (Wang 2014). When land expropriation for industrial use and industrial waste dumping threatened farming and aquaculture, farmers and fishermen took their cases to court, with the assistance of the Environmental Jurists Association (EJA) and Citizen of the Earth. Notable cases include actions taken against converting the Hsinyuan Farm to industrial use and turning Chisan farmland into a slag waste dump site.

In terms of legislative reform and political lobbying, Citizen of the Earth and other environmental organizations active nationwide have seized the momentum created by pollution incidents, such as working to set a new effluent standard for the petrochemical industry in 2012 after confirming the Formosa Plastic Group's Renwu Plant water contamination and amending the Water Pollution Control Regulation in 2014 after the Advanced Semiconductor Engineering pollution scandal. Further, due to the fact that many polluters in Kaohsiung are export-oriented corporations, the environmental groups have built up connections with international environmental organizations. For example, in the campaign against Advanced Semiconductor Engineering pollution, Citizen of the Earth collected endorsements from over fifty member organizations in the International Campaign for Responsible Technology to persuade

Apple to pressure Advanced Semiconductor Engineering to take responsibility for the restoration of Houjin River (Chiu 2014b).

The movement now has greater capacity to construct movement discourse in order to buttress the frames of environmental justice and industrial transition. Along with the increasing concern over the uneven distribution of environmental costs and health risks, activists frequently criticize the lack of information transparency and citizen participation in policy decision-making. Since the mid-aughts, various campaigns have emphasized the appeal of communities' right to know as well as the idea of treating local communities and environmental organizations as stakeholders in environmental governance. In addition, Kaohsiung's environmental movement has advocated for a citywide transition toward nuclear-free and low-carbon economy. Requests to downsize the petrochemical industry, other high-polluting industries, and power plants have gained legitimacy since the 2014 gas explosion and more urgent public concern over air pollution. The need for an energy transition has been amplified by the success of the antinuclear power campaign. The revitalized antinuclear movement in Taiwan gained unprecedented momentum after the 2011 Fukushima Nuclear Disaster, and subsequent demonstrations in 2014 terminated construction of the country's Fourth Nuclear Power Plant (see chapter 12). In 2016, newly elected president Tsai Ing-wen promised to carry out the "nuclear go zero" policy called for by environmental groups, which have also articulated an energy transition model that favors renewable energy and energy democracy by encouraging citizens and communities to participate in decentralized forms of energy production and consumption. The example of Germany's energy transition and the success of Seoul's One Less Nuclear Power Plant initiative have informed the thinking of Taiwanese activists and through outreach efforts become known to the public and Kaohsiung city government. However, whether these efforts will help Kaohsiung progress toward energy transition at a municipal level remains unclear.

Political Obstacles to Environmentalism

It is obvious that the new antipollution activism in Kaohsiung is the consequence of series of industrial incidents, the government's ongoing plans for industrial expansion, and growing public awareness of the threats of industrial hazards and air pollution.

The recent characteristics of the environmentalism movement highlight the experiences of local residents, farmers, and fishermen and connect local pollution to the broader national context, such as urban development planning, energy, and industrial transition. Another area in which a similar movement might occur is central Taiwan, including Taichung City, Changhwa County, and Yunlin County where new industrial parks, large power plants, steel factories, and Taiwan's biggest petrochemical complex—the Formosa Plastics Group's 6th Naphtha Cracker Plant—are located. In those areas, along with the community-based activists, more and more middle-class professionals participate in antipollution movements.

While the Kaohsiung environmental movement has encountered numerous obstacles, it has evolved in ways that have given it demonstrable influence. Key changes involve the composition of activists, diverse advocacy strategies, and the heightened capacity to frame movement discourses since the late 1990s. The movement's human and financial resources, however, remain limited.

In addition, with Taiwan having been a model of the East Asian developmental state for half a century, the pro-business orientation of central and local governments can make activist participation through official channels ineffective or even futile. When urban environmental activism in Kaohsiung gradually morphed into a movement pursuing environmental justice and an urban transition, the movement's goals at times conflicted with the ideologies of mainstream political parties. Following Taiwan's democratization, the change of ruling parties has provided political opportunities for the movement to forge new alliances in the context of environmental campaigns. However, both mainstream parties have failed to effectively counteract the effects of industrial development. They generally favor the interests of industries over citizens and have been reluctant to pursue the objective of an urban industrial transition.

Before the 2016 general election, the environmental movement leveraged its influence to persuade local DPP government and councilors to challenge the Nationalist Party's central government's plans for the expansion of Kaohsiung's petrochemical industry and power plants.

From 1998 to 2018, the DPP municipal government has also improved its capability of risk management and pollution control and has delivered urban plans to make certain area of the city to be more "livable." These changes, however, were apparently insufficient to pursue the objective of a profound urban industrial transition.

From the perspectives of environmental activists, the change in ruling parties at the national level has demonstrated that the two mainstream parties may be different in some respects—their political stance on China, for example—but they share a similar vision of economic development; their policy preferences show an addiction to petrochemical industries that consume tremendous amounts of energy and emit great amounts of pollution. It is urgent for the environmental movement to promote alternative economic and ecological perspectives. This is why some environmentalists participated in or supported the Alliance of the Green Party and the Social Democratic Party in the 2016 legislative election, rather than the Nationalist Party or the DPP. Citizen of the Earth's general secretary and one of its board members ran as candidates in the Green Party-Social Democratic Party Alliance. The alliance failed, however, to win any seats in 2016.

In both 2016 and 2020, the DPP won both the presidency and the majority in the Legislative Yuan. Tsai Ing-wen's government has committed to energy transition in the blueprint for a nuclear-free and decarbonized economy, addressed the model of circular economy and created some governance frameworks with civic participation. However, the DPP government has continued to advocate the development and use of petrochemicals. It has not yet shown the determination to decouple Kaohsiung-area development from petrochemical and other high-pollution industries. Building up the requisite political influence to reconstruct the Kaohsiung economy remains a key challenge for the environmental movement in Kaohsiung as well as in Taiwan generally. The answer could lie in the new complementarities created by collaboration between professional environmental groups and community-based organizations and the broader network-building made possible by full-time environmental campaigners, community-based activists, lawyers, scholars, and volunteers. Interaction among increasingly diverse activist groups has helped the environmental movement to identify the risks and full costs of pollution, to reframe discourses to emphasize just and sustainable development, and to secure a greater role in future decision-making in the democratic process. It is this new environmental activism that will play a pivotal role in continuing the transformation of the developmental state into an eco-developmental state in the future.

Notes

1   "Antipollution self-help protests" (*fan wuran zili jiuji*) is a term that has been commonly used by scholars and mass media to describe community-based, antipollution protests in Taiwan, which erupted in communities that long suffered the effects of heavy pollution levels (Hsiao 1988).

2   The National Kaohsiung Marine University merged with two other universities in 2018 and is now part of the National Kaohsiung University of Science and Technology.

3   Interview with community activist Hsu Shun-liang, October 27, 2014.

12

Indigenous Attitudes toward Nuclear Waste in Taiwan

HSI-WEN CHANG (LENGLENGMAN ROVANIYAW)

IN 1980, TAO PEOPLE ON LANYU (ORCHID ISLAND OR PONGSO NO Tao), off the southeast coast of Taiwan, were informed that the Taiwanese government was building a "fish canning plant" on the coast of their island. Tao people, however, discovered that it was in fact a nuclear waste repository. Although Tao people have resolutely opposed storing nuclear waste and have firmly rejected the government's request to extend the storage period, more than one hundred thousand barrels of nuclear waste are still quietly stored on the island.

In contrast, after Taiwan Power Company (TPC) announced that Nantian, on the southeastern coast of Taiwan, was twice selected as the candidate site for nuclear waste in 2008 and 2010, a majority of Nantian villagers, most of whom are Paiwan indigenous people, have been willing to accept nuclear waste in their homeland, despite suspicion expressed by one chieftain of Nantian Village: "If the nuclear waste is good stuff, why don't they [governmental officials] put it in the presidential office in Taipei? They wouldn't give really good stuff to us, the poorest people in Taiwan." What explains the difference between Lanyu and Nantian?

Nuclear Power in Taiwan

After the oil crisis of the early 1970s, Taiwan immediately committed to developing a controversial energy source—nuclear power, which was strategically important because it reduced Taiwan's need for imported energy after its coal mines were basically exhausted in the 1970s (Wu 2007, 993).

Map 12.1 shows the locations of Taiwan's nuclear power plants, all built in the 1970s and 1980s. There were no protests against the construction of the first three nuclear power plants, something that would have been risky given Taiwan's authoritarian government at the time. In the 1980s, a few years before and after the Nationalist government proposed the fourth nuclear power plant at Lungmen, Taiwan, was in the process of abolishing martial law. Pro-environment and antinuclear protests were part of challenges to the authoritarian state (Fan 2007, 39; Liu and Hsu 2012, 13–14). In 2014, the central government eventually agreed to seal the fourth plant prior to putting it into operation. Like other countries that use nuclear power, Taiwan has struggled to assuage the public's safety concerns as well as to come up with satisfactory plans for nuclear waste disposal.

Lanyu, a tiny island located off the southeastern coast of Taiwan, is the first and only external site chosen to store waste from the three nuclear power plants. Lanyu's Tao indigenous people rely on fishing and farming to make a living. The Republic of China Atomic Energy Council began planning the Lanyu nuclear waste repository in 1974, and construction started in 1979. It received its first batch of 10,008 barrels of nuclear waste in May 1982. From 1982 to 1996, TPC stored 97,672 barrels of low-level radioactive nuclear waste in the repository (Kuan 2007).

From Deception to Embellishment of Nuclear Waste

Even though construction began in 1979, most Tao people knew nothing about the project, even while witnessing the ongoing construction. Only a year later did Dung Senyong, a Tao Presbyterian minister, notice a report about the nuclear waste repository project in a corner of a newspaper. A few Tao people heard that the repository was a fish cannery and that the nearby harbor was being used for military purposes instead of the transportation of nuclear waste (Kuan 2007, 96–98). Even now, while all islanders and most Taiwanese people know the real purpose of the repository, the sign at the entrance simply says "Lanyu Repository," and does not mention nuclear waste. The experience of this betrayal not only attracts concern and support from Taiwan and international environmental

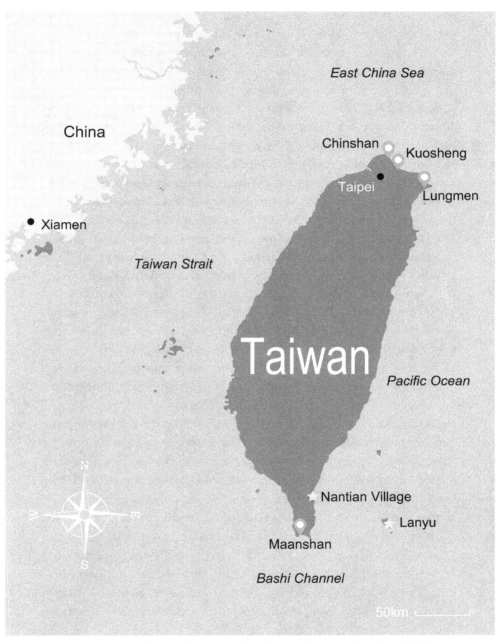

MAP 12.1 Taiwan, showing locations of nuclear power plants (pins) and field research sites (stars). The Lungmen plant, sometimes called the Fourth Nuclear Power Plant, was built but never operated.

protection groups but has also contributed to the subsequent resistance to the construction of the fourth nuclear power plant.

In the past four decades, Taiwan's government and society have paid a lot of attention to the nuclear waste issue, while neglecting other historical wrongs made by the Taiwan government. Several factors help to explain this. Firstly, environmental movements in Taiwan began in the democratization era of the 1980s. After 1990, the Taiwan government began to moderate its emphasis on growth and incorporated environmental restoration and preservation into its policies and practices (see the Introduction to this volume). Secondly, as part of 1980s indigenous movements, both cultural consciousness and a multi-tribal indigenous rights movement arose among Taiwan's indigenous intellectuals (Hsieh 1987, 137; Hsieh 2004, 69). Lastly, Rukai indigenous anthropologist Taiban Sasala (chapter 7) was the first scholar to propose the concept of tribalism (*buluo zhuyi*), leading to indigenous cultural revitalization and switching the focus of attention from nationalism to localism, in parallel to other localisms in Han society in Taiwan. (Chen and Chang 2009, 15). These three contextual factors together contributed to the Taiwanese state's transition to eco-developmentalism and helped Lanyu people link to the broader civil society, enabling them to continue their resistance.

Under pressure from the public outcry of environmental protection groups and local people, in 2006 the Atomic Energy Council promulgated the Act on Sites for Establishment of Final Disposal Facilities for Low-Level Radioactive Waste, whereby the Taiwanese government aims to deal with the issue of nuclear waste sites in accordance with the principle of justice. Thirty years after Tao people were deceived by the state, and after the Lanyu repository was filled to capacity, a small village, Nantian, in southeastern Taiwan, was twice selected in accordance with this law (in 2008 and 2011) as a candidate for the new nuclear waste site.

Using paradise as a metaphor to describe the life surrounding the nuclear waste repository and comparing its role to that of a minister delivering the gospel, TPC gave hope of improvement to Nantian villagers suffering from poor living conditions. In 2013, the heir to the chieftainship of Nantian Village told me angrily in broken Mandarin about how the TPC workers have successfully manipulated the Christian religion to deliver the "gospel of nuclear waste." At a village barbecue night on the Moon Festival in 2013 sponsored by TPC in the Nantian's community center, a TPC official enthusiastically gave a speech promising to provide Nantian villagers free meals, medical care, a community leisure center, and all the necessary infrastructure for developing ecological and cultural tourism. Under the TPC's description of "paradise" at Nantian, after accepting nuclear waste, life would become much easier for villagers. However, a majority of the villagers hesitated to restate their support for the proposal because villagers have heard too many similar speeches from TPC.

In spite of the obvious environmental injustice involved, these two Taiwanese indigenous communities clearly have different attitudes toward nuclear waste. To understand why, we need to examine how specific indigenous people's relationships to their lands have been changed historically by sociopolitical contextual factors, including colonial history, the economic system, and religion.

Colonial Rule and Resistance in Lanyu

Tao people in Lanyu do not identify as Taiwan indigenous people, but instead emphasize their ethnic relationship with Batanes islanders, who have similar culture and language but Philippine nationality. In Tao people's eyes, both the Japanese colonial government and the government of the Republic of China are definitely outsiders. Under threat from "strangers" with hegemonic power, the relationship between Tao people and land has become closer rather than more distant, and their desire to be autonomous and independent is getting stronger and stronger.

From 1895 to 1945, the Japanese colonial government's policy of "preserving" Lanyu as a field for Japanese scholars to study Tao culture helped to maintain the close relationship between Tao people and the land and ocean. After Japan was defeated in World War II, the Chinese Nationalist government came to Taiwan and started its own colonial project of hegemonic Han cultural invasion of Lanyu. In order to bring Tao people a modernized, cultivated, and sinicized life, the state appropriated some Lanyu land for state use, including prisons and the nuclear waste repository. The also redistributed Lanyu space for land administration and bureaucratic control.

The history of Lanyu under colonial administration has thus conditioned Tao people to resist state hegemony. Their disobedience to the governmental policies and laws can range from passive daily practices (Kantor 2002) to large-scale demonstrations.

Passive resistance takes several forms, mostly involving obedience to customary law rather than state law. For example, state land regulations are unsuited to the customs of Lanyu. Ninety percent of Tao people have not registered their land because to them relationships between people and the land/ocean are self-evident. Both ownership and usufruct of land are based clearly on both rights and obligations; Tao people do not regard land as a kind of capital that can be owned or traded using money. There are clear boundaries for both privately held land and village commons in fields, forests, fresh water for irrigation and daily needs, and ocean fishing rights delineated through landmarks. Boundaries are flexible, depending on changes in interpersonal relationships (gifts or punishments) and in family relationships (marriage or divorce). State attempts to use land registration to replace Tao customary laws have been largely unsuccessful. Most Tao people still follow the traditional mode of interacting with the land and the ocean and retain their traditional ecological knowledge, including men's knowledge of ocean ecology and women's knowledge of the ecology of water taro fields and tidelands.

Another example is traffic regulation. There are many cars and motorcycles without plates on the round-the-island road of Lanyu. Even though motorcyclists are required to wear helmets, Tao people still don't wear them. Construction regulations are also unsuited to Lanyu. One person told me, "Our underground houses have existed over thousands of years without construction permits and have protected our Tao people from the typhoon threats year by year. It is those houses with construction permits built by Han people that cannot resist the threats from typhoons."

Lot number seven at Iranmeylek Village is another example of aggressive resistance to state authority. In 2013, the county government selected Lot number seven as the site for a ready-mixed concrete plant, claiming that the land belonged to the Republic of China, but the villagers of Iranmeylek rejected the project. According to the principle of village independence, it was an affair of Iranmeylek only, and other villages were not supposed to get involved. But the county government sent around sixty policemen to suppress the Iranmeylek villagers' protest, and Tao people felt bullied. Around two hundred people from the whole island spontaneously went with weapons to support Iranmeylek villagers. Tao people asked the county government "Where was the Republic of China two hundred years ago?" Tao people were only owners of the island long before the government of the Republic of China came to Lanyu, even during the Japanese Imperial period. The event eventually became an issue of land across villages.

It is noteworthy that the antinuclear movement, which has lasted for over thirty years, was the first and longest form of active collective resistance in the Lanyu region. It began in the 1980s when civil society has become active and Taiwan began to turn to eco-developmentalism. A lot of graffiti in public places reflect Tao people's antinuclear sentiments. Nuclear waste is an issue about which everyone can easily express opinions in public. In restaurants, the airport, and other public places, news related to nuclear waste is easily accessible in the newspaper published by Lan An Cultural and Educational Foundation. The rejection of nuclear waste is so strong that it even led President Tsai Ing-wen to apologize publicly to the Tao people in 2016 for forcing them to accept the nuclear waste (Central News Agency, Taiwan. 2016).

Forming a consensus requires access to diversified and updated information. Unlike most Taiwanese aboriginal communities, Lanyu has independent media including the Lanyu radio station, the biweekly local newspaper, and magazines published by young Tao writers; these local media help form a consensus to reject nuclear waste at Lanyu. Although Taiwan Power Company also publishes a monthly magazine, *Good Neighbors*, its impact is far less significant than the ones created by Tao people.

Tao people have not only already found a common economic interest in their dependence on a safe and clean physical environment for farming, fishing, and tourism, but more importantly, they have understood that they must unite to defend their traditional sovereignty in Lanyu. The churches have played a role in awakening this understanding, allowing Tao people with different beliefs and political interests to cooperate in fighting against external threats to Lanyu's mountains and ocean, which they believe are God's gifts.

The unique joint faith worship meeting, Tao's "Lanyu Joint Christian Lord Praising Evangelism," is a rare activity in which the indigenous community can close the gap between believers of different religions. By treating all islanders as a living community and gaining strength by emphasizing their shared Tao ethnic identity, joint evangelism integrates superficially different denominations into a unit. Leaders from different Christian religions take turns preaching to the congregation to soothe the historical trauma from colonial injuries and enhance their strength to fight the external disturbing forces.

Indigenous tourism, the contemporary antinuclear movement, environmental protection, and economic transformation are developing simultaneously on Lanyu. The government removed restrictions on travel to Lanyu in 1967 and allowed the development of tourism in 1971. Since 1972, there has been regular sea and air transportation between Taiwan and Lanyu, which has opened the door for the tourism industry in Lanyu (Yang 2012, 61).

Modern antinuclear protesters believe that Tao people have to pursue economic independence in advance so that they are able to continue the antinuclear movement. When leading tourists around Lanyu, Tao tour guides equate nuclear waste with the litter that inconsiderate tourists are prone to leave on the roadsides and beaches. They tell tourists to protect the environment and get rid of garbage, including the garbage of daily life (i.e., pick up their trash) and the garbage of nuclear waste (i.e., support the Tao people's antinuclear movement), to avoid polluting the land and ocean.

In the 1970s, the tourism industry was completely controlled by Han people (Hsieh 1994). However, in the last decade, many Tao people have devoted themselves to developing indigenous tourism and have recovered their autonomy in tourism management. They build their own guesthouses and restaurants, train Tao tour guides, and maintain a website with information on lodging and other services in Lanyu as well as guidelines for tourists about how to behave respectfully in the indigenous territory (table 12.1). Ninety percent of guest houses in Lanyu are operated by Tao people, even though they are all technically illegal because it is very difficult for them to meet the legal requirements for permits. To solve this problem, both Tao people and the local government hope that the state can modify (localize/adapt) the laws to help Lanyu tourism obtain legal legitimacy.

The development of indigenous tourism has encouraged Tao people to return to Lanyu. Tao people can decide what cultural content, such as traditional ecological knowledge, they would like to share with tourists,

Table 12.1   Tao leaders' important reminders to tourists on Lanyu Island

MUTUAL RESPECT AND PEACEFUL COMMUNICATION	RESPECT RITES AND OBEY TABOOS
Since all villages at Lanyu are connected by the round-the-island road, tourists may not avoid coming into contact with the living area of Tao people. The culture of Tao people is very different from that of Taiwan. When entering Lanyu, tourists should behave as Tao people do and respect Lanyu customs. Do not intentionally criticize, mutually respect each other, and proceed to friendly communication.	Tao people have their own lunar calendar, seasonal rites, and a set of taboos, which are the bases of their cultural norms. Tourists should hold a respectful attitude in learning and experiencing Tao customs. When holding a traditional rite, please respect the local customs and taboos, and do not intentionally interfere with rites.
Do not enter or loiter at local residents' houses. Do not peep at or point at the local people.	The flying fish season runs from March to June or July every year. Please be attentive that female tourists are not allowed to touch the *tatala* (Tao canoe), and do not get on the *tatala* to take photos.
Villagers always eat meals at the *takakal* (Tao resting pavilion). Tourists should not interfere with their eating or observe and comment on their meals.	If there is a funeral in a village, please do not speak loudly. *Barringtonia asiatica* is regarded as one kind of evil tree by Tao people. Tourists must not bring their branches or leaves to Tao people's houses or intentionally put them on the *takakal*. Do not bring oranges to the seashore (especially in the flying fish season).
RESPECT PRIVACY, NO PHOTOS WITHOUT PERMISSION	CHERISH NATURE AND CARE FOR THE ENVIRONMENT
Tao traditional underground house, *takakal*, and indigenous people with traditional clothes are Tao features that attract tourists' eyes. Do ask for permission from the aborigine(s) before taking photos of them in order to avoid conflicts.	Lanyu has abundant and valuable natural resources. The Tao lifestyle that focuses on using natural resources sustainably maintains the original natural appearance.

(continued)

Table 12.1   Tao leaders' important reminders to tourists on Lanyu Island (continued)

RESPECT PRIVACY, NO PHOTOS WITHOUT PERMISSION	CHERISH NATURE AND CARE FOR THE ENVIRONMENT
Ask permission: Do not arbitrarily take photos of underground houses, *takakal*, and locals in order to avoid conflicts.	Do not arbitrarily pick or collect living things, discard garbage, or damage the natural environment when entering Lanyu.
Communication and coordination: Ask the tour guide to help communicate with locals and take photos only after obtaining permission.	Collecting Lanyu's animals and plants and bringing them out of Lanyu is not allowed according to the regulation of Taitung County government.

Sources: Blue Door n.d.; Lanyu n.d.

which is a process to recover their culture and also a process to strengthen their ethnic identity. Through the introduction of indigenous tourism to Lanyu Island, the Tao are able to teach tourists how to understand their culture and how to protect their land and ocean, echoing the development of ecological consciousness among the general population in the age of eco-development.

In sum, geographic isolation, cultural integrity, indigenous-tourism economy, mutual tolerance among religions, accessible communication channels, and support from the broader civil society are critical factors that help Tao people maintain the intimate relationship between humans and the land/ocean, which further consolidates Tao people's environmental autonomy. Environmental autonomy empowers Tao people to consistently insist on rejecting nuclear waste, but it also challenges Tao people to find the balance between economic development and environmental sustainability in the future.

Colonization at Nantian, a Paiwan Village

In contrast to the nonhierarchical structure of Tao communities, traditional Paiwan governance depended on a system of chiefship, by which hereditary chiefs had prestige and political power to assign subsistence rights (to land and sometimes water). When this solid structure of human-land relationships was loosened or even destroyed by colonial regimes, the characteristics of land ownership changed as the land governed by the chieftains was seized by the state or was redistributed through the government's privatization policy. Although there were a number of waves of indigenous movements of cultural renascence after 1980s in Taiwan, chieftains have never had the chance to recover their authority in substantive matters. Ironically, chieftains have now become a symbol at festivals.

Nantian is a Paiwan immigrant village, or perhaps more accurately a resettlement village with residents from different villages subject to a few different officially recognized chieftains (and their families), whose power is now only symbolic. As the legitimacy of the chieftains has been questioned, Nantian people have not been able to develop alternative leadership structures that could mount an effective opposition to the nuclear waste repository. Unlike Lanyu's stable social structure, the far greater disruption of life in Nantian has left the community bereft of effective leaders who might organize a meaningful political protest.

Given that the chieftains have no authority to organize resistance, the task of leading the rejection of nuclear waste would fall to bureaucratic and church leaders. But in fact, many Paiwan officials simply obey the national nuclear power policies and hence are inclined to support TPC's decision to site the nuclear waste repository in Nantian. They do so because they are promised economic development in return, and most of the local officials are members of the Nationalist Party, which gives more weight to economic development than environmental protection and hence has long supported the nuclear power policy. As a result, the developmental side of eco-developmentalism still dominates in Nantian Village.

There are two small Christian churches at Nantian. The first was established in the Navi neighborhood around 1970, and the second in the Vili neighborhood soon thereafter. There is no Catholic church at Nantian, but some Catholics go to Mass at churches in neighboring villages. Both local churches are informally affiliated with the Presbyterian Church in Taiwan but have not paid the fees to join the larger assembly, making it difficult for the Presbyterian Church in Taiwan to mobilize the antinuclear movement at Nantian. In general, the Nantian churches are indifferent to public affairs, including political activities.

The economic marginalization of Nantian began when the Japanese colonial government seized Paiwan traditional lands, first by force and later by law. The Chinese government followed the previous colonial government's land policies, seizing indigenous lands and limiting the use of indigenous reserve lands. As a result, the chieftains lost their right to distribute lands, and Paiwan people also lost their autonomy to make a living from the natural environment. Eventually, most Paiwan people have been forced to leave their homeland and become bottom-level workers in the mainstream (Han) society, and the elderly and infirm living in the villages have become a marginalized group who must rely solely on government social welfare.

The relationship between the Taiwan government and Nantian Village is thus one of "welfare colonialism," in which the government distributes welfare to marginalized groups, ostensibly for their benefit (Paine 1977). Ironically, welfare subsidies or development aid from the state have the adverse effect of making the colonized groups less able to develop autonomously, resulting in a situation of dependency (Amundsen 2011).

The Nantian village official responsible for social welfare affairs told me that around 80% of households are low-income families and that shrimp farming is an important industry at Nantian Village. The owners of the shrimp farms are all outsiders who rent the township's public property, while the indigenous reserve lands in the mountains are less valuable for economic development. Most Nantian villagers rely on the social welfare system, and younger villagers have to find jobs in cities.

In summer 2013, the Nantian village head brought me along with reporters from a public television station to the coast of Nantian village. He pointed out the wasted, empty, and shaky houses, half of whose foundations had been washed away by ocean waves, and which would be entirely consumed by the sea in the near future. In an anxious tone, he told us,

> There are only 100 meters from the coast to the village. Even if the
> tsunami would not attack us, there is still a huge threat to the village
> due to the erosion by the strong waves at high tide, especially when a
> typhoon is approaching. . . . The candidate site for the nuclear waste
> repository . . . is located at the top of a mountain in Nantian. Taiwan
> Power Company plans to adopt the tunnel approach to store nuclear

waste in a mountain with 40 hectares. . . . Of course, there are voices supporting and rejecting the plan. Those who reject the plan are elders of our village, who have a kind of love or adherence to the ancestor spirits and homeland which is our Paiwan people's belief. With this feeling of homeland protection, chieftains and elders think they are obligated to protect this piece of land. But there are some practical aspects that we have to face and consider. We are so remote, our fields are not very fertile, and there are not many job opportunities for us. Most economic pillars of the households are forced to work in outside cities to support their families. When they notice that nuclear waste would be possibly stored at Nantian village accompanied by a huge compensation fund, it [the repository] turns out to be a hope. . . . The biggest worry of Nantian village is the issue of erosion, while the government has not shown any concern about it. So, what we can do is switch our focus to TPC's compensation, which may help us protect our properties and lives, and provide a better welfare system and more job opportunities. Outside people who are against nuclear waste don't understand our predicament.

Because of pervasive poverty and the lack of education, Nantian villagers have been pushed to accept nuclear waste stored on their homeland in exchange for the TPC's compensation money, a case of what Blaikie and Brookfield refer to as poverty-driven "desperate ecocide" (Blaikie and Brookfield 1987, 240).

Up to now, although many Nantian villagers support the nuclear waste repository project, the Taitung County government is unwilling to hold a county-wide referendum because it considers the potential negative effects of the nuclear waste repository on the development of local tourism.

Culturally, compared to Lanyu's location, isolated from Taiwan, Nantian's geographic closeness to Han people has resulted in Nantian villagers' higher degree of sinicization. Han people's values about the land have changed Paiwan traditional ones and have brought about huge impacts on the relationship between Paiwan people and the land.

In a 2013 interview, a Nantian Township officer who governs land administration told me that the total area of Nantian Village is 1,122 hectares (2,781 acres), of which 1,109 hectares (2,772 acres), or 99.87% is comprised of aboriginal reserves. There are 807 land parcels registered in the names of villagers, 770 of them by indigenous people. The Nantian villagers are highly willing to participate in the aboriginal reserves' registration system, which is quite different from Lanyu, where 90% of Tao people are not willing to register their land.

This phenomenon reveals two important kinds of changes in the relationship between the people and the land. First, the state has seized most indigenous lands or redefined them as indigenous reserve lands with restricted right to use, which means that people can no longer use them for agriculture, hence lessening the intimate human-land relationship. Second, indigenous lands have become one kind of capital that can be freely traded among indigenous people or between indigenous people and Han people through the black market.

Both these changes have severely reduced Nantian Paiwan people's environmental autonomy and distanced them from their land. Low environmental autonomy has led directly to Nantian villagers' inability to continue traditional farming and hunting, which is also harmful to the development of local tourism based on traditional Paiwanese ecological

Table 12.2   *Differences in media usage between Nantian and Lanyu*

	NANTIAN VILLAGE	LANYU ISLAND
Demographic structure	Primarily elders, children, and people with disabilities, as young adults work in the cities	Attracted by the prosperity of the tourism industries, more younger generations are returning
Access to information	Weak	Strong
Communication forms: traditional vs. contemporary	• Face-to-face conversation. • Local public affairs information is diffused by the village head office. • Only one private group on Facebook for public affairs. • Outside information mainly from national TV channels and newspapers.	• Face-to-face conversation. • Different types of local media: — Biweekly newspaper since 1985 — Local radio station — Many self-initiated blogs and Facebook platforms

knowledge. Because Paiwan indigenous people, including Nantian villagers, cannot make a living on their homeland, this predicament forces them to become economically marginalized people in urban cities and eventually weakens Nantian villagers' determination to reject the nuclear waste repository project.

Nantian people are also limited by their lack of indigenous media. Table 12.2 shows the differences in media usage between these two sites. Compared to Lanyu Island, the abnormal demographic structure of Nantian Village, where most full-time residents are old people and children, impedes residents' access to information, resulting in a greater reliance on traditional communication channels. This results in a vicious cycle of an uninformed population.

In sum, the Tao, who have lived for forty years with nuclear waste, which has caused them no actual physical harm, are still resisting the blandishments of the power company, whereas the Paiwan, who have a chance to actually resist (since the nuclear waste repository has not been built yet), would rather accept the waste and the blandishments. The Tao have solidarity, have kept the government at a distance from their society (if not off their island altogether), still act according to their customary laws, and believe that nuclear waste is an affront to their autonomy and to their land, with which they feel a very literal kinship. The four-decade antinuclear movement has evolved alongside some critical contextual factors including environmental movements, Taiwan indigenous movements and the development of tribalism and other forms of localism. Moreover, the Tao antinuclear movement has obtained both domestic and international support through media connections and linkages with religious organizations. However, even though these three contextual factors operate in both communities, why does Nantian have a different attitude toward nuclear waste than Lanyu?

The community characteristics of Nantian play a pivotal role in shaping villagers' attitude toward nuclear waste. The Nantian villagers have a disintegrated and dysfunctional social order, little economic achievement or progress, and no unity and are living as refugees. In Nantian village, most of the valuable land belongs to the local government and newcomers; the villagers don't know how to help themselves, but they do know they need roads, schools, and clinics.

When Nantian villagers lost their relationship to the land, they had no reason to object to nuclear waste. By contrast, Tao people on Lanyu have continued to reject nuclear waste through a positive self-reinforcing process—securing the rights to land and ocean, maintaining their environmental autonomy, and developing local tourism.

Environmental autonomy is deeply influenced by the intimate relationship between the people and the land. Simply put, the relationship between the people and the land shapes the indigenous people's environmental autonomy, and the environmental autonomy subsequently influences their attitudes toward nuclear waste.

Reconnecting people with the land may be a critical factor to enhance indigenous resilience. Indigenous peoples cannot forget or overlook the wounds from the history of colonialism, self-pity, and passive discourse that would not help them recover from the existing social issues such as suicide, alcohol abuse, and poverty. But, more importantly, we should try to find the factors that motivate indigenous people to unleash positive resilient forces after oppression (Denham 2008, 391–414). The Lanyu case is a typical example of strong resilience to historical and contemporary social issues. Compared to indigenous ethnic groups in Taiwan, Tao people maintain the close relationship with the land and the ocean, which helps them develop a strong antinuclear attitude and powerful resilience. When the state tried to persuade Tao people to accept the governmental policies for the purpose of management or development, Tao people have firmly defended their core values on the basis of the intimate, intersubjective relationship between the people, the land, and the ocean and determinedly rejected the state's interferences.

The sovereignty of indigenous people has always been an important issue of indigenous movements, and the returning of land rights remains the most critical in Taiwan. Notably, indigenous peoples should not only aim to recover the right of land management but also to rebuild the relationship between the people and the land to establish their environmental autonomy and build a more sustainable future.

13

The Battle over GMOs in Korea and Japan

YVES TIBERGHIEN

THE REGULATION OF AGRICULTURAL BIOTECHNOLOGY, OR GENET-
ically modified organisms (GMOs), is a fruitful lens to study the changing relationships and influence of business, government, and civil
society in all East Asian countries (Bernauer 2003; Pollack and Shaffer
2009; Tiberghien 2012; Vogel 2012). Owing to the multifunctional nature of
GMOs, regulatory debates connect questions of scientific development,
economic competitiveness, consumer rights, public health, environmental impacts and long-term biodiversity, national culture, trade, and the
ethics of the relationship between humans and nature.

After the introduction of GM seeds and the start of GMO trade in
1996, a battle has played out at regional, national, and global levels in
every region of the planet around the search for the proper balance of
regulations required to support innovative food and health science, while
protecting biodiversity and local ecosystems, as well as long-term health,
culture, and consumer rights. Complicating matters, the biotech industry
had the first-mover advantage and initial control over information,
leading to early regulatory victories in the US but also in Europe, Japan,
and Korea, as well as in the Organization for Economic Cooperation and
Development (OECD) and the World Trade Organization (WTO). Thus,
by 1996, global and national regulations were in the process of converging toward the principle of "substantial equivalence," according to which
GMOs should not be regulated in any more stringent ways than regular
crops. This initial consensus included Japan, Korea, Taiwan, and China,

where economic and trade ministries, as well as scientists and business, supported the "pro-science" and "pro-trade" approach.

This consensus began to fray in 1997–98 with policy reversal in the European Union and the start of a moratorium in 1998 banning new approval of GM crops and seeds for planting and consumption. The EU went on to develop strict new regulations, enshrining the "precautionary principle," according to which more data on environmental and health impacts should be gathered over time and safeguards applied until independently collected data corroborates the view that GM crops do not negatively affect human health. Initially, it appeared that the precautionary approach would mostly be confined to Europe. Northeast Asia, with its developmental state consensus, was holding firm in the pro-US "substantial equivalence" camp.

However, between 1999 and 2001, Japan, Korea, and even China, all experienced policy reversals and began to adopt rules and laws that required mandatory labeling, imposed environmental assessments and tough guidelines on new approvals, and restricted experimental tests of GM crops in real open fields (Tiberghien 2012). These national and international regulatory steps were significant departures from the status quo in trade relations with the US. They put additional burdens on US exporters to avoid including unapproved seeds in export batches and subjected US and other foreign seed companies (such as Monsanto) to lengthy approval processes. Even more significantly, the US feared that mandatory labeling of GM products would lead to a reduction in consumer buy-in and to significant export reductions, as happened in the case of corn in Europe. Indeed, major trade disruptions happened at the time of introduction of new GMO regulations in Korea and China, generating very tense negotiations with the US. Japan managed to negotiate *ex ante* with the US and to ease into the new regulations without major impact on trade. Yet, the US has consistently fought against all mandatory labeling and additional approval requirements in all Asian countries. Asian countries studied in this chapter also all saw their biotech industry suffer as a result of the additional regulations.

All three countries signed the 2000 UN-sponsored Cartagena Protocol on Biosafety (which includes protections for biodiversity and mandatory labeling guidelines for cross-border GMOs), although Korea only ratified it in 2007, taking longer than Japan (2003) and China (2005).[1] In all three cases, the policy shift followed large-scale mobilization by civil society. Given its high dependence on US soy and corn imports and unable to sign the Cartagena Protocol as non-UN member, Taiwan initially hesitated. Yet, Taiwan similarly passed a mandatory labeling law in 2001, implemented in 2003 and patterned after the Japanese blueprint (with limited scope and the same high 5% threshold for inadvertent GM content below which labeling is not required). The legislation was expanded in 2007 and 2014, and non-GMO labels started to appear on the market.[2]

Japan and South Korea, two large democratic developmental states with strong biotech and chemical industries, making them tough places to implement an anti-biotech shift, provide useful case studies for exploring the following questions: (1) When do developmental trading states choose to move away from significant trade commitments and introduce costly regulatory obstacles to both trade and industrial development? and (2) Given the structural impediments against civil society in Asian developmental states (both state institutions and economic corporatist structures), under what conditions does civil society succeed in shifting policy outcomes?

The comparative politics literature offers a range of possible explanations for costly regulatory shifts. Partisanship and elections would be a classic first plausible lens, as it did shift outcomes on GMO regulations in countries like Germany and France when the Green Party entered governing coalitions. However, there was no partisan divide and no electoral saliency to the issue in Japan (1996, 1998, 2001, 2005) or in Korea (1998, 2003). Business and science elites held strong positions in all key parties. A second explanation might be public opinion (itself shaped by culture). However, the record shows a divided and poorly informed public opinion, which only became mobilized and salient after a series of civil society actions and policy responses. Thus, public opinion itself proved to be an outcome of other determining factors, rather than an independent factor in itself. A third plausible explanation often invoked in debates on GMOs by scholars and policy leaders is protectionism. However, the record shows that large farmers and business groups with influence in the Korean and Japanese economies were in fact in favor of GMOs and lobbied accordingly. The groups who lobbied against GMOs were small organic farmers, consumer groups, or NGOs that did not have a voice in traditional policy making.

The patterns observed in Korean and Japanese GMO regulatory shifts illustrate neatly the shift of these countries from pure developmental states to eco-developmental states concerned with social legitimacy in addition to economic growth. The cases explored here feature enlarged policy coalitions that begin to embed civil society groups or their ideas as part of the quest for political legitimacy.

We cannot understand the policy shifts that took place in Korea and Japan without focusing on the role of civil society as a conditional catalyst for change under the right institutional conditions. In both Korea and Japan, NGO actions challenged the legitimacy of existing policy networks. Their effectiveness relied on three primary instruments. First, they demonstrated a significant framing power, as they triggered an institutional legitimacy crisis and a new process of normative formation, with the support of the media. Second, they were successful in developing effective political linkages, relying both on local governments and on urban policy entrepreneurs, both of whom used the issue to increase their voice and power. In both Korea and Japan, civil society benefitted from a period of political transformation and party change, which created fluidity and space for new coalitions. When Japan's Liberal Democratic Party (LDP) was dependent on minor parties to govern, or fragmented, it opened space for new environmental or social agendas. When the LDP is under the powerful and unified leadership of a conservative leader, space for new environmental ideas that do not fit in the leader's vision is very narrow. For example, change is much more difficult now, under the unified leadership and pro-business leanings of Prime Minister Shinzō Abe in Japan. Third, they successfully used the platforms of international institutions by importing international norms and mobilization examples, from Europe in particular, to the domestic setting.

With these instruments, civil society was able to trigger an anti-GMO tipping point in policy making in both Korea and Japan. However, going beyond agenda setting to the regulatory phase proved to be a more difficult endeavor. In both cases, the bureaucratic apparatus refused to incorporate civil society into formal committees (as was done in Europe). In Korea, NGOs benefitted initially from stronger political leadership thanks to the presence of Agricultural Minister Kim Sung Hoon, who came from civil society; but the Ministry of Economy was able to reassert its control and delay ratification of the Cartagena Protocol once that minister left office. In Japan, the presence of a favorable Committee for Consumer Affairs in the Diet gave a bit more institutional momentum to the precautionary voice. Yet, even there, pro-business interests were eventually able to shut down the committee itself, even though the anti-GMO legislation has endured to this day.

Development States vs. Civil Society: Conditions for Civil Society's Catalytic Impact

Civil society's possibility of success as a catalyst for environmental policy change in developmental states hinges on three key factors. The first is the ability of civil society coalitions to frame an issue in a compellingly novel way, in opposition to the official frame, and in resonance with latent public expectations. In essence, civil society coalitions act as arbitrage entrepreneurs. They identify latent gaps between policy outputs and legitimacy expectations of the public in hopes of triggering a process of institutional change (Aoki 2001). The success of civil society in triggering this legitimacy change requires in turn a degree of coherence within the coalition, good leadership, and creative capacity (which may be spurred by international models).

The second factor is the presence of political allies and of opportunities for multilevel reinforcement, once public opinion has been activated by the new frame (Schreurs and Tiberghien 2007). It is easier for NGOs to mobilize public opinion when politics have been decentralized, since civil society has easier access to local governments. They also have greater opportunity when there is fluidity in the political system, such as when new elites are being recruited into high-level positions (cf. the Kim Dae-Jung moment in 1999–2000 in Korea or political transition in Japan from 1993 to 2011), or when existing elites are fragmenting.

The puzzle can be understood only through a political lens, rather than an economic interest lens. In both Korea and Japan, the anti-GMO (and anti-beef) mobilization by civil society was partially successful because it became a vector for a larger battle over governance and democracy. It was a clash of governing paradigms, pitting old-style, opaque network policy making against new expectations of transparency and inclusion. In Korea, both the GMO battle of 2000 and 2002 and the beef battle of 2008[3] became a battle for the maturation of democratization started in the late 1980s. According to civil society, the next step of democratization required the full opening of policy making to new actors, such as women's groups, environmental groups, labor, and urban consumers. In Japan, the GMO battle pitted local governments against an overbearing central bureaucracy and newly elected urban politicians against traditional LDP networks. It became a battle for more inclusive policy making and for renewal of voices within the governance paradigm.

The third factor is the presence of international linkages. Cross-national NGOs linkages play a growing role in empowering domestic NGOs in difficult environments and in accelerating the diffusion of new norms (Finnemore and Sikkink 1998; Keck and Sikkink 1998). Also, the creation of new international treaties broadly signed by governments in order to retain their global image can provide extremely valuable tools and repertoires to civil society—what I call Trojan horses. The Cartagena Protocol for Biosafety became such a Trojan horse in Japan and Korea after 2000.

During the regulatory phase, an additional factor becomes significant: long-lasting voice in shaping the details of regulations requires civil society representatives to be included in deliberation committees or parliamentary deliberations in a way that is rarely seen in Northeast Asian democracies. For example, the committee created by the Ministry of Agriculture in Japan between 1999 and 2000 to advise the ministry on writing the new mandated GMO law included scientists linked to the biotech industry and one consumer representative, but no member from environmental or health related NGOs. In the European Commission, things are different, and civil society members are embedded in the advisory committees that help draft EU regulations.

Civil Society Coalitions Working on GMOs in Japan and Korea

Both Japan and Korea presented more constrained environments than Europe for civil society mobilization on GMO issues. For starters, both countries have a very low food self-sufficiency rate (40% for Japan overall and 44% for South Korea).[4] The rate hovers in single digits in both countries when it comes to corn, soy, and canola, making both countries extremely dependent on imports from large producers, such as the US, Canada, Brazil, and Argentina. Additionally, economic, scientific, and agricultural ministries invested significantly in biotechnology beginning in the 1980s and supported the OECD and WTO consensus on

Table 13.1 *Selected anti-GMO-network and other main NGOs taking part in anti-GMO movement in Korea*

ANTI-GMO NETWORK			
NGOS	FOCUS	DETAILS	RELATED RELIGIOUS GROUP
Farmers' Association for Environmental Agriculture on Ganghwa Island (Ganghwado Hwan'gyeong Nong'eop Nongminhui)	Cooperative agricultural community	Farmers' community for organic farming in Ganghwa Island	n/a
Indramang Life Community (Indramang Saengmyeong Gongdongche), www.indramang.org	Environment	Environmental movement for ecological farming	Buddhist
Hansalim (Hansalim), www.hansalim.co.kr	Environment	Environmental movement for ecological farming	n/a
National Association for Korean Farmers (Jeon'guk Nongminhui Chongyeonmaeng), www.ijunnong.net	Korean farmers' union	Anti-import, anti-WTO movement	n/a
JUMIN Consumers' Cooperation Union (JUMIN Saenghyoep), http://coop.jinbo.net	Consumer rights	Consumers' organization	Protestant
Korean Catholic Farmers' Meeting (Han'guk CATHOLIC Nongminhui), www.kcfm.or.kr	Farmers' union	Anti-import, anti-WTO movement	Catholic

(continued)

Table 13.1   Selected anti-GMO-network and other main NGOs taking part in anti-GMO movement in Korea (continued)

	OTHER NGOS		
NGOs	FOCUS	DETAILS	RELATED RELIGIOUS GROUP
Korean Womenlink (Han'guk Yeoseong Minwuhui), www .womenlink.or.kr	Women	Women's movement	n/a
Green Korea (Noksaek Yeonhap), www .greenkorea.org	Environment	Environmental movement	n/a
Catholic Environmental Network (CATHOLIC Hwan'gyeong'yeondea), www.cen.or.kr	Environment	Environmental movement	Catholic
Korean Federation for Environmental Movement (Hwan'gyeong'undong Yeonhap), http:// english.kfem.or.kr	Environment	Environmental movement	n/a

Source: Thanks to research assistant Dr. Hyunji Lee.

substantial equivalence. However, new civil society actors sprung up after 1996 in both countries and started presenting new information the public, eliciting media interest. Who were these anti-GMO coalitions and how different were they in Japan and Korea?

In Japan, science journalist Amagasa Keisuke and consumer activist Yasuda Setsuko formed an NGO federation called "No GMO! Campaign" in 1996, operating out of very small and cramped headquarters near Waseda University. Amagasa closely studied EU and Swiss developments, attending civil society events there. He introduced significant written material into Japan (Amagasa 2000, 2003, 2004, 2005). The campaign formed a tactical alliance with the Seikatsu Club (Daily Life Club) Consumers' Cooperative

Union providing alternative food products through mail orders to housewives around Japan. The Seikatsu Club counted 22 million members, almost all women. The Seikatsu Club could not agree on an anti-GMO campaign, as it counted many poorer members but agreed with Amagasa on the need to provide information to consumers and thus the need for mandatory labeling. Therefore, unlike in Europe, the initial NGO core in Japan was formed by a coalition focused on consumer rights and health issues rather than environmental concerns.[5] In subsequent years, after 2000, other civil society groups joined the larger coalition related to food security, including groups working on the provision of quality and healthy food for urban residents, such as the Soybean Trust, the Rice Trust, and Slow Food Cafés.[6] After 2001, the alliance further grew to include organic farmers, environmental NGOs, and anti-globalization NGOs (weaker in Japan).

By contrast, the civil society coalition that sprang up in Korea in 1999–2001 was much larger and more broad-based, gathering strong farmer cooperatives, environmental groups, anti-globalization groups, and consumer rights groups into a large anti-GMO network counting nineteen different organizations. This coalition received the further support of other women's movements, environmental groups and religious groups (table 13.1).[7] Unlike Japan, the coalition was broad-based and fragmented, but organized around a focus on antiauthoritarian and anti-globalization mobilization. In that sense, it was a clear outgrowth of the democratization movement and the accompanying explosion of civil society groups advocating democracy and human rights.

Causal Mechanisms and Tipping Points in the Two Countries

The No GMO! Campaign managed to shift the ground in Japan on GMO policy in two key steps. First, the coalition organized a massive petition drive (reaching two million individual sheets sent to the Ministry of Agriculture and jamming its corridors by 1998), thanks to its links to the Seikatsu Club. It also succeeded in orchestrating a cascade of resolutions by 1,600 out of 3,000 local government assemblies requesting mandatory labeling of GMOs. The first one to pass the resolution was the Tokyo Assembly (December 1996). Second, the campaign successfully spurred the formation of a cross-party coalition in a key Diet committee encompassing almost entirely female opposition MPs from the Democratic Party of Japan, the Komeito, the Japan Communist Party, and Social Democratic Party (Shaminto). However, when the "subcommittee on the issue of labeling of GMOs as part of the special committee on consumer issues" took up the issue in December 1997, Kono Taro joined the female opposition coalition and tilted the majority in favor of mandatory labeling.[8] Kono, a rising star from the governing LDP from an urban district with a strong interest in food and environmental issues, later rose to become the minister of foreign affairs and defense minister (at the time of writing). Ironically, The Minister of Economy, Trade, and Industry (METI) managed to mobilize enough political capital in both the LDP and the Democratic Party of Japan (DPJ) to have party leaders from the two parties agree to shut down the subcommittee in 2001. Even though the committee shut down quickly, it was open long enough to allow GMO opponents to demand that the Ministry of Agriculture draft new mandatory labeling rules for GMOs.

By contrast, the trigger mechanism behind the 2001 Law on Mandatory Labeling (which led to trade conflict with the US) was very different in Korea. Despite strong civil society mobilization and parliamentary interest (including activist Members of Parliament such as Kang Ki Gap), the process leading to legal or regulatory change relied on the linkage between civil society and a key policy entrepreneur. The presence of Dr. Kim Sung-Hoon as the minister of agriculture under President Kim Dae-Jung (1998–2002) made a key difference. Dr. Kim was not only a professor of agriculture and resource economics, he was also deeply active in Korea's burgeoning civil society. Of course, President Kim Dae-Jung appointed him in this ministerial position both for his competence and in recognition of the growing political importance of civil society groups. Dr. Kim had played active roles in organizations working on forest conservation, sustainable agriculture, and consumer rights in Korea. After his term in office, he went on to serve as the president of South Korea's Citizens Movement for Environmental Justice. In Minister Kim's own admission, the South Korean government is usually good at insulating itself from NGO pressures, and environmental ministers tend to be weak (as was the case during the 2000–2002 period). In 2000–2001, even though there was pro-GMO lobbying from the biotech industry, and the Ministry of Health and Environment was weak, President Kim Dae-Jung and his prime minister essentially delegated to GMO-skeptic Minister Kim Sung-Hoon the task of drafting the legislation on GMO labeling. Since he was a long-serving minister with strong credibility, he could win the agreement of the Cabinet over the need to give priority to transparency and to quality over price.[9] His presence and decisive intervention led to rapid action on the GMO file. It also meant that the victory would be fragile and open to backsliding once he left office. Indeed, the Ministry of Economy and Trade later managed to delay the ratification of the Cartagena Protocol until 2007 and commitments to dilute stringent GMO regulations were later made part of the Free Trade Agreement (FTA) negotiations with the US under President Lee Myung-Bak. In sum, the Kim Dae-Jung presidency provided a window of opportunity during which the developmental state coalition was vulnerable. The pro-biotech coalition encompassing the Ministry of Economy and Trade, the Ministry of Science, large companies, and pro-business politicians gradually reasserted itself after 2003 and especially after 2008, ensuring the continuation of intense conflicts between civil society and the developmental state. Under President Moon Jae-In after 2017, space for civil society and environmental movements has opened up again, given the close connections between Moon and such organizations. President Moon promised in his 2017 campaign to strengthen GMO labeling regulations, leading to a limited amendment issued in June 2019.

Civil Society Coalitions as Catalysts for Change

The issue of GMO regulation in Korea and Japan is a struggle over the paradigm of governance between traditional developmental state elites and emerging civil society groups. It is a battle over political accountability and domestic governance rather than one about trade and international openness or science.

In both Korea and Japan, civil society coalitions were able to score significant policy victories due to the successful linkages between civil society coalitions and political allies. In both cases, however, the regulatory shifts were partial and prone to policy reversal. Korea still has not reached a political equilibrium between its enduring developmental coalition and its lively civil society clamoring for inclusiveness and environmental accountability. In Japan, space for civil society impact has decreased after 2012, even though the public and the media never back-tracked from their skeptical view toward GMOs after 2000. In Korea, civil society has remained highly mobilized around agriculture issues (including GMOs) and the precautionary frame has held firm, despite continuing efforts by the economic bureaucracy to erode this frame.

More battles can be expected over the next generations of GMOs, such as GM fish, GM animals, and pharmacrops (GM crops that can produce enzymes or proteins used in drugs or vaccines). These will further test the relationship between developmental elites and civil society as the two sides seek to reconfigure their relationship and policies in accordance with eco-developmentalism in both countries.

Notes

1 Convention on Biological Diversity, "Parties to the Cartagena Protocol and Its Supplementary Protocol on Liability and Redress," https://bch.cbd.int/protocol/parties/, accessed April 2020.
2 US Department of Agriculture, Global Agricultural Information Network, Report #TW1052, December 2001.
3 In spring 2008, the newly negotiated beef trade deal between the US and Korea triggered massive spontaneous protests across universities and high schools around South Korea. Young people opposed the reopening of free imports of US beef because of fears of mad cow disease. The protests escalated into massive sit-ins and candlelight vigils in Seoul, earning majority public support. Newly elected President Lee Myung-Bak lost a huge amount of popularity within weeks and resorted to firing his entire National Security Council and ministers to save his presidency. He also revised the agreement with the US to allay public concerns.
4 Ministry of Agriculture, Forestry and Fisheries, Japan, Annual Report, 2010, p. 11, https://www.maff.go.jp/e/annual_report/2010/pdf/e_1.pdf, accessed April 2020.
5 Interviews by the author with Amagasa Keisuke, Tokyo, November 15, 2005, and with Shimizu Ryoko (Seikatsu Club), November 16, 2005.
6 Interview by the author with Abe Fumiko, Rice Trust leader, November 10, 2005.
7 Interviews conducted by the author and Dr. Hyunji Li with Korean Federation of Environment, anti-GMO network, farmers, and members of Parliament in January 2007 in Seoul.
8 Interviews by the author with Ishige Eiko and Kono Taro, 2006, Tokyo.
9 Interview by the author and Dr. Hyunji Lee with former minister Kim Sung-Hoon, August 2011, Vancouver.

14

Grassroots NGOs and Environmental Advocacy in China

JINGYUN DAI AND ANTHONY J. SPIRES

FROM UNDRINKABLE WATER TO HAZARDOUS AIR, CHINA FACES daunting environmental problems. In reaction, the Chinese public has been taking individual measures—putting on masks, buying filters, or even fleeing the country (for the rich)—but its frustration with pollution has also grown into demands directed at the state, sometimes in the form of protests. Amid this, China has seen a growing number of environmental nongovernmental organizations (ENGOs) that have been advocating for change in government policy. In the broader Chinese civil society, ENGOs have been pioneers in such advocacy (Hildebrandt 2013; Wu 2013).

While prior studies have documented incidents of some larger, more famous Chinese ENGOs opposing dam building that have drawn national or even international attention (e.g., Johnson 2010; Mertha 2008; Han, Swedlow, and Unger 2014), we show that lesser-known Chinese grassroots ENGOs also regularly employ a variety of advocacy strategies to influence local-level government policy. Based on in-depth interviews with ENGOs active in Guangdong, this study examines these groups' advocacy efforts and considers their implications for the further development of Chinese civil society. These groups employ three main advocacy strategies: (1) cultivating a stable, interactive relationship with government while using existing institutional means to communicate their concerns; (2) carefully selecting the "frames" used to present their preferred policy goals and outcomes; and (3) obtaining media exposure to mobilize societal support for their goals in order to put pressure on the state. ENGOs use these strategies concurrently, though concrete choices vary case by case. Taken as a whole, such practices suggest the ability of civil society to carve out more political space than the state is commonly believed to grant. While this increased policy engagement by ENGOs could lead to stronger state "governance" and thus help sustain China's authoritarian system, it may also open up new pathways for robust civic engagement by ordinary citizens and civil society organizations.

The Context of ENGO Advocacy: Shrinking Political Space, Favorable Policy Lines

Though China has witnessed a surge in NGOs since the 1990s, observers believe it is now a dark time for Chinese civil society (Yuen 2015). Censorship of the mass media and cyberspace has increased; human rights lawyers and activists have recently been detained and interrogated; and several labor NGOs in Guangdong were suddenly repressed in December 2015. The Overseas NGO Management Law, passed in April 2016, places unprecedented restrictions on international NGOs (INGOs) that operate in China and may cut off already-dwindling foreign funding for domestic NGOs. The state is also restricting NGO contacts with foreign organizations and personnel. NGOs that focus on environmental protection have not been spared by the recently deteriorating political climate. In October 2016, for instance, one ENGO leader was detained for ten days by a city-level Bureau of State Security for "leaking state secrets," after the ENGO had collected and widely publicized pollution data (RFA 2016).

Nevertheless, there are countercurrents in national policies and laws, many of which originated well before the recent crackdown on civil society. New official rhetoric promoting "social management innovation" has encouraged local and provincial governments to cooperate with civil society and has also led to the registration of more "social organizations." Starting in 2012, Guangdong was the first province to reform registration regulations, allowing NGOs to register with the Ministry of Civil Affairs without first needing to be sponsored by a government-affiliated supervisory agency. The greening of the Chinese state is also well underway. The State Environmental Protection Administration was elevated to ministry level in 2008—now the Ministry of Environmental Protection (MEP). The National People's Congress, China's legislature, amended the Environmental Protection Law in 2014, strengthening the MEP's enforcement power and emphasizing the government's responsibility to address environmental problems. The amended law also allows for public interest litigation, and NGOs are qualified to be complainants. Overall, Chinese ENGOs work in a complex and ever-changing environment, with contradictory political currents but also a general trend towards greater recognition of and participation by NGOs.

More broadly, although Chinese civil society is growing and making changes on the margins, it remains weak, not rebellious, and lacks the capacity to promote larger political and social change (Gasemyr 2016). NGO efforts to alleviate social problems can also improve the state's responsiveness and accountability, ironically strengthening favorable views of the state's performance and legitimacy and thereby contributing to "better governance under authoritarianism" (Teets 2014). In the environmental realm, the growth of environmental organizations has been attributed to the state's recognition of the many environmental problems arising alongside economic development and to the weakness of the state's own environmental protection bureaucracy (Schwartz 2004).

Nevertheless, a few established ENGOs have been involved in advocacy campaigns, exemplified in a series of anti-dam campaigns in Southwest China (Johnson 2010; Mertha 2009; Han, Swedlow, and Unger 2014). These campaigns marked the most successful and influential cases in which grassroots ENGOs have influenced government decisions. These campaigns also demonstrated that ENGOs are able to make use of the Environmental Impact Assessment Law and the Administrative Licensing Law, and to mobilize social support to pressure the government to open up its decision-making process and allow for a greater degree of policy deliberation (Han 2014). In contrast to studies suggesting that well-connected ENGOs with government ties and funding are best positioned to engage in this sort of advocacy (Li, Lo, and Tang 2017), in this chapter we show how more autonomous grassroots ENGOs have made local-level advocacy a regular part of their work.

Methods and Data

The research analyzes interviews conducted in 2016 with leaders of eight grassroots ENGOs (four of whom were interviewed twice) in Guangzhou and Shenzhen, two major cities in Guangdong. Famous for its relatively open political environment, Guangdong has been a locus of grassroots NGO activity over the past decade and a half (Spires, Tao, and Chan 2014). Interviews were supplemented by analysis of the ENGOs' websites, blogs, written reports, and social media platforms, as well as news reports about these ENGOs and government documents. We believe the eight groups generally depict the situation of ENGOs in Guangzhou and Shenzhen. ENGOs in the same city know each other well; when asked to name other ENGOs they knew, their responses generated almost the same exact list.

All eight groups are legally registered and are relatively young, having registered in some form between 2012 and 2015. At the time of our interviews, one group, registered as a business, had tried but had been unable to register as a "proper" NGO. The eight NGOs are mostly medium-sized grassroots groups, with six to nine full-time salaried staff, while the smallest has three full-time and two part-time staff. Their budgets range from hundreds of thousands to several million yuan, mostly coming from domestic foundations, businesses, and to a lesser extent, government. They work on a wide range of issues and demonstrate a fair degree of specialization, with three working exclusively on water, one on industrial pollution prevention, one on waste, one on nature education, one on green transportation, and one on wetland conservation, water, and community engagement.

When asked about their work, interviewees from four of the groups stated that "policy advocacy" is an integral part of what they do, while one group, though not specifically mentioning policy advocacy, has nevertheless had major accomplishments in policy advocacy and deals with the government frequently. Two groups do not consider advocacy as an integral part of their work, although they do work to expand public participation. An interviewee from the final group specifically mentioned "monitoring of the government" as their job. For these eight groups, the simplest and most common advocacy activity is to request the government to address specific environmental problems—for instance, to punish a polluting factory. Most of these ENGOs also offer policy suggestions and initiatives to the city government and promote disclosure of information by government and business. Two ENGO leaders often write newspaper columns critiquing government policies, and four of the groups have initiated or participated in campaigns against government decisions and policies. In seeking to influence the government, ENGOs as a whole typically resort to three main strategies.

Strategy 1: Using Formal Institutional Means and Building an Interactive Relationship

The government cannot deny the legitimacy of using institutional channels and is generally obligated to follow official procedures when responding. ENGOs send out research reports and open letters, submit proposals to the city-level People's Congress or Political Consultative Conference, apply for information disclosure, and make use of channels that the local government has established to show its commitment to communicating with citizens, such as government "office visiting" days, the Committee of Public Consultation and Supervision, and the "mayor's mailbox" in Guangzhou.

It was somewhat surprising to find that most grassroots ENGOs were able to directly communicate with the government through formal means using few prior personal connections (*guanxi*). One group sent a letter to the mayor through the "mayor's mailbox" online and eventually had the problem resolved by the mayor's order. One ENGO leader commented, "If you are not familiar with certain departments, you can still send them something." When asked how he got in touch with the government the first time, another leader who was experienced in working with local governments nationwide said: "You just go and make an appointment. You just need to find them directly." This was not easy, though; he waited for months before the Guangzhou Bureau of Environmental Protection met him for an initial, two-hour conversation. Similarly, the ENGO that appealed to the mayor had previously approached several city departments that had passed the buck, and the ENGO was also ignored or turned down by city-level People's Congress deputies.

ENGOs sometimes favor formal channels even though they also have informal talks with certain government officials. One group led by a former city-level Bureau of Environmental Protection official failed to talk formally with the bureau but emphasized the importance of "following the official procedures" and "using official channels" when advocating for information disclosure. The group had begun seeking formal meetings with the bureau, arguing, "It is to let the Bureau get accustomed to dealing with ENGOs publicly, to improve their administrative efficiency . . . to learn how to face skepticism from the public."

Filing an administrative appeal (*xingzheng fuyi*) is relatively common when ENGOs request local government to disclose information. A successful appeal to a superior government agency would force the subordinate agency to again review the ENGO's requests. But none of the eight ENGOs regularly resorted to administrative litigation (*xingzheng susong*), that is, suing a government agency in court. A leader of one group said they view litigation as their last resort, yet they have been carefully watching the government to identify any law violations in preparation for an administrative lawsuit if need be. In a rare case, one group had filed an administrative lawsuit against a district-level bureau for its failure to publicize environmental data. The ENGO refused the bureau's request for a private settlement, and despite lacking confidence in its chance of winning, the leader emphasized the broader implications of the case—"to let the law become the most important criterion of national governance" and to clarify the Regulation on the Disclosure of Government Information, according to interviews with the leader and also *Caixin* news reports (June 2, 2016). The ENGO eventually won the case and later organized a workshop to share its experience about seeking information disclosure and administrative litigation.

Grassroots ENGOs also consciously try to cultivate a long-term, stable, and interactive relationship with local governments. Rather than relying on preexisting *guanxi*, they actively seek to nurture new relationships, pursuing frequent communication with the government with the goal of building mutual trust. Underpinning communication is the government's realization that it needs ENGOs to monitor pollution and to gather local information. One group leader who had pushed for reforms in Environmental Impact Assessment regulations explained how gaining authorities' trust enabled efficient cooperation: "With trust . . . then it's simple and efficient. For example, if I discover a polluting enterprise, without good communication [the government] would need to spend a lot of time to verify it. . . . But with trust, it would know that our organization's investigation is free of problems, that we must have sufficient evidence. All it has to do is penalize [the rule breaker]. So having trust saves costs and makes both our work more efficient. The government used to handle thirty cases per month, but now it can handle sixty."

This relationship with government is reciprocal, and the government sometimes initiates communications with ENGOs. It is relatively common for relevant city government departments to invite ENGOs to forums and meetings to ask for suggestions and feedback. After gaining a level of prominence through exposure in the media, a group that registered in 2015 described how the Water Authority in Guangzhou started to engage with them: "From time to time, every one or two months, the Water Authority invites us [to meetings], and the director of the bureau will come and sit there and ask if we have any questions. We then make a series of complaints. He will do what he can, assign this or that to somebody to deal with it. . . . They all diligently take notes about what we say . . . but we do not know if they can really deal with it satisfactorily."

Another ENGO reported, "People who are concerned with politics or who are within the system, when they notice your organization . . . they take the initiative to ask if you have any proposals this year." Partly because of these invitations, this group handed in sixteen policy proposals before the 2016 meetings of the National People's Congress and Chinese People's Political Consultative Conference.

Strategy 2: Framing Issues: Not Blaming, but Assisting
the Government

The ENGOs in this study are careful about the way they frame issues when communicating with the local government. They have learned through experience that aligning advocacy with central policies and local interests substantially increases the chance of success. An ENGO that advocates for green transportation wrote to the mayor and received a positive reply because, the NGO believes, the mayor supported public transportation and bicycles to alleviate traffic congestion. The group acknowledged, "When asking him to bike with us, we took advantage of his policy line." Another group agreed that ENGOs should "keep a close eye on central policy trends and the government's work, combine your advocacy with that and grab the opportunity." All of the ENGOs recognized that the national government has placed increasing emphasis on environmental protection, and that, as a result, environmental issues in general are now considered less sensitive in comparison with other rights-related issues. Framing their advocacy as aligned with the state's commitment to environmental protection allows ENGOs to gain legitimacy. Specifically, they present their advocacy as a form of public participation, which the state expressly encourages and is written into the Environmental Protection Law.

Following the central policy line, however, is far from enough. Even when ENGOs report a pollution case to the Bureau for Environmental Protection, officials may interpret this as criticism of the government. But ENGOs in Guangdong do more than report on pollution violations. One vital strategy is to emphasize the ENGO's eagerness to partner with the state in tackling what both see as common problems and to "reduce" environmental justice to concrete problems to be solved. A group that met with the Water Authority, for example, presented its case in a way that did not accuse the government of wrongdoing but rather expressed a desire to assist in solving a particular environmental problem: "The first time we communicated with each other, both sides were nervous. . . . A deputy head attended, with the bureau's scientists and experts. They stood in the shape of a fan, and only three of us were allowed to be there. We explained to them that we are a social organization working on environmental protection in Guangzhou who came here not to find out who is responsible for what, but just in the hope of offering assistance. We can cooperate with each other to let your work be smoother. We just hope rivers and the environment will get cleaner."

These framing tactics mean that ENGOs avoid potentially antagonistic relations over sensitive issues. As one group put it, "Don't say anything oppositional. You should rather focus on good aspects" of government work. When the media cover problems and negative cases, ENGOs are careful to promote positive exemplary cases, in order not to "make the public and officials pessimistic." In a similar vein, the two ENGO leaders who regularly contribute to newspaper columns, though writing mostly critical pieces, do not forget to praise the government's improvements in its handling of environmental issues or any positive policies and regulations. Other groups use the same tactics on their websites and social media platforms.

Strategy 3: Mobilizing Social Support

None of these eight groups engaged in "street mobilization" of local citizens, not even indirectly. While some of the groups' staff and volunteers had been involved in Guangzhou's Panyu District incinerator protests of 2009 (Steinhardt and Wu 2015), the ENGOs they now belong to choose to mobilize social support via mass media and the internet to bolster their influence, to expose problems, and to exert pressure on the government when necessary. Their newspaper commentaries on the environment are a "dialogue with government at a distance," according to one ENGO's leader, for "the government reads these commentaries and collects public opinions" and sometimes publishes responses in newspapers. In addition, social media is increasingly important in shaping public opinion in China. The self-proclaimed advocacy ENGO is adept at launching campaigns and creating polls on social media to mobilize public support and attract authorities' attention.

In some cases, when ENGOs fail to influence the government through institutional means or direct communications—for instance, when the government simply ignores the problems, their critical voices, and their policy suggestions—they resort to the media to "force the government to do something. If the government ignores us, we use more radical means to force it to attend to us." For instance, when an ENGO reported that the red mud produced by subway construction was directly poured into a river, an investigator from the Bureau of Environmental Protection responded by saying, "Do not call us over such a trifle." So the group "made it a big deal. We put this information online, and the mass media followed up. Because of this incident, the government adjusted its policy to 'guard the river' and reinforced its implementation. . . . Later, the construction company was penalized."

The "nature education" ENGO usually does not interact with the government but once used the media to force a government-backed tourism development corporation to stop building roads in the core areas of a regional nature reserve. Initially, the group wrote an open letter to the Forestry Bureau, but this did not have much effect: "In fact, we shouldered pressures and didn't receive a positive response. Our volunteers would receive phone calls saying, 'Do not do this anymore.'" In contrast, the pressure the non-local mass media exerted on the government was effective: "Local media was under pressure to prohibit coverage on this, so we found some news media from Beijing, and held a conference to explain the situation. After that, the media in Beijing covered the incident. After the coverage, very quickly the local government made a response. . . . The corporation promised to stop construction immediately and to start to restore vegetation."

Another ENGO found that a sewage treatment plant, located only one kilometer upstream from a water supply facility, was failing to meet quality standards each year about 20% of the time. The plant's environmental impact assessment (EIA) report was also deeply flawed, and the company that conducted the EIA had already lost its official qualification to do so because of its own poor performance. Several ENGOs informed local Political Consultative Conference representatives and journalists about this, but their entreaties initially failed to generate any action or publicity. Several months later, however, a journalist finally reported on it and very soon other media pursued it, putting public pressure on the government. One ENGO leader heard from a government contact that after this incident had come to the attention of the Guangzhou mayor and the city's party secretary, the government organized a team to prepare a lengthy report and took action to resolve the problems.

The aforementioned three advocacy strategies, however useful, cannot ensure success. When ENGOs advocate for change through institutional channels, a substantial portion of their suggestions are simply ignored. Delayed responses and passing the buck are common practices. Moreover, pursuing a stable, interactive relationship with the government can also risk diminishing the advocacy function of ENGOs; some groups might end up working for the government or a particular government department. One ENGO in the sample has become content with reporting pollution cases, asking businesses to disclose information, and providing policy suggestions. While this approach may help achieve the group's immediate goals, it has ceased making efforts to elicit any wider civic participation that engages ordinary citizens.

Not all of the ENGOs in our sample took the same approach or agreed on the effectiveness of working directly with government versus focusing on public participation. In general, the ENGOs that actively seek an interactive relationship with the government tend to emphasize that forcing the government to take action and to be more competent is the most efficient way to realize environmental protection. In contrast, some groups prefer more direct on-site activities and raising public awareness—work they believe to be more fundamental to environmental protection. But on the whole we found that these groups work to encourage citizens' participation in a variety of ways, by persuading them to patrol and test rivers, by showing them environmentally harmful products in supermarkets, and by forming online discussion groups. Through online and offline activities, ENGOs teach the public how to apply for government information disclosure, how to report problems to the local bureau of Environmental Protection, and how to write letters to the bureau, even offering a letter template to build on.

Multiple Advocacy Strategies: Protecting Guangzhou's Liuxi River

A campaign to preserve the "protected zone" designation of the lower course of the Liuxi River, which runs through Guangzhou, is illustrative of how ENGOs deployed multiple advocacy strategies simultaneously to influence the decisions of city and provincial governments. In January 2015, the Guangzhou Water Bureau proposed removing the protected zone designation, arguing that the water quality had fallen short of the standard for drinking water for a long time and that Guangzhou no longer relied on the river for drinking water. This proposal was supposed to be agreed upon by the Guangzhou Bureau of Environmental Protection and eventually finalized by the Guangdong provincial government.

The Water Bureau only allowed seven days for public comments on the proposal, but five water pollution ENGOs joined forces to voice their opposition and managed to submit opinions collected from five hundred residents along with letters by the ENGOs. They also succeeded in getting a series of news stories and opinion articles published in newspapers and social media. In published comments to the Water Bureau, they openly questioned the government's true motive for seeking to remove the protected zone designation: "Several key industrial projects are to be located in the river's water source protection zone. Is this proposal to make way for those projects?" The Water Bureau later invited several ENGOs to join a roundtable to talk about the bureau's proposal, but it was a tense meeting where both parties insisted on their own positions, and at the end of the meeting the bureau's plan remained unchanged. To press their view, the three water ENGOs identified sympathetic allies in the city-level Political Consultative Conference and sought attention for the issue at the annual meeting of the local People's Congress.

Facing constant opposition, the Water Bureau and the Bureau of Environmental Protection responded through newspapers, repeatedly promising to improve the Liuxi River's water quality even after removing the protected zone. ENGOs, doubting their sincerity, responded by publishing opinion pieces. In March 2016, the Guangzhou city government announced a plan for water treatment specifically for this local river. However, ENGOs still demanded that the protected zone "not be reduced even one inch."

During the second phase of the protection zone adjustment, the city Bureau of Environmental Protection followed official administrative procedures to organize a public hearing. In June 2016, one month before the hearing, the bureau revealed that the protection zone would remain but be significantly reduced in size. When preparing for the hearing, ENGOs collected and sent thousands of people's messages to the mayor and continued to publish opinion articles, arguing for keeping the original protection zone.

In October, the provincial government made the final decision to reduce the official protection zone but promised that the original area would be maintained as a "quasi-protection" zone, a status that still prohibits polluting industrial projects. In this case of protracted and collective advocacy, ENGOs were unsuccessful in their fight to preserve the original protection zone in its entirety, but the city government also made concessions. As one ENGO leader commented: "The next time they plan to develop the economy in a fashion that's unfriendly to the environment, they'll know these ENGOs are going to oppose them and form obstacles."

Discussion and Conclusion

The ENGOs in our study have cooperated with the state in ways that increase transparency and bring residents' voices into policy making, improving government performance and perhaps helping the state maintain social stability (Teets 2014). However, as exemplified in the case of the Liuxi River above, most of these ENGOs are not limited to playing the role of service providers or policy participants assigned to them by the government. They also engage in critical activities to change government actions.

It can be argued, of course, that the Chinese state permits ENGOs to serve as outlets for discontent so that critical voices can be more easily contained. In this line of thinking, inviting civil society into the policy making process can be a way to co-opt these groups. This may contain some truth, but it overemphasizes the omnipotence of the local state while overlooking subtle dynamics in civil society's relations with the state. Our findings suggest that the consultative authoritarianism model (Teets 2014) is more of an ideal the authoritarian state wishes to realize than a reflection of the actual dynamics between ENGOs and the government. Once the state opens up channels of communication with ENGOs, ENGOs use these channels in ways not fully under the control of the state. While their actions demonstrate the importance of the agency of civil society, in interviews most ENGOs went out of their way to emphasize that their major goal is environmental protection. Some also argued that ENGOs should "balance" the government and "provide a societal perspective to policies" or that "policies have to be deliberated." One group was bolder, asserting that its proper role is to "monitor the government, otherwise government power is boundless." These ideas support the argument that ENGOs are promoting policy deliberation with the government as an end in itself (Han 2014).

Nevertheless, ENGO advocacy in China at present is cautious, piecemeal, and limited to environmental governance issues. Groups are careful to avoid fundamental political issues, and the state remains both the agenda setter and final decision maker. Moreover, few groups exclusively work on policy advocacy, and most are engaging—at times—in mutually beneficial cooperation with the government. As one group's leader described his strategy about publishing commentaries in newspapers: "I think a line does exist. Some articles cannot get published, but I keep writing so that I know where the bottom line is. The next time I try to touch that bottom line . . . if it gets published, I think I can go on writing, pushing that line a little further."

Notes

This chapter is adapted in part from "Advocacy in an Authoritarian State: How Grassroots Environmental NGOs Influence Local Governments in China," *China Journal* 79 (January 2018).

PART V

OUTCOMES

15

The Eco-developmental State and the Environmental Kuznets Curve

STEVAN HARRELL

IN THE 1960S JAPAN WAS KNOWN AS THE "TOXIC ARCHIPELAGO." Not only was the air in the big cities unbreathable, toxic chemicals in the environment sickened thousands and became infamous around the world. Now its air is clean by world standards, rivers flow clear, forested area has increased, and citizens are environmentally conscious. Similarly, in my diary from 1991, I refer to Taiwan as "garbage island"—the air was terrible, and foods were pesticide-laden. Yet nowadays the streets are clean, the air is cleaner, and the environmental movement is active everywhere and is a major factor in national and local politics. Korea at the same time experienced severe pollution and environmental diseases from its rapid development of heavy industry, but its environment is much cleaner now.

Today, however, it is still easy to see China as a billion-hectare environmental disaster. Every day, media—from WeChat groups to censored documentaries to state newspapers to foreigners' blogs—pour forth an unremitting litany of "air-pocalypses," oily rivers, algal blooms, cadmium-laden soils, desertification, landslides, mountains of waste, pika-riddled grasslands, disappearing aquatic creatures, and more. One wonders at times how anyone could live there at all. At the same time, China is a world leader in developing and installing renewable energy, has some of the world's most progressive environmental laws, and trumpets such slogans such as "ecological civilization." Villagers stage successful protests against toxic factories; authorities shut down steel mills and coal-burning power stations. There are credible reports that air quality has seen its worst days and is improving around the country.

The trajectories illustrated in this book, from severely polluted and degraded environments to various degrees of improvement, suggest that the environment in East Asian countries might follow a pattern of getting worse and then getting better as processes of economic growth eventually lead to the emergence of the eco-developmental state.

The Environmental Kuznets Curve

In 1993 a group of economists working for the World Employment Programme proposed an analytical device called the Environmental Kuznets Curve (Grossman and Krueger 1994; Panayotou 1993).[1] It posited a universal progression of economic growth and development, starting with unregulated industrialization and resource extraction, causing environmental degradation: pollution increases, landscapes are degraded, resources are depleted, environmental diseases increase. But as the economy continues to grow, it becomes more service-oriented, and the populace begins to value environmental quality and health along with increased production, whereupon a combination of regulation and market incentives leads to remediation of environmental damage and general improvement in environmental quality (figure 15.1). The evolution of a developmental state into an eco-developmental state is part of this upward turn in environmental quality (Kaika and Zervas 2013; Dinda 2004).

The Environmental Kuznets Curve (EKC) is not without its problems (Stern 2004). First, it assumes a universal trajectory of economic growth, a materialist teleology pointing toward the current condition of the wealthy countries of Western Europe and North America. Second, it assumes that prosperity can be measured by a linear economic metric, namely gross domestic product, per capita income, or a near equivalent. Third and most disturbingly, if it is adopted as a basis for policy, the EKC presents a moral hazard. Because, according to the EKC model, post-industrial or high-tech economic growth invariably happens and inevitably leads to environmental remediation, economies can pollute first and grow their way out of pollution later, and the EKC becomes a "license to pollute."

Despite these problems, environmental degradation at present is fastest in late-industrializing countries, particularly those that are dependent

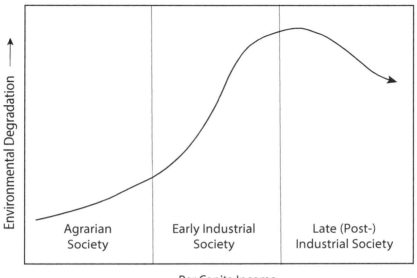

Environmental Degradation →

Per Capita Income

| Agrarian Society | Early Industrial Society | Late (Post-) Industrial Society |

FIGURE 15.1   The Environmental Kuznets Curve. (Adapted from Kaika and Zervas 2013, 1394)

on neocolonial resource extraction (Costantini and Monni 2007), and environmental remediation is happening in many of the wealthiest countries. A crude measure like the Environmental Performance Index (EPI), compiled by the Yale School of Forestry and Environmental Sciences (Yale Center 2018), shows this, scoring 180 countries from 0 to 100 on a series of environmental indicators: air quality, water and sanitation, water resources, health impacts, forests, agriculture, fisheries, energy and climate, and biodiversity. On this index in 2017, Japan ranked 20th, Taiwan 23rd, Korea 60th, and China 120th. Plotting these countries' EPI against GDP per capita shows that wealthier countries score higher (figure 15.2). That Japan's EPI is slightly higher than Taiwan's is perhaps explained by the earlier timing of Japan's economic growth.

If we look at individual aspects of the environment, however, the picture is more complex. Sectoral change, shifting state priorities, and environmentalist action have led to material improvements in many but not all aspects of the environment in many countries. As David Stern, Michael S. Common, and Edward B. Barbier (1996) state, "A more fruitful

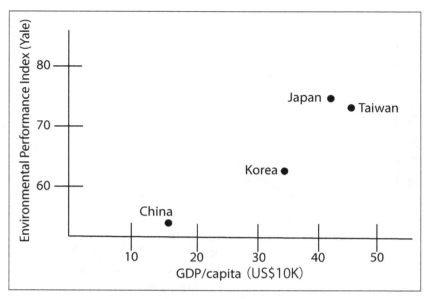

FIGURE 15.2   Environmental Performance Index 2018 and per capita 2017 GDP for four East Asian countries. (World Bank 2019 and CIA n.d., tabulated at Wikipedia 2019)

approach to the analysis of the relationship between economic growth and environmental impact would be the examination of the historical experience of individual countries, using econometric and also qualitative historical analysis" (1159).

This approach leads to several questions about not just the past but also the present and future of East Asian environmental degradation. First, what are the proximate causes of initial degradation and later remediation? Second, what are the particular biophysical, political, economic, or cultural changes that bring about environmental change when an economy moves from preindustrial through industrial to "postindustrial" phases? Finally, what particular types of environmental degradation and remediation follow this curvilinear pattern? Figure 15.3 shows the logic behind this approach to the EKC by superimposing certain specific drivers of environmental change.

- Increasing energy use drives environmental degradation in early stages, and increasing energy efficiency enables environmental remediation in later stages. The degree of sensitivity to energy use is a factor in whether any form of degradation is likely to be remediable in the postindustrial transition. However, gains in energy efficiency must be great enough to offset increases in energy use promoted by increased consumption.

- State efforts to mobilize for remediation are related to three kinds of factors:

  —Availability of remediation technology and cost-benefit balance of installing it. For example, replacing fossil-fuel energy with renewables was very costly until relatively efficient forms of wind and solar power generation were developed.

  —Political costs or benefits of implementing policies of remediation. Environmental problems that are linked to industries with economic growth potential are more likely to be addressed by the government.

  —The degree of state influence over the sources of pollution. For example, it is easier for governments to mandate pollution reduction efforts at power plants that they control than to require millions of new drivers to take their cars off the road.

- In both democratic and authoritarian countries, citizen pressure and popular activism play important roles in environmental remediation. Individuals and communities can modify their own consumption patterns. Consumer activism can pressure corporations to curb pollution. Citizen activism can pressure governments to give environmental remediation higher priority in policy making. Activism is particularly important when undertaken by politically influential groups. If the state/party views the activism as a political threat, it is more likely to take action to address the environmental problem. Protests by urban elites usually worry rulers more than do marginalized indigenous people's protests in the hinterland.

- High-income countries are often able to export their environmental problems to lower-income countries, where the environment is not a high citizen priority and the state prioritizes economic development and is thus unable or unwilling to mobilize for environmental improvement (Stern, Common, and Barbier 1996: 1155–56). The downward turn of the EKC in wealthier countries can exacerbate the upward turn in poorer countries or regions, particularly those dependent on resource extraction, and thus may not be sufficient to turn back environmental degradation on a global scale (Jha and Murthy 2003).

- Some environmental problems by their nature take longer to correct than others; each has a "biophysical remediation time scale," ranging from days to geologic epochs. Air pollution, for example, blows away with the next big storm, and if we don't pump the pollutants back into the air, the air won't be polluted. At the other end of the scale, species extinction is permanent.

All of these factors affect the remediability of specific environmental problems, as summarized in table 15.1.

The history of specific environmental problems in Japan, Taiwan, China, and the Republic of Korea (hereafter, Korea) reflects both their remediation time scale and their susceptibility to the drivers shown in figure 15.3, and thus their relative remediability. Certain aspects of the previously degraded environment have already improved considerably in Japan, Taiwan, and Korea as economic growth has brought sectoral shifts,

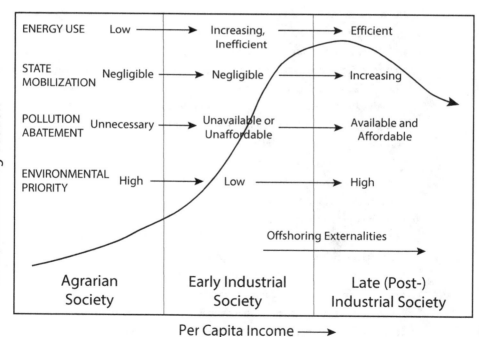

FIGURE 15.3   Drivers of environmental improvement in the transition to the eco-developmental state. (Adapted and expanded from Kaika and Zervas 2013, 1394)

Table 15.1   *Environmental problems and aspects of their remediability*

ENVIRONMENTAL PROBLEM	BIOPHYSICAL REMEDIATION TIME SCALE	ENERGY RELATED?	COST OF REMEDIATION	STATE WILLINGNESS TO MOBILIZE?	POPULAR PRESSURE?	EXPORTABLE?
Air pollution	*Days*	*Yes*	*Inexpensive*	*Yes*	*Extreme*	*Partially*
Water pollution	Months–decades	Somewhat	Moderate	Yes	Strong	Partially
Environmental health	Decades	Somewhat	Moderate	Yes	Strong	Partially
Deforestation	*Decades–centuries*	*Tangential*	*Inexpensive*	*Yes*	*Weak*	*Yes*
Soil contamination	*Decades–centuries, depending on cost*	*Tangential*	*Very expensive*	*Weak*	*Strong*	*Partially*
Soil transport (erosion)	Centuries	Tangential	Inexpensive	Weak	Weak	Partially
Groundwater depletion	Centuries–millennia	Somewhat	Inexpensive	Yes	Weak or none	No
Climate change	Millennia	Yes	Expensive	Variable	Weak	No
Biodiversity loss	Geologic epochs	No	Expensive	Weak	Weak	Partially

Note: Problems analyzed in detail in this chapter are shown in *italics*.

new energy sources, and technological capabilities, along with new political and community pressures, while other elements of the environment have not improved. These changes have also very recently begun to happen in China. The pattern of improvement and non-improvement is very different from the pattern of overall improvement that the EKC predicts; this is partly due to the evolution of the developmental state into an eco-developmental one that considers environmental sustainability along with growth, especially in areas that directly affect human health and can enhance economic growth.

The history of three representative environmental problems—air pollution, deforestation, and soil contamination—in Japan, Korea, Taiwan, and China, shows the utility of this analysis of remediability.

Air Pollution: Public Pressure Forces Change

Air pollution[2] is the most remediable of the environmental problems listed in table 15.1, and thus most liable to follow the EKC trajectory. It is highly salient politically and has a short remediation time, so political gains from addressing the problem can be reaped quickly. Air pollution negatively effects the economy through rising healthcare costs, lost crops, and lost workdays, while renewable energy and efficiency-related technologies offer the potential for economic growth. Finally, many of the greatest polluters are controlled by the government or industry, and affordable technical solutions are available, making it easier for industry and the government to work together.

In the 1960s the air in Japanese cities was terrible—comparable to the early 2020s air quality in Beijing, Taiyuan, Shenyang, Lanzhou, and other highly polluted cities in China. Today, however, Japan's air quality is much improved. As late as 1984, only 50.1% of general air monitoring stations and only 16.7% of motor vehicle exhaust monitoring stations nationwide met Japan's Ministry of the Environment criteria for total suspended particulate (TSP), but since then, compliance rates have improved almost yearly, and by 2013, 97.3% of the general monitoring stations and 94.7% of the roadside exhaust monitoring stations met the MOE criteria; and average levels of TSP were less than a third of those in 1977 (MOE Japan 2015, 308). However, the number of days per year on which at least one prefecture reported a warning for high ozone levels hardly decreased at all between 1972 and 2012 (ibid., 319).

At two monitoring stations in Tokyo, from 1970 to the 2010s, there has been a sharp decline in maximum concentrations of carbon monoxide, sulfur dioxide, and total suspended particulate, and $PM_{2.5}$ has similarly decreased since measurements began in 2000. Oxides of nitrogen, however, have shown a more modest decline, and there has been no significant trend since 1980 for oxidants including ozone, the most important in air pollution (California Air Resources Board 2005). This general improvement coincides with a long series of increasingly stringent air pollution standards and laws (Wakamatsu, Morikawa, and Ito 2013). Declines in nitrogen dioxide are associated with a series of regulations on factory soot and smoke, and on exhaust from gasoline and diesel vehicles. Declines in sulfur dioxide are associated with explicit regulations concerning sulfur content of diesel oil.

Air pollution trends are similar in Taiwan and Korea, if over a shorter period. In the central Taiwan cities of Taichung, Chiayi, and Tainan, levels of sulfur dioxide, oxides of nitrogen, and suspended particulate fell by over half from 1996 to 2005 (Kuo et al. 2009). In Taipei and Kaohsiung, pollutant values in November, during the dry season, almost all declined drastically from 1990 to 2019. Average values of PM_{10} declined from 72 and 129 to 32 and 71 micrograms per cubic meter ($\mu g/m^3$). Sulfur dioxide declined from 31.1 and 27.6 parts per billion (ppb) in 1990 to 2.2 and 2.4 ppb in 2019; and oxides of nitrogen from 86 and 67 ppb in 1990 to 21 and 19 ppb in 2019 (EPA Taiwan n.d.). Kuo et al. (2009, 3933) attribute this decline to laws limiting industrial and vehicle emissions, restricting the sulfur content of fuels, and taxing industrial emissions. As in Japan, however, ozone concentrations have increased if anything over the same twenty-nine-year period; levels in Taipei and Kaohsiung were 13 and 23 ppb in 1990 and 31.1 and 37.0 2019, and over 90% of unhealthy Air Quality Index readings nationwide in 2019 were due to ozone, and the rest to PM_{10} or $PM_{2.5}$ (EPA Taiwan 2019b, 3:6).

The recent history of air pollution in Korea varies from site to site and is thus less supportive of the EKC model but does not directly contradict it. Nationally, carbon monoxide declined from 2000 to 2013, nitrogen dioxide and PM_{10} stayed the same, and ozone rose slightly (Ray and Kim

2014). Lead pollution has declined greatly, from .09µg/m³ to only .04 in 2013 (MOE ROK 2014, 14). In the four largest cities—Seoul, Busan, Taegu, and Kwangju—sulfur dioxide levels have not changed appreciably (ibid., 15), while nitrogen dioxide levels have declined in Seoul and Busan, and Taegu and Kwangju have shown no clear trend (ibid., 16). Particulate matter declined in Seoul, Busan, and Taegu, while in Kwangju it rose dramatically between 2003 and 2006 but has declined since then (ibid., 17). Korea's trajectory may reflect the later emergence of its environmental movements in general as compared to Taiwan (Liu 2016). As in Japan and Taiwan, ozone in Korea has shown no clear trend (MOE ROK 2014, 18).

In sum, the air has gotten steadily better in Japan since the 1960s and has improved in Taiwan and Korea at least since the turn of the millennium. This improvement appears to be due to increasingly stringent regulations and in some cases, to economic incentives including Pigovian taxes on polluters. Environmental activism has also played a role (Chiu, chapter 11). But none of the earlier-industrializing Asian countries have managed to do much about ozone pollution, which comes primarily from motor vehicle exhaust, a dispersed pollution source that governments have difficulty controlling except through incentives to decrease driving or encourage switching to electric vehicles, something that is just beginning to take place.

China is probably better known for air pollution than for any other environmental problem, and progress against it is recent and tentative (J.P. 2018). At the same time, there is hope that China may follow the EKC trajectories of its East Asian neighbors, as several posited drivers of the EKC may be moving China in the right direction. As in the other countries, public pressure on local and national authorities to do something may be very important. For example, after the US Embassy in Beijing began posting hourly readings of particulate matter levels in 2008 (Roberts 2015), the Beijing municipal government first replied by greenwashing—posting alternative readings from a site, still within Beijing's boundaries, that had lower pollution levels. But, with the advent of smartphone apps like AQI (air quality index) and BlueSky, average citizens now have easy access to both sets of readings, providing scientific proof of particulate levels that cannot be greenwashed by the Chinese government. Investigative journalist Chai Jing's 2015 documentary

"Under the Dome" (Qiongding zhi xia) was viewed over two hundred million times before it was officially banned (Gardner 2015), and probably at least as many times afterward. There is now open public discussion of air pollution, putting pressure on governments at all levels to take concrete measures (Schmitt 2016).

State mobilization to remediate air pollution came late in China, but since the 2008 Olympics, state efforts have been broad and concerted, focused on the transition toward cleaner forms of energy and more efficient energy use (Lewis, chapter 2). One concrete measure (pun intended) is the forced shutdown of cement plants that are over capacity, along with inefficient steel mills and outdated coal-fired power plants in Beijing, Tianjin, and Hebei (Burns 2017; Mathews and Tan 2016; Winters 2016). China now leads the world by wide margins in installed capacity of low-pollution hydroelectric, wind, and photovoltaic power generation (IEA 2019, 21, 23, 25). Many coal-fired plants that were planned in 2014 and 2015 were either never built or never started up, and China's coal consumption dropped for three years after a historic high in 2013, though it leveled off in 2017 and 2018 (Qi et al. 2016; Enerdata 2019b). However, plans now being considered for new coal-fired generating plants have raised alarms that coal consumption may rise again in the 2020s (Walsh 2019).

Measures to limit traffic congestion and vehicle-generated pollution are also important. Leaded gasoline was phased out in 1999, and progressively tighter limits on sulfur emissions from gasoline and diesel fuels were implemented starting in 2002. In 2008, cities began to restrict vehicles with certain license plate numbers from driving on certain days. Emissions-controls and fuel-consumption standards were similarly tightened for all classes of vehicles over the same time period (Transport Policy 2018). The smoke-spewing Dongfeng and Jiefang brand diesel stake trucks of yore have mostly been replaced, even in rural areas, by newer and cleaner models. Rapid-transit systems have been built in almost all of China's large cities, beginning with Beijing in 1991; it is not yet clear whether the recent explosive growth of bike-share programs and bike lanes actually represents a partial return to the pedal-powered urban society that flourished in the time of state socialism (Wang 2018).

However, short-term solutions that mitigate visible air pollution may be exacerbating long-term environmental problems. Hydroelectric power is a favorite of developmental states, and has expanded rapidly, enabling China to replace a lot of coal power (Tilt 2015, 30). Many in the Chinese hydroelectric industry passionately defend their dams, pointing out that every kilowatt hour generated in a hydro plant replaces both air pollution and greenhouse gas emissions from fossil fuel-powered plants. At the same time, dams create a diversity of additional environmental problems, including submersion of agricultural lands (and the forced migration of their inhabitants), polluted water and accompanying diseases, microclimate changes, biodiversity loss (*China Green News* 2011), small earthquakes (Huang Rong et al. 2018), and massive accumulation of trash on the surface of reservoirs (Cao and Wang 2010; Nelson 2014).

Coal gasification facilities built in the extensive coal fields of Inner Mongolia and Shanxi bring another tradeoff. Much of the coal mined in those basins goes to fuel power plants in the heavily populated and polluted Beijing-Tianjin-Hebei region. Replacing or converting those power plants to burn much cleaner and more efficient coal gas reduces visible air pollution in Beijing, Tianjin, and the many large cities in Hebei, but it generates more greenhouse gas, exacerbating the much less visible and longer-term problem of climate change (Ding et al. 2013).

As in the other East Asian countries, the problem of ozone, mainly from motor vehicle exhaust, will take longer to solve. Ozone concentrations are rising in the three most densely populated regions of the North China Plain, the Yangtze Delta, and the Pearl River Delta, exceeding maximum levels in the Los Angeles Basin over the same period by a factor of two to three (Wang et al. 2017, 1585–87).

China's air crisis has thus stimulated a combination of public pressure, regulatory tightening, and infrastructural construction, all designed to alleviate the problems of air pollution. Given that reductions in air pollution in Japan, Taiwan, and Korea have happened as their economies have made structural changes similar to those now happening in China, recent slight improvements (Greenpeace 2018) may be harbingers of a fairly quick improvement in many aspects of China's air quality, and in twenty years people may look back upon China's air-pocalypses of the early twenty-first century as a regrettable but perhaps unavoidable historical interval, just as the EKC would predict.

Deforestation and Reforestation: A Shift Earlier than Predicted

East Asia's forests recovered sooner than the EKC would predict from both long-term deforestation due to population growth and shorter-term forest losses due to the expansion of agriculture and industry (figure 15.4). Reforestation did not wait for the predicted "turning point" from an industrial to a service-oriented economy (see figures 15.1 and 15.3). Rather, as the eco-developmental state model would predict, the important drivers of reforestation have primarily been economic shifts in the energy and construction industries, which made cutting down trees less economically profitable; the political and economic costs of the negative consequences of deforestation, such as increasing landslides and other disasters; and the fairly high concentration of forestry in the state sector, allowing state policy to effectively dictate quick reforestation.

As soon as the major fuel source shifted from forest biomass to fossil fuels, and as soon as agricultural yields increased somewhat from pre-industrial levels, there was less incentive to cut down forests for reasons other than lumber and pulp (Mather 1992). Thus, cutting down trees began to contribute less to economic growth than letting them stand, or even replanting them. Additionally, since forests have been primarily state-owned in all four countries, it was easy for the entire industry to adjust once the financial incentives shifted. Finally, although public pressure to remediate deforestation is typically light, governments elsewhere, including nineteenth century German states, postrevolutionary France, and even the famously prodigal United States have felt the imperative to restore their forests well before they have felt the imperative to clean their air (Hölzl 2010; Wulf, Sommer, and Schmidt 2010; Mather 1992, 369; Pinchot 2017 [1906]).

Japan, Taiwan, and Korea all show a similar pattern of deforestation and reforestation. Japan's forests were severely cut during the militarist era and immediately after World War II, resulting in landslides, siltation, and downstream floods, as well as a nearly complete depletion of the nation's timber supplies (Knight 1995: 715). In response, the postwar government began a national reforestation program, highlighted by the emperor's tree-planting visits to a different forested prefecture each year (Knight 1995; Ouchi 1987). As a result, during the forty postwar years, at

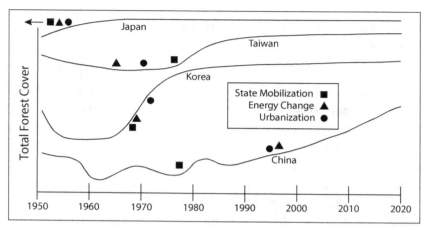

FIGURE 15.4   Environmental Kuznets Curve trajectories for forest cover in four East Asian countries, showing posited drivers of reforestation. Shapes are conceptual, not to scale.

least 10 million hectares (25 million acres), or over 25% of the entire country, were reforested (ibid.), and the current 68% forest cover rate has remained stable for the past several decades.

In Taiwan, reforestation has coincided with its "economic miracle" and eventual democratization. The island has never been severely deforested, but forest cover decreased from 54.1% in 1967 to 50.8% in 1976, before recovering to 58.5% in 1992 and 60.9% in 2012, including an increase in "natural forest" (*tianran lin*) from about 1.35 million hectares (3.4 million acres) in 1974 to about 1.7 million hectares (4.25 million acres) in 2009 (Lin Wu Ju 2017). Taiwan has always had a market economy, but forests have been under state control, so state agencies have controlled reforestation. Coupled with sufficient food and thus no pressure to cut forests for agriculture, there were few obstacles, even before post-industrialization, to state-led reforestation in Taiwan.

Korea also shows that state-led programs can bring about reforestation under suitable economic circumstances. The peninsula was severely deforested during the latter part of the Japanese colonial occupation (after 1930) and during the Korean War in 1950–53, but now 61% of the country is forested. Much of this happened under authoritarian rule, particularly as part of dictator Park Chung-hee's New Village Campaign, or Saemaul Undong (Kim, chapter 9), starting in 1972. Villagers all over the country were required to convert their housing from traditional wooden structures to "modern" concrete and glass buildings, replace fuelwood with coal, petroleum, and natural gas (Kim 2015, 126; Kim and Kim 2005), and reforest the nonagricultural lands around their villages; in total they reforested over 500,000 hectares (1.25 million acres) between 1962 and 1987 (ibid., 127–28; Kim, chapter 9). In addition, because the campaign coincided with rapid industrialization, population distribution changed from 64.2% rural in 1960 to 86.4% urban in 1995 (Kim Yong-woong 1999, 44–45), reinforcing the move away from wood products and the commitment to regrow force-planted forests.[3]

As in other East Asian countries, Korea's reforestation occurred well before the EKC model would predict, but it is compatible with the logic of the evolution of the eco-developmental state. As the economic benefits of cutting down forests were reduced in favor of other energy sources and building materials, reforestation was no obstacle to economic growth, and it was easy for the government to promote reforestation and for the building industry to shift away from forest products. The story of Korea's early and rapid reforestation is not entirely a happy one, however. As with air pollution mitigation in China, reforestation in Korea was one side of an environmental tradeoff. Both the New Villages and the cities to which former peasants moved were built of energy-intensive concrete, steel, and glass. Because Korea has few energy sources of its own, this along with industrialization contributed to making more than 90% of Korea's energy imported (Kim 2015, 130), making Korea a major source of greenhouse gas emissions, as are Japan and Taiwan for the same reasons.

China was already heavily deforested at the founding of the PRC—a survey conducted by the Nationalist Party (Guomindang) in 1936–37 showed only 11%–12% forest cover. In the early years of the People's Republic, the rapid increase of cultivated area, along with the exploitation of timber for construction, may have reduced the forest coverage to as low as 8% (table 15.2).

After bottoming out in the 1960s, China's forest area has been increasing since, albeit with a noticeable downturn from the mid-1970s to the early 1980s, when state forestry bureaus were changed into state-owned forestry enterprises that could make quick money by cutting wood for the construction boom that was part of the rapid economic expansion of the time (Song et al. 1997; Albers, Rozelle, and Li 1998). Thus in China as

Table 15.2   Forested area and standing biomass in China, 1949–2018

YEAR	FORESTED AREA (MILLION HECTARES)	SHARE OF TOTAL AREA (%)	CHANGE FROM PREVIOUS PERIOD (%)	STANDING BIOMASS (BILLION M³)	CHANGE FROM PREVIOUS PERIOD (%)
1949	109.01	11			
1962	80–113	8–12	−27 to +4		
1973–1976	121.86	12	+8 to +52	8.66	
1977–1981	115.28	12	−5	9.03	+4
1984–1988	124.65	13	+8	9.14	+1
1989–1993	133.70	14	+7	10.14	+11
1994–1998	158.94	16	+19	11.27	+11
1999–2003	174.91	18	+10	12.46	+11
2004–2008	195.45	20	+12	13.72	+10
2009–2013	208	21.63	+11	15.31	+11
2014–2018	220	22.96	+10.6	17.56	+15

Source: Adapted and expanded from Robbins and Harrell 2014, 384.
Notes: Data before the 1970s are unreliable and controversial. Data from 1973 onward are based on National Forest Inventories and can be assumed to be more reliable. See He et al. 2008; Démurger, Hou, and Yang 2007; Dai et al. 2011; He et al. 2011; Ministry of Forestry 2014, 2019. The large increase between the fourth and fifth inventories (1989–93 and 1994–98) partly reflects a change in the definition of forested area from a minimum of 30% to 20% canopy cover.

elsewhere, the transition to reforestation predates the timing predicted by the classical EKC, which ties environmental remediation efforts to a shift to a postindustrial economy. But the obvious environmental harm done by previous agricultural expansion, along with state control of forestry, made it relatively easy for government policy to shift quickly to address deforestation even before the turn to post-industry.

China's reforestation is not, however, focused primarily on improving the forest ecosystem. Replanted forests have generally been monocultures, less biodiverse than natural second-growth (let alone old-growth) forests; even orchards are included in figures for forest coverage in China.[4]

East Asian reforestation was also facilitated by the ability to outsource wood production. Japan is now one of the world's largest importers of wood (Chang and Gaston 2016), and Korea also imports large amounts of logs, thus exporting deforestation to other countries (MOE ROK 2014, 397). China too has left itself short of wood: the demands of China's construction and wood-product industries have made it the world's largest importer of logs, depleting forests in such far-flung countries as Malaysia, New Zealand, Papua New Guinea, and even Gabon, but most of all, in Siberia (Robbins and Harrell 2014, 396–98). All East Asian countries thus export their deforestation internationally, in the same way that Beijing, Tianjin, and Hebei export their air pollution to less-populated parts of the country. This reinforces the observation that the downward phase of the EKC in economically wealthy countries is partly dependent on poorer countries' EKCs continuing to climb.

Soil Contamination: Remediation Remains Difficult

Soil contamination, while arguably the most important ecologically of the three issues examined here, continues to present challenges to East Asian countries. Although the EKC model would suggest that this highly toxic problem, which does great harm to human health, should be one of the first to improve with the overall economy, that is not what we find in East Asia.

Unlike air pollution and deforestation, soil contamination has a long biophysical remediation time; it is technically difficult and costly to remediate; it is caused by multiple sources of pollution, thus challenging state and industry capacity to address the problem; and it arouses little public pressure on anything but a local scale. China's soil contamination problems are severe and are likely to remain so for a long time, and the other East Asian countries have not dealt with the problem particularly well either.

A multiyear, nationwide survey of over sixty thousand sites in China examined soil contamination by heavy metals (contamination by organic hydrocarbons from agricultural pesticides exists but is relatively minor). The survey report stated that about 8 million hectares (20 million acres), or 6% of China's agricultural land, should not be used for growing food crops at all, and that a total of 22 million hectares (55 million acres), or 17% of the China's total, was "severely polluted" (MEP and MLR 2014).

These results are frightening. Cadmium is particularly concerning, with 7% of the samples tested exceeding the national standard. On top of this, the acidity of much of China's rice-growing soil, combined with the high cadmium uptake of common southern Chinese rice varieties, means that the percentage of rice containing unacceptably high levels of cadmium is even higher than the percentage of soil containing the element. Similar problems exist with arsenic and lead, though to a lesser degree (Zhao et al. 2014). Industry and mining continue to deposit heavy metals through airborne and waterborne routes. Without remediation, levels of soil pollution are destined to remain high and probably rise.

Soil contamination is not permanent. Crops take up heavy metals in soils; if deposition stops, each year's crop will take up a small percentage of the contaminants, and eventually the metals will be removed. There is, however, a tradeoff; crops that take up heavy metals are dangers to public health. And, if deposition continues at present levels, uptake will never catch up. Many measures can slow deposition, including controls on industrial and mining sources and avoiding fertilizers that contain metals, such as some animal manures. But unless and until deposition stops altogether, there have to be ways to take contaminants out of the soil. Unfortunately, each of these involves a tradeoff of its own. Liming the soil increases the pH, which decreases the uptake of cadmium by rice plants, but it may increase the uptake of arsenic and lead; keeping fields flooded for greater-than-customary portions of the rice-growing cycle also increases the pH but puts extra stress on often-precarious irrigation supplies in dry years or seasons; planting varieties that take up less of the undesirable contaminant has fewer side effects, but leaves the soil unmitigated; bioremediation with nonfood crops that take up metals more quickly than rice takes agricultural land out of food production and may threaten food security, especially if crop yields in unmitigated areas are low. Measures often used in nonagricultural areas, such as capping with uncontaminated soil, are inapplicable for farmland, and all of the measures are very costly when applied on a large scale (ibid.).

Experiences of other East Asian countries might serve as rough forecasts for alleviating soil contamination in China. In Japan, the *itai-itai* (ow ow!) disease broke out in the 1910s in Toyama Prefecture due to cadmium deposition by irrigation water contaminated by tailings from a nearby zinc mine. Pregnant women and lactating mothers in particular suffered severe joint and bone pain. Several other parts of the country also reported outbreaks of the disease. In the postwar period, changes in mining technology actually increased cadmium deposition and raised the incidence of the disease. After a lawsuit found the mining company liable for medical expenses and environmental mitigation, discharge of cadmium was severely reduced, and about 1,000 hectares (2,500 acres) of farmland was mitigated by capping the soil. The cost of the soil mitigation (which was only a fraction of the total cost of pollution mitigation) was close to ¥45 billion—almost half a billion dollars (Yoshida, Hata, and Tonegawa 1999).

The 7% of China's farmland that exceeds the cadmium standard amounts to about 9 million hectares (22.5 million acres). Even if China could mitigate only the "moderately" and "severely" contaminated lands, about 1% of total farmland, or around 1.3 million hectares (3.25 million acres), at one-tenth of the cost per acre incurred by Japan, it would still cost around US$43 billion; if the cost per acre rose to half of Japan's, the cost would rise to US$200 billion, just for the areas most severely affected by cadmium, not including areas affected by other soil contaminants.

As in Japan, Taiwan's efforts, though successful, have been very small scale. In 2002 the government established the Soil and Groundwater Pollution Governing Board, which between 2003 and 2010, supervised the cleanup of sites in every agricultural county; after ten years of effort, they had remediated a total of 466 hectares (1,165 acres) of farmland, much of it contaminated by relatively low toxicity copper and nickel, using inexpensive soil dilution methods; more expensive methods were used for areas contaminated by cadmium, lead, and mercury (EPA Taiwan 2016).

Concern with soil contamination is also relatively new in Korea. Korea established its first law on soil and groundwater contamination in 1995, and in 2011, the government completed a study of 2,470 sites spread across the country, finding 41 sites that exceeded the "worrisome standard," among which 12 were judged to require immediate remediation. Plans for remediation have focused on neighborhoods near chemical plants and petroleum facilities (MOE ROK 2012, 2017a). Early surveys also found contamination near abandoned metal and coal mines, but comprehensive surveys were not planned to be completed until 2023 (MOE ROK 2017b). Korea is, in other words, still in the early stages of what promises to be a long and expensive effort toward mitigating soil contamination.

Although the EKC would predict that soil contamination would be an environmental problem quickly remediated—it is highly toxic to human health, is typically one of the first problems to be the subject of citizen demands (albeit mostly local) for remediation, and diminishes with the general shift from industrial/agricultural economies to more service-oriented economies—this is not what we have seen in East Asia. The model of the eco-developmental state may help explain why remediation of soil contamination has been so slow. Aside from its long biophysical remediation time, sources of pollution are not consolidated, and agricultural land, though it is technically state-owned in China, is privately worked in all four countries, so state capacity to address the issue is low. Sources of contaminants and methods of mitigating each contaminant are also diverse, so a single technical/economic shift will not mitigate the entire problem. Political pressure remains localized, so state interest in addressing the issue is low.

The way forward for East Asia's contaminated farmlands, particularly the extensive contaminated areas in China, thus appears very unsure. Effective mitigation measures over millions of hectares seem prohibitively expensive, and at present deposition of heavy metals from industry and mining, via both air and water, continues apace. If curtailing deposition—which will require considerable investment in technological improvements in factories and mines—is successful, selective mitigation could gradually reduce the concentrations of dangerous heavy metals, but it will take a long time, and it really hasn't started yet.

One area of hope is the explosive growth of the niche organic food movement, which is active across East Asia and has been spurred in China by recent food safety issues (Abramson, chapter 10; Zhang Chun 2018). As with other environmental problems, when an industry, in this case agriculture, can benefit economically from more environmentally friendly policies, it becomes much easier for the eco-developmental state to facilitate that transition. Since the organic food market is growing rapidly (a fivefold increase since 2000) and China has been one of the fastest growing producers and consumers of organic food, it seems possible that greater attention to soil contamination issues may be just beyond the horizon, even if they are costly and take a long time to implement.

Conclusion: Eco-developmental State Transitions and the EKC

When we turn to other environmental problems listed in table 15.1, above, we can see patterns consistent with the factors that we have emphasized as important to the evolution of the eco-developmental state: biophysical remediation time scale, potential contributions to economic growth, availability and affordability of remediation technology, state capacity to address the issue (diversity of pollution sources and state influence over industry), and citizen political pressure. For example, water pollution, which has more varied sources, is not as visible as air pollution, is less susceptible to public pressure, and has a much more mixed record. Rivers in Japan have been cleaned up (MOE Japan 2015, 5.05), but Korea's have farther to go (MOE ROK 2014), and Taiwan's have a very mixed record (EPA Taiwan 2019a, 1:15). Lake and reservoir eutrophication has, if anything, increased in all three places (MOE ROK 2014; MOE Japan 2015; EPA Taiwan 2019a, 3:15). China's rivers are susceptible to campaign-style cleanups, as happened with the Huai in the late 1990s, but then often fall victim to neglect, and pollution returns (Economy 2004a).

For forms of environmental degradation whose biophysical remediation time is counted in centuries or longer, the EKC might apply in a very restricted sense: the degradation process may slow or stop with the transition to a service-oriented economy. But because it takes so long to remediate the damage already done, the other proposed drivers of the EKC are nearly irrelevant to understanding whether the status quo before industrialization can be restored in the near future. The lowering of the water table on the North China Plain is irremediable in the short run, since the rate of recharge is only about 10% of the rate of withdrawal over the last half of the twentieth century (Foster et al. 2003). More efficient methods of irrigation or alternative means of industrial cooling can reduce the rate at which water is withdrawn, but the biophysical time needed for remediation means that the water table will remain low for centuries. The EKC is doubly inappropriate for analysis of greenhouse gas emissions. Not only have emissions not yet peaked in any of the East

Asian countries but also, even if they do, the net effects of twentieth and twenty-first century GHG emissions are predicted to last for thousands of years (Hausfather 2010; IPCC 2013, 21–23).

It is thus perhaps no coincidence that the original formulators of the EKC applied their insight to deforestation and air pollution, which turn out to be the forms of environmental degradation most likely to follow the EKC pattern. Air pollution follows most closely, primarily because of citizen pressure, state mobilization, and energy change, all factors that accompany the evolution of the eco-developmental state. Deforestation follows the EKC pattern principally through energy change, state mobilization, and urbanization, all factors that arise in the course of state-led development before the economy post-industrializes or environmental problems become a major factor in state policy or a citizen concern. Hence reforestation starts earlier than the EKC logic would predict. It is quite possible that water pollution will follow a pattern similar to that of air pollution, given its relatively short biophysical remediation time scale and the fact that there are already several cases where citizen activism and state regulation have effectively mediated pollution in specific rivers. We have not, however, seen evidence of water pollution remediation in East Asia on a national scale. Still, the EKC pattern for air and forests is by no means insignificant and points again to the importance of the developmental state's increasing inclusion of environmental goals as economic development continues.

All the studies in this book, despite their varied scales, methods, and topics, illustrate clearly why we think the idea of the eco-developmental state is useful both in analyzing the recent past, present, and near future of the environment in East Asia and in pointing out the uses and limitations of the EKC model. On the one hand, the formulators of the EKC were right: as societies become more affluent, environmental problems become more important to their citizenry and hence to their governments. Less energy-intensive and less-polluting methods of resource extraction, manufacture, and transportation become possible as technology develops, and environmental mitigation becomes affordable. First citizens, and then governments, become aware that further economic growth speeds up when they use energy more efficiently and implement lower-energy processes. All this gives developmental states a reason to become eco-developmental. But "eco-developmental" is still a variety of "developmental"—a huge amount of political legitimacy continues to derive from economic growth. As a result, no state has foresworn economic growth as a goal, and herein lies the first problem with the EKC. States ordinarily attempt to mitigate environmental degradation only when it is so serious as to have widespread health effects or when it does not conflict with their persistent developmental goals.

The second problem with the EKC has little to do with the evolution of the state and more to do with the physical world. Some things once changed exhibit hysteresis—they are not easy to change back. It is possible to clean up smokestack emissions, regulate river discharges, and replant forests. But once the finless porpoise is gone, no amount of genetic engineering is going to bring it back. The same goes for the climate. We can eliminate fossil fuels altogether, and eventually the warming will level off. But once the planet is 2° or 3° or 4° Celsius warmer than its current state, only slow geological processes and changes in the earth's orbit are ever going to cool it again. Thus the EKC, formulated according to a sociopolitical and economic logic, cannot change the laws of nature, and this further limits its explanatory powers.

Nevertheless, many aspects of the environment do get better, as Japan, Korea, and Taiwan show, and as China looks to be turning a corner in air pollution, forest ecology, public awareness, and state policy. But they do not get better automatically, which is the third problem with the EKC. Moving a country from polluted to "clean" requires active participation from citizens, businesses, and governments. Citizens must demand better products and better policies. Businesses must innovate to find cleaner ways to produce their "dirty" products and build new markets for green products. Governments must adopt policies that help shift individual and corporate incentives in ways that encourage more environmentally responsible behavior and discourage actions that harm our ecosystems.

The cases in this book demonstrate that it is possible for concerned citizens to work at both grassroots and elite levels to affect positive changes to environmental policy, even under very difficult circumstances. They also illustrate how challenging those efforts are and how resourceful and creative the activists must be to succeed. Whether it is Japanese lawyers formulating new notions of rights (Avenell, chapter 5); Indigenous Taiwanese activists establishing forest patrols (Taiban et al., chapter 7), Chinese educators inducing parents to let their children play with bugs and climb trees (Efird, chapter 8), Korean engineers improving the efficiency of electrical grids (Lim, chapter 3) or any of the other case studies in this book, we see not only how activism of all kinds puts pressure on the state but also how the state's turn to eco-developmentalism creates further openings for innovation and change.

The concept of eco-developmentalism can help us understand the conditions under which activists' efforts are more likely to succeed, as well as the policy areas that governments are more likely to pursue. While East Asia's eco-developmentalism has emerged organically from its developmentalism, the basic principle—that environmental progress can contribute to economic development with government assistance—is applicable everywhere. Indeed, we see countless examples around the world of governments adopting policies to support better environmental outcomes and of companies developing environmental tech, organic food, and green finance as methods for generating profit even as they improve environmental outcomes.

Unfortunately, eco-developmentalism also helps us understand the policy areas where such win-win outcomes are impossible—where a company's gains can only happen on the backs of an indigenous population, or where a seemingly incessant need for more energy threatens the ecosystem of the planet. Despite the greening of its energy mix, China's overall greenhouse gas emissions continue to rise, and despite its government's green platforms, Taiwan's petrochemical industry districts continue to be toxic places (Chiu, chapter 11).

Whether they are focusing on the win-win areas in which economic and environmental progress can positively reinforce each other or seeking to mitigate the negative effects of exploitation in areas where economic and environmental goals are in opposition, the examples drawn from East Asia are useful. East Asia is at the forefront of challenges that communities around the world are facing, and the East Asian experience can help inform us not only about what is happening but also about what is possible. Activists, scholars, and policy makers can learn from counterparts in East Asia which of their efforts might be more successful, which allies they can cultivate, and which political avenues might be the most fruitful. Climate change is a global problem that can only be solved if people around the world move very quickly to implement as many successful solutions as they can. East Asia offers some suggestions and some hope. Now we all need to move a bit faster to implement them.

It is worth stating that the outlook is far from hopeless. If we do move faster, the combined effects of the rise of popular environmental consciousness and the eventual emergence of the "eco" in the eco-environmental state, which are described in this volume, allow us to hope that by 2040 or so, Beijing, Shanghai, and Chengdu will follow the examples of Tokyo and Taipei; that rivers and lakes all over the East Asian region will be cleaner; and that most of East Asia's forests will be flourishing and sustainable.

Notes

1   The name comes from the original (nonenvironmental) curve proposed by Simon Kuznets, who observed that economic inequality increases in the early stages of industrialization but then decreases again with further economic growth (Kuznets 1955). The fact that this pattern has not always held since Kuznets's time is not particularly important for the environmental equivalent.

2   "Air pollution" refers to the presence of pollutants in the troposphere, where they directly affect human and animal life and well-being, not to greenhouse gases, which have their effect in the stratosphere.

3   For a detailed analysis of the Saemaul Undong and its environmental effects, see Kim (chapter 9, this volume).

4   There are also problems with data quality: local officials have incentives to report progress on a wide variety of fronts, and they sometimes report successful reforestation when trees have been planted, even though they may not have actually survived the seedling stage (Trac et al. 2007).

REFERENCES

Abramson, Daniel Benjamin. 2016. "Periurbanization and the Politics of Development-as-City-Building in China." *Cities* 53 (April): 156–62.

———. 2019. "Ancient and Current Resilience in the Chengdu Plain: Agropolitan Development Re-'revisited.'" *Urban Studies* (June 20, online first).

Acton, James M. 2015. "A Realistic Approach to Solving Japan's Plutonium Problem." Carnegie Endowment for International Peace Policy Outlook, September 29. https://carnegieendowment.org/2015/09/29/realistic -approach-to-solving-japan-s-plutonium-problem-pub-61430.

Agrawal, Arun, and Maria Carmen Lemos. 2007. "A Greener Revolution in the Making? Environmental Governance in the 21st Century." *Environment: Science and Policy for Sustainable Development* 49 (5): 36–45.

Alagappa, Muthiah, ed. 2004. *Civil Society and Political Change in Asia: Expanding and Contracting Democratic Space*. Stanford, CA: Stanford University Press.

Albers, Heidi, Scott Rozelle, and Guo Li. 1998. "China's Forests under Economic Reform: Timber Supplies, Environmental Protection, and Rural Resource Access." *Contemporary Economic Policy* 16 (1): 22–33.

Alexander, Jeffrey C. 2010. *The Performance of Politics: Obama's Victory and the Democratic Struggle for Power*. New York: Oxford University Press.

Almeida, Paul, and Linda Brewster Stearns. 1998. "Political Opportunities and Local Grassroots Environmental Movements: The Case of Minamata." *Social Problems* 45 (1): 47–60.

Amagasa, Keisuke. 2000. *Idenshi Kumikae Shokuin (GMOs)*. Tokyo: Ryokufu Shuppan.

———. 2003. "Declaration of Victory: Citizens Succeed in Stopping Iwate Prefecture's GM Rice!" No! GMO Campaign Japan website, accessed 2003.

———. 2004. "Monsanto Suspends Development of Herbicide-Resistant GM Wheat: Japanese Consumer Petition Stops GM Wheat." No! GMO Campaign Japan website, accessed 2004.

———. 2005. "The Opposition Movement to GMOs in Japan." Paper presented at EU GMO Free International Conference, January 22–23, 2005, Berlin.

Amundsen, Ingri Kværne. 2011. "Chinese Tibet: Tibet Autonomous Region's Path to Welfare Colonialism." Master's thesis, University of Oslo.

Aoki, Masahiko. 2001. *Toward a Comparative Institutional Analysis*. Cambridge, MA: MIT Press.

Armitage, Derek. R. 2003. "Traditional Agroecological Knowledge, Adaptive Management and the Socio-politics of Conservation in Central Sulawesi, Indonesia." *Environmental Conservation* 30:79–90.

Arthur, W. Brian. 1990. "Positive Feedbacks in the Economy." *Scientific American* 262 (2): 92–99.

Asahi shinbun. 1970a. "Ningen ni 'kankyōke—Atarashii hōritsu kaishaku teian; Nichibenren ga kōgai shinpojiumu" (Environmental rights for people—Proposal for a new legal interpretation; Nichibenren's pollution symposium). September 22, evening edition.

———. 1970b. "'Kankyōken' hōtei e: Fukui Chisai—'Jigo hoshō dewa muimi' kōgyō chitai zōsei, jūmin ga torikeshi motomeru" ("Environmental rights" to the courtroom: The Fukui District Court—"Retrospective compensation meaningless" creation of industrial regions, residents seek revocation). September 26, morning edition.

Asian Development Bank. 2012. *The Saemaul Undong Movement in the Republic of Korea: Sharing Knowledge on Community-Driven Development*. Mandaluyong City, Philippines: Asian Development Bank.

Avenell, Simon. 2012. "Japan's Long Environmental Sixties and the Birth of a Green Leviathan." *Japanese Studies* 32 (3): 423–44.

———. 2013. "The Borderless Archipelago: Toward a Transnational History of Japanese Environmentalism." *Environment and History* 19:397–425.

Awaji, Takehisa. 1995. "Shizen hogo to kankyōken: Kankyōken e no tetsuzuki-teki apurōchi" (Nature preservation and environmental rights: An administrative approach to environmental rights). *Kankyō to kōgai* (Environment and pollution) 25 (2): 8–12.

Bebbington, Anthony. 2000. "Reencountering Development: Livelihood Transactions and Place Transformations in the Andes." *Annals of the Association of American Geographers* 90 (3): 495–520.

Becker, C. Dustin, and Kabita Ghimire. 2003. "Synergy between Traditional Ecological Knowledge and Conservation Science Supports Forest Preservation in Ecuador." *Conservation Ecology* 8 (1). http://www.consecol.org/vol8/iss1/art1/.

Becker, Jasper. 1998. *Hungry Ghosts: Mao's Secret Famine*. New York: Macmillan.

Beeson, Mark. 2004. "The Rise and Fall (?) of the Developmental State: The Vicissitudes and Implications of East Asian Interventionism." Western Australia University. http://rrojasdatabank.info/beeson04.pdf.

Bellini, Emiliano. 2019. "Global Cumulative PV Capacity Tops 480 GW, IRENA Says." *PV Magazine International*, April 2. https://www.pv-magazine.com/2019/04/02/global-cumulative-pv-capacity-tops-480-gw-irena-says/.

Berkes, Fikret. 1999. *Sacred Ecology: Traditional Ecological Knowledge and Resource Management*. Philadelphia: Taylor and Francis.

Berkes, Fikret, and Carl Folke. 2002. "Back to the Future: Ecosystem Dynamics and Local Knowledge." In Lance. H. Gunderson and C. S. Holling, eds., *Panarchy: Understanding Transformations in Human and Natural Systems*, 121–46. Washington, DC: Island Press.

Bernauer, Thomas. 2003. *Genes, Trade, and Regulation: The Seeds of Conflict in Food Biotechnology*. Princeton, NJ: Princeton University Press.

Bernstein, Thomas P. 1984. "Stalinism, Famine, and Chinese Peasants." *Theory and Society* 13 (3): 339–77.

Birnbaum, S. Elizabeth, and Xiubo Yu. 2006. "NGO Strategies to Promote River Protection and Restoration." In *China Environment Series 8 Special Report*, 185–90. Washington, DC: Woodrow Wilson International Center for Scholars. https://www.wilsoncenter.org/sites/default/files/media /documents/publication/CEF_SpecialReport.2.pdf.

Blaikie, Piers. 2000. "Development, Post-, Anti-, and Populist: A Critical Review." *Environment and Planning A: Economy and Space* 32 (6): 1033–50.

Blaikie, Piers, and Harold C. Brookfield. 1987. *Land Degradation and Society*. London: Methuen.

Blalock, Garrick, Vrinda Kadiyali, and Daniel H. Simon. 2007. "The Impact of Post-9/11 Airport Security Measures on the Demand of Air Travel." *Journal of Law and Economics* 50 (4): 731–55.

Bloomberg News Editors. 2018. "China Hopes to Lessen Solar, Wind Curtailment in 2019." *Renewable Energy World*. December 3. https://www.renew ableenergyworld.com/articles/2018/12/china-hopes-to-lessen-solar-wind -curtailment-in-2019.html.

Blue Door (Lansi Damen). n.d. "Lanyu lüyou zhuyi shixiang" (Things to pay attention to when traveling in Lanyu). https://travel.lanyu.info/trip-info/. Accessed April 2017.

BNEF (Bloomberg New Energy Finance). 2019. "Clean Energy Investment Exceeded $300 Billion Once Again in 2018." January 16. https://about.bnef .com/blog/clean-energy-investment-exceeded-300-billion-2018/.

Boden, T. A., G. Marland, and R. J. Andres. 2017. "Global, Regional, and National Fossil-Fuel CO_2 Emissions (1751–2014)." Carbon Dioxide Information Analysis Center, Oak Ridge National Laboratory, US Department of Energy. https://doi.org/10.3334/CDIAC/00001_V2017.

Borrini-Feyerabend, Grazia. 1996. *Collaborative Management of Protected Areas: Tailoring the Approach to the Context*. Gland, Switzerland: IUCN.

Bosso, Christopher J. 2005. *Environment, Inc.* Lawrence: University Press of Kansas.

Boyle, Alan. 2007. "Human Rights or Environmental Rights: A Reassessment." *Fordham Environmental Law Review* 18:471–511.

BP Global. 2017. *BP Statistical Review of World Energy*. 2017 edition. http://large .stanford.edu/courses/2018/ph241/kuet2/docs/bp-2017.pdf.

Bray, David. 2013. "Urban Planning Goes Rural: Conceptualising the 'New Village.'" *China Perspectives* (3): 53–62.

Broadbent, Jeffrey, and Vicky Brockman. 2010. *East Asian Social Movements: Power, Protest, and Change in a Dynamic Region*. New York: Springer.

Brodt, Sonja B. 2001. "A Systems Perspective on the Conservation and Erosion of Indigenous Agricultural Knowledge in Central India." *Human Ecology* 29:99–120.

Buckley, Chris, and Javier C. Hernandez. 2016. "China Seeks to Avoid Mass Layoffs while Cutting Production." *New York Times*, March 16.

Burns, Stuart. 2017. "How Much Is China's Steel and Aluminum Capacity Really Shrinking?" *MetalMiner*, July 13. https://agmetalminer.com/2017/07/13/how-much-is-chinas-steel-and-aluminum-capacity-really-shrinking/.

Busch, Per-Olof, Helge Jörgens, and Kerstin Tews. 2005. "The Global Diffusion of Regulatory Instruments: The Making of a New International Environmental Regime." *Annals of the American Academy of Political and Social Science* 598:146–67.

Cai, Shaotian. 2007. "Xin nongcun jianshe zhong de linpan baohu guihua" (Plan for preserving *linpan* in new rural reconstruction). *Sichuan jianzhu* (Sichuan architecture) (5): 4–6.

Cai, Shouqiu, and Mark Voigts. 1993. "The Development of China's Environmental Diplomacy." *Pacific Rim Law and Policy Journal* 3:18–42.

California Air Resources Board. 2005. "History of Ozone and Oxidant Ambient Air Quality Standards." https://www.arb.ca.gov/research/aaqs/caaqs/ozone/o-hist/o-hist.htm.

Cao, Ling, Yong Chen, Shuanglin Dong, Arthur Hanson, Bo Huang, Duncan Leadbitter, David C. Little, Ellen K. Pikitch, Yongsong Qiu, Yvonne Sadovy de Mitcheson, Ussif Rashid Sumaila, Meryl Williams, Guifang Xue, Yimin Ye, Wenbo Zhang, Yingqi Zhou, Ping Zhuang, and Rosamond L. Naylor. 2017. "Opportunity for Marine Fisheries Reform in China." *Proceedings of the National Academy of Sciences* 114 (3): 435–42.

Cao Li and Wang Qian. 2010. "Floating Trash Threatens Three Gorges Dam." *China Daily*, August 2. www.chinadaily.com.cn/m/hubei/2010-08/02/content_11083052.htm.

Carter, Neil T., and Arthur P. J. Mol. 2008. *Environmental Governance in China*. New York: Routledge.

CEIC Data. n.d. "Taiwan Gross National Product, 1961–2019." https://www.ceicdata.com/en/indicator/taiwan/gross-national-product. Accessed March 2020.

Central News Agency, Taiwan. 2016. "Full Text of President Tsai Ing-Wen's Apology to Indigenous People." *Taiwan News*, August 1. https://www.taiwannews.com.tw/en/news/2960528.

Chai Jing. n.d. *Under the Dome* (Qiongding zhi xia). Documentary film. https://www.youtube.com/watch?v=V5bHb3ljjbc. Accessed March 2020.

Chan Chang-Chuan. 2014. "Shihua yuanliao guanxian bugai jin shiqu" (Petrochemical pipelines should not exist in the city center). In Chou Kuei-Tien, ed., *Yongxu zhishang: Cong Gaoxiong qibao jiexi huanjing zhengyi yu zhuanxing daiduo* (The swan song of sustainable development: Environmental justice and transitional inertia in Kaohsiung gas blast), 195–98. Taipei: Wunan Chubanshe.

Chang, Hsi-wen. 2017. "Wounded Land and Wounded Peoples: Attitudes of Paiwan People and Tao People toward Nuclear Waste." PhD dissertation, University of Washington, Seattle.

Chang, Wei-yew, and Chris Gaston. 2016. "A Trade Flow Analysis of the Global Softwood Log Market: Implications of Russian Log Export Tax Reduction and New Zealand Log Production Restriction." *Forestry: An International Journal of Forest Research* 89 (1): 20–35.

Chao, Lucy. 2017. "Green Energy, Green Economy Avert Decline." *Common-Wealth* (Taiwan). https://english.cw.com.tw/article/article.action?id=1601.

Ch-aviation. 2019. "South Korea Launches New Policy to Boost Aviation Industry." https://www.ch-aviation.com/portal/news/84562-south-korea -launches-new-policy-to-boost-aviation-industry.

Chawla, Louise, and Victoria Derr. 2012. "The Development of Conservation Behaviors in Childhood and Youth." In Susan Clayton, ed., *Oxford Handbook of Environmental and Conservation Psychology*, 527–55. Oxford: Oxford University Press.

Chen, Yi-Feng, and Chang, Wei-Qi. 2009. "From Colonization to Development." Paper presented at the First Development Annual Conference at National Chengchi University, Taipei.

Chen Qibing. 2011. *Chuanxi linpan jingguan ziyuan baohu yu fazhan moshi yanjiu* (Research on the preservation and development of West Sichuan *linpan* landscape resources). Beijing: Zhongguo Linye Chubanshe.

Chen Yann-juin (Chen Yanzhen) and Chen Ying-shih (Chen Yingshi). 2014. "Lieren xuexiao zhong de xingsu wenhua: Yi Taidong Luanshan, Lalaolan Buluo, Hualian Shuilian Buluo wei li" (Revitalizing indigenous culture: Hunter School from tribes of Lalaolan, Ciwadianm, and Sazasa). *Taiwan Yuanzhumin Yanjiu* (Journal of indigenous studies) 7 (3): 39–81.

Chengdu Municipal Bureau of Statistics. 2014. "Grain Output of Counties Each Year, 1949–1998." In *Chengdu tongji nianjian* (Chengdu statistical yearbook). Chengdu: Chengdu Municipal Bureau of Statistics. This volume and subsequent years available from aggregated database at http://www.stats .gov.cn/. Accessed November 2014.

Chengdu Municipal People's Government. 2008. *Sichuan sheng Chengdu Shi Renmin Zhengfu Bangongting zhuanfa Shi Jian Wei "guanyu tuijin wo shi Chuanxi linpan baohu shishi yijian" de tongzhi* (Sichuan Province Chengdu Municipal People's Government General Office forwards the Municipal Construction Commission announcement of "opinions on promoting the implementation of our municipality's preservation of West Sichuan *linpan*"). Municipal Government Document no. 233, promulgated September 4. Chengdu: Chengdu Municipal People's Government.

Chengdu Urban and Rural Construction Commission. 2007. "Chengdu bianzhi guihua baohu chuanxi linpan fengmao" (The plan for Chengdu's transformation preserves the spirit of West Sichuan *linpan*). *Chengshi guihua tongxun* (Urban planning news report) (17): 8–9.

Chi, Chun-chieh (Ji Junjie). 2005. "Yuanzhumin yanjiu yu Yuanhan Guanxi: Hou zhimin guandian zhi lu" (Research on Taiwan's indigenous people and indigenous-Han relationship: A postcolonial critique). *Guojia Zhengce Jikan* (National policy quarterly) 4 (3): 5–28.

China Daily. 2017. "Water Quality Improvements Visible with River Chief System." December 11.

China Green News. 2011. "The 'War between Fire and Water' Continues: Is Hydroelectric Development in China an Opportunity, or a Catastrophe?" January 28. http://eng.greensos.cn/showArticle.aspx?articleId=755.

Chiu, Hua-mei. 2014a. "Communities Have Right to Know." *Taipei Times*, August 15. https://www.taipeitimes.com/News/editorials/archives/2014/08/15/2003597431.

———. 2014b. "The Movement against Science Park Expansion and Electronics Hazards in Taiwan." *China Perspectives* (3): 15–22.

———. 2018. "Yancong xia de jiaoshi: Huanjing de xingdong zhuyi" (The school under chimneys: Environmental activism). In Lin Wen-yuan et al., eds., *Keji, shehui, ren* (Science-technology, society and human), 194–205. Hsinchu: National Chiao Tung University Chubanshe.

Cho, Hong Sik. 1999. "An Overview of Korean Environmental Law." *Environmental Law* 29 (3): 501–14.

Choi, Hyun-jung, and Lee Soo-hyun. 2015. "Not Good Enough: South Korea's 2030 Carbon Mitigation Target and the INDC." *Asan Issue Brief*, October 29.

Choi, Yoo-sung, and Deil S. Wright. 2004. "Intergovernmental Relation (IGR) In Korea and Japan: Phases, Patterns, and Progress toward Decentralization (Local Autonomy) in a Trans-Pacific Context." *International Review of Public Administration* 9 (1): 1–22.

CIA (US Central Intelligence Agency). n.d. "CIA World Factbook, GDP per capita." https://www.cia.gov/library/publications/the-world-factbook/fields/211rank.html. Accessed August 2020.

Citizen of the Earth Taiwan and Houjin Social-Welfare Foundation. 2015. *Jianchi* (Perseverance). Kaohsiung: Diqiu Gongmin Jijinhui (Citizen of the Earth Taiwan).

Climate Action Tracker. 2017. "Countries." http://climateactiontracker.org/countries.html. Accessed July 2017.

Cohen, Myron L. 1993. "Cultural and Political Inventions in Modern China: The Case of the Chinese 'Peasant.'" *Daedalus* 122 (2): 151–70.

Costantini, Valeria, and Salvatore Monni. 2007. "Environment, Human Development, and Economic Growth." *Ecological Economics* 64 (4): 867–80.

Courtney, Chris. 2016. "Governing Disasters: A Comparative Analysis of the 1931, 1954 and 1998 Middle-Yangzi Floods in Hubei." In Jean Marc F. Blanchard and Kun-Chin Lin, eds., *Governance, Domestic Change, and Social Policy in China: 100 Years after the Xinhai Revolution*, 67–102. New York: Palgrave Macmillan.

Dai, Jingyun, and Anthony J. Spires. 2018. "Advocacy in an Authoritarian State: How Grassroots Environmental NGOs Influence Local Governments in China." *China Journal* 79:62–83.

Dai, Limin, Yue Wang, Dongkai Su, Li Zhou, Daopu Yu, Bernard J. Lewis, and Lin Qi. 2011. "Major Forest Types and the Evolution of Sustainable Forestry in China." *Environmental Management* 48:1066–78.

Dalton, Russell J., Steve Recchia, and Robert Rohrschneider. 2003. "The Environmental Movement and the Modes of Political Action." *Comparative Political Studies* 36:743–71.

Daly, Tom, and Muyu Xu. 2019. "China's 2018 Coal Usage Rises 1 Percent, but Share of Energy Mix Falls." Reuters, February 28.

Davenport, Coral. 2016. "Nations, Fighting Powerful Refrigerant That Warms Planet, Reach Landmark Deal." *New York Times*, October 15.

Davidson, Michael, Fredrich Kahrl, and Valerie Karplus. 2016. "Towards a Political Economy Framework for Wind Power: Does China Break the Mould?" WIDER Working Paper no. 2016/32. United Nations University World Institute for Development Economics Research (UNU-WIDER), Helsinki, Finland.

Davis, Julie Hirschfeld, and Coral Davenport. 2015. "China to Announce Cap-and-Trade Program to Limit Emissions." *New York Times*, September 24.

Delman, Jorgen. 2018. "Ecological Civilization Politics and Governance in Hangzhou: New Pathways to Green Urban Development?" *Asia Pacific Journal* 16 (17.1).

Démurger, Sylvie, Yuanzhao Hou, and Weiyong Yang. 2009. "Forest Management Policies and Resource Balance in China: An Assessment of the Current Situation." *Journal of Environment and Development* 18 (1): 17–41.

Denham, Aaron R. 2008. "Rethinking Historical Trauma: Narratives of Resilience." *Transcultural Psychiatry* 45 (3): 391–414.

Dinda, Soumanyanda. 2004. "Environmental Kuznets Curve Hypothesis: A Survey." *Ecological Economics* 49:431–55.

Ding, Iza. Forthcoming. "Performative Governance." *World Politics*.

Ding, Yanjun, Weijian Han, Qinhu Cai, Shuhong Yang, and Wei Shen. 2013. "Coal-Based Synthetic Natural Gas (SNG): A Solution to China's Energy Security and CO_2 Reduction?" *Energy Policy* 55:445–53.

Dudek, Dan. 2013. "To Understand China's Environmental Solutions, You Have to Think Big." *Environmental Defense Fund Blog*. https://www.edf.org/blog/2014/01/03/understand-chinas-environmental-solutions-you-have-think-big.

Economy, Elizabeth. 1997. "Chinese Policy-Making and Global Climate Change: Two-Front Diplomacy and the International Community." In Elizabeth Economy and Miranda A. Schreurs, eds., *The Internationalization of Environmental Protection*. Cambridge: Cambridge University Press.

———. 1998. "China's Environmental Diplomacy." In Samuel S. Kim, ed., *China and the World: Chinese Foreign Policy Faces the New Millennium*, 264–65. Boulder, CO: Westview Press.

———. 2004a. "Environmental Enforcement in China." In Kristen A. Day, ed., *China's Environment and the Challenge of Sustainable Development*, 102–20. Armonk, NY: M. E. Sharpe.

———. 2004b. *The River Runs Black: The Environmental Challenge to China's Future*. Ithaca, NY: Cornell University Press.

Economy, Elizabeth, and Miranda A. Schreurs. 1997. "Domestic and International Linkages in Environmental Politics." In Elizabeth Economy and Miranda A. Schreurs, eds., *The Internationalization of Environmental Protection*. Cambridge: Cambridge University Press.

Edahiro, Junko. 2009. "A Brief History of the Environmental Movement in Japan." Parts 1 and 2. *JFS Newsletter* (82, 83) (June, July). www.japanfs.org/en/news/archives/news_id029180.html and www.japanfs.org/en/news/archives/news_id029265.html.

———. 2016. "Fukushima Evacuees Still Unable to Go Home Over 5 Years after Earthquake, Nuclear Accident." *JFS Newsletter* (170) (October). www.japanfs.org/en/news/archives/news_id035681.html.

Edahiro, Junko, and Kozuko Kojima. 2011. "Open Platform for Energy Policy Discussion Launched." *JFS Newsletter* (108) (August). www.japanfs.org/en/news/archives/news_id031245.html.

Efird, Rob. 2011. "Learning by Heart: An Anthropological Perspective on Environmental Learning in Lijiang." In Helen Kopnina and Eleanor Shoreman-Ouimet, eds. *Environmental Anthropology Today*, 253–66. New York: Routledge.

———. 2012. "Learning the Land beneath Our Feet: The Place of NGO-Led Environmental Education in Yunnan Province." *Journal of Contemporary China* 21 (76): 569–83.

———. 2014. "Closing the Green Gap: Policy and Practice in Chinese Environmental Education." In John Chi-kin Lee and Rob Efird, eds., *Schooling for Sustainable Development across the Pacific*, 279–92. Dordrecht: Springer.

———. 2015. "Learning Places and 'Little Volunteers': An Assessment of Place- and Community-Based Education in China." *Environmental Education Research* 21 (8): 1143–54.

EIA (US Energy Information Administration). 2011. *International Energy Outlook 2011*. https://www.eia.gov/outlooks/archive/ieo11/.

———. 2017. *Country Analysis Brief: Japan*. February 2. https://www.eia.gov/beta/international/analysis.cfm?iso=JPN.

————. 2018. *Country Analysis Brief: South Korea*. July 16. https://www.eia.gov/beta/international/analysis.cfm?iso=KOR.

————. 2019. *International Energy Outlook 2019*. https://www.eia.gov/outlooks/ieo/pdf/ieo2019.pdf.

Eisner, Mark Allen. 2006. *Governing the Environment*. New York: Lynne Reinner.

Elvin, Mark. 2004. *The Retreat of the Elephants: An Environmental History of China*. New Haven, CT: Yale University Press.

Enerdata. 2019a. *Global Energy Statistical Yearbook 2019: Coal and Lignite Balance of Trade*. https://yearbook.enerdata.net/coal-lignite/balance-trade-data.html.

————. 2019b. *Global Energy Statistical Yearbook 2019: Coal and Lignite Domestic Consumption*. https://yearbook.enerdata.net/coal-lignite/coal-world-consumption-data.html.

————. 2019c. *Global Energy Statistical Yearbook 2019: Natural Gas Domestic Consumption*. https://yearbook.enerdata.net/natural-gas/gas-consumption-data.html.

————. 2019d. *Global Energy Statistical Yearbook 2019: Oil Products Domestic Consumption*. https://yearbook.enerdata.net/oil-products/world-oil-domestic-consumption-statistics.html.

————. 2019e. *Global Energy Statistical Yearbook 2019: Total Energy Consumption*. https://yearbook.enerdata.net/total-energy/world-consumption-statistics.html.

————. 2019f. *World Energy Statistical Yearbook 2019: Energy Balance of Trade*. https://yearbook.enerdata.net/total-energy/world-import-export-statistics.html.

EPA Taiwan (Environmental Protection Administration, Executive Yuan, Taiwan). 2016. "Heavy Metal Pollution in Farmland." https://sgw.epa.gov.tw/en/accomplishments/farmland.

————. 2019a. *Minguo 107 nian Huanjing Shuizhi Jiance Nianbao* (Annual report of environmental water quality measurements for 2018). Taipei: Environmental Protection Administration.

————. 2019b. *Zhonghua Minguo Kongqi Pinzhi Jiance Baogao* (Air quality annual report of ROC [Taiwan], 2019). Taipei: Environmental Protection Administration.

————. n.d. "Huanjing ziyuan ziliao ku: kongqi pinzhi jiance yuezhi" (Environmental resources database: Monthly measurement records of air quality). https://www.epa.gov.tw/ct.asp?xItem=61195&CtNode=35638&mp=epaen. Accessed March 2020.

EPA US (US Environmental Protection Agency). 2018. "Global Greenhouse Gas Emissions Data." https://www.epa.gov/ghgemissions/global-greenhouse-gas-emissions-data#Country.

Escobar, Arturo. 1999. "The Invention of Development." *Current History* 98 (631): 381–86.

Esherick, Joseph W., and Jeffrey N. Wasserstrom. 1990. "Acting Out Democracy: Political Theater in Modern China." *Journal of Asian Studies* 49 (4): 835–65.

Ewing, Jackson. 2018. "Tough Tasks for China's New Environment Ministry." *Diplomat*, March 17. https://thediplomat.com/2018/03/tough-tasks-for-chinas-new-environment-ministry.

Falcus, Max, and Maggie Hiufu Wong. 2019. "Beijing Is Building Hundreds of Airports as Millions of Chinese Take to the Skies." *CNN Travel*, May 25. https://www.cnn.com/travel/article/china-new-airports/index.html.

Fan Shuoming. 2007. *Minzuhua xia Taiwan de shehui yundong waibu celüe yanjiu* (A study of the external strategy of social movements in Taiwan's democratization). Taipei: National Cheng-Chi University.

Fedman, David. 2018. "Wartime Forestry and the 'Low Temperature Lifestyle' in Late Colonial Korea, 1937–1945." *Journal of Asian Studies* 77 (2): 333–50.

Feldman, Eric. A. 2000. *The Ritual of Rights in Japan: Law, Society, and Health Policy*. Cambridge: Cambridge University Press.

Fell, Dafydd. 2017. "The Evolution of the Anti-nuclear Movement in Taiwan since 2008." In Dafydd Fell, ed., *Taiwan's Social Movements under Ma Ying-Jeou: From the Wild Strawberries to the Sunflowers*, 170–92. New York: Routledge.

Fewsmith, Joseph. 2004. "Promoting the Scientific Development Concept." *China Leadership Monitor* 11.

Finnemore, Martha, and Kathryn Sikkink. 1998. "International Norm Dynamics and Political Change." *International Organization* 52 (4): 887–917.

Foote, Daniel H. 2014. "Cause Lawyering in Japan: Reflections on the Case Studies and Justice Reform." In Patricia G. Steinhoff, ed., *Going to Court to Change Japan: Social Movements and the Law in Contemporary Japan*, 165–80. Ann Arbor: Center for Japanese Studies, University of Michigan.

Foster, Stephen, Hector Garduno, Richard Evans, Doug Olson, Yuan Tian, Weizhen Zhang, and Zaisheng Han. 2003. "Quaternary Aquifer of the North China Plain: Assessing and Achieving Groundwater Resource Sustainability." *Hydroecology Journal* 12:81–93.

Frumkin, Howard., Gregory N. Bratman, Sara Jo Breslow, Bobby Cochran, Peter H. Kahn, Jr., Joshua J. Lawler, Philip. S. Levin, Pooja. S. Tandon, Usha Varanasi, Kathleen. L. Wolf, and Spencer. A. Wood. 2017. "Nature Contact and Human Health: A Research Agenda." *Environmental Health Perspectives* 125 (7). https://ehp.niehs.nih.gov/EHP1663/.

Fujikawa, Ken. 2013. "Kankyō soshō to jinken: Kankyō mondai o meguru kenri kakudai to shakaiteki sekinin" (Environmental lawsuits and human rights:Expansion of environmental rights and social responsibility). *Prime = Puraimu* (36): 33–47.

Gardner, Daniel K. 2015. "China's 'Silent Spring' Moment? Why 'Under the Dome' Found a Ready Audience in China." *New York Times*, March 18.

Gasemyr, Hans Jorgen. 2016. "Networks and Campaigns but Not Movements: Collective Action in the Disciplining Chinese State." *Journal of Civil Society* 12 (4): 394–410.

Geertz, Clifford. 1980. *Negara: The Theater State in Nineteenth-Century Bali.* Princeton, NJ: Princeton University Press.

Ghimire, Krishna B., and Michel P. Pimbert. 1997. "Social Change and Conservation: An Overview of Issues and Concepts." In Krishna B. Ghimire and Michel P. Pimbert, eds., *Social Change and Conservation: Environmental Politics and Impacts of National Parks and Protected Areas,* 1–45. London: Earthscan.

Gold, Thomas B. 1986. *State and Society in the Taiwan Miracle.* Armonk, NY: M. E. Sharpe.

Gómez-Baggethun, Erik., Esteve Corbera, and Victoria Reyes-García. 2013. "Traditional Ecological Knowledge and Global Environmental Change: Research Findings and Policy Implications." *Ecology and Society* 18 (4): 72.

Gómez-Pompa, Arturo, and Andrea Kaus. 1992. "Taming the Wilderness Myth." *BioScience* 42 (4): 271–79.

Government of Canada and Government of China. 2017. "Canada-China Joint Statement on Climate Change and Clean Growth." Prime Minister of Canada, December 4. https://pm.gc.ca/eng/news/2017/12/04/canada-china -joint-statement-climate-change-and-clean-growth.

Government of the People's Republic of China. 2010. "Guowuyuan guanyu jiakuai peiyu he fazhan zhanlüexing xinxing qiye dejueding: Guofa 2010, 32 hao" (State Council decision on accelerating the development of the strategic emerging industries: Communique of the State Council, no. 32). www.gov.cn/zwgk/2010-10/18/content_1724848.htm.

Government of the Republic of Korea. 2008. *The First Basic Plans for Energy* (August). Seoul: Government of the Republic of Korea.

———. 2015. *The Promotion Plans for Setting Post-2020 Goals of Reducing Green-house Gas Emissions* (June). Seoul: Government of the Republic of Korea.

Grano, Simona A. 2015. *Environmental Governance in Taiwan: A New Generation of Activists and Stakeholders.* New York: Routledge.

Green, Fergus, and Nicholas Stern. 2016. "China's Changing Economy: Implications for Its Carbon Dioxide Emissions." *Climate Policy* (March, online first). https://doi.org/10.1080/14693062.2016.1156515.

Greenpeace. 2018. *Analysis of Air Quality Trends in 2017.* https://storage. googleapis.com/planet4-eastasia-stateless/2019/11/2aad5961-2aad5961 -analysis-of-air-quality-trends-in-2017.pdf.

Greenpeace Japan. 2014. "Nuclear Free Japan One Year." September. Reprinted in *JFS Newsletter* (146) (October). https://www.japanfs.org/en /news/archives/news_id035087.html.

Gresser, Julian, Koichiro Fujikura, and Akio Morishima. 1981. *Environmental Law in Japan.* London: MIT Press.

Grossman, Gene M., and Alan B. Krueger. 1994. "Environmental Impacts of a North American Free Trade Agreement." In P. Garber, ed., *The US-Mexico Free Trade Agreeement*, 13–56. Cambridge, MA: MIT Press.

Gu, Hallie, and Naveen Thukral. 2018. "Soy Source: Brazil's Share of Soybean Exports to China Hits Record." Reuters, January 25.

Guan, Dabo, Zhu Liu, Yong Geng, Sören Lindner, and Klaus Hubacek. 2012. "The Gigatonne Gap in China's Carbon Dioxide Inventories." *Nature Climate Change* 2:672–75.

GWEC (Global Wind Energy Council). 2019. *Global Wind Report 2018*. https://gwec.net/global-wind-report-2018/.

Haddad, Mary Alice. 2015a. "From Backyard Environmental Advocacy to National Democratisation: The Cases of South Korea and Taiwan." In Carol Hager and Mary Alice Haddad, eds., *NIMBY Is Beautiful: Cases of Local Activism and Environmental Innovation around the World*, 179–99. New York: Berghahn Books.

———. 2015b. "Increasing Environmental Performance in a Context of Low Governmental Enforcement: Evidence from China," *Journal of Environment and Development* 24:3–25.

———. 2015c. "Paradoxes of Democratization: Environmental Politics in East Asia." In Paul G. Harris and Graeme Lang, eds., *Routledge Handbook of East Asia and the Environment*, 86–104. New York: Routledge.

———. 2017. "Environmental Advocacy: Insights from East Asia." *Asian Journal of Political Science* 25 (3): 401–19.

Hager, Carol, and Mary Alice Haddad, eds. 2015. *NIMBY Is Beautiful: Cases of Local Activism and Environmental Innovation around the World*. New York: Berghahn Books.

Haggard, Stephan, and Chung In Moon. 1997. "The State, Politics, and Economic Development in Post-war South Korea." In Hagen Koo, ed., *State and Society in Contemporary Korea*, 51–94. Ithaca, NY: Cornell University Press.

Hale, Matthew A. 2013. "Reconstructing the Rural: Peasant Organizations in a Chinese Movement for Alternative Development." PhD dissertation, University of Washington, Seattle.

Han, Heejin. 2014. "Policy Deliberation as a Goal: The Case of Chinese ENGO Activism." *Journal of Chinese Political Science* 19 (2): 173–90.

Han, Heejin, Brendon Swedlow, and Danny Unger. 2014. "Policy Advocacy Coalitions as Causes of Policy Change in China? Analyzing Evidence from Contemporary Environmental Politics." *Journal of Comparative Policy Analysis: Research and Practice* 16 (4): 313–34.

Han Hongyun and Yingde Hu. 2011. "Zhejiang sheng qiye paiwuquan jiaoyi canyu yiyuan de yingxiang yinsu yanjiu" (Factors affecting firms' participation willingness in tradable emissions permits in Zhejiang Province." *Zhongguo huanjing kexue* (China environmental science) 31 (3): 510–15.

Hanna, Susan, Carl Folke, and Karl-Göran Maler, eds. 1996. *Rights to Nature: Ecological, Economic, Cultural, and Political Principles of Institutions for the Environment.* New York: Island Press.

Harris, Paul G., and Graeme Lang, eds. 2015. *Routledge Handbook of Environment and Society in Asia.* New York: Routledge.

Hatch, Walter, and Kozo Yamamura. 1996. *Asia in Japan's Embrace: Building a Regional Production Alliance.* New York: Cambridge University Press.

Hausfather, Zeke. 2010. "Common Climate Misconceptions: Atmospheric Carbon Dioxide." *Yale Climate Connections.* https://www.yaleclimateconnec tions.org/2010/12/common-climate-misconceptions-atmospheric-carbon -dioxide/.

He, Fanneng, Quansheng Ge, Jianru Dai, and Yujuan Rao. 2008. "Forest Change of China in Recent 300 Years." *Journal of Geographical Sciences* 18:59–72.

He, Hong S., Stephen R. Shiffley, and Frank R. Thompson. 2011. "Overview of Contemporary Issues of Forest Research and Management in China." *Environmental Management* 48:1061–65.

Heilmann, Sebastian. 2008. "Policy Experimentation in China's Economic Rise." *Studies in Comparative International Development* 43 (1): 1–26.

———. 2011. "Policy-Making through Experimentation: The Formation of a Distinctive Policy Process." In Sebastian Heilmann and Elizabeth J. Perry, eds., *Mao's Invisible Hand: The Political Foundation of Adaptive Governance in China*, 62–102. Cambridge, MA: Asia Center, Harvard University Press.

Hellier, Augustine, Adrian Newton, and Susana Gaona. 1999. "Use of Indigenous Knowledge for Rapidly Assessing Trends in Biodiversity: A Case Study from Chiapas, Mexico." *Biodiversity and Conservation* 8:869–89.

Henck, Amanda C., Katharine W. Huntington, John O. Stone, David R. Montgomery, and Bernard Hallet. 2011. "Spatial Controls on Erosion in the Three Rivers Region, Southeastern Tibet and Southwestern China." *Earth and Planetary Science Letters* 303 (1): 71–83.

Hildebrandt, Timothy. 2013. *Social Organizations and the Authoritarian State in China.* New York: Cambridge University Press.

Hildebrandt, Timothy, and Jennifer Turner. 2009. "Green Activism? Reassessing the Role of Environmental Ngos in China." In Jonathan Schwartz and Shawn Shieh, eds., *State and Society Responses to Social Welfare Needs in China: Serving the People*, 88–110. New York: Routledge.

Hiwatashi, Shun'ichi. 1992. "40 shūnen ni atatte: iinkai no tatakai wa tsuzuku" (On our 40th anniversary: The struggle continues). *Kōgai-kankyō* (Pollution-environment) 46 (3).

Ho, Ming-Sho. 2005. "Protest as Community Revival: Folk Religion in a Taiwanese Anti-pollution Movement." *African and Asian Studies* 4 (3): 237–69.

———. 2010. "Co-opting Social Ties: How the Taiwanese Petrochemical Industry Neutralized Environmental Opposition." *Mobilization: An International Journal* 15 (4): 447–63.

———. 2011. "Environmental Movement in Democratizing Taiwan (1980–2004): A Political Opportunity Structure Perspective." In Jeffrey Broadbent and Vickie Brockman, eds, *East Asian Social Movements*, 283–314. New York: Springer.

Ho, Peter. 2007. "Embedded Activism and Political Change in a Semiauthoritarian Context." *China Information* 21:187–209.

Ho, Samuel P. S. 1975. "The Economic Development of Colonial Taiwan: Evidence and Interpretation." *Journal of Asian Studies* 34 (2): 417–39.

Holdgate, Martin, and Adrian Philips. 1999. "Protected Areas in Context." In Ian R. Swingland, Mike Walkey, and Shaun Russell, eds., *Integrated Protected Area Management*, 1–24. Boston: Springer US.

Hölzl, Richard. 2010. "Historicizing Sustainability: German Scientific Forestry in the Eighteenth and Nineteenth Centuries." *Science as Culture* 4:431–60.

Hong, Sun-Kee, In-Ju Song, and Jianguo Wu. 2007. "Fengshui Theory in Urban Landscape Planning." *Urban Ecosystems* 10 (3): 221–37.

Hsiao Hsin-Huang. 1988. "Qiling niandai fan wuran zili jiuji de jiegou yu guocheng fenxi" (An analysis of the structure and process of spontaneous anti-pollution protest in the '70s decade [1980s]). Taipei: Environmental Protection Administration.

Hsieh Shih-Chung (Xie Shizhong). 1987. *Rentong de wuming: Taiwan Yuanzhumin de zuqun bianqian* (Stigmatized identity: A study on ethnic change of Taiwan indigenous peoples). Taipei: *Independence Evening Post*.

———. 1994. "Shenghuo qu de shanbao guanguang: Lanyu moshi" (The tourism mode in an aboriginal area: The Lanyu mode. In *Shanbao guanguang dangdai shandi wenhua zhanxian de renlei quanshi* (Aboriginal tourism: The anthropologic interpretation of local native culture exhibitions). Taipei: *Independence Evening Post*.

———. 2004. *Zuqun renleixue de hongguan tansuo: Taiwan Yuanzhumin junji* (Macro-viewpoints of ethnic anthropology: Collected essays on Taiwan indigenous peoples). Taipei: National Taiwan University Press.

Hsu Hui-Tsung. 2014. "Shihua gongyequ de kongqi wuran wenti yu jiankang fengxian" (Air pollution and health risk of petrochemical industrial parks). In Chou Kuei-Tien, ed., *Yongxu zhishang: Cong Gaoxiong qibao jiexi huanjing zhengyi yu zhuanxing daiduo* (The swan song of sustainable development: Environmental justice and transitional inertia in Kaohsiung gas blast), 53–70. Taipei: Wunan Chubanshe.

Hu, Jiawen. 2015. "Coming Home to the Land: Natural Farming as Therapeutic Landscape Experience in Chengdu Plain, China." PhD dissertation, University of Washington, Seattle.

Hu, Jiawen, and Daniel B. Abramson. 2015. "Visions of New Urban-Rural Relations and Alternative Definitions of Well-Being in Rapidly Urbanizing China: The Case of Chengdu, Sichuan." In Fritz Wagner, Riad Mahayni, and Andreas Piller, eds., *Transforming Distressed Global Communities: Making*

Inclusive, Safe, Resilient, and Sustainable Cities, 317–37. Farnham, Surrey, UK: Ashgate.

Hu, Wen-cheng, Shih-ming Chung, Jui-chu Lin, Chien-te Fan, and Chen-An Lien. 2017. "An Accelerating Green Growth for Taiwan's Climate Ambition." *Renewable and Sustainable Energy Reviews* 79:286–92.

Huang, Chun, Liangji Deng, Xuesong Gao, Yi Luo, Shirong Zhang, and Li Liu. 2013. "Rural Housing Land Consolidation and Transformation of Rural Villages under the 'Coordinating Urban and Rural Construction Land' Policy: A Case of Chengdu City, China." *Low Carbon Economy* 4 (3): 95–103.

Huang, Rong, Lupei Zhu, John Encarnacion, Yixian Xu, Chi-Chia Song Luo, and Xiaohuan Jiang. 2018. "Seismic and Geologic Evidence of Water-Induced Earthquakes in the Three Gorges Reservoir Region of China." *Geophysical Research Letters* 45 (12): 5929–36.

ICAO (International Civil Aviation Organization). 2016. "Historic Agreement Reached to Mitigate International Aviation Emissions." October 6. https://www.icao.int/Newsroom/Pages/Historic-agreement-reached-to-mitigate-international-aviation-emissions.aspx.

IEA (International Energy Agency). 2019. *Key World Energy Statistics 2017*. https://webstore.iea.org/download/direct/2831.

Iijima, Nobuko. 2000. *Kankyō mondai no shakaishi* (The social history of environmental problems). Tokyo: Yūhikaku.

IPCC (Intergovernmental Panel on Climate Change). 2013. *Fifth Assessment Report, Summary for Policymakers*. https://www.ipcc.ch/pdf/assessment-report/ar5/wg1/WG1AR5_SPM_FINAL.pdf.

Isoyama, Tomoyuki. 2016. "Jiritsu no seishin o torimodosu itoshiro no shōsuiryoku hatsuden" (Reclaiming the spirit of autonomy: Small-scale hydropower in Itoshiro). *Wedge Infinity* (June 11). http://wedge.ismedia.jp/articles/-/6318?page=3.

IUCN (International Union for Conservation of Nature). 1993. *Parks and Progress*. Gland, Switzerland: IUCN.

Jeon, Bong-hee. 1992. "A Study on Architectural Characteristics and Immanent Regularity of Lineage Village in Choson Dynasty, Korea." PhD thesis, Seoul National University.

———. 2016. *A Cultural History of the Korean House*. Seoul: Seoul Selection.

JFS (Japan for Sustainability). 2012. "Company Helping Revitalize a Local Community after Japan Earthquake through Energy Self-Sufficiency." *JFS Newsletter* (June 9). www.japanfs.org/en/news/archives/news_id031976.html.

———. 2013. "Local Energy Meeting Held in Odawara, Japan. *JFS Newsletter* (July 19). www.japanfs.org/en/news/archives/news_id032938.html.

———. 2014. "Community-Led Energy Association Launched to Promote Renewable Energy." *JFS Newsletter* (August 26). www.japanfs.org/en/news/archives/news_id035025.html.

———. 2015. "Community Happy Solar!" *JFS Newsletter* (159) (November). https://www.japanfs.org/en/news/archives/news_id035404.html.

Jha, Raghbendra, and K. V. Bhanu Murthy. 2003. "An Inverse Global Enviornmental Kuznets Curve." *Journal of Comparative Economics* 31 (2): 352–68.

Jiang, Li, Xiangzheng Deng, and Karen C. Seto. 2012. "Multi-level Modeling of Urban Expansion and Cultivated Land Conversion for Urban Hotspot Counties in China." *Landscape and Urban Planning* 108 (2): 131–39.

Jiang, Tao, Junzhuo Li, Fengjing Zhang, Ahmad Hassan, and Qibing Chen. 2016. "Linpan Community: A Framework of Protection and Development of Rural Landscape in Chengdu Plain." In *Proceedings of the 2016 International Conference on Arts, Design and Contemporary Education.* Atlantis Press. https://doi.org/10.2991/icadce-16.2016.165.

Jiangsu Price Association. 2016. "Paiwuquan youshang shiyong he jiaoyi lujing chutan" (A path for paid use of emissions quota and emissions trading). www.jsjgxh.org/col3/articleinfo.php?infoid=57.

Johnson, Chalmers. 1982. *MITI and the Japanese Miracle.* Stanford, CA: Stanford University Press.

———. 1986. "The Nonsocialist NICs: East Asia." *International Organization* 40 (2): 557–65.

Johnson, Thomas. 2010. "Environmentalism and NIMBYism in China: Promoting a Rules-Based Approach to Public Participation." *Environmental Politics* 19 (3): 430–48.

J.P. 2018. "How China Cut Its Air Pollution." *Economist*, January 25.

JPC (Japan Policy Council). n.d. "Zenkoku shiku chōson-betsu '20~39-sai josei' no shōrai suikei jinkō" (Projected population of 20- to 39-year-old women: National, urban, ward, and village). www.policycouncil.jp/pdf/prop03/prop03_2_1.pdf. Accessed April 2020.

Kaika, Dimitra, and Efthimios Zervas. 2013. "The Environmental Kuznets Curve (EKC) Theory—Part A: Concept, Causes and the CO_2 Emissions Case." *Energy Policy* 62:1392–1402.

Kantor, M. 2002. *Passive-Aggression: A Guide for the Therapist, the Patient and the Victim.* Westport, CT: Praeger.

Keck, Margaret E., and Kathryn Sikkink. 1998. *Activists beyond Borders: Advocacy Networks in International Politics.* Ithaca, NY: Cornell University Press.

KEEI (Korea Energy Economics Institute). 2016. *Monthly Energy Statistics.* Ulsan: KEEI.

KFEM (Korean Federation for Environmental Movement). n.d. "Who We Are." http://kfem.org/who-we-are. Accessed March 2020.

Kim, Chung Ho. 2015. "The Ecological Impact of the Korean Saemaul (New Rural Community) Movement, 1970–79." In Xueming Chen and Qisheng Pan, eds., *Building Resilient Cities in China: The Nexus between Planning and Science,* 119–132. Cham, Switzerland: Springer International.

———. 2017. "Community Resilience of the Korean New Village Movement, 1970–1979: Historical Interpretation and Resilience Assessment." PhD dissertation, University of Washington, Seattle.

Kim, Da-sol. 2017a. "70% of Korea's Fine Dust Particles Come from China." *Korea Herald*, January 3. www.koreaherald.com/view.php?ud =20170103000745.

———. 2017b. "Moon Jae-in Orders Shutdown of Old Coal-Fired Power Plants." *Korea Herald*, May 15. www.koreaherald.com/view.php?ud =20170515000815.

———. 2017c. "Korea to Shut Down Oldest Nuclear Reactor." *Korea Herald*, June 9. www.koreaherald.com/view.php?ud=20170609000651.

Kim, Euiyoung. 2009. "The Limits of NGO-Government Relations in South Korea." *Asian Survey* 49 (5): 873–94.

Kim, Eui-gyeong, and Kim Dong-jun. 2005. "Historical Changes and Characteristics of Rehabilitation, Management, and Utilization of Forest Resources in South Korea." *Journal of Mountain Science* 2 (2): 164–72.

Kim, Su Min. 2014. "Shunning the Authority: Symbolic Purity and Autonomy in Consuming Non-certified Organic Foods in Chengdu, China." BA honors thesis, University of Washington, Seattle.

Kim Yong-woong. 1999. "Industrialization and Urbanization in Korea." *Korea Journal* 39 (3): 35–62.

King, Betty L. 1975. "Japanese Colonialism and Korean Economic Development, 1910–1945." *Asian Studies: Journal of Critical Perspectives on Asia* 13 (3): 1–15.

Kingdon, John W. 1984. *Agendas, Alternatives, and Public Policies*. New York: Harper Collins.

Knight, John. 1997. "A Tale of Two Forests: Reforestation Discourse in Japan and Beyond." *Journal of the Royal Anthropological Institute* 3 (4): 711–30.

Kobayashi, Yasuaki. 2017. "The U.S.-Japan Nuclear Agreement and the Nuclear Fuel Cycle: Past, Present, and Future." Occasional Paper Series. Edwin O. Reischauer Center for East Asian Studies, Johns Hopkins SAIS, Washington, DC.

Koiwai, Hironori. 2012. "'Kenri' toshite no 'kankyōken' no saikō: Shihōjō no kankyōken e no sekkin" (A reconsideration of environmental rights as "rights": Responsibility for environmental rights in the administration of justice). *Hikaku hōsei kenkyū* (Kokushikan Daigaku) (Research in comparative law [Kokushikan University]) 35:53–78.

Kono, Shigemi. 2011. "Confronting the Demographic Trilemma of Low Fertility, Ageing, and Depopulation." In Florian Coulmas and Ralph Lützeler, eds., *Imploding Populations in Japan and Germany: A Comparison*, 35–54. Leiden: Brill.

Koshida, Kiyokazu. 2005. "Teikō o seidoka suru: Hokkaidō-Date no keiken kara kangaeru" (Institutionalizing resistance: Considerations from the experience in Date, Hokkaido). *Takagi Kikin josei hōkokushū* (Reports of the Takagi Foundation grants) 2:17–20.

Ku, Do-wan. 1996. "The Structural Change of the Korean Environmental Movement." *Korea Journal of Population and Development* 25:155–80.

————. 2002. "Environmental Movement and Policies during High Economic Growth in Korea." In Yuko Arayama, ed., *Environment and Our Sustainability in the 21st Century: Understanding and Cooperation between Developed and Developing Countries*. Nagoya: Nagoya University.

————. 2004. "The Korean Environmental Movement: Green Politics through Social Movement." *Korea Journal* (Autumn): 185–219.

Kuan Hsiao-Jung (Guan Xiaorong). 2007. *Lanyu baogao, 1987–2007* (A report on Lanyu, 1987–2007). Taipei: Jen-Chien Press.

Kung, James, and Chen Shuo. 2011. "The Tragedy of the Nomenklatura: Career Incentives and Political Radicalism during China's Great Leap Famine." *American Political Science Review* 105:27–45.

Kuo, Lily. 2019. "Chengdu Is Blossoming as China's 'Park City,' but Its Residents Pay the Price of Beautification." *South China Morning Post*, February 7. https://web.archive.org/web/20190708192039/https://www.scmp.com/magazines/post-magazine/long-reads/article/2185246/chengdu-blossoming-chinas-park-city.

Kuo, Ming, Michael Barnes, and Catherine Jordan. 2019. "Do Experiences with Nature Promote Learning? Converging Evidence of a Cause-and-Effect Relationship." *Frontiers in Psychology* 10:305. https://doi.org/10.3389/fpsyg.2019.00305.

Kuo, Pei-Hsuan, Pei-Chen Ni, Andrew Keats, Ben-Jei Tsuang, Yung-Yao Lan, Min-Der Lin, Chien-Lung Chen, Yueh-Yuan Tu, Len-Fu Chang, and Ken-Hui Chang. 2009. "Retrospective Analysis of Air Quality Management Practices in Taiwan." *Atmospheric Environment* 43:3925–34.

Kuznets, Simon. 1955. "Economic Growth and Income Inequality." *American Economic Review* 45:1–28.

Kyunghyang shinmun. 1972. "Model nongchon burak geonseol" (Constructing model rural villages). March 8.

Lanyu Township Office. n.d. "Zhuyi shixiang" (Things to pay attention to) www.lanyu.gov.tw/iframcontent_edit.php?menu=2557&typeid=2594. Accessed April 2020.

Lee, Hsin-Yin. 2018. "Taiwan Adds 30 Routes in 2018 amid Strong Aviation Market." *Focus Taiwan.* https://focustaiwan.tw/business/201810130006.

Lee, John Chi-Kin. 2010. "Education for Sustainable Development in China: Experiences of the Environmental Educators' Initiative (EEI)." *Chinese Education and Society* 43:63–81.

Lee, Keun-young, and Jung-ae, Lee. 2017. "Shin-Kori 5 & 6 Public Task Force Recommends Proceeding with Construction." *Hankyoreh*, October 21. http://happyvil.hani.co.kr/arti/english_edition/e_national/815444.html.

Lee, See-Jae. 2000. "The Environmental Movement and Its Political Empowerment." *Korea Journal* 40:131–60.

Lee, Su-Hoon, Hsin-Huang Michael Hsiao, Hwa-Jen Liu, On-Kwok Lai, Francisco A. Magno, and Alvin Y. So. 1999. "The Impact of Democratization on Environmental Movements." In Yok-shiu F. Lee and Alvin Y. So, eds., *Asia's Environmental Movements*, 230–51. Armonk, NY: M. E. Sharpe.

Lee, Wei-i (Li Weiyi). 2014. "Zuqun zhanshi de fansi: Hou quanwei Taiwande guancha" (Reflections on the exhibition of ethnicity: Observations from post-authoritarian Taiwan). *Journal of Archaeology and Anthropology* 80:221–50.

Lee, Yok-shiu F., and Alvin Y So, eds. 1999. *Asia's Environmental Movements: Comparative Perspectives*. Armonk, NY: M. E. Sharpe.

Lee, Yoo-soo. 2015. *A Study on Institutional Obstacles against the New Energy Industry in Korea*. Ulsan: KEEI.

Lee Chien-liang (Li Jianliang). 2010. *Huanjing gongmin susong xin dianfan: Jianxi taibei gaodeng xingzheng fayuan 98 niandu suzi di 504 hao panjue* (The new paradigm of environmental citizen lawsuits: Analysis of Taipei High Administrative Court decision 98-Su-504]. *Taiwan Law Journal* 152:57–67.

Lee Ken-cheng (Li Genzheng). 2007. "Gongye he haoshui, nongye he dushui" (While industry is consuming clean water, farmland is irrigated with toxic water). http://leekc-95kh.blogspot.tw/2008/03/blog-post_18.html.

———. 2009. "Toushi chaoliao duzai shijian" (Review of the hazardous accident in Chaoliao). Diqiu Gongmin Jijin Hui (Citizen of the Earth Taiwan). www.cet-taiwan.org/node/439.

———. 2014. "Chanye zhuanxing haigei gaoxiong shimin lishi zhengyi" (Industrial transition: Bring back historical justice to people of Kaohsiung). *Ziyou Shibao* (Liberty times). August 5. http://talk.ltn.com.tw/article/paper/801596.

———. 2015. "Houjin qishi" (Inspirations from Houjin). In Citizen of the Earth Taiwan and Houjin Social-Welfare Foundation, eds., *Jianchi* (Perseverance). Kaohsiung: Diqiu Gongmin Jijinhui (Citizen of the Earth Taiwan).

Lee Yu-chin. 2016. "Gaoshifu qingxiang she shihua zhuanqu Huantuan: Yu qiancun yiti tuogou, xian gaishan wuran" (Kaohsiung city government intends to establish special petrochemical industrial zone, environmental groups: Improve the pollution first and delay the issue of relocation). Taiwan Huanjing Zixun Zhongxin (Taiwan Environmental Information Center), June 2. http://e-info.org.tw/node/115907.

Leftwich, Adrian. 1994. "Governance, the State and the Politics of Development." *Development and Change* 25:363–86.

Lemos, Maria Carmen, and Arun Agrawal. 2006. "Environmental Governance." *Annual Review of Environmental Resources* 31:297–325.

Lewis, Joanna I. 2007. "China's Strategic Priorities in International Climate Negotiations." *Washington Quarterly* 31 (1): 155–74.

———. 2013a. "China's Environmental Diplomacy: Climate Change, Domestic Politics and International Engagement." In Rosemary Foot, ed., *China across the Divide: The Domestic and Global in Politics and Society*. Oxford: Oxford University Press.

———. 2013b. *Green Innovation in China: China's Wind Power Industry and the Global Transition to a Low-Carbon Economy*. New York: Columbia University Press.

———. 2014. "The Rise of Renewable Energy Protectionism: Emerging Trade Conflicts and Implications for Low Carbon Development." *Global Environmental Politics* 14 (4): 10–35.

———. 2016. "Wind Energy in China: Getting More from Wind Farms." *Nature Energy* 1 (6): 16076. https://doi.org/10.1038/nenergy.2016.76.

———. 2017. "Green Energy Innovation in China." In Eva Sternfeld, ed., *Routledge Handbook of Environmental Policy in China*. London: Routledge.

Lewis, Joanna, and Shuo Li. 2017. "As the US Steps Back, China Must Step Up on Climate Leadership." *China Dialogue*, June 4. https://www.chinadialogue.net/article/show/single/en/9722-As-the-US-steps-back-China-must-step-up-on-climate-leadership.

Li, Hui, Carlos Wing-Hung Lo, and Shui-Yan Tang. 2017. "Nonprofit Policy Advocacy under Authoritarianism." *Public Administration Review* 77 (1): 103–17.

Li, Jing. 2018. "China's New Environment Ministry Unveiled, with Huge Staff Boost." *China Dialogue*, April 19. https://www.chinadialogue.net/article/show/single/en/10599-China-s-new-environment-ministry-unveiled-with-huge-staff-boost.

Li, Lillian M. 2007. *Fighting Famine in North China: State, Market, and Environmental Decline, 1690s–1990s*. Stanford, CA: Stanford University Press.

Liang, Hao. 2015. "Toward a Resilient Landscape: The Eco-cultural Redevelopment in Rural Chengdu Plain." Master's thesis, University of Washington, Seattle.

Lifayuan. 2016. "Lifayuan di 9 jie di 1 huiqi di 11 cihuiyi yian guanxi wenshu yuan zong di 887 hao" (Documents no. 887 for 11th meeting, 1st term, April 27, 2016, Legislative Yuan).

———. 2017. "Lifayuan di 9 jie di 3 huiqi di 5 ci huiyi yian guanxi wenshu yuan zong di 887 hao" (Documents no. 887 for 5th meeting, 3rd term, March 15, 2017, Legislative Yuan).

Lim, Eunjung. 2016. "Japan's Nuclear Trilemma." *IGAS Journal of Energy Security* (January 19). www.ensec.org/index.php?option=com_content&view=article&id=591:japansnucleartrilemma&catid=131:esupdates&Itemid=414.

———. 2018. "Japan's Energy Policy under Abe: Liberalization of the Energy Market and Nuclear U-turn." *Seoul Journal of Japanese Studies* 4 (1): 103–31.

———. 2019. "South Korea's Nuclear Dilemmas." *Journal for Peace and Nuclear Disarmament* (April 11): 297–318.

Lin, Hsuta (Lin Xuda). 2011. "'Yi/yi' wenhua mailuo: Zaidi zhishi yu quwending de renleixue yundong" (Cultural context: The uses of local knowledge and destabilization). *Chuanbo Yanjiu yu Shijian* (Journal of communication research and practice) 1 (2): 1–11.

Lin, Yih-Ren. 2005. "Whose Tradition? Whose Territory? A Critical Review of Indigenous Ancestral Domain Mapping Project in Taiwan." Paper presented at Mapping for Change: International Conference on Participatory Spatial Information Management and Communication, Nairobi, Kenya.

Lin Wu Ju (Bureau of Forestry, ROC). 2017. "Senlin mianji bianqian" (Changes in forest area). https://www.forest.gov.tw/0001502.

Ling, Daxie. 1983. "Woguo senlin ziyuan bianqian" (Changes in our country's forest resources). *Zhongguo nongshi* (China Forest History) 2:26–36.

Litzinger, Ralph A. 2004. "The Mobilization of 'Nature': Perspectives from Northwest Yunnan." *China Quarterly* 178:488–504.

Liu, Huajie. 2012. *Bowu rensheng* (Life as a naturalist). Beijing: Beijing University Press.

Liu, Hwa-jen. 2016. *Leverage of the Weak: Labor and Environmental Movements in Taiwan and South Korea*. Minneapolis: University of Minnesota Press.

Liu, Jianguo. 2010. "China's Road to Sustainability." *Science* 328 (5974): 50.

Liu Ming-Te (Liu Mingde) and Hsu Yu-Chen (Xu Yuzhen). 2012. "Taiwan jixu you yuanjian de zaisheng nengyuan zhengce yu zuofa: Deguo jingyan de qishi" (The urgent needs of forward-looking policies to develop renewable energy in Taiwan: Enlightenment from Germany's experience). *Journal of Public Administration* 43:127–50.

Liu Qin, Wang Yukuan, Guo Yingman, and Peng Peihao. 2017. "Chengdu Pingyuan linpan de yanjiu jinzhan yu zhanwang" (The current state and outlook of research on *linpan* in the Chengdu Plain). *Zhongguo nongxue tongbao* (Chinese agricultural science bulletin) 33 (29): 150–56.

Lo, Alex Y. 2016. "Challenges to the Development of Carbon Markets in China." *Climate Policy* 16 (1): 109–24.

Looney, Kristin E. 2012. "The Rural Developmental State: Modernization Campaigns and Peasant Politics in China, Taiwan, and South Korea." PhD dissertation, Harvard University, Cambridge, MA.

———. 2015. "China's Campaign to Build a New Socialist Countryside: Village Modernization, Peasant Councils, and the Ganzhou Model of Rural Development." *China Quarterly* 224: 909–32.

Lora-Wainwright, Anna. 2017. *Resigned Activism: Living with Pollution in Rural China*. Cambridge, MA: MIT Press.

Louv, Richard. 2005. *Last Child in the Woods: Saving our Children from Nature-Deficit Disorder*. Chapel Hill, NC: Algonquin Books.

———. 2014. *Linjian zui hou de xiaohai: Zhengjiu ziran queshizheng de ertong* (Last child in the woods: Rescuing children with nature deficit syndrome). Translated by Friends of Nature and Wang Ximin. Beijing: Zhongguo Fazhan Chubanshe.

———. 2016. *Vitamin N: The Essential Guide to a Nature-Rich Life*. Chapel Hill, NC: Algonquin Books.

Lu, Hsin-yi. 2009. "Place and Environmental Movement in Houjin, Kaohsiung." *Journal of Archaeology and Anthropology* 70:47–78.

Lu Hsin-yi (Lü Xinyi). 2016. "Tudi shequn xinyang: Jiexi sumin huanjing lunshu" (Land, community, and faith: An analytical model of folk environmental discourse). *Keji yiliao yu shehui* (Taiwanese journal for studies of science, technology and medicine) 22:63–108.

Lungu, Andrei. 2017. "A New G2: China and the EU?" *Diplomat* (August). https://thediplomat.com/2017/08/a-new-g2-china-and-the-eu/.

Lyons, David. 2009. "The Two-Headed Dragon: Environmental Policy and Progress under Rising Democracy in Taiwan." *East Asia* 26:57–76.

Maclachlan, Patricia L. 2014. "Suing for Redress: Japanese Consumer Organizations and the Courts." In Patricia G. Steinhoff, ed., *Going to Court to Change Japan: Social Movements and the Law in Contemporary Japan*, 129–46. Ann Arbor: Center for Japanese Studies, University of Michigan.

Manufacturing Institute. 2013. "The US Is Losing Export Market Share." www.themanufacturinginstitute.org/~/media/2769E16B279F4E6FBC65B228C69658D6.ashx.

MAREX (Maritime-Executive). 2018. "China Surpasses U.S. as Largest Crude Oil Importer." https://www.maritime-executive.com/article/china-surpasses-u-s-as-largest-crude-oil-importer.

Mather, A. S. 1992. "The Forest Transition." *Area* 24 (4): 367–79.

Mathews, John A., and Hao Tan. 2016. "A 'Great Reversal' in China? Coal Continues to Decline with Enforcement of Environmental Laws." *Asia Pacific Journal* 13 (34.1). https://apjjf.org/2015/13/34/John-A.-Mathews/4365.html.

Matsubara, Hironao. 2013. "Community Power Revolution Spreads in Japan." *JFS Newsletter* (June 3). www.japanfs.org/en/news/archives/news_id032838.html.

Matsushita, Ryūichi. 1999. *Matsushita Ryūichi sono shigoto: Kurayami no shisō o* (The works of Matsushita Ryūichi: Toward a philosophy of the dark). Tokyo: Kawade Shobō Shinsha.

———. 2008. *Kankyōken no katei: Matsushita Ryūichi mikankō chosakushū 4* (The process of environmental rights: Matsushita Ryūichi unpublished collected works 4). Fukuoka: Kaichōsha.

Matsushita, Ryūichi, and Kankyōken Soshō o Susumeru Kai, eds. 1975. *Kankyōken te nanda: Hatsudensho wa mō iranai* (What are environmental rights? We don't want any more power plants). Tokyo: Daiamondosha.

McCrone, Angus, Ulf Moslener, Francoise d'Estais, and Christine Gruning, eds. 2018. *Global Trends in Renewable Energy Investment Report 2018*. FS-UNEP Collaborating Centre for Climate and Sustainable Energy Finance. https://www.greengrowthknowledge.org/resource/global-trends-renewable-energy-investment-report-2018.

McKean, Margaret A. 1981. *Environmental Protest and Citizen Politics in Japan*. Berkeley: University of California Press.

McNeely, Jeffrey. 1994. "Protected Areas for the 21st Century: Working to Provide Benefits to Society." *Biodiversity and Conservation* 3 (5): 390–405.

MEP (Ministry of Environmental Protection) and MLR (Ministry of Land Resources) (China). 2014. *Quanguo turang wuran zhuangkuang diaocha kongbao* (Public report on the nationwide situation of soil contamination). http://www.zhb.gov.cn/gkml/hbb/qt/201404/W020140417558995804588.pdf.

Mertha, Andrew C. 2008. *China's Water Warriors: Citizen Action and Policy Change*. Ithaca, NY: Cornell University Press.

METI (Ministry of Economy, Trade, and Industry) (Japan). 2014. *The Fourth Basic Plan for Energy* (April). Tokyo: METI.

———. 2017a. "Collection of Case Examples Concerning Smart Communities Compiled." https://www.meti.go.jp/english/press/2017/0623_002.html.

———. 2017b. *The 2017 Edition of Energy White Paper*. Tokyo: METI.

———. 2018. *The Fifth Basic Plan for Energy*. Tokyo: METI.

Mettler, Suzanne. 2011. *The Submerged State: How Invisible Government Policies Undermine American Democracy*. Chicago: University of Chicago Press.

Miller, Norman. 2002. *Environmental Politics: Interest Group, the Media, and the Making of Policy*. New York: Taylor and Francis.

Ministry of Economic Affairs (Republic of China). n.d. "Energy Statistical Annual Reports by Bureau of Energy." https://www.moeaboe.gov.tw/ECW/english/content/ContentLink.aspx?menu_id=1540. Accessed April 2020.

Ministry of Education (People's Republic of China). 2003a. "Zhongxiaoxue huanjing jiaoyu shishi zhinan (shixing)" (Guidelines for implementing primary and secondary environmental education [trial]). http://xjs.mep.gov.cn/download/sszn.pdf. Accessed August 2017.

———. 2003b. "Zhongxiaoxuesheng huanjing jiaoyu zhuanti jiaoyu dagang" (Special topic education outline for primary and secondary school children's environmental education). http://xjs.mep.gov.cn/xjwx/200511/t20051118_71829.htm. Accessed August 2017.

Ministry of Forestry (People's Republic of China). 2014. "Zhongguo senlin ziyuan (2008–2013)" (China's forest resources [2008–2013]). www.forestry.gov.cn/main/58/20140225/660036.html.

———. 2019. "Zhongguo senlin fugai lü 22.96%" (China's forest cover 22.96%). www.forestry.gov.cn/main/65/20190620/103419043834596.html.

Ministry of Home Affairs (Republic of Korea). 1972. "Saemaeul nongchon geonseol gyehoek: Sibeom chwirak bunsan nongga jipdanhwa gyehoek" (*Saemaul* countryside construction plan: Constructing model rural villages). Seoul: Ministry of Home Affairs.

Mission Innovation. 2017. "Second Mission Innovation Ministerial: Mission Innovation." http://mission-innovation.net/our-work/mi-2/.

Miyazaki, Shōgo. 1975. *Ima "kōkyōsei" o utsu: Dokyumento yokohama shinkamotsusen hantai undō* (Striking at the public interest now: Documenting the new freight line opposition movement). Tokyo: Shinsensha.

Modelski, George. 2003. *World Cities: –3000 to 2000*. Washington, DC: FAROS2000.

MOE Japan (Ministry of the Environment) (Japan). 2015. *Annual Report on Environmental Statistics*. Tokyo: MOE Japan.

MOE ROK (Ministry of the Environment, Republic of Korea). 2012. "2011 Soil Contamination Investigations Show 43 Areas Exceed Standard." http://eng

.me.go.kr/eng/web/board/read.do?menuId=21&boardMasterId=522&boardId
=777&searchKey=titleOrContent&searchValue=soil%20contamination.

———. 2014. *Environmental Statistics Yearbook*. Seoul: MOE ROK.

———. 2017a. "Major Policies: Soil Contamination." http://eng.me.go.kr/eng
/web/index.do?menuId=330.

———. 2017b. "Soil Contamination Prevention and Restoration." http://eng
.me.go.kr/eng/web/index.do?menuId=313.

Mol, Arthur P. J., and Neil T. Carter. 2006. "China's Environmental Governance in Transition." *Environmental Politics* 15 (2): 149–70.

Montgomery, David R. 2007. *Dirt: The Erosion of Civilizations*. Berkeley:
University of California Press.

Moseley, Robert K, and Renée B. Mullin. 2014. "The Nature Conservancy in
Shangrila: Transnational Conservation and its Critiques." In Emily T. Yeh
and Chris Coggins, eds., *Mapping Shangrila*, 129–52. Seattle: University of
Washington Press.

MOTIE (Ministry of Trade, Industry, and Energy, Republic of Korea). 2014. *The
Second Basic Plan for Energy*. Sejong: MOTIE.

———. 2015. *The Seventh Basic Plan on Electricity Demand and Supply*. Sejong:
MOTIE.

———. 2016. *The 2016 Edition of New and Renewable Energy White Paper*. Sejong:
MOTIE.

———. 2017. *The Eighth Basic Plan on Electricity Demand and Supply*. Sejong:
MOTIE.

———. 2019. *The Third Basic Plan for Energy*. Sejong: MOTIE.

Munnings, Clayton, Richard D. Morgenstern, Zhongmin Wang, and Xu Liu.
2016. "Assessing the Design of Three Carbon Trading Pilot Programs in
China." *Energy Policy* 96:688–99.

Murphree, Marshall W. 1994. "The Role of Institutions in Community-Based
Conservation." In David Western and R. Michael Wright, eds., *Natural
Connections: Perspectives in Community-Based Conservation*, 403–27.
Washington, DC: Island Press.

Museum of the City. n.d. "Nuclear Power in Taiwan." www.museumofthecity
.org/project/nuclear-power-in-taiwan/.

Nace, Trevor. 2017. "China Shuts Down Tens of Thousands of Factories in
Widespread Pollution Crackdown." *Forbes*, October 24.

Nakajima, Akira. 2010. "Kōgai-kankyō hakai ni tachimukatta bengoshi no
torikumi" (Lawyers' initiatives for resisting pollution and environmental
destruction). In Nihon Bengoshi Rengōkai Kōgai Taisaku-Kankyō Hozen
Iinkai, ed., *Kōgai-kankyō soshō to bengoshi no chōsen* (Pollution-environmental
litigation and the challenge of lawyers), 3–27. Kyoto: Hōritsubunkasha.

Nasu, Toshiki. 2007. *Kankyōken no ronten (Chōsa shiryō: 2006-2-b. Shirīzu kenpō
no ronten 14)* (Issues in environmental rights [Survey materials: 2006-2-b.
Series constitutional issues 14]). Tokyo: Kokuritsu Kokkai Toshokan Chōsa
oyobi Rippō Kōsakyoku.

National People's Congress. 2016. *The 13th Five-Year Plan for Economic and Social Development of the People's Republic of China (2016–2020)*. http://en.ndrc.gov .cn/newsrelease/201612/P020161207645765233498.pdf.

The Nature Conservancy. n.d. "The Land Trust Reserve: A New Model of Nature Conservation in China." https://www.nature.org/en-us/about-us/where-we -work/asia-pacific/china/stories-in-china/the-land-trust-reserve/. Accessed March 2020.

NBS (National Bureau of Statistics). 2017. *China Energy Statistical Yearbook 2016*. Beijing: China Statistics Press.

——. 2019. *China Energy Statistical Yearbook 2018*. Beijing: China Statistics Press.

NDRC (National Development and Reform Commission). 2011. "Guojia fazhangaigewei Bangongting Guanyu Kaizhan Tan Paifangquan Jiaoyi Shi Dian Gongzuo de Tongzhi" (NDRC Notice on Pilot Trading Programs for the Development of Carbon Emissions Rights). Notice 2601." www.ndrc .gov.cn/zcfb/zcfbtz/2011tz/t20120113_456506.htm.

NDRC (National Development and Reform Commission), Department of Climate Change. 2015. "Enhanced Actions on Climate Change: China's Intended Nationally Determined Contributions." June 30. https://www4 .unfccc.int/sites/submissions/INDC/Published%20Documents/China/1 /China's%20INDC%20-%20on%2030%20June%202015.pdf.

NEA (National Energy Administration). 2019. "Gongbu 2019 nian diyipi fengdian, guangfufadian pingjia shang wang xiangmu de tongzhi" (NEA announces the first batch of wind and PV power generation projects for 2019). http://zfxxgk.nea.gov.cn/auto87/201905/t20190522 _3664.htm.

Nelson, Katie. 2014. "Reservoir at Hubei's Three Gorges Dam Is a Garbage-Strewn Pool of Hell. *Shanghaiist*, October 7. http://shanghaiist.com/2014 /10/07/reservoir-three-gorges-dam-pool-of-hell.php.

Nemeth, David J. 2008. "Blame Walt Rostow: The Sacrifice of South Korea's Natural Villages." In Timothy R. Tangherlini and Sallie Yea, eds., *Sitings: Critical Approaches to Korean Geography*, 83–97. Honolulu: University of Hawai'i Press; Center for Korean Studies, University of Hawai'i.

Nichibenren (Nihon Bengoshi Rengōkai). 1978. *Kōgai kara ningen no songen o mamoru tame ni: Nichibenren jinken yōgo no ayumi* (Defending human dignity against pollution: The history of Nichibenren human rights advocacy). Tokyo: Nihon Bengoshi Rengōkai.

——. 1988. *Chikyū kankyō hozen Kōbe sengen* (The Kobe declaration on global environmental protection). https://www.nichibenren.or.jp/activity /document/civil_liberties/year/1988/1988_2.html.

——. 2010. *Soshite inochi o mamoru tatakai wa tsuzuku: Kōgai-kankyō mondai ni okeru 40nen no kiseki to shōrai senryaku* (And the struggle to defend lives continues: The forty-year history of pollution and environmental problems and future strategies). Tokyo: Nihon Bengoshi Rengōkai.

Nichibenren Kōgai-Kankyō (Nihon Bengoshi Rengōkai, Kōgai Taisaku-Kankyō Hozen Iinkai), ed. 1991. *Nihon no kōgai yushutsu to kankyō hakai: Tōnan Ajia ni okeru kigyō shinshutsu to ODA* (Japan's pollution export and environmental destruction: The expansion of industry into Southeast Asia). Tokyo: Nihonhyōronsha.

Niitsu, Naoko. 2015. "Everyday Shopping Can Promote Local Economies, Says JFS Survey." *JFS Newsletter* (150) (February). www.japanfs.org/en/news/archives/news_ido35190.html.

Nishimura, Hitoshi. 2006. "Nihon ni okeru 'shizen gakkō' no dōkō" (Trends in "nature schools" in Japan). *Dōshisha daigaku sōgō seisaku kagaku kenkyūka* (Doshisha University School of Policy and Management) 8 (2): 31–44.

Nitō, Hajime, and Ikeo Takayoshi. 1973. "'Kankyōken' no hōri" (Legal principles of environmental rights). In Ōsaka Bengoshikai Kankyōken Kenkyūkai, ed., *Kankyōken* (Environmental rights), 41–60. Tokyo: Nihonhyōronsha.

NRDC (Natural Resources Defense Council). 2016. "The China Coal Consumption Cap Plan and Research Project." Issue brief, March 14. https://www.nrdc.org/resources/china-coal-consumption-cap-plan-and-policy-research-project.

O, Won-chol. 2009. *The Korea Story: President Park Jung-hee's Leadership and the Korean Industrial Revolution*. Seoul, Korea: Wisdom Tree.

OICA (International Organization of Motor Vehicle Manufacturers). n.d. "World Motor Vehicle Production by Country and Type, 2017–2018." www.oica.net/wp-content/uploads/By-country-2018.pdf.

Olsson, Marie, Aaron Atteridge, Karl Hallding, and Joakim Hellberg. 2010. "Together Alone? Brazil, South Africa, India, China (BASIC) and the Climate Change Conundrum." Policy brief, Stockholm Environment Institute. https://www.sei.org/publications/together-alone-brazil-south-africa-india-china-basic-climate-change-conundrum/.

O'Neill, Michael. 1997. *Green Parties and Political Change in Contemproary Europe: New Politics, Old Predicaments*. Burlington, VT: Ashgate.

Osaka Bengoshikai (Kankyōken Kenkyūkai). 1973. *Kankyōken* (Environmental rights). Tokyo: Nihonhyōronsha.

Ostrom, Elinor. 1990. *Governing the Commons: The Evolution of Institutions for Collective Action*. Cambridge: Cambridge University Press.

Ōsugi, Mami. 2012. "Shizen kankyōken no hogo" (Protection of natural environmental rights) *Nihon Fudōsan gakkaishi* (Journal of the Japan Real Estate Association) 26 (3): 29–34.

Ouchi, Yukio. 1987. "Kakudai zōrin seikatsu no rekishiteki tenkai katei" (The historical process of development of the broad forestation policy). *Ringyō keizai kenkyu* (Forest economics research) 111:3–11.

Paine, Robert, ed. 1977. *The White Arctic. Anthropological Essays on Tutelage and Ethnicity*. St. Johns: Institute of Social and Economic Research, Memorial University of Newfoundland.

Pan, Chen, Glen P. Peters, Robbie M. Andrew, Jan Ivar Korsbakken, Shantong Li, Dequn Zhou, and Peng Zhou. 2017. "Emissions Embodied in Global Trade Have Plateaued Due to Structural Changes in China." *Earth's Future* 5 (9): 934–46. https://doi.org/10.1002/2017EF000625.

Panayotou, Theodore. 1993. "Empirical Tests and Policy Analysis of Environmental Degradation at Different Stages of Economic Development." World Employment Programme Research Working Paper, Geneva.

PCP (Partners for Community Development). 2012. "Internal Project Funding Application YN12-GNRBS001, Hong Kong–Based NGO Partnerships for Community Development." www.pcd.org.hk/en.

Pearson, Margaret M. 1999. "The Major Multilateral Economic Institutions Engage China." In Alistair Iain Johnston and Robert S. Ross, eds., *Engaging China: The Management of an Emerging Power*. New York: Routledge.

People's Daily Online. 2004a. "China Sets Energy, Resources Saving as One of Key Economic Targets." December 6. http://english.peopledaily.com.cn /200412/06/eng20041206_166239.html.

———. 2004b. "Put Into Effect Scientific Viewpoint of Development in an All-Round Way." December 15. http://english.peopledaily.com.cn/200412 /14/eng20041214_167332.html.

Perry, Elizabeth J. 2008. "Chinese Conceptions of 'Rights': From Mencius to Mao—and Now." *Perspectives on Politics* 6 (1): 37–50.

———. 2011. "From Mass Campaigns to Managed Campaigns: Constructing a New Socialist Countryside." In Sebastian Heilmann and Elizabeth J. Perry, eds., *Mao's Invisible Hand: The Political Foundations of Adaptive Governance in China*, 30–61. Cambridge, MA: Asia Center, Harvard University Press.

Perry, Elizabeth J., and Stevan Harrell. 1983. "Syncretic Sects in Chinese History: A Symposium." *Modern China* 8 (3–4).

Pi County People's Government. 2007. *Pi Xian Renmin Zhengfu Bangongshi guanyu yinfa "Chuanxi Nongju Fengmao Baohu Jianshe Qu Pi Xian Shifan Dian jianshe shishi Fangan" de tongzhi* (Pi County People's Government General Office prints "Construction Implementation Scheme for the Pi County West Sichuan Farmhouse Character Preservation and Construction District Pilot Project"). Chengdu: Pi County People's Government.

———. 2011. "Tudi zhengzhi xiangmu guihua tu (jianshe yongdi)" (Land improvement project planning map [built land]). In Pi County Land and Resources Bureau, ed., *Pi Xian tudi zhengzhi guihua (2011–2015)* (Pi County land improvement plan [2011–2015]). Chengdu: Pi County People's Government.

Pietz, David A. 2015. *The Yellow River: The Problem of Water in Modern China*. Cambridge, MA: Harvard University Press.

Pinchot, Gifford. 2017 [1906]. "The Proposed Eastern Forest Reserves." In Char Miller, ed., *Gifford Pinchot: Selected Writings*, 43–49. University Park, PA: Penn State University Press.

Pittman, Russell. 2014. "Which Direction for South Korea Electricity Policy?" *Korea Energy Economic Review* 13 (1): 145–78.

Pizer, William A., and Xiliang Zhang. 2018. "China's New National Carbon Market." *AEA Papers and Proceedings* 108:463–67. https://doi.org/10.1257/pandp.20181029.

Plecher, H. 2019. "Gross Domestic Product (GDP) in Taiwan 2024." Statista. https://www.statista.com/statistics/727589/gross-domestic-product-gdp-in-taiwan.

Pollack, Mark A. and Gregory C. Shaffer. 2009. *When Cooperation Fails: The International Law and Politics of Genetically Modified Foods.* New York: Oxford University Press.

President, Office of the (Republic of China). 2016. "President Tsai Apologizes to Indigenous Peoples on Behalf of Government." https://english.president.gov.tw/NEWS/4950.

Qi, Ye, Wenjuan Dong, Changgui Dong, and Caiwei Huang. 2018. *Fixing Wind Curtailment with Electric Power System Reform in China.* Washington, DC: Brookings Institution. https://www.brookings.edu/research/fixing-wind-curtailment-with-electric-power-system-reform-in-china.

Qi, Yeh, Nicholas Stern, Tong Wu, Jiaqi Liu, and Fergus Green. 2016. "China's Post-coal Growth." *Nature Geoscience* 9 (8): 564–66.

Rapoza, Kenneth. 2015. "Are Chinese Investments in Argentina Destroying the Environment?" *Forbes*, May 30.

Ray, Sharmila, and Ki-Hyun Kim. 2014. "The Pollution Status of Sulfur Dioxide in Major Urban Areas of Korea between 1989 and 2010." *Atmospheric Research* 147–48:101–10.

Reardon-Anderson, James. 1997. *Pollution, Politics, and Foreign Investment in Taiwan: The Lukang Rebellion.* Armonk, NY: M. E. Sharpe.

REN21 (Renewable Energy Policy Network for the 21st Century). 2019. *Renewables 2018: Global Status Report.* Paris: REN21 Secretariat. www.ren21.net/gsr-2018.

Reuters. 2018. "China Coal Imports Highest Since 2014—Customs." January 12.
———. 2019. "China Installed 18 Percent Less Solar Power Capacity in 2018." January 17.

RFA (Radio Free Asia). 2016. "Pilu wuran shuju huanbao NGO fuzeren Liu Shu beibu" (Environmental NGO leader Liu Shu detained for disclosing pollution data). October 11. www.rfa.org/cantonese/news/arrest-10112016073626.html.

Robbins, Alicia S. T., and Stevan Harrell. 2014. "Paradoxes and Challenges for China's Forests in the Reform Era." *China Quarterly* 218:381–403.

Roberts, David. 2015. "Opinion: How the US Embassy Tweeted to Clear Beijing's Air." *Wired*, March 6.

Rodrigues, Maria Guadalupe Moog. 2003. *Global Environmentalism and Local Politics: Transnational Advocacy Networks in Brazil, Ecuador, and India.* Albany: State University of New York Press.

Rostow, Walt Whitman. 1960. *The Stages of Economic Growth: A Non-Communist Manifesto,* Cambridge: Cambridge University Press.

Rural Development Administration (Republic of Korea). n.d. "Hanguk nongeop geunhyeondaehwa 100 nyeon" (100 years of modernized agriculture in Korea). www.rda.go.kr/.

Saitō, Kiyoaki. 2001. "Kankyō mondai to borantia" (Environmental problems and volunteers). In Utsumi Seiji, ed., *Borantiagaku no susume* (An encouragement of volunteering), 2–23. Kyoto: Shōwadō.

Sarat, Austin, and Stuart A. Scheingold. 2006. "What Cause Lawyers Do *For,* and *To,* Social Movements: An Introduction." In Austin Sarat and Stuart Scheingold, eds., *Cause Lawyers and Social Movements,* 1–36. Stanford, CA: Stanford University Press.

Sax, Joseph L. 1971a. *Defending the Environment: A Strategy for Citizen Action.* New York: Knopf.

———. 1971b. "Legal Redress of Environmental Disruption in the United States: The Role of the Courts." In Tsuru Shigeto, ed., *Proceedings of International Symposium on Environmental Disruption: A Challenge to Social Scientists,* 223–32. Paris: International Social Science Council.

———. 1990. "The Search for Environmental Rights." *Journal of Land Use and Environmental Law* 6 (93): 91–105.

Scheingold, Stuart A. 2004. *The Politics of Rights: Lawyers, Public Policy, and Political Change.* Ann Arbor: University of Michigan Press.

Schmitt, Edwin. 2016. "The Atmosphere of an Ecological Civilization: A Study of Ideology, Perception, and Action in Chengdu, China." PhD thesis, Chinese University of Hong Kong.

Schneider, Annemarie, Karen C. Seto, and Douglas R. Webster. 2005. "Urban Growth in Chengdu, Western China: Application of Remote Sensing to Assess Planning and Policy Outcomes." *Environment and Planning B: Planning and Design* 32 (3): 323–45.

Schneier, Bruce. 2006. *Beyond Fear: Thinking Sensibly about Security in an Uncertain World.* New York: Copernicus Books.

Schreurs, Miranda A. 2002. *Environmental Politics in Japan, Germany, and the United States.* New York: Cambridge University Press.

Schreurs, Miranda A., and Yves Tiberghien. 2007. "Multi-level Reinforcement: Explaining European Union Leadership in Climate Change Mitigation." *Global Environmental Politics* 7 (4): 19–46.

Schroeder, Patrick. 2014. "Assessing Effectiveness of Governance Approaches for Sustainable Consumption and Production in China." *Journal of Cleaner Production* 63 (Supplement C): 64–73.

Schwartz, Jonathan. 2004. "Environmental NGOs in China: Roles and Limits." *Pacific Affairs* 77 (1): 28–49.

Scott, James C. 1998. *Seeing Like a State: How Certain Schemes to Improve the Human Condition Have Failed.* New Haven, CT: Yale University Press.

Seligsohn, Deborah, and Angel Hsu. 2016. "How China's 13th Five-Year Plan Addresses Energy and the Environment." *ChinaFile*, March 10. https://www.chinafile.com/reporting-opinion/environment/how-chinas-13th-five-year-plan-addresses-energy-and-environment.

Senba, Junko. 1989. "OO-ken to iu kotoba no seisei to hatten" (The origins and development of terms for XX-Rights). *Waseda Daigaku Nihongo Kenkyū Kyōiku Sentā Kiyō* (Bulletin of the Center for Japanese Language, Waseda University) 1:42–64.

Shan, Yuli, Dabo Guan, Heran Zheng, Jiamin Ou, Yuan Li, Jing Meng, Zhifu Mi, Zhu Liu, and Qiang Zhang. 2018. "China CO_2 Emission Accounts 1997–2015." *Scientific Data* 5 (January): 170201. https://doi.org/10.1038/sdata.2017.201.

Shapiro, Judith. 2001. *Mao's War against Nature: Politics and the Environment in Revolutionary China*. Cambridge: Cambridge University Press.

Shelton, Dinah. 2009. "Draft Paper on Human Rights and Environment: Past, Present and Future Linkages and the Value of a Declaration." Background paper prepared for High Level Expert Meeting on the New Future of Human Rights and Environment: Moving the Global Agenda Forward, co-organized by UNEP and OHCHR, Nairobi, November 30–December 1.

Shi Ju Zhi Ku (Anonymous staff of Chengdu agricultural agency) and Li Chuyue, eds. 2014. "Dang Tianfu Zhi Guo xuyao jinkou liangshi, Zhongguo zenme ban?" (When the Land of Heavenly Abundance must import grain, what is China to do?). *Guancha zhe* (Observer). www.guancha.cn/ShiJuZhiKu/2014_04_05_219104.shtml (archived at https://web.archive.org/save/https://www.guancha.cn/ShiJuZhiKu/2014_04_05_219104.shtml). Accessed April 2020.

Shim, Woo-hyun. 2017. "[Moon in Office] Moon Jae-in to Push for Renewable Energy Policies." *Korea Herald*, May 10. www.koreaherald.com/view.php?ud=20170510000794.

Shimizu, Makoto, Uchikawa Yoshikazu, Masaki Hiroshi, Awaji Takehisa, and Nagai Susumu. 1981. "Kankyōken kakuritsu e no michinori" (The process of realizing environmental rights). *Kōgai kenkyū* (Environmental research) 10 (3): 58–69.

Shin, Gi-Wook. 1996. *Peasant Protest and Social Change in Colonial Korea*. Seattle: University of Washington Press.

———. 1998. "Agrarian Conflict and the Origins of Korean Capitalism." *American Journal of Sociology* 103 (5): 1309–51.

Shin, Jin-Dong, Woo-Jong Lee, and Chang-Soo Lee. 2008. "Iphyangseong-gyeok mit sigie ttareun jeontong maeul ipjiteukseong yeongu" (A study on the characteristics of the locations of traditional Korea villages.) *Gukto Gyehoek* (Journal of Korea Planner Association) 43 (1): 7–25.

Shin, Sangbum. 2013. "China's Failure of Policy Innovation: The Case of Sulphur Dioxide Emission Trading." *Environmental Politics* 22 (6): 918–34.

Si, Zhenzhong. 2017. "Rebuilding Consumers' Trust in Food: Community-Supported Agriculture in China." In Jessica Duncan and Megan Bailey, eds., *Sustainable Food Futures: Multidisciplinary Solutions*, 34–45. London: Taylor and Francis.

Silverstein, Helena. 1996. *Unleashing Rights: Law, Meaning, and the Animal Rights Movement*. Ann Arbor: University of Michigan Press.

Smil, Václav. 1993. *China's Environmental Crisis. An Inquiry into the Limits of National Development*. Armonk, NY: M. E. Sharpe.

Smith, Eric A. 2001. "On the Coevolution of Cultural, Linguistic, and Biological Diversity." In Luisa Maffi, ed., *Language, Knowledge, and the Environment: The Interdependence of Biological and Cultural Diversity*. Washington, DC: Smithsonian Institution Press.

Somusho (General Affairs Office). 2017a. "Kaso kankei shichōson kyōdofuken betsu bunpuzu" (Map of the distribution by prefecture of cities, townships, and villages affected by depopulation). https://www.soumu.go.jp/main_content/000456268.pdf. Accessed April 2020.

———. 2017b. "Kaso taisaku no genkyō" (The current state of depopulation policies). www.soumu.go.jp/main_content/000473003.pdf. Accessed April 2020.

Song, Yajie, William Burch Jr., Gordon Geballe, and Liping Geng. 1997. "New Organizational Strategy for Managing the Forests of Southeast China: The Shareholding Integrated Forestry Tenure (SHIFT) System." *Forest Ecology and Management* 91 (2–3): 183–94.

Songster, E. Elena. 2018. *Panda Nation: The Construction and Conservation of China's Modern Icon*. New York: Oxford University Press.

Spires, Anthony J., Lin Tao, and Kin-man Chan. 2014. "Societal Support for China's Grass-Roots NGOs: Evidence from Yunnan, Guangdong and Beijing." *China Journal* 71:65–90.

State Council of the People's Republic of China. 2005. "Zhonghua Renmin Gongheguo kezaisheng nengyuan fa" (Renewable energy law of the People's Republic of China). www.gov.cn/ziliao/flfg/2005-06/21/content_8275.htm.

Statistics Times. 2018. "List of Countries by Projected GDP." http://statisticstimes.com/economy/countries-by-projected-gdp.php.

Stavins, Robert N. 2008. A Meaningful US Cap-and-Trade System to Address Climate Change." *Harvard Environmental Law Review* 32:293.

Steinhardt, H. Christoph, and Fengshi Wu. 2015. "In the Name of the Public: Environmental Protest and the Changing Landscape of Popular Contention in China." *China Journal* 75:61–82.

Stern, David I. 2004. "The Rise and Fall of the Environmental Kuznets Curve." *World Development* 32 (8): 1419–39.

Stern, David I., Michael S. Common, and Edward B. Barbier. 1996. "Economic Growth and Environmental Degradation: The Environmental Kuznets Curve and Sustainable Development." *World Development* 24 (7): 1151–60.

Sugimoto, Kyoko. 2016. "Tokushima chiiki enerugī Toyooka Kazumi-san ga yaritai no wa kankyōmondai ya enerugī mondai no kaiketsude wa naku, akumademo 'jizoku kanōna chiiki-dzukuri'" (Even though this was not the solution to environmental and energy problems that Ms. Toyooka Kazumi wanted, she will continue to pursue the creation of a sustainable region). *Greenz Japan*, October 24. https://greenz.jp/2016/10/24/tene/.

Suh, Chung-Sok, and Seung-Ho Kwon. 2014. "Wither the Developmental State in South Korea? Balancing Welfare and Neoliberalism." *Asian Studies Review* 38 (4): 676–92.

Taiban, Sasala. 2006. "The Lost Lily: State, Social Change, and the Decline of Hunting Culture in Haocha, Taiwan." PhD dissertation, University of Washington, Seattle.

———. 2008. "Chuantong lingyu de liejie yu chonggou: Kucapungane ren di tu pu yu bianqian de zai jianshi" (The division and re-construction of traditional territory: Reexamining human-land configuration and spatial change of Kucapungane). *Kaogu renleixue yanjiu* (Journal of archaeology and anthropology) 69:9–44.

Taiban, Sasala, Kurtis Pei, Dau-jye Lu, and Hwa-sheng Gau. 2015. "Disaster and Cultural Revitalization: The Practice of Community-Based Conservation at Wutai Township post Typhoon Morakot, Taiwan." *Macrotheme Review* 4 (6): 213–26.

Taiwan Today. 2014. "ROC Legislature OKs Food Act Amendments." January 29. https://taiwantoday.tw/news.php?unit=2,23,45&post=3282.

Takeuchi, Kazuhiko, Robert D. Brown, Izumi Washitani, Atsushi Tsunekawa, and Makoto Yokohari. 2003. *Satoyama: The Traditional Rural Landscape of Japan*. Tokyo: Springer.

Tam, Vivian W. Y. 2009. "Comparing the Implementation of Concrete Recycling in the Australian and Japanese Construction Industries." *Journal of Cleaner Production* 17 (7): 688–702.

Tamura, Kentaro, and Eric Zusman. 2011. "The Politics of Climate Policy in China: Interests, Institutions and Ideas." Working paper. Institute for Global Environmental Strategies, Kanagawa. https://www.iges.or.jp/en/pub/politics-climate-policy-china-interests/en.

Tao, Julia, and Daphne Ngar-yin Mah. 2009. "Between Market and State: Dilemmas of Environmental Governance in China's Sulphur Dioxide Emission Trading System." *Environment and Planning C: Government and Policy* 27 (1): 175–88.

Teets, Jessica C. 2014. *Civil Society under Authoritarianism: The China Model.* New York: Cambridge University Press.

———. 2018. "The Power of Policy Networks in Authoritarian Regimes: Changing Environmental Policy in China." *Governance* 31 (1): 125–31.

Telegraph. 2019. "How Japan Became the World's Fastest Growing Travel Destination." September 25.

Terao, Tadayoshi, and Kenji Otsuka, eds. 2007. *Development of Environmental Policy in Japan and Asian Countries*. New York: Palgrave Macmillan and IDE-JETRO.

Thompson, E. P. 1974. "Patrician Society, Plebeian Culture." *Journal of Social History* 7 (4): 382–405.

Tiberghien, Yves. 2012. "The Global Battle over the Governance of Agricultural Biotechnology: The Roles of Japan, Korea, and China." In Michael Howlett and David Laycock, eds., *Regulating Next Generation Agri-food Biotechnologies: Lessons from European, North American and Asian Experiences*, 111–25. London: Routledge.

Tilly, Charles. 2008. *Contentious Performances*. New York: Cambridge University Press.

Tilt, Bryan. 2015. *Dams and Development in China: The Moral Economy of Water and Power*. New York: Columbia University Press.

Tippins, Jennifer L. 2013. "Planning for Resilience: A Proposed Landscape Evaluation for Redevelopment Planning in the Linpan Landscape." Master's thesis, University of Washington, Seattle.

Toyota. 2018. "Toyota Sells 1.52 Million Electrified Vehicles in 2017, Three Years ahead of 2020 Target." https://newsroom.toyota.co.jp/en/corporate/20966057.html.

Trac, Christine J., Stevan Harrell, Thomas M. Hinckley, and Amanda C. Henck. 2007. "Reforestation Programs in Southwest China: Reported Success, Observed Failure, and the Reasons Why." *Journal of Mountain Science* 4 (4): 275–92.

Transport Policy. 2018. "Regions: China." https://www.transportpolicy.net/region/asia/china/.

Tsuang, Ben-Jei. 2014. "$PM_{2.5}$ yu shihua chanye." ($PM_{2.5}$ and the petrochemical industry). In Chou Kuei-Tien, ed., *Yongxu zhishang: Cong Gaoxiong qibao jiexi huanjing zhengyi yu zhuanxing daiduo* (The swan song of sustainable development: Environmental justice and transitional iinertia in Kaohsiung gas blast), 71–107. Taipei: Wunan Chubanshe.

Tsuji, Hiroshi. 2008. "Hekichi nōson gyoson ni okeru shizen taiken kyōiku katsudō" (Nature experience educational activities in remote agricultural and fishing communities). *Hokkaidō daigaku daigakuin kyōikugaku kenkyū kiyō* (Hokkaido University Graduate School pedagogical research notes) 104:149–167.

Tsuru, Shigeto, ed. 1971. *Proceedings of International Symposium on Environmental Disruption: A Challenge to Social Scientists*. Paris: International Social Science Council.

———. 1999. *The Political Economy of the Environment: The Case of Japan*. London: Athlone Press.

Tu, Shih-Yun (Du Shiyun). 2012. "Yuanzhumin shengtai zhishi yu tudi liyong guanxi zhi yanjiu: Yi liangge Paiwan Zu buluo nongye yu shoulie huodong wei li" (The study of the relationship between indigenous ecological knowledge and land use: Two Paiwan villages' agricultural and hunting activities as examples). Master's thesis, National Dong Hwa University, Hualien, Taiwan.

Tu, Wei-Ming. 1989. *Centrality and Commonality: An Essay on Confucian Religiousness* Albany: State University of New York Press.

Tyers, Roger. 2017. "It's Time to Wake Up to the Devastating Impact Flying Has on the Environment." *The Conversation.* https://theconversation.com /its-time-to-wake-up-to-the-devastating-impact-flying-has-on-the-envi ronment-70953.

Tyson, Elizabeth, and Kate Logan. 2016. "Tracking China's 'Filthy Rivers' with Citizen Science." *New Security Beat.* https://www.newsecuritybeat.org /2016/04/tracking-chinas-foul-filthy-rivers-citizen-science/.

Ui, Jun, ed. 1992. *Industrial Pollution in Japan.* Tokyo: United Nations University Press.

UNCHA (UN Office for the Coordination of Humanitarian Affairs). 1998. "Final Report on 1998 Floods in the People's Republic of China." https://reliefweb .int/report/china/final-report-1998-floods-peoples-republic-china.

UNEP (UN Environment Programme). 1972. "Declaration of the United Nations Conference on the Human Environment." http://webarchive.loc .gov/all/20150314024203/http%3A//www.unep.org/Documents .Multilingual/Default.asp?documentid%3D97%26articleid%3D1503.

UN-ESCAP (Economic and Social Commission for Asia and the Pacific). n.d. "A Paradigm Shift for Economic Growth: Republic of Korea's National Strategy for Green Growth and Five-Year Plan." https://www.unescap.org /sites/default/files/35.%20CS-Republic-of-Korea-National-Strategy-for -Green-Growth-and-Five9Year-Plan.pdf. Accessed March 2020.

UNFCCC (United Nations Framework Convention on Climate Change). 1992. "UNFCCC, Article 2: Objective." http://unfccc.int/essential_background /convention/background/items/1353.php.

———. 2019. "Decision 18/CMA.1: Modalities, Procedures and Guidelines for the Transparency Framework for Action and Support Referred to in Article 13 of the Paris Agreement." https://unfccc.int/documents /193408.

Upham, Frank K. 2009. *Law and Social Change in Postwar Japan.* Cambridge, MA: Harvard University Press.

US-China Economic and Security Review Commission. 2017. "The 13th Five-Year Plan." February 14. https://www.uscc.gov/Research/13th-five-year-plan.

van der Kamp, Denise. 2017. "Clean Air at What Cost? The Rise of 'Blunt Force' Pollution Regulation in China." PhD dissertation, University of California, Berkeley.

Vogel, David. 2012. *The Politics of Precaution.* Princeton, NJ: Princeton University Press.

Wakamatsu, Shinji, Tazuko Morikawa, and Akiyoshi Ito. 2013. "Air Pollution Trends in Japan between 1970 and 2012 and Impact of Urban Air

Pollution Countermeasures." *Asian Journal of Atmospheric Environment* 7 (4): 177–90.

Walker, Brett L. 2011. *Toxic Archipelago: A History of Industrial Disease in Japan.* Seattle: University of Washington Press.

Walsh, Matthew. 2019. "Climate Experts Raise Alarm on China's Coal Power Plants." *Caixin Global.* November 26.

Wang, Chin-Shou. 2014. "Taiwan huanjing yundong de falü dong yuan: cong san jian huanjing xiangguan panjue tan qi" (The legal mobilization of Taiwanese environmental Movements: Discussion from three cases related to the environment). *Taiwan zhengzhi xuekan* (Taiwan political science review) 18(1): 1–72.

Wang, Qiang, and Rongrong Li. 2017. "Decline in China's Coal Consumption: An Evidence of Peak Coal or a Temporary Blip?" *Energy Policy* 108 (September): 696–701. https://doi.org/10.1016/j.enpol.2017.06.041.

Wang, Qingchun, and Zhengyuan Liu. 2017. "2016nian ziran jiaoyu hangye diaocha baogao: Di sanjie ziran jiaoyu luntan" (2016 report on a survey of the nature education profession: 3rd Nature Education Forum). www .chinanatureeducation.org. Reposted in 2018 to https://wenku.baidu.com /view/4f6f8d22854769eae009581b6bd97f192279bfba.html. Accessed August 2020.

Wang, Tao, Likun Xue, Peter Brimblecome, Yun Fat Lim, Li Li, and Li Zhang. 2017. "Ozone Pollution in China: A Review of Concentrations, Meteorological Influences, Chemical Precursors, and Effects." *Science of the Total Environment* 575:1582–96.

Wang, Yue. 2018. "After Bike Sharing Explodes in China, Local Authorities Now Move to Clamp Down." *Forbes,* January 26.

Wedeen, Lisa. 2015. *Ambiguities of Domination: Politics, Rhetoric, and Symbols in Contemporary Syria.* 2nd ed. Chicago: University of Chicago Press.

Weller, Robert P. 1999. *Alternate Civilities: Democracy and Culture in China and Taiwan.* Boulder, CO: Westview Press.

———. 2006. *Discovering Nature: Globalization and Environmental Culture in China and Taiwan.* Cambridge: Cambridge University Press.

Western, David, and R. Michael Wright. 1994. "The Background to Community-Based Conservation." In David Western and R. Michael Wright, eds., *Natural Connections: Perspectives in Community-Based Conservation,* 1–14. Washington, DC: Island Press.

Whiting, Susan, Daniel Abramson, Shang Yuan, and Stevan Harrell. 2019. "A Long View of Resilience in the Chengdu Plain, China." *Journal of Asian Studies* 7 (2): 257–84.

Whitney, Joseph B. R. 1973. "Ecology and Environmental Control." In Michel Oksenberg, ed., *China's Developmental Experience,* 93–109. New York: Praeger.

WHO (World Health Organization). 2018. "Global Health Observatory (GHO) Data: Exposure to Ambient Air Pollution." https://www.who.int/gho/phe /outdoor_air_pollution/exposure/en/.

Wikipedia. 2019. "List of Countries by GDP (PPP) per capita." https://en
.wikipedia.org/wiki/List_of_countries_by_GDP_%28PPP%29_per_capita.

Wilkening, Kenneth E. 2004. *Acid Rain Science and Politics in Japan*. Cambridge,
MA: MIT Press.

Winters, Carrie. 2016. "China's Declining Cement Production? Can Environment Take a Breather?" *Eurasia Review*, May 6.

WNA (World Nuclear Association). 2019. "Nuclear Power in Japan." www
.world-nuclear.org/information-library/country-profiles/countries-g-n
/japan-nuclear-power.aspx.

Woodall, Brian. 1996. *Japan under Construction: Corruption, Politics, and Public
Works*. Berkeley: University of California Press.

Workman, Daniel. 2019. "Car Exports by Country." World's Top Exports. www
.worldstopexports.com/car-exports-country/.

World Bank. 2019. "Gross Domestic Product 2018." https://databank
.worldbank.org/data/download/GDP.pdf. Accessed July 2019.

———. n.d., a. "Air Transport, Passengers Carried—China." https://data
.worldbank.org/indicator/IS.AIR.PSGR?contextual=aggregate&locations
=CN. Accessed March 2020.

———. n.d., b. "GDP (Current US$)." https://data.worldbank.org/indicator/NY
.GDP.MKTP.CD. Accessed March 2020.

———. n.d., c. "International Tourism, Number of Arrivals—China." https://
data.worldbank.org/indicator/ST.INT.ARVL?contextual=aggregate&locations
=CN. Accessed March 2020.

———. n.d., d. "Japan." https://data.worldbank.org/country/japan.

———. n.d., e. "Korea, Rep." https://data.worldbank.org/country/korea-rep
?view=chart.

World Nuclear News. 2018. "Early Closure for Korea's Oldest Operating Reactor." June 15. www.world-nuclear-news.org/C-Early-closure-for-Koreas
-oldest-operating-reactor-1506184.html.

World Steel Association. 2018. "World Steel in Figures 2018." https://www
.worldsteel.org/en/dam/jcr:f9359dff-9546-4d6b-bed0-996201185b12
/World+Steel+in+Figures+2018.pdf.

———. 2019. "World Crude Steel Production—Summary." January 25. https://
www.worldsteel.org/en/dam/jcr:dcd93336-2756-486e-aa7f-64f6be8e6b1e/20
18%2520global%2520crude%2520steel%2520production.pdf.

———. 2020. "Crude Steel Production Monthly." https://www.worldsteel.org
/internet-2017/steel-by-topic/statistics/steel-data-viewer/MCSP_crude
_steel_monthly/CHN/IND/WORLD_ALL/TWN/JPN/KOR.

WTO (World Trade Organization). 2017. "WTO Statistics Database." http://stat
.wto.org. Accessed December 2017.

———. 2018. "World Trade Statistical Review." https://www.wto.org/english
/res_e/statis_e/wts2018_e/wts2018_e.pdf.

Wu, Fengshi. 2013. "Environmental Activism in Provincial China." *Journal of
Environmental Policy and Planning* 15 (1): 89–108.

Wu, Yu-Shan. 2007. "Taiwan's Developmental State: After the Economic and Political Turmoil." *Asian Survey* 47 (6): 977–1001.

Wulf, Monika, Michael Sommer, and Rolf Schmidt. 2010. "Forest Cover Changes in the Prignitz Region (NE Germany) between 1790 and 1960 in Relation to Soils and Other Driving Forces." *Landscape Ecology* 25 (2): 299–313.

Xi Jinping. 2017. "Jointly Shoulder Responsibility of Our Times, Promote Global Growth." Keynote speech at the Opening Session of the World Economic Forum Annual Meeting. CGTN America, January 17. https://america.cgtn.com/2017/01/17/full-text-of-xi-jinping-keynote-at-the-world-economic-forum.

Xiao, Lei. 2015. "Buying Time for the Farmers of Chengdu: Settlement Form, Labor Time Allocation, and Their Implications for Resilient Land Use Planning in a Rapidly Urbanizing Region." Master's thesis, University of Washington, Seattle.

Xiao, Yuan. 2014. "Making Land Fly: The Institutionalization of China's Land Quota Markets and Its Implications for Urbanization, Property Rights, and Intergovernmental Politics." PhD dissertation, Massachusetts Institute of Technology, Cambridge, MA.

Xinhua Net. 2017. "China Promises further Cuts to Steel, Coal Capacity." March 5. http://news.xinhuanet.com/english/2017-03/05/c_136104886.htm.

———. 2018. "Explanation of the State Council Institutional Reform Plan." March 14. www.xinhuanet.com/politics/2018lh/2018-03/14/c_1122533011.htm.

Xu, Xinliang, Liang Wang, Hongyan Cai, Luyao Wang, Luo Liu, and Hongzhi Wang. 2017. "The Influences of Spatiotemporal Change of Cultivated Land on Food Crop Production Potential in China." *Food Security* 9 (3): 485–95.

Yale Center for Environmental Law and Policy. 2018. "Environmental Performance Index 2018." https://epi.envirocenter.yale.edu/2018-epi-report/executive-summary.

Yamamura, Tsunetoshi. 1994. *Shizen hogo no hō to senryaku* (The law and strategy of nature protection). Tokyo: Yūhikyaku.

———, ed. 1998. *Kankyō NGO: Sono katsudō, rinen, to kadai* (Environmental NGOs: Their activities, principles, and challenges). Tokyo: Shinzansha.

Yan, Baohua. 2015. "Nature Education in China: Growing Demand, Greater Business Involvement, and a New Model for Conservation." Children and Nature Network, December 14. www.childrenandnature.org/2015/12/14/nature-education-in-china-growing-demand-greater-business-involvement-and-a-new-model-for-conservation/.

Yan Hairong. 2008. *New Masters, New Servants: Migration, Development, and Women Workers in China*. Durham, NC: Duke University Press.

Yang, Dali. 1998. *Calamity and Reform in China: State, Rural Society, and Institutional Change since the Great Leap Forward*. Stanford, CA: Stanford University Press.

Yang, Mary. 2018. "COP 24 Round-Up Part One: The Paris Rulebook." Inside Energy and Environment, December 18. https://www.insideenergy

andenvironment.com/2018/12/cop-24-round-up-part-one-the-paris
-rulebook/.

Yang, Qingjuan. 2014. "Chengdu Shi xinxing nongcun jujudian xuanzhi
pingjia tixi yanjiu" (Research on the system for evaluating the choice of
locations of concentrated new village housing in Chengdu). *Sichuan Daxue
xuebao (shehui kexue ban)*. (Journal of Sichuan University [social science
edition]) (1): 135–41.

Yang, Qingjuan, Bei Li, and Kui Li. 2011. "The Rural Landscape Research in
Chengdu's Urban-Rural Intergration Development." *Procedia Engineering*
21:780–88.

Yang, Rongjie, Jun Cai, Li Wang, and Dianquan Hu. 2012. "Analysis of
Protective Planning and Design of Suburban Linpan of Chengdu City in
China." *Journal of Landscape Research* 4 (3): 22–24, 28.

Yang Cheng-Hsien (Yang Zhengxian). 2012. *Dao, guo zhijian de "zuqun": Taiwan
Lanyu Tao, Feilübin Badan Dao Ivatan guanxi shi de dangdai xiangxiang* (The
ethnic group between islands and nations: The contemporary imagination
of the relationship history of the Tao of Taiwan's Lanyu and the Ivatan of
the Philippines' Batan). Hualien, Taiwan: National Dong Hwa University.

Yasuda, John Kojiro. 2013. "The Scale Problem: Food Safety, Scale Politics, and
Coherence Deficits in China." PhD dissertation, University of California,
Berkeley.

Ye, Yumin, and Richard LeGates. 2013. *Coordinating Urban and Rural Development in China: Learning from Chengdu*. Northampton, MA: Edward Elgar.

Yoneda, Yuriko. 2012. "Transition Towns in Japan and a Try for Local Energy
Independence by Fujino Denryoku." *JFS Newsletter* 121 (September). www
.japanfs.org/en/news/archives/news_id032303.html.

Yoon, Hong-key. 2006. *The Culture of Fengshui in Korea: An Exploration of East
Asian Geomancy*. Lanham, MD: Lexington Books.

Yoshida, Fumikazu, Akio Hata, and Haruo Tonegawa. 1999. "Itai-itai Disease
and the Countermeasures against Cadmium Pollution by the Kamioka
Mine." *Environmental Economics and Policy Studies* 1999 (3): 215–29.

Yoshimura, Ryōichi. 2010. "Kōgai-kankyō hō riron no seisei-hatten to bengoshi no yakuwari" (The origins and development of the legal theory of
pollution and environmental law and the role of lawyers). In Nihon
Bengoshi Rengōkai Kōgai Taisaku-Kankyō Hozen Iinkai, ed., *Kōgai-kankyō
soshō to bengoshi no chōsen* (Pollution-environmental litigation and the
challenge of lawyers), 52–65. Kyoto: Hōritsubunkasha.

Yuan, Lin, and Lin Yuan. 2013. "Problems and Countermeasures of Dujiangyan
Agricultural Area Protection during the Rapid Urbanization in Chengdu."
Paper presented at the 49th ISOCARP Congress 2013, Frontiers of Plan-
ning: Evolving and Declining Models of City Planning, Brisbane, Australia,
October 1–4.

Yuan, Lin. 2018. *Shengtai diqu de chuangzao: Dujiangyan guanqu de bentu renju
zhihui yu dangdai jiazhi* (Creating ecological regions: Indigenous wisdom for

sustainable living in Dujiangyan irrigation region). Beijing: Zhongguo
Jianzhu Gongye Chubanshe.

Yuen, Samson. 2015. "Friend or Foe? The Diminishing Space of China's Civil
Society." *China Perspectives* 3:51–56.

Zensho Eisuke. 1933. *Chosen no jūroku* (Human settlements of Korea). Keijo:
Chosen Sōtokufu.

Zhan, Shaohuo, and Lingli Huang. 2017. "Internal Spatial Fix: China's Geographical Solution to Food Supply and Its Limits." *Geoforum* 85 (Supplement C): 140–52.

Zhang, Bing, Hanxun Fei, Pan He, Yuan Xu, Zhanfeng Dong, and Oran R.
Young. 2016. "The Indecisive Role of the Market in China's SO_2 and COD
Emissions Trading." *Environmental Politics* 25 (5): 875–98.

Zhang, Jianfeng. 2018. "China Announces Cabinet Reshuffle Plan to Streamline Govt Work." CCTV, March 13. http://english.cctv.com/2018/03/13
/ARTISPxEr8uomw9YsaYjmHrG180313.shtml.

Zhang, Qian Forrest, and Jianling Wu. 2017. "Providing Rural Public Services
through Land Commodification: Policy Innovations and Rural-Urban
Integration in Chengdu." In Yijia Jing and Stephen P. Osborne, eds., *Public
Service Innovations in China*, 67–91. Singapore: Springer.

Zhang, Shoushuai. 2017. "Chengdu jiang dong jin, nan tuo, xi kong, bei gai,
zhong you" (Chengdu to advance east, extend south, control the west,
improve the north, and optimize the center). *Sichuan ribao* (Sichuan daily),
April 25. Archived at https://web.archive.org/save/http://sc.sina.com.cn
/news/b/2017-04-25/detail-ifyepsch3166648.shtml.

Zhang Chun. 2018. "China's Middle Class Gets a Taste for Healthy Eating."
ChinaDialogue, January 19.

Zhao, Fengjie, Yibing Ma, Yong-Guan Zhu, Zhong Tang, and Steve P. McGrath.
2014. "Soil Contamination in China: Current Status and Mitigation
Strategies." *Environmental Science and Technology* 49:750–59.

Zhou, Kate Xiao. 1996. *How the Farmers Changed China: Power of the People*.
Boulder, CO: Westview Press.

Zhao, Rui. 2013. *Solving the Problem of Urban River Pollution: Protect the River
from the Headwater and Restore the Ecosystem*. China NGO Case Study
Series 3. New Brunswick, NJ: Rutgers School of Social Work, Huamin
Research Center, Huamin Charity Foundation, Tsinghua University School
of Public Management.

Zhou, Ru. 2011. *Shijian huanjing jiaoyu: Huanjing xuexi zhongxin* (Environmental
education practice: Environmental learning centers). Taibei: Wunan Press.

———. 2013. *Ziran shi zui hao de xuexiao: Taiwan huanjing jiaoyu shijian* (Nature
is the best school: Taiwanese environmental education practice). Shanghai:
Shanghai Kexue Jishu Chubanshe.

CONTRIBUTORS

DANIEL BENJAMIN ABRAMSON is associate professor of urban planning and design and a member of the China studies faculty at the University of Washington. He has led numerous international planning collaborations in China and held a part-time visiting lectureship at Sichuan University in Chengdu (2012–17) focusing on rural and peri-urban community resilience.

SIMON AVENELL is associate professor at the Australian National University. His research interests include civil society, Japan and Asia, environmentalism, transnational activism, and political thought. His most recent book, *Transnational Japan in the Global Environmental Movement* (2017), recasts the history of Japanese environmental activism through a transnational lens.

HSI-WEN CHANG (LENGLENGMAN ROVANIYAW) is a Paiwan indigenous scholar and assistant professor in the Department of Indigenous Affairs and Ethno-development, National Dong Hwa University, Taiwan. She obtained her PhD in anthropology at the University of Washington in June 2017. Her research interests include environmental anthropology, tourism, place/space, and indigenous health.

HUA-MEI CHIU is associate professor of sociology at National Sun Yat-sen University, Taiwan. She is the author of the articles "Conflict and Compromise between Market and Social Forces" (2018) and "The Movement against Science Park Expansion and Electronics Hazards in Taiwan" (2014). She serves as a board member of Citizen of the Earth Taiwan.

JINGYUN DAI is a PhD student in sociology at Harvard University. She is broadly interested in political sociology and development. She has researched environmental NGOs in China and is currently working on left-leaning activism in China.

IZA DING is assistant professor of political science at the University of Pittsburgh. She is working on a book on environmental governance in China.

ROB EFIRD is professor of anthropology and asian studies at Seattle University. His community-based research focuses on children's environmental learning in China and the Pacific Northwest. He was a Fulbright Senior Research Scholar in China (2011–12) and a National Committee on US-China Relations Public Intellectual Program Fellow (2014–16).

ASHLEY ESAREY is assistant professor of political science at the University of Alberta and academic advisor to the China Institute. He is the coauthor of *My Fight for a New Taiwan: One Woman's Journey from Prison to Power* (2014) and coeditor of *The Internet in China: Cultural, Political, and Social Dimensions* (2014) and *Taiwan in Dynamic Transition: Nation Building and Democratization* (2020).

HWA-SHENG GAU is associate professor in the Institute of Cultural and Creative Industries at Tajen University, Taiwan. His long-time research interests include indigenous traditional territory, community tourism, and local, cultural, and creative industries.

MARY ALICE HADDAD is chair of the College of East Asian Studies and professor of government, East Asian studies, and environmental studies at Wesleyan University. She is the author of *Building Democracy in Japan* (2012) and *Politics and Volunteering in Japan: A Global Perspective* (2007).

STEVAN HARRELL is professor emeritus of anthropology and environmental and forest sciences at the University of Washington. His research focuses on human ecology, family and demography, ethnic relations, material culture, and elementary education in China and Taiwan. He is writing a book on the ecological history of modern China.

CHUNG HO KIM is an architect, urban scholar, and assistant professor of urban planning and design at the University of Seoul. His recent research focuses on East Asia's rapid urbanization and built-environment-driven developments in terms of long-term sustainability and social-ecological resilience. He is the author of *Desire City, Seoul* (2017) and *Birth of Space, 1968–2018* (2019).

JOANNA I. LEWIS is associate professor of energy and environment and director of the Science, Technology, and International Affairs Program at Georgetown University's School of Foreign Service. She has worked on energy and climate issues in China for two decades and is the author of *Green Innovation in China: China's Wind Power Industry and the Global Transition to a Low-Carbon Economy* (2013).

EUNJUNG LIM is associate professor in the Division of International Studies, Kongju National University. Her areas of specialization include energy and climate change policies of East Asian countries and nuclear governance. She previously taught at Johns Hopkins University and Ritsumeikan University.

HUI-NIEN LIN is associate professor in the Indigenous Program of the College of Tourism and Hospitality at I-Shou University, Taiwan. Her research focuses on indigenous studies related to traditional ecological knowledge and resilience.

DAU-JYE LU is associate professor in the Department of Forestry and Resources at National Taiwan University. His research interests include community-based conservation, community forestry, and indigenous natural resource management.

KURTIS JIA-CHYI PEI is professor at the Institute of Wildlife Conservation, National Pingtung University, Taiwan. His research fields include wildlife population ecology, mammalogy, and human dimensions of natural conservation. He has worked on traditional hunting knowledge and natural resource management in indigenous communities for three decades.

NORIKO SAKAMOTO spent twelve years as communications director of Japan for Sustainability, a Japanese NGO committed to improving education about environmental sustainability. She now works for Japan's Ministry of Education, Culture, Sports, Science, and Technology.

ANTHONY J. SPIRES is deputy director of the Centre for Contemporary Chinese Studies and a senior lecturer at the University of Melbourne's Asia Institute. He holds a PhD in sociology from Yale University. His research focuses on the development of civil society in China.

SASALA TAIBAN is a Rukai indigenous scholar and professor in the Department of Sociology at National Sun Yat-sen University, Taiwan. He obtained his PhD in anthropology at the University of Washington in June 2006 and has worked on natural disaster and community resilience issues in southern Taiwan for decades.

YVES TIBERGHIEN is professor of political science, director emeritus of the Institute of Asian Research, and codirector of the Center for Japanese Research at the University of British Columbia. He holds a PhD from Stanford University. His work focuses on global environmental and economic governance in East Asia, including climate change, agriculture biotechnology, and biodiversity.

INDEX

A

Abe, Shinzō, 68, 72; and GMO controversy, 216
aboriginal land reserves (Taiwan), 209–10
aborigines. *See* indigenous people
academic success: conflict of nature schools with, 139
accidents, industrial, 181, 186, 187
Act on Sites for Establishment of Final Disposal Facilities for Low-Level Radioactive Waste, 200
activism: and air pollution, 35, 38, 150, 250; citizen, 245, 262; and climate change, 188; comparisons to rest of the world, 33; consumer, 245; and eco-developmental state, 264; and Environmental Kuznets Curve, 245; in Kaohsiung, 181–96; lawyers in, 92–93, 105; low levels in East Asia, 13; restricted to local level, 16; urban elite, 245
activists: collaboration with professionals, 195; types of, 181, 183, 190–91. *See also* protest
adaptive capacity: in Chengdu Plain, 165, 175–76; China's low, 165; and climate change, 175
administrative appeals, 230

Administrative Licensing Law (China), 227
Advanced Semiconductor Engineering, 187, 192–93
advocacy, 12; differences among NGOs, 235; issues addressed, 35–37; modes of, 33–35; multiple strategies, 235–36; and policymakers, 35; strategies of environmental, 32–43, 225–37; success and failure of strategies, 234–35
Agency for Natural Resources and Energy (Japan), 67
Agongdian River (Kaohsiung), 187
agriculture: and biodiversity, 171, 174; commercialization of, 166; community supported (CSA), 170–72; ecological, obstacles to, 175; farm consolidation in China, 166, 167; increasing yields and reforestation, 252; organic, 170, 171, 172, 174, 216, 260–61; sustainable, 166; and water quality, 171, 174–75
agritourism, 168, 173
air pollution, 6; apps for monitoring, 250; China's affects Korea, 71; criteria for, 248–49; and economic

diesel oil: reduced use of, 251; sulfur content of, 249

disasters, natural: mapping of, 129, 131. *See also* Fukushima triple disaster; Typhoon Morakot

Dongfeng brand trucks, 251

Duoli Organic Farm Conglomerate, 174

Dudek, Dan, 83, 90n6

Dujiangyan irrigation system, 165; changes in New Socialist Countryside, 167; as cultural heritage, 176; ecological function of, 176

Dung Senyung, Rev., 198

dust storms, 10

directed experimentation. *See* pilot programs

E

East Asia: compared to rest of world, 37–40; consumption and pollution in, 6; importance as a region, 6–13; interconnections within, 10; international influence of, 8–9; lessons to be learned from, 264–65; resource poverty of, 7; variation within, 13–17

eco-developmental state: and adaptive capacity, 175–77; broad applicability of concept, 264; in China, 149, 151, 164–77; civil society and, 6; as compromise, 24, 28, 30; defined, 6; and deforestation, 253; evolution of, 23–30, 256, 261; factors in formation of, 28–30; in Japan, 24, 74, 92–94, 106, 110, 121, 224; in Korea, 24–25, 74, 224; lack of historical awareness, 176; limitations on concept, 264; and nature education, 149; opportunities for activism, 274; and organic food, 260; role of

lawyers in, 91, 106; and soil contamination, 260; in Taiwan, 123, 196, 200, 203, 207; transition to, 5–6, 13, 15–16, 17–18, 32, 42, 74, 92–94, 106, 196, 200, 203, 216–17, 242–48, 261–66; utility of concept, 262–63; as a variety of developmental state, 262–63. *See also* developmental state

"ecological civilization," 12, 22, 27, 173, 241

economic restructuring, 58

ecotourism: indigenous, 132, 134

education: access to, 158; as advocacy, 12, 36–37, 39–40; and developmental state, 19; lack of, as impediment to environmental activism, 209; about pollution, 181. *See also* environmental education

electricity, 13–14; community managed, 111–21; curtailment, 51; decentralization, 111; demand management, 69, 73; diversification of sources, 65; efficiency, 65–66, 73; hydroelectric, 251; integration of, 51; market liberalization in, 110–11; markets, 66–67, 72, 73, 74n4, 75n5; solar, 50–51, 118–21, 251; stabilization, 69; wind, 50–51, 120, 151

electroplating, 187

Elvin, Mark, 165

emissions trading: adoption of, 82–83; compared to command-and-control, 77, 83, 85, 87; disincentives to participation in, 84–85; evaluation of, 80–81; feedback distortion in, 86, 87; incentives for, 80–81; lack of success, 82, 84–85, 87–89; pilot programs, 83–86. *See also* carbon emissions; carbon emissions trading; pollution trading endangered species, 8–9; as advocacy issue, 33–35, 38–39; and community-based conservation, 127–29; litigation on behalf of, 104–5; and population density, 11; recording of, 129

energy, 6; as advocacy issue, 33–35, 38–39; centrality of, to environmental issues, 42; clean, 48; conservation after Fukushima, 110; conservation in Japan, 66, 68, 72; conservation in Taiwan, 189; conservation technologies, 68; consumption, 48–49; and development, 47, 48–49; and Environmental Kuznets Curve, 244–45; imports of, 7, 62–63, 255; intensity, 48–49, 54, 55–56; intensity targets, 56; Japan's white papers on, 67–68; Korea's white papers on, 68–69, 71, 75n8; national mixes of, 63, 65; nuclear, 13–14; policy, 62–75; and reforestation, 254–55; renewable, 50–51; transition, 193; use rights, 78. *See also* renewable energy

ENGOs (environmental nongovernmental organizations). *See* NGOs (nongovernmental organizations)

environmental colonies, 189

environmental consciousness, rise of, 20–23

Environmental Defense Fund, 83

environmental diplomacy: China's role in, 51–54

environmental education: conflict with academic (test) success, 139, 142–45; as curricular requirement, 142–43; deficiency of in China, 138–39; guidelines for, 142, 146; lack of field experience, 142–43; parent-child conflicts and, 141; and sacrifice, 142; safety concerns as impediment to, 143; school-based, contrasted to nature schools, 142–45; teacher training, 145–46. *See also* nature education

environmental forums, 8; China's role in, 51–52. *See also* Paris Agreement; Rio Conference

environmental health: remediability of, 247

environmental impact assessments: in China, 84, 234; in Kaohsiung, 187–89; law of, in Japan, 92

Environmental Impact Assessment Law (China), 227

Environmental Jurists Association (Taiwan), 192

environmental justice: as advocacy issue, 33–35, 38–39, 183, 189; sensitivity as issue, 232

Environmental Kuznets Curve (EKC), 164, 241–65; and air pollution, 248–52; and climate change, 247, 261–62, 263; and deforestation, 253–57, 262; diagrammed, 243; differential applicability of, 261–62; drivers of, 244–46, 261–62; factors affecting, 244–46; and greenhouse gas emissions, 247, 261–62; and groundwater depletion, 247, 261; history of, 242; and materialist teleology, 242; and moral hazard, 242; not automatic, 263; physical limits on, 263; problems with, 242, 262–63; and soil contamination, 257–61; timing of, 246–47; and water pollution, 247, 261, 262

Environmental Monitoring Alliance (Kaoshiung), 184

environmental movements: and democracy, 16–17, 200; in China, 23, 166; in Japan, 20–21; in Korea, 21–22; obstacles to, 193–96; rise

forest cover, 7; in China, 28, 255–56; in Japan, 253; in Korea, 254–55; in Taiwan, 254. *See also* deforestation; reforestation

Forestry Bureau (China), 233, 255–56

Formosa Plastics Group, 186–87, 192, 194

fossil fuels:; dependency on, 26, 37, 47–48, 62, 65, 155; imports of, 7; increases in, 75; replacing with renewables, 245, 252, 263; transition to, 155, 162, 261. *See also* coal; greenhouse gases; natural gas; petroleum

Free Trade Agreement, US-Korea, 223

Friends of Nature (Ziran zhi You), 140, 143, 144, 146

Fukui, Masahiro, 119

Fukushima triple disaster, 13–14, 26, 63, 66; blackouts, 109; death tolls, 109; destroyed buildings, 109; effects in Taiwan, 193; and energy imports, 70; evacuation from, 109; and regulation, 68; safety concerns in Korea after, 71

G

Gabon, 7

Gaia Nature School, 137–38, 140–42; ecological garden, 140; founding, 140; influence of, 140. *See also* nature education

Gaoligongshan Nature Reserve, 146

gas. *See* natural gas

GDP (gross domestic product), 5, 62; calculation of, 31n2; carbon intensity of, 55; and emissions, 48; and energy, 48; and Environmental Performance Index, 243–44; growth rates, 66, 74n3; increases in, 48; as misleading indicator, 242; rankings, 62

genetically modified organisms. *See* GMOs (genetically modified organisms)

geomancy. *See* fengshui

Gifu Prefecture, 113–18; water resources of, 116

glass: and energy, 255

global-local interactions, 41–42

GMOs (genetically modified organisms), 9–10, 213–24; Cartagena Protocol on, 214–15; constrained environment for opposition to, 218–20; and consumer rights, 221; Diet opponents in Japan, 221–22; EU opposition to, 214; and food security, 221; and health issues, 221; inadvertent content limits on, 215; lack of electoral salience of, 216; mandatory labeling of, 214–15, 221, 223; "precautionary principle" approach to, 214; "pro-science" approach to, 213–14; protectionism and, 216; "pro-trade" approach to, 213–14; public opinion on, 216; resolutions against, 221–22; "substantial equivalence" consensus on, 213–14; US support of, 214

Golden Chimney Association, 188–89

governance: civic participation in, 195; climate, 59; competing forms of, 217, 223; differences in, 14–15; environmental, 237; and law, 230; local, 12, 166, 193; indigenous, 206; and state strength, 226–27; strategies of, 17; street level, 82. *See also* authoritarianism; bureaucracy; command-and-control; democracy

government restructuring, 59–60

GPS (global positioning systems): in conservation, 127–29

Great Leap Forward, 86

252; micro-scale community, 113–18; targets for, 56. *See also* dams

I

Ikeo Takayoshi, 97–98
imports: beef, 224n3; coal, 63; corn, 215, 218; energy, 62–63, 255; natural gas, 72; petroleum, 63; soy, 215, 218; wood, 257
incinerators: protests against, 233
Indigenous Are the Protectors of the Forest Symposium, 131
indigenous knowledge. *See* TEK (traditional ecological knowledge)
indigenous people: in China, 23; intellectuals among, 200; relationship to land, 201, 212; social disfunction among colonized, 212; in Taiwan, 22, 122–36, 197–212; tribalism among, 200. *See also* Paiwan indigenous people; Rukai indigenous people; Tao indigenous people
Indigenous Traditional Sites and Ecological Resources Maintenance Project, 130
Indonesia, 7
Indramang Life Community, 219
industrial policy: in China, 48
industrial transition, 189, 193, 194
industrial refugees, 188
industrial zones, 189–90
industry: control of polluting, 248; and deforestation, 253, 255; development of in Taiwan, 183, 188; eliminating polluting, 77–78; green, 30; as policymaker, 35; pollution in Taiwan, 181–96; recycling in, 9; and soil contamination, 257–58; strategic emerging, 50; support and rise of eco-developmental state, 28–29;

transition away from heavy, 58; value of polluting, 96; variation in pollution payments, 79; water consumption by, 186
information asymmetry: in emissions trading, 86, 88–89
injunctions: against development, 98, 99
Inner Mongolia: goal gasification in coalfields of, 252
Institute for Sustainable Energy Policies, 111
international agreements, 53, 54
International Campaign for Responsible Technology, 192–93
International Civil Aviation Organization (ICAO), 59
international connections: and biodiversity, 52; and climate change, 51–53, 55, 91, 103–4, 106; and emissions trading, 79–80; and pollution abatement, 192–93
international examples: in emissions trading, 82–83; in environmental rights, 97
international movements, 16. *See also* NGOs (nongovernmental organizations)
international reputation, 81, 88
International Symposium on Environmental Disruption (1970), 97
Iranmeylek Village, Lanyu, 202–3
irrigation, 25–26; canals repurposed for hydro generation, 116–18
Irrigation Canal Agricultural Cooperative, 117
itai-itai (ow ow!) disease, 21, 258–59
Itoshiro Village, 113–18; café serving local foods, 115; climate, 114; community association, 117; community hydro project, 115–18; cooperative culture of, 114; crops, 114; food processing in, 115;

markets (*continued*)
77–78, 81, 88; in pollution trading,
14–15, 55, 81, 83, 84–85, 87–88;
real estate, 172–74; similarity to
command-and-control, 85. *See also*
emissions trading
martial law: abolition of, 198
Marxism: explanation of
environmental degradation, 20, 23
Matsushita Ryūichi, 102–3
"mayor's mailbox," 229
media: as advocacy strategy, 46,
225–26; digital, 135; environmental
advocacy in, 100, 188, 191, 216,
220, 224, 233–34; environmental
reporting in, 241; and
environmental rights, 100;
indigenous, 203, 210–11;
mobilization of, 37, 188, 191,
225–26, 232–33, 235; social, 191,
233, 235
middle class: and conservation, 184;
and environmental activism,
184–85
migration: rural-to-urban, 169;
urban-to-rural, 162
Miki Takeo, 101–2
Minamata disease, 21, 95; litigation
and, 95
mining: and soil contamination,
258–60
Ministry of Agriculture (Japan), 218,
222
Ministry of Ecology and
Environment (MEE; China), 60,
78; establishment of, 89; relative
weakness of, 80
Ministry of Economy and Trade
(Korea), 216, 223
Ministry of Economy, Trade, and
Industry (METI; Japan), 222
Ministry of Education (China), 143
Ministry of Environmental
Protection (China), 60, 77–78, 227

Ministry of Internal Affairs
and Communication (Japan),
112–13
Ministry of Natural Resources
(China), 149
Ministry of Science (Korea), 223
Ministry of the Environment
(Japan), 248
Mitsui company, 21
model villages, 153
Monsanto, 214
Moon Jae-in, 69, 70, 72, 75n10; and
civil society, 223
motor vehicles, 8, 63; and air
pollution, 250, 251; exports and
imports, 63; in First Saemaul
Village, 159; ownership of, in
Korea, 159
Mountain Forest Patrol (Taiwan),
126–31; activities of, 129–31;
challenges to work, 134–35; change
of name, 130; composition of, 127;
creation of, 127; dependence on
government financing, 135; and
illegal logging, 130; landslides
discovered by, 130; patrol routes,
130; training, 127–29
Mugi Town, 119
multinational corporations, 19–20
"myth of rights," 93–94

N

Nanjing, 79
Nantian Village (Taiwan), 197;
chiefship system, 206–7; Christian
churches in, 207; colonization in,
206–12; compared to Lanyu,
210–11; dependency of, 208–9; lack
of indigenous media, 211;
migration from, 208, 209, 210–11;
powerlessness of chiefs, 207–8;
reduction of local autonomy in,
211–12; as resettlement/refugee

village, 207, 211; selected as nuclear waste site, 200; shrimp farming in, 208; sinicization in, 209; support for nuclear waste site, 208–9, 211–12; Taiwan Power Company promises to, 200–201, 207. *See also* Paiwan indigenous people

Nanzih Export Processing Zone, 186

Naphtha Cracker Plants, 184–85, 190, 194

Naruto City, 120

National Association for Korean Farmers, 219

National Local Energy Association (Japan), 111

National Nature Education Forum (China), 147–48

National People's Congress, 59–60, 227, 231. *See also* People's Congress

Nationalist Party (Taiwan), 25, 26; as colonial power, 201–2; as obstacle to environmentalism, 194; promotion of nuclear power by, 198; promotion of polluting industry by, 187, 189, 194; similarity of environmental positions to Democratic Progressive Party, 194–95

natural gas, 6; expansion in Korea, 71, 72; in First Saemaul Village, 160; imports to Japan, 63, 70, 72; in Japan, 63; spill disaster, 185

natural resources: common pool, 148; conservation of, 9; Environmental Kuznets Curve and, 242–43; imports of, 63, 72; inclusive management of, 123–25; indigenous people and, 122, 126, 127–31, 133–34, 205; limits on, 98; local, 111, 113, 116, 126, 127–31; and nuclear power, 25–26; poverty of, 7, 13, 17, 25–26, 62, 72, 74;

self-sufficiency of, 13; tourism and, 29

Natural Resources Defense Council, 27

nature: in childrearing, 137–49; and human health, 104, 138, 143, 148; and hunters, 132; lost connections to, 125; mastery of, 152; rediscovery of, 148–49; responsibilities to, 104; right to enjoy, 104; rights of, 104–5

Nature Conservancy, The, 9, 27

nature education, 137–49, 233; access to, 149; adaptation of, to China, 145; as aspect of environmental education, 141–42; contrast to classroom environmental education, 141, 142, 142–45, 148–49; and eco-developmental state, 149; and environmental stewardship, 142; growth of in China, 143, 148–49; growth of in Japan, 147; Hong Kong, Japan, and Taiwan influence on China's, 146–48; and human health, 143, 148–49; importance of parents in, 140–41, 143–44, 145, 148; in national parks, 149; and "nature deficit disorder," 139; NGOs and, 228, 233; parent-child, 137–38, 139, 140–42, 145; as pleasurable experience, 142; as supplement to formal education, 138–39; sustainability of, 140–41. *See also* Gaia Nature School; Maolin Hunter School; Shicheng Nature School

nature reserves, 233

nature schools. *See* nature education

nature-deficit disorder, 139, 143–44

NDRC (National Development and Reform Commission), 54, 60, 76, 89; relative strength of, 80

Nemeth, David, 176

neocolonialism: and resource extraction, 243

neo-Confucianism: and village structure, 151–52

networks, business-government-nonprofit, 35–36, 41

New Rural Reconstructionist (NRR) Movement, 170, 175, 177n2

New Socialist Countryside/Village Campaign (China). *See* Socialist New Countryside Construction (SNCC) Campaign

New Village Movement (Korea), 25, 150–63; as inspiration for China's New Socialist Countryside, 163, 175; leadership training in, 155; marginalization of the rural, 162; sacrifice of resilience by, 175; urban dependency created in, 162–63

NGOs (nongovernmental organizations): absence of national scale in China, 27; anti-globalization, 221; anti-GMO, 216–21; approached by governments, 231; budgets of, 228; cautious nature of in China, 237; and conservation, 8–9; co-optation of, by government, 237; detention of leaders of, 226; and education, 140; framing of issues of, 216, 225, 231–32; government sponsors of, 226–27; and governments, 216, 217; governments' dependence on, 230; grassroots, 225–37; interactive relations with governments, 225, 226–27, 229–31; international, 8–9, 9–10, 27, 35–36, 226; and international linkages, 216, 218, 226; labor, 226; limits on, 237; and media exposure, 37, 188, 191, 225–26, 229, 233–35; mobilization of social support, 233–35; and nature education, 228, 233;

nature-focused, growth of, 147; opposition to dams, 225, 228; for organic agriculture, 170; and public education, 235; registration of, 226, 228; and renewable energy, 111–12, 114–15; repression of, 226; rise of, 16; and sensitive issues, 232; specialization among, 228; strategies used by, 229–36

NIMBY logic, 96

Nitō Hajime, 97–98

nitrogen oxides (NO_x), 78; modest decline in, 249; regulations on, 249

No GMO! Campaign (Japan), 220–22

North China Plain: air pollution in, 252; groundwater depletion on, 261

NPOs (nonprofit organizations). *See* NGOs (nongovernmental organizations)

nuclear power, 13; and GHG reduction, 68; in Japan, 63, 65, 66, 67; in Korea, 63–65, 67; phaseout in Korea, 69, 71, 75n10; and reducing import dependency, 72; restarting after Fukushima, 68, 70; shutdown after Fukushima, 110; spent fuel, 73; strategic importance, 197–98; in Taiwan, 25–26, 193, 197–212; Taiwan plant locations, 198, 199; targets for, 56; waste, 75n9, 197–212. *See also* antinuclear movements; nuclear waste

Nuclear Regulation Authority (Japan), 70

nuclear waste: acceptance in Nantian, 206–12; as bringer of "paradise," 200–201; equated with garbage, 204; and opposition to fourth nuclear plant, 198–200; repository construction, 198; repository signage, 198; salience as political issue, 200; in Taiwan, 197–212

O

OECD (Organization for Economic Cooperation and Development), 213, 218–19
office visiting, 229
oil. *See* petroleum
one child policy. *See* planned-birth policy
Onsan disease, 24
Orchid Island. *See* Lanyu (Orchid Island, Pongso no Tao); Tao indigenous people
Osaka Airport Case, 99, 100, 101
Osaka Federation of Lawyers, 97–98
overcapacity, 58
Overseas NGO Management Law, 226
ozone: compared to Los Angeles, 252; as intractable problem, 252; lack of decline in, 249–50

P

Paik Un-gyu, 71
Paiwan indigenous people, 197; acceptance of land registration, 209–10; change in land values, 209–10; chiefship system, 206–7. *See also* Nantian Village (Taiwan)
pandas, 9
Panyu District: incinerator protests in, 233
parental overprotectiveness, 139, 146
Park Chung-hee, 25, 152–53; and reforestation, 254–55
Partners for Community Development, 146
partnerships: interparty, 25; NGO-government, 146, 232; NGO-local

as advocacy strategy, 39–40, 170–71; NGO-local in conservation, 126; private-business as advocacy strategy, 39–40; private-government as advocacy strategy, 35–37, 39–40; trading, 10
party incentive: and rise of eco-developmental state, 29–30
Paris Agreement, 53, 55, 59, 63–65; targets, 70, 72, 74nn1,2; US withdrawal from, 90n11
path-dependency: in ecosystems, 165; in emissions trading, 87
patriliny: and village structure, 152; in Yangdong Village, 155–56
People's Congress, 229, 236. *See also* National People's Congress
performance evaluation: of local environment bureaus, 86
petrochemicals: downsizing of Taiwan's industry, 193; industry zone, 189; remediation of damage from, 186; water pollution from, 186
petroleum: refining and processing, 183, 184–85; and soil contamination, 259. *See also* petrochemicals
photovoltaic power. *See* solar power
Pi County (Sichuan): decline of grain cultivation in, 169; decline of rapeseed cultivation in, 170
Pigovian taxes, 250
pigs: growth in Chengdu, 169–70
pilot programs, 37, 39, 41, 55, 77; in carbon emissions trading, 55, 80; information asymmetry and, 86; in *linpan* preservation, 171; in pollution trading, 79–80, 81, 83–86, 88–89, 90n3, 91n17; sulfur dioxide trading, 79; variation in, 84

pipelines: explosions of, 189, 193
planned-birth policy: and nature
    schools, 139; and parental
    overprotectiveness, 139; and
    selfishness, 141
plutonium, 73
$PM_{2.5}$: reduction in, 249
PM_{10}: decline in, 249
"point-to-surface" (*you dian dao
    mian*). *See* pilot programs
policy advocacy: as NGO focus,
    228–29
policy entrepreneurs, 216–17, 222
policy experimentation. *See* central-
    local relations; pilot programs
policy papers: as advocacy strategy,
    36–37, 39–40, 229
policy theater, 77, 81–89; negative
    effects of, 88
pollution: as advocacy issue, 33–35,
    38–39, 95–96; compensation for,
    95; compensation to victims of,
    184; and conservation, 183; and
    economic growth, 96; and human
    health, 187; as impetus for
    environmental rights, 95–97;
    litigation concerning, 95–97; and
    population density, 11; protests
    against, 181–96; as sacrifice,
    23–24; timing of, 34–35; "tolerable
    limits," 96. *See also* air pollution;
    pollution trading; soil
    contamination; water pollution
pollution trading, 76–91; auctions,
    84, 85; and carbon emissions
    trading, 79–80; exchange centers,
    84; expansion, lack of in, 86–89;
    in Hubei, 85; in Jiaxing, 85; lack of
    success in, 88; local initiative in,
    84; low level of participation in,
    85; market mechanisms in, 84;
    pilot programs of, 79, 86; and
    pollution permits, 84, 87; price-
    setting, 84; variation in, 84; in

Zhejiang, 87. *See also* emissions
    trading; pollution
Pongso no Tao. *See* Lanyu (Orchid
    Island, Pongso no Tao); Tao
    indigenous people
population, 6; aging of Japanese,
    112–13; animal, 134; East Asian as
    percentage of world, 5–6; decline in
    Japan, 66, 112, 113–14; decline of
    rural, 113–16, 119–20, 255; density
    and environmental degradation,
    11, 164; forecast decline in Korea,
    66, 73; growth and deforestation,
    253; growth rates, 66; health of, 23;
    indigenous, 35, 122, 126
"post-industrial" economies, 244
precautionary principle: and GMOs,
    213, 217, 224
Prius, 9
protection zones, 235–36
protectionism, 216
protest: as advocacy strategy, 12,
    36–37; against beef imports, 224n3;
    against incinerators, 233; against
    nuclear power, 14, 26, 198, 204;
    against pollution, 21, 181–96, 202–3,
    225, 241–42; as challenge to
    authoritarianism, 198; community-
    based, 23, 183–85, 187, 196n1; and
    democracy, 25–26, 198; differential
    effectiveness of, 246; and
    environmental rights, 97, 101;
    farmers and fishers' roles in, 191;
    lawyers' role in, 92, 105; limited
    occurrence in East Asia, 37, 40; local
    focus of, 23, 26; and media, 188;
    urban vs. rural, 245; vocabulary of
    social, 94. *See also* activists
Purple Butterfly Research Society, 132

Q

Qinggangshu Village, 173
Quanjia Heba, 171–72, 174–75, 176

Super Ministries Reform, 89
sustainability: of agriculture, 166, 169, 222; and authoritarianism, 164–65; and community power, 112; contradiction with development, 18, 58; and energy, 111; and environmental education, 140–41; global, vii–viii; of landscapes, 164, 166; and legitimacy, 6; and/of nature education, 140–41, 147–48; of New Villages, 150–63; and pollution, 195–96; of rural development, 158–59, 162–64; and rural livelihoods, 18; sacrifice of, for growth, 164; and switch to eco-developmental state, 15, 17, 28, 248; and technological lock-in, 165; and TEK, 127, 133, 205–6; and urban design, 32

T

Taegu: air pollution in, 250
Taiban Sasala, 200
Taicang City, 79
Taichung: air pollution decline in, 249
Tainan: air pollution decline in, 249
Taipei: air pollution decline in, 249
Taiwan Power Company, 187, 197; compensation for nuclear waste storage, 209; magazine published by, 203
Taling Coal Power Plant (Kaoshiung), 187–88
Tao indigenous people, 197; Christianity among, 203–4; customs and taboos, 205–6; deceived about nuclear waste repository, 198–99; independent media among, 203, 210–11; lack of identification with Taiwan, 201; land rights among, 202; relation to Batanes Islanders,

201; relationship to land and ocean, 201–3; resilience in the face of colonialism, 212; resistance to laws and regulations, 202–3; resistance to nuclear waste, 201–6, 211; return to Lanyu, 204; Tsai Ing-wen apology to, 203; underground houses, 202. *See also* Lanyu (Orchid Island, Pongso no Tao)
Tashe petrochemical complex (Kaohsiung), 186
technological lock-in: and agricultural modernization, 166–67; and labor inputs, 165; new forms of, 175; in sustainable agriculture, 165
TEK (traditional ecological knowledge): and conservation, 127; contemporary relevance of, 133; in hunter school, 133; and natural resources, 125, 127; recording of, 129; in Rio Declaration, 132; and sustainability, 127, 133; synergy with scientific knowledge, 127–29, 130, 131; in UN Council for Science report, 133
"three concentrations," 167–69
Tianjin: air pollution in, 251, 252; shutdown of polluting industries in, 251
tipping points, 24, 216, 221–23
Tokushima Prefecture, 118–20; depopulation in, 119
Tokushima Regional Energy General Incorporated Association (TREGIA), 118–20
Tokyo: air pollution in, 249
top-down management. *See* command-and-control
total suspended particulate. *See* TSP (total suspended particulate)
tourism, 28–29; on Lanyu, 203–6
"toxic archipelago," 241

CPSIA information can be obtained
at www.ICGtesting.com
Printed in the USA
BVHW030114101120
592941BV00002B/5